Patrolling Baghdad

Patrolling Baghdad

A Military Police Company
and the War in Iraq

Mark R. DePue

 UNIVERSITY PRESS OF KANSAS

© 2007 by the University Press of Kansas

Published by the University Press of Kansas
(Lawrence, Kansas 66049), which was
organized by the Kansas Board of Regents
and is operated and funded by Emporia
State University, Fort Hays State University,
Kansas State University, Pittsburg State
University, the University of Kansas, and
Wichita State University

Library of Congress Cataloging-in-
Publication Data

DePue, Mark R.
    Patrolling Baghdad: a military police
company and the war in Iraq / Mark R.
DePue.
        p.   cm. — (Modern war studies)
    Includes bibliographical references and
index.
    ISBN-13: 978-0-7006-1498-1 (cloth : alk.
paper)
    1. Iraq War, 2003—Campaigns. 2. Iraq
War, 2003—Personal narratives, American.
3. United States—Armed Forces—Military
police.   I. Title.
    DS79.764.U6D34 2007
    956.7044′31—dc22   2006034429

British Library Cataloguing-in-Publication
Data is available.

Printed in the United States of America

10 9 8 7 6 5 4 3 2 1

The paper used in this publication meets
the minimum requirements of the American
National Standard for Permanence of Paper
for Printed Library Materials Z39.48-1984.

To the men and women of the 233rd

Contents

A photo section appears following page 102.

Preface

Rich Miller, a Chicago-based journalist, figured it was time for a vacation in the summer of 2003. The rough-and-tumble world of Chicago politics, his normal beat, was enough to give anyone a jaded view of humanity, and he found it healthy to occasionally take a break. He thought British Columbia would be the perfect place to unwind, but as he scanned the region's road-maps his mind kept drifting to Iraq, where the American military was struggling to bring democracy. He was a journalist, and this was the biggest story in the world. Unable to shake the idea, Miller changed his plans: instead of heading to Canada, he made his way to Iraq in September 2003. There, he toured the midnight streets of Baghdad in the back of a Humvee belonging to the 2nd Squad of the 1st Platoon of the 233rd Military Police Company, a National Guard unit from Springfield, Illinois.

In some respects, Miller had already seen more than he wanted to since arriving in Iraq. His initial report was filed from Fallujah after observing a nasty incident involving an infantry unit. That city sat in the middle of the volatile Sunni triangle and possessed a well-deserved reputation as Iraq's version of the wild, wild west. There he observed a bloody firefight that resulted in eleven Iraqi police dying after an accidental exchange of fire with American infantrymen at a roadside checkpoint, triggered when several insurgents, crammed into a BMW, pulled up in front of an Iraqi police station, sprayed the station with gunfire, and sped away. The police immediately piled into cars and gave chase, racing through the streets until they encountered the American checkpoint. The infantrymen stationed there were already jumpy, having just survived a near miss from a rocket-propelled grenade attack. When they saw the police cars speeding toward them, they instinctively opened fire and kept firing despite the Iraqi policemen's desperate pleas, suspecting that the whole thing was only a ruse. It wasn't the first time that insurgents had disguised themselves as policemen.

It was an uneven fight, explained Miller in his report, especially since the police never returned fire. Eight Iraqi policemen died outright, as did a Jordanian who was cut down while standing guard outside a nearby hospital. Within minutes, rumors of a conspiracy were circulating in the streets—a story that the Americans had contrived the whole incident. It wasn't true, of course, but in postwar Iraq, perception usually trumped reality. Two days later, American authorities broadcast an apology over the radio, but it was too little, too late. Miller found the whole episode disconcerting. He concluded that in Fallujah, at least, the Americans were losing the war for the Iraqis' hearts and minds.

His midnight patrol in Baghdad with the military police (MP) a few days later stood in stark contrast to the incident in Fallujah. He was a passenger that night in a convoy consisting of only two light-skinned Humvees, a convoy that threaded its way through the empty streets of Baghdad. Commanding the convoy was Sergeant Ryan Getz of tiny Mount Carroll, Illinois. His job that evening was to conduct a roving patrol in eastern Baghdad, through some of the most treacherous streets in the world.[1]

Because the city was under a curfew, it was no big deal when the convoy headed the wrong way down a four-lane boulevard. Suddenly, wrote Miller, "a dark-colored van came speeding toward them from around a curve. The van's driver, perhaps blinded by the oncoming headlights, did not stop immediately, but slammed on his brakes shortly before slamming into one of the squad's two Hummers." With a head-on collision barely averted, the MPs dismounted and headed toward the van while Miller watched from his vantage point inside the Humvee, scribbling in his notepad. Sergeant Getz coolly ordered a man out of the van, then patted him down while other MPs searched the van. Finding nothing, they sent the Iraqi on his way with a firm rebuke, but also "with smiles on their faces." With the patrol on the move again, Miller asked his escorts what would have happened if the man had encountered an infantry patrol instead of the MPs. He'd probably be dead, came the terse reply. This encounter stood in stark contrast to the troubling incident he'd observed just a few days before.

Miller reached a conclusion that night. "Critically short of experienced military police," he wrote, "the Americans have been forced to rely mostly on infantry soldiers to patrol Iraqi streets. The infantry is trained for full-scale war." What was now needed, he believed, was a more subtle approach, one for which the MPs were much better suited.[2] He closed his article with this. "If you're looking for some good news in Iraq the 233rd might just be it."[3]

This is their story.

Acknowledgments

This book is about the 233rd Military Police Company and their year-long odyssey in Baghdad from the fall of Saddam's statues in April 2003 to spring 2004. As much as possible, the story is told from their perspective, using their words, letters, and pictures, as well as the unit's extensive official documents.

The narrative is based on a series of interviews that I began in August 2004, just months after the unit's return from Iraq. Through it all, I often felt like an intruder, living vicariously on their courage, pain, and sacrifice. They did not have to talk to me. Most came back determined to move on with their lives, to put the bad memories behind them while embracing the good ones. There is a very human reluctance for soldiers to share their experiences with those who have not experienced their hardships and traumas. That reticence is understandable given the unwillingness to relive painful memories with those who could not possibly understand what it was really like.

Thankfully, the soldiers of the 233rd were, for the most part, willing to share their experiences with me. Their cooperation grew out of an intense pride in their unit and a strong belief in the justness of their mission in Baghdad. They also wanted to make sure I got the story right. They spoke candidly of their experiences, and they went above and beyond in doing so. That was characteristic of the 233rd—they routinely did more than was expected of them; they strove to do better than just OK. That spirit makes their story compelling. It is to them and thousands of others just like them in the Illinois National Guard and the U.S. Army that this book is dedicated.

This book is fundamentally an oral history, based on eighty interviews I conducted with the members of the 233rd Military Police Company from August 2004 through mid-2005. Whenever possible, I corroborated the MPs' comments with other interviews, as well as official documents, newspaper and magazine articles, and other, more traditional sources. Having said that, it should be noted that oral histories always have an element of subjectivity about them.

Others who were in Baghdad during that tumultuous first year might remember things differently than what I have portrayed here. But this is not their story. It is the 233rd's story, the story of their experiences and recollections, told as much as possible with their voices. For that I offer no apologies, merely a caution. Human memory is a frail thing. Details like names, dates, the specific sequence of events, and other facts quickly become fuzzy, while emotions and general impressions are often seared more permanently in memory. When I discovered inconsistencies, I sorted them out as best as I could, and indicated as much in the endnotes. Yet truth is an elusive thing, especially in the heat of combat. There are probably "facts" presented in the book that others who read this will want to challenge. In acknowledging that possibility, I am confident that this is, in the aggregate, an accurate portrayal of the 233rd's experiences in Iraq.

This book started as an article entitled "Typical Day" that I wrote for the Pritzker Military Library, newly opened in downtown Chicago. Accordingly, I want to thank Colonel (Illinois) Jim Pritzker and everyone at the library for allowing me to use much of the material from that article for this book. Just as important to me, Jim and the library's staff have been unfailingly generous in their support and assistance. Indeed, Jim has proven himself to be one of the military historian's best friends. He created the Pritzker Military Library in 2003 expressly for the purpose of mentoring military historians while promoting a better understanding of our nation's rich military history.

There are many others to thank, starting with Colonel (Retired) John Raschke, a dear friend who also possesses a keen eye for detail and a passion for the subject, who served as editor for the early drafts. Jean Welch did much of the interview transcription, a taxing job if ever there was one, and the folks at Mapping Specialists of Madison, Wisconsin, proved very helpful and timely in preparing the map of Baghdad. I also thank Mike Briggs, Larisa Martin, and the rest of the people at the University Press of Kansas, who helped shepherd a novice through the intricacies of publishing, and especially for connecting me with the likes of Professor James Corum of the Command and General Staff College and Dr. Mike Doubler. Both read the manuscript and provided the kind of insightful criticism that helped improve the book.

This book would not have been possible without the cooperation of Journalist Marcus Stern and the staff of the Springfield *State Journal-Register* and Copley News Service. Their stories on the 223rd provided the inspiration for the book; their support throughout the book's development was crucial to its completion. Equally important is the support I received from several photographers, most notably Nelvin Cepeda, who took so many superb photos of the unit while he and Stern spent a week with the 233rd in Baghdad, and two of the unit's most prolific photogrraphers, Sergeant George Martin and Staff Sergeant Jim Mayes.

Finally, I thank my "gate-keepers" for this project, the people who proved so helpful in pointing me in the right direction, who invariably helped me dig up the facts, to whom I repeatedly turned for assistance: Captain Jeff Royer, First Sergeant Robert Elmore, and Sergeant First Class Lawrence Wilson. They embody the professionalism and dedication I learned to expect from all of those in the 233rd.

Glossary

AAR	After Action Review, the formal review process the Army uses after operations to ensure each lesson is learned, geared to improving future operations.
AIT	Advanced Individual Training, the course of training after basic training, where soldiers learn their specific military skill.
APC	Armored Personnel Carriers. These vehicles are designed to carry a squad of eight to eleven infantrymen. They are much lighter than tanks, and their armor is designed to stop small arms fire, but not tank rounds.
ASAP	As Soon As Possible.
AT	Annual Training, typically two weeks of extended training traditionally conducted during the summer.
BC	Battalion Commander.
BIAP	Baghdad International Airport, the city's major air link to the world, located on the southwestern outskirts of the city.
CENTCOM	Central Command, the American theater command responsible for operations in South and Southwest Asia.
CPA	Coalition Provisional Authority, the United States–backed governing authority that temporarily governed Iraq in the months after the overthrow of Saddam's regime. L. Paul Bremer served as the administer for the CPA.
CSH	Combat Support Hospital, pronounced "cash."
Deadlined	Vehicles and equipment that are nonoperational are declared "deadlined."
Drill	The traditional term used by National Guard units for their weekend training sessions.
DCU	Desert Camouflage Uniform, the style of fatigue uniforms worn by American troops in Iraq.
EOD	Explosive Ordnance Demolition.
FOB	Forward Operating Base.
FRAGO	Fragmentary Order. A change or elaboration to an Operations Order, which is the more formal document.
FRG	Family Readiness Group.

GPS	Global Positioning System. Many of the soldiers had purchased commercial GPSs before their departure, most commonly the Garmin brand.
HIPAA	Health Insurance Portability and Accountability Act of 1996, which, among other things, imposed privacy guidelines on health records that limited the information parents and other relatives could receive on the status of injured loved ones.
IED	Improvised Explosive Device, the makeshift bombs that became the preferred weapon of insurgents.
IP	Iraqi Police, sometimes referred to as IPS, short for Iraqi Police Service.
LSA	Life Support Area, the acronym the MPs used when referring to Viper Base, the unit's compound and base of operation next to the Tigris River.
MOUT	Military Operations in Urban Terrain. Army training centers often include MOUT sites, where units learn to fight in an urban environment.
MP	Military Police.
MRE	Meals Ready to Eat, the military's current field ration, which requires no preparation.
MSR	Main Supply Route, designating the highway or rail line used to supply the forward units.
MWR	Morale, Welfare, and Recreation.
NBC	Nuclear, Biological, and Chemical.
NCO	Noncommissioned Officer.
NVG	Night Vision Goggles. The American Army was well supplied with various night-vision devices, most of which relied on either ambient light sources or heat sources.
OML	Order of Merit List. The OML was the list that commanders developed to determine who in the unit would first take an environmental leave.
OPORD	Operations Order, the document the Army uses to issue daily and mission-oriented operational guidance.
ORHA	Office of Reconstruction and Humanitarian Assistance.
PT	Physical Training.
PTSD	Post-traumatic Stress Disorder, the psychological ailment those in a traumatic event so often experience.
QRF	Quick Reaction Force, a team of soldiers positioned and prepared to respond in the event of an emergency or incident.

REFORGER	A training maneuver held each year in West Germany involving U.S. units based in Germany, units from the continental United States, and troops from other NATO nations.
RIP	Relief in Place, the process by which one unit hands off its mission to a follow-on unit.
Rock drills	Exercises designed to help commanders and key staff personnel visualize an operation by allowing them to move on a giant-sized replica of the operation's terrain laid out on the ground.
RPG	Rocket-Propelled Grenade. The most common RPG encountered was the Soviet-manufactured RPG-7 and its variants.
SAW	Squad Automatic Weapon, the acronym used for the M-249 5.56-millimeter machine gun used throughout the army.
SOP	Standard Operating Procedure.
snafu	A classic (and informal) military acronym for Situation Normal, All Fouled Up.
SRP	Soldier Readiness Processing, the procedure all soldiers go through before deployment to ensure that they meet the medical and administrative deployment standards, and to ensure that all pay and administrative paperwork are up to date.
TAG	The Adjutant General, the commander of both the Army and Air National Guard for each state.
TCP	Traffic Control Points, set up by MPs at road intersections, where they would conduct random searches.
TOC	Tactical Operations Center, a unit's command post.
TTP	Tactics, Techniques, and Procedures.

Prominent Locations
A - Al-Sa'ad School
B - Baghdad University
C - BIAP (Baghdad International Airport)
D - Green Zone
E - Muleskinner
F - House of Love Orphanage
G - Provider
H - UN HQs
I - Sadr City
J - Viper Base
K - 14th of July Bridge
L - Double-Decker Bridge

Police Stations
1 - Abu Ghraib Prison
2 - Al-Alawyah (Camelot)
3 - Al-Mesbah (White Castle)
4 - Al-Sa'adoun (Boondocks)
5 - Diyala Bridge Police Station
6 - New Baghdad Police HQs (Grayskull)
7 - New Baghdad Police Station (Tombstone)
8 - Police Academy
9 - Tas Ferrat (Across street to south of Academy)

Location of Incidents
a - Chop Shop
b - Firefighters
c - From Medic to MP
d - LT Ferris' Raid
e - LT Rice Injury
f - Railway Firefight
g - SGT Carroll & IED
h - SGT Cunningham's Incident (Christian Market)

Map of Baghdad

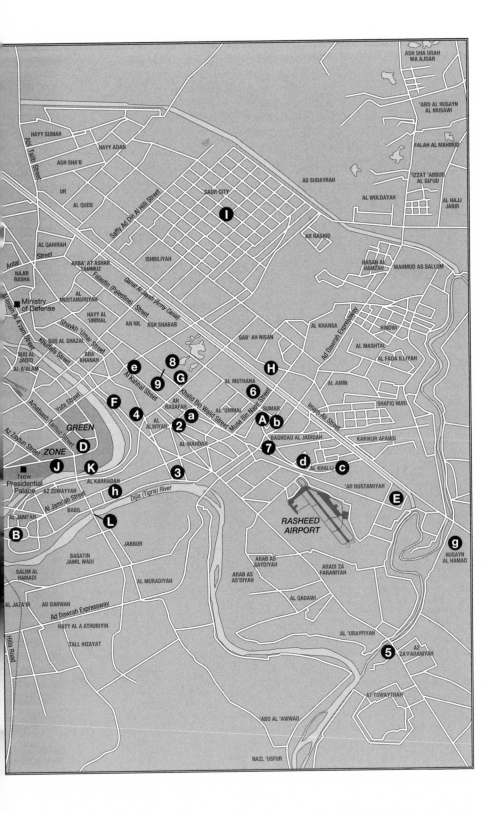

Patrolling Baghdad

1
The Early Years

The 233rd Military Police Company was born in 1968, a tumultuous year for Chicago, torn by both the Martin Luther King riots and the Democratic National Convention. That year, the Illinois National Guard leadership decided to station the 233rd and several other new military police (MP) units in downtown Chicago in a decaying old armory near the heart of the city's commercial district. The cavernous Chicago Avenue Armory, originally built in 1916, was one of the Illinois National Guard's gems when it was first constructed. It overlooked Lake Michigan and scenic Lake Shore Drive. During its heyday, it hosted polo games on the armory drill floor and lavish military dances in the rooftop ballroom. But by the late 1960s, the armory had become an eyesore. By the late 1970s, the building cowered in the shadows of the majestic John Hancock Building, one of the world's tallest buildings. Not surprisingly, the 233rd's leadership struggled to fill its ranks.[1]

In spring 1978, after many years of recruiting shortfalls, Major General John Phipps, the state's adjutant general, told Captain Edwin T. "Terry" Lucas that the 233rd MP Company was moving 150 miles south to Springfield, and that he would be the unit's new commander. In his civilian job, Lucas worked for the Illinois state police. When in military uniform, he served as the supply officer for the 1144th Transportation Battalion in Springfield. What General Phipps offered Lucas was the kind of assignment that every self-respecting captain dreamed of: command of a company. Commanding an MP company was especially appealing to Lucas because he could combine his skills as a police officer with his military career. There was one hitch, however. None of the unit's current members would be making the move to Springfield. They would be absorbed into other Chicago-area MP units. It was Lucas's job to build the 233rd from scratch. He went after the assignment with vigor.

Not surprisingly, Lucas looked first to his old unit, the 1144th Transportation Battalion, to find recruits for his new command, raiding the unit of some of its best noncommissioned officers (NCOs). Many were Korean War veterans—just the type of seasoned leaders whom Lucas hoped to build the unit around. He enticed a couple more NCOs out of a local Air National Guard unit and aggressively recruited from the area's many law enforcement agencies. Because Springfield, a city of 100,000 located in the heart of central Illinois, was the state capital, it boasted the state police headquarters. The state police academy was only 10 miles further south, and a surprising number of state agencies claimed their own police forces. In other words, Springfield was a police-rich environment.

Lucas was particular about the type of recruit he sought. He insisted on quality, and because of it, he occasionally weathered criticism from his superiors for not filling the unit quickly enough. Despite the criticism, he never regretted his decision, and as the unit's ranks gradually filled, it began to receive challenging missions.[2]

During the 1970s, Illinois Army National Guard units typically spent their two weeks of annual training (AT) at Fort McCoy, Wisconsin, engaged in mundane and often unambitious training exercises. In contrast, the 233rd MP Company drew a real-world mission for its very first AT in 1979. The unit was ordered to Fort Riley, Kansas, with orders to augment the post's Regular Army MPs. Lucas and his NCOs soon had the MPs standing tall. Their military appearance, bearing, uniforms, and military courtesy were excellent. They looked so good, in fact, that during a formation of the post's MPs, their senior NCO asked Lucas to leave the area while he addressed his troops in private. Lucas was still in earshot when he overheard the NCO dress down his own troops for allowing a bunch of National Guardsmen to show them up. The story soon circulated among the 233rd's MPs. It became a source of pride, one Lucas made sure they did not forget.[3]

The 233rd faced an even bigger challenge during their next AT in summer 1980. The entire unit, numbering about 50 at the time against an authorized strength of 150, spent three weeks at Fort McCoy assisting Regular Army MPs guard Cuban refugees from the Mariel boat lift. These were some of Cuba's most reprehensible outcasts—prisoners and reprobates whom Castro had purged from his prisons. The 233rd's specific mission was to keep the Cubans contained in the makeshift prison compound, which consisted of converted World War II wooden barracks, now surrounded by a barbed wire fence rimmed with concertina wire. The Cuban prisoners proved resourceful both in fabricating handmade weapons and in finding ways to slip out of the compound at night, sending the MPs hustling after them until they could once again be incarcerated. Fortunately, many of the 233rd's soldiers were policemen or correctional officers in civilian life, a fact that gave them a reservoir of skills that helped immeasurably with this assignment. Once again, the MPs impressed their Regular Army counterparts, so much so that one Regular Army commander asked Lucas if the 233rd NCOs could teach his soldiers some of the classes he'd observed the guardsmen conduct for their own recruits. Lucas of course obliged. The Fort McCoy mission was tough, but it accelerated the unit's maturation.[4] By 1981, the unit had earned a reputation for competence and professionalism, gaining the reputation as a good unit to join. The 233rd built on its early successes and began to fill more quickly, attracting high-quality recruits.

There were many reasons for the unit's popularity. Springfield was a cop-rich town, and policemen were often inclined to serve in the military. It also helped that the 233rd was the closest MP unit to Western Illinois University in Macomb, located less than 100 miles to the northwest. The university boasted one of the Midwest's best law enforcement administration programs, and the school's ROTC program regularly fed the 233rd with recruits, especially officers.

The MPs met one weekend a month at Camp Lincoln, a thin slice of land in northern Springfield. Weekend drills were carefully orchestrated affairs, concentrating on soldier-level training and administrative tasks, with intermittent stretches of down time that acclimated new recruits to the army tradition of "hurry up and wait." The armory was an angular two-story affair built in the shadow of the Illinois National Guard headquarters. There was nothing fancy about the boxy brick building, which was dominated by an eminently utilitarian and austere drill floor. It certainly wasn't the building that drew the MPs to their monthly drills. And it wasn't the fact that the unit met at a site close to the state headquarters. If anything, that was an impediment. As far as their training and readiness were concerned, the MPs were expected to clear the same hurdles their Regular Army counterparts faced: the same series of military schools, the same physical fitness test and weight control standards—and they had to do all this while also holding down a civilian job.

Although the first two AT periods tested the soldiers' abilities as garrison MPs, that was only one facet of their overall mission. The 233rd MP Company was organized as a combat MP unit, designed with the cold war and the huge Soviet army in mind. Its primary mission in combat was to maintain "battlefield circulation control." In layman's terms, the unit was responsible, in the event of a full-scale war, to provide security for the Army's rear area. The MPs were expected to be much more than traffic cops for the rear, however; they were more like infantry. If, for example, isolated pockets of enemy soldiers suddenly emerged in the rear area, it was the MPs' job to either destroy them outright or to contain them until an infantry force could arrive to take them out. This tall order was accompanied by a long list of sub-ordinate tasks, including securing the main supply routes, forwarding damage reports, and providing security for key assets, ranging from command posts to bridges, dams, road intersections, and communications nodes.

As the years rolled by, the 233rd continued to receive challenging AT assignments. While Illinois' infantry and artillery units typically headed to Fort McCoy for their two weeks of summer camp, the MPs became world travelers.[5] The unit headed to Subic Bay in the Philippines in 1986, and the next year, First Lieutenant Tom Bowman, brand new to command, took the 233rd to Europe for the Army's annual REFORGER exercise. Bowman, a Vietnam veteran, was also one of the NCOs Lucas recruited back in 1978. He received a direct commission in 1984, a rarity in the National Guard, then worked his way up to company command.

The MPs' first challenge during their REFORGER mission was to pack every piece of the unit's equipment and prepare it for shipment to the Neth-erlands. Weeks later, the MPs crammed onto a flight to Amsterdam along with elements from several other units. Bowman spent the flight fretting over how his troops would link up with the unit's equipment and mulling over the unit's ambitious mission, which required him to spread the company between four sites in three different countries.

Fifteen minutes before landing in Amsterdam, a crewman informed him that a group of dignitaries, including the queen of the Netherlands, a three-star general, a military band, and a cluster of reporters were all waiting to greet the soldiers on the tarmac. Bowman's flight just happened to be the first contingent to arrive for that year's REFORGER, and he was the senior man aboard. (He drew the ceremonial mission only because the plane carrying the official party had been delayed for repairs.) He quickly huddled with another lieutenant on the plane, and together, they planned an impromptu ceremony involving the plane's 200 passengers. The resulting ceremony wasn't pretty, but they managed to pull it off. Immediately after the ceremony, a two-star general cornered Bowman and told him to send a detachment of twenty MPs to an army aviation base in Germany, an assignment that further divided his unit. That meant Bowman now had to divide his troops between five far-flung locations, and the number of sites they covered only grew over the next several days.

Bowman chalked up the unit's REFORGER experience as another in a string of important milestones. The exercise allowed the unit to train over a huge piece of northern Europe, performing just the kind of mission they were designed to do in the event of war. It accelerated the unit's development and gave the officers and NCOs a chance to develop their skills and confidence. The Army would make good use of those skills over the next few years.

CPT Bowman served as the unit's commander until October 1990, far longer than the customary two-year command hitch. During that time, he logged several trips to Panama, his first in December 1989, one week after the overthrow of Panamanian strongman Manuel Noriega. He had had a great ride as commander, and he loved every minute of it. Then came Saddam Hussein's invasion of Kuwait.

Desert Storm

On a cold December morning in 1990, Captain Bowman watched the 233rd MP Company pass through Camp Lincoln's front gate, heading for service in the gulf war. He had reluctantly turned over his command a few weeks before to First Lieutenant Kevin Keen, just before the unit's formal mobilization for the gulf. Despite being out of command, Bowman struggled to find a way—any way—to be with his troops in the desert, even asking for a reduction in rank to sergeant first class if only he could accompany the 233rd into combat. The state's leadership would hear nothing of it, so Bowman stood by helplessly as the buses carrying the MPs drove out the gate. "Here goes everybody I've know in the military for the last ten years, . . . all these people I was responsible for," he stated years later. "I didn't know whether to cry, or scream, or . . . cuss."[6]

Kevin Keen, the new commander, was a relatively junior lieutenant when he received his new post. He joined the 233rd just before the 1987 RE-FORGER, leading a contingent of MPs guarding an aviation base in Germany. Now he was about to get a crash course in command. The 233rd was officially alerted for war on November 21, just before Thanksgiving. Within days, the unit took a bone-chilling ride to Fort Benjamin Harrison, Indiana (their mobilization station), riding in the unit's dilapidated quarter-ton jeeps and trailers. Once at Ben Harrison, they were overjoyed to turn in their jeeps for brand-new, fresh-from-the-factory Humvees. The next few weeks flew by, the days filled with mind-numbing briefings, physicals, mountains of paperwork, inspections, training, packing, and more training. With their preparations complete, the unit flew directly from Indiana to the deserts of northeast Saudi Arabia, where they soon found themselves assigned to the VIIth Corps sector. They arrived on January 17, one day after the allied air offensive began.

When the ground phase began, the MPs set up an enemy prisoner of war collection site in the VIIth Corps rear area just south of the Iraqi border. Given their mission, they expected to keep busy processing plenty of Iraqi prisoners once the war kicked off. The ground phase began with a relentless and devastating bombardment of the Iraqi forward positions, a lethal combination of an aerial and artillery bombardment that left the survivors shell-shocked. Once the armored columns surged forward, they sliced easily through the Iraqi defenses. The MPs were soon inundated by a flood of prisoners, far exceeding what they had expected. The reason was simple. The Iraqi soldiers had been sent straight from city streets to the front lines, assigned one rifle for every three men, and then left to their fate in a foxhole. They were hemmed in with a line of minefields to the front and another to the rear to prevent them from fleeing. The first chance they got, they surrendered en masse, straggling into American positions looking like "anything but a soldier." Said Keen years later, "we had guys in blue jeans and T-shirts, leisure suits, 3-piece suits." Another 233rd veteran was amazed when he saw an Iraqi approach his position wearing a University of Illinois "Illini" T-shirt. The man, in excellent English, patiently explained that he was a graduate of the University's medical school.[7]

The 233rd followed in the VIIth Corps' wake as the armored juggernaut penetrated deep into Iraq. Once there, the armored columns swung to the right like an enormous gate, with its hinge fixed firmly at the confluence of the Iraq, Kuwait, and Saudi border. As the war drew to a close, the 233rd found itself patrolling the northern portion of the infamous Highway of Death, the stretch of four-lane road that connected Kuwait City with Iraq—the road where the Iraqi occupation forces had met their violent death at the hands of allied pilots. The MPs patrolled north of the site where most of the destruction had occurred, but they occasionally ventured far enough south to catch a glimpse of the massive destruction. And everywhere they looked, Kuwait's burning oil wells lit up the sky like smoky torches, casting a dark pall on the landscape.

After Desert Storm

The 233rd stayed busy in the years after Desert Storm. They chalked up several more overseas deployments, plus a couple of stints on state active duty. Their first state active duty came after the Chicago Bulls' "Three-Peat," when they assembled in a Chicago-area armory in case overexuberant Chicagoans got out of hand. Later that year, Governor Jim Edgar called them out to fight the great flood of 1993. And throughout the 1990s, the MPs continued their role as military globetrotters, including AT deployments to Panama, Belize, and Italy.

The 233rd enjoyed an excellent reputation throughout the 1990s, and their busy schedule of worldwide travel appealed to many prospective recruits. The strength of the unit centered on an excellent core of NCOs, just as Terry Lucas had intended in 1978. These were seasoned professionals who took their jobs seriously and prided themselves in being a cut above the average Guardsman. Meanwhile, officers regularly came and went. Captain Wendell Lowry felt fortunate to get his command time in the 233rd. When he arrived to take command, Master Sergeant Michael Nuding, the unit's operations sergeant, pulled him aside and gave him a piece of advice. "Sit back, relax, and enjoy the ride," Nuding bluntly declared. Lowry neither sat back nor relaxed during his two-year command, but he did enjoy the ride. And looking back at the experience, he admitted that the sergeants of the 233rd were "among the best NCOs I've ever worked with after 23 years in the military, including [four years on] active duty."[8]

After 9/11 in 2001, the 233rd's operations tempo picked up another notch. Scores of unit members were sent to bolster security at several Illinois airports. Others pulled duty at other critical assets throughout the state. Those missions were on top of the unit's AT requirements, which included trips to Nicaragua and Italy. By late 2002, when the Bush administration began to build up forces in the Middle East for an attack on Iraq, the MPs speculated endlessly about when they might be called up. The old hands knew it was just a matter of time.

2

Mobilization and Train-up

It was a gorgeous October afternoon in central Illinois. Like so many Fridays, Sister Beth Murphy of the Dominican Sisters of Springfield manned her normal station outside the Old Capital building in downtown Springfield with several other sisters. They were there in civilian attire to protest "the U.S. drumbeat for war against Iraq," carrying handmade signs and brochures they handed out to sympathetic passers-by. On this particular day, however, Sister Beth watched apprehensively as a police car pulled to a stop nearby. A policeman soon emerged and approached the group. She was pleasantly surprised when he greeted the group cordially and then politely perused the brochure Sister Beth handed him. He introduced himself as Jeff, then stated matter-of-factly, "I'm in the Guard. I've been in war zones before, and I expect to go again if there is a war. I appreciate your efforts." The two talked for a bit, but it was soon time for the sisters to leave. It was their tradition to end the protest with a prayer. So a group of Dominican sisters and a Springfield police officer formed a circle and prayed. When Jeff finally left the group, Sister Beth called after him with a promise to keep him in her prayers.

When President Bush took the nation to war a few months later, Sister Beth often wondered about the young soldier she had encountered on that beautiful fall afternoon. She remained true to her pledge; she often prayed for him. Their brief encounter put a human face to the war she so strongly opposed. She was convinced that President Bush had made a tragic mistake when he decided to overthrow Saddam. She believed that the war would lead only to more violence and suffering for a people who had already suffered too much. She knew of the Iraqis' heartaches firsthand: she had visited Iraq several times over the preceding years. The Dominican sisters had a presence in Iraq, and whenever Sister Beth visited them, they expressed their hope and belief that the Iraqi people would remove Saddam of their own accord. Sister Beth ardently shared that hope, but Bush had preempted that, and now Iraq was torn by war. She inherently distrusted the American military, but she was confident that Jeff would conduct himself honorably.

By the fall of 2003, as Sister Beth planned a return trip to Iraq that Christmas, the war was very much on her mind. She followed the war in the news and was especially drawn to a series of articles in Springfield's newspaper about the community's own 233rd Military Police Company, then serving in Baghdad. Even so, Sister Beth was startled by the *State Journal-Register*'s front-page photo on October 24. There, staring out at her from above the fold was the police officer she had met a year before. Captain Jeff Royer, the commander of the 233rd MP Company, was addressing his troops in Baghdad.[1]

Notification

Ever since October 10, 2002, the date Congress gave President Bush authorization to use armed force against Saddam Hussein, the rumors had flown thick and fast among the members of the 233rd. It seemed that everyone had a different tidbit of inside information they were eager to share. There was a rumor about Bosnia. Another had them heading to Germany to backfill regulars. There were also plenty of rumors that had them going to Iraq. With the war fast approaching and the buildup in Kuwait underway, many were certain it was just a matter of time before they were called. With mobilization appearing certain, the Thanksgiving and Christmas holidays were especially poignant that year.[2]

The company's strength stood at a robust 243 in October against an authorized strength of 180. It was a testament to the unit's solid reputation and history of success. The company was so large, in fact, that state headquarters had authorized the creation of an additional platoon.

By the December drill, Royer felt compelled to address his troops and let them know what he knew, which wasn't much. He had received no indication on whether they were going to be alerted any time soon, Royer informed the troops, let alone what their mission or destination might be. Even so, he warned them to get their "personal affairs in order and keep them in order and be prepared to move out." Not until February 3 did Royer finally get the long-expected call. When he answered his cell phone, he recognized the voice of Lieutenant Colonel Timothy Hodge, his battalion commander. The brigade commander and a staff officer from state headquarters were also on the line. Effective February 7, stated Hodge, the 233rd was being mobilized for the war on terror. Royer was told to get his people assembled, lead them through the mandatory predeployment soldier readiness processing, and report to Fort McCoy, Wisconsin, for further training not later than February 10. Hodge said nothing about where the unit was going, what the MPs would be doing once they got there, or how long they might be gone. Even so, the phone call was a relief. "Finally the guessing game is over."[3]

The next few days passed in a whirlwind of activity. Armed with such vague information, there wasn't much Royer could tell the troops except to prepare for any contingency. Everyone wanted to know where the unit was headed, and especially how long they would be gone, but no one knew—not Royer, not his commanders, not the state headquarters, not even those at the National Guard Bureau headquarters in Washington, D.C., where the order had originated. Rumors once again raced through the company: were they headed to the desert, or to Europe, or maybe somewhere in the states to guard a power plant or some other high-value terrorist target? The most persistent question the unit's family members asked was, "When will you be back?" The official order read, "for an initial period of up to 365 days," but the president had the authority to extend that time by another year if the situation required it. Most soldiers assumed that because the unit was back home after only six months during Desert Storm, they could expect the same for this war.[4]

Train-up

The MPs poured into the armory on Wednesday, February 5, and soon piled onto buses and headed to the Marseilles training area, a National Guard training area located 100 miles north. They spent two days at Marseilles going through the formal soldier readiness processing (SRP), a series of stations where the MPs filled out forms, received physical checkups, reviewed their wills and other legal documents, and verified their financial status. Marseilles was conveniently located in the center of the state, accessible to all of the Illinois National Guard units that the Army called up. They joined seven other units that were also going through their own SRP, including two other military police companies (the 333rd from Freeport and the 933rd from Chicago), a truck company, two aviation units, and a medical company.

No one was surprised when several soldiers washed out as the unit worked its way through the SRP stations. Some were removed for medical reasons, others because of complications with their dependents, and one because she was pregnant. A score or more of the unit's youngest soldiers would not be going because they had not yet finished their initial training. The Guard aggressively recruited high school juniors and seniors and allowed them to drill even though they had not attended basic training or advanced individual training. Not until they completed both blocks of instruction, however, were recruits eligible for deployment. It was a compromise the National Guard was willing to make to ensure they had a steady supply of new enlistees. To compensate for these known losses, units were allowed to carry excess personnel, and no unit in Illinois had more excess personnel than the 233rd.

Even with these losses, the unit had more than enough troops to fill its ranks. This included several former members, veterans of the gulf war who had left the National Guard but now lobbied the state's leadership to let them rejoin their unit. Several were successful, including Specialist Chris Cunningham, a police officer from Springfield, and Sergeant Richard Carroll, a police officer from Champaign. The unit was so fat, in fact, that Captain Royer was directed to transfer some of his soldiers to the state's other two MP companies then being mobilized. The 233rd lost twenty-one soldiers to the 933rd MP Company and another six to the 333rd MP Company. Their loss was a sore point for Royer, and especially for many of the soldiers being transferred, but it was an argument they could not win.[5]

Many of those being mobilized were scheduled to complete their tour of duty during the next several months. The army could ill afford to ship units overseas and then watch their ranks decline as the soldiers' terms of enlistment ended. For that reason, the secretary of defense, Donald Rumsfeld, invoked the stop-loss provision, which was part of President Bush's statutory war powers. That meant that when a unit mobilized, soldiers whose enlistments were due to expire in the next few months were automatically and involuntarily extended. In one fell swoop, scores of the soldiers were involuntarily extended for the duration of the deployment. Specialist Andrew Moore, only days from his discharge, was one of those. The provision had been invoked before, and it was no surprise to the old hands, but it was a bitter pill to swallow. Still, most of those caught in the stop-loss net got over it pretty quickly. After all, this was their company, and they were not about to let their fellow soldiers down.[6]

Once soldier readiness processing was completed, the company returned to Springfield on Thursday evening to gather up their equipment, prepare for deployment, and spend a few more nights with their loved ones. Everything was rushed, and it didn't help that the individual packing list kept changing every day, the inevitable consequence of not knowing where they were headed. On Sunday, February 9, the entire company formed on the armory drill floor. The drill floor was spartan, even by National Guard standards, and the acoustics were atrocious. The soldiers of the 233rd stood tall in front of an assembly of family members, dignitaries, and well-wishers. It was an emotional send-off.

Included in the crowd were scores of wives, children, parents, girlfriends, coworkers, and even a few husbands. Several wives in attendance that day were pregnant, including Monica Hildebrandt, two months pregnant with her second child, with seven-month Caleb in her arms. Her husband, Paul Hildebrandt, served as a team leader in 1st Platoon, and her brother-in-law, Keith, was the unit's maintenance sergeant. Paul found it tough to say goodbye, especially since he didn't know when he would return. Monica took some comfort in knowing that the unit's mobilization order stated they would be gone for no more than a year. She promised Paul that she would send him monthly photos to chronicle her progress. Captain Royer left his six-month-old son behind, and Robert Elmore, the unit's no-nonsense first sergeant, left his wife at home with three sons. His eldest, Robert Paul Elmore, was assigned as a gunner in 2nd Platoon.

The next morning, 180 members of the 233rd MP Company headed north for Fort McCoy, Wisconsin, to an uncertain future.[7]

The Command Team

Captain Jeff Royer was a thirty-four-year-old police officer from Springfield, one of the city's handful of K-9 cops. He had a medium build—he wasn't lean, but he was well within the Army's weight standards. He kept his light brown hair trimmed tight to the side—a "high and tight," in the army's vernacular. Jeff carried himself with an air of self-assurance, a fact that helped earn his soldiers' confidence. Born and raised in Springfield, he became interested in law enforcement while attending Southeast high school. He joined the Illinois Army National Guard in 1986 and began his military career as an infantryman in Litchfield, Illinois. After basic training and advanced individual training, Royer headed to Western Illinois University in Macomb. Western was typical of most state universities. It was located in the middle of fertile farm country, and it was far enough from Chicago to serve as a refuge for kids from the Chicago suburbs who were determined to keep their parents at arms' length. Because of that, Western had earned a reputation as a party school, but it also boasted the best law enforcement administration program in the Midwest, the feature that drew Jeff to the school. It also had one of the best and the largest ROTC programs in the Midwest.

Jeff graduated from Western in 1992 and received his commission as a second lieutenant that same year. Like so many adventurous young officers, he wanted to fly, and he hoped for a flying billet with an aviation unit in Peoria. When that opportunity slipped away, he sought an assignment with the 233rd MP Company, a position that would combine his two interests, law enforcement and the military. Because the 233rd had no vacancies, Royer was assigned to the infantry: Charlie Company of the 1st Battalion, 123rd Infantry in Litchfield, Illinois.

It was not until 2001, after his infantry unit had been reorganized, that Royer finally got his chance to transfer to an MP unit, and then under the worst of circumstances. He was named as the 233rd's new commander to replace Captain Doug Livingston, a popular commander who had died in a motorcycle accident. Royer likened the experience to "following a ghost." By that time, he had also worked his way up through the ranks at the Springfield police department. He started as a dispatcher following his graduation from Western Illinois, and in 1996 he attended the Illinois state police academy. A few years later, he successfully competed for one of the department's coveted K-9 positions. His new partner was Lux, a German shepherd bomb dog from the Czech Republic who was also adept at crowd control. Although Royer was a relative newcomer to the 233rd, he was soon accepted as the commander. Being a cop helped, but his infantry background didn't hurt either. It was deemed as a worthy alternative to the military police. He also shared something else in common with many of his soldiers. With a wife and a brand-new son back home, it gave urgency to his overriding concern as commander. He was determined to get all of his soldiers back home.[8]

First Sergeant Robert Elmore made up the other half of the unit's command team. He went by the nickname "Top" much of the time, the traditional name given to first sergeants in the Army. Gruff, taciturn, and often cool toward his troops, Elmore worked as a correction officer in the civilian world. A newspaper reporter likened him to Lee Van Cleef playing Angel Eyes in a spaghetti Western, a reference both he and Royer found amusing. The reporter had turned him into a character from a Harlequin romance, a transformation he found a bit over the top. For many of Elmore's soldiers, he epitomized what a first sergeant was supposed to be. He trained and worked them hard, and did not hesitate to share in the work. He was also a good listener, an invaluable trait for a first sergeant. Still, most of his troops were surprised when they read in a newspaper article that his wife described him as a "marshmallow." "My soldiers say she's out of her ever-loving mind," he later commented.

The first sergeant position was a venerable one in the United States Army. Elmore was the unit's senior noncommissioned officer (NCO), and by design, he was the commander's most trusted advisor and assistant. A good first sergeant was the glue that bound a unit together—the link between the officers and soldiers. It was typical in the National Guard for enlisted men to spend their entire career in the same unit, a contrast to the officers, who tended to move from unit to unit as they moved up through the ranks. And although the officers spent much of their day pushing a desk, attending meetings, or doing "brain work," the first sergeant and his fellow NCOs were expected to execute whatever plans the officers and commanders developed. The NCOs were the backbone of America's Army; they were the doers while the officers were the thinkers and planners. That was certainly the case for the 233rd's NCOs. Royer expected his NCOs to work independently and take initiative when confronted by a challenge. They had a reputation for doing just that!

First Sergeant Elmore joined the 233rd in 1985 along with his two brothers, then worked his way up through the ranks. He had been groomed by some superb NCOs along the way, and now he was charged with leading a uniquely strong and capable group of NCOs. Ultimately, it was Elmore's job to make sure the commander succeeded. "If he fails, the company fails, and I will not allow the company to fail," he told a reporter matter-of-factly. So it was that Elmore shared his commander's vision of success. He was committed to keeping his soldiers focused on their mission by focusing his attentions on their training and morale. His quest was to get all of his soldiers back alive—and make no mistake, they were *his* soldiers.[9]

Unit Profile

The 180 soldiers that Captain Royer and First Sergeant Elmore took to Wisconsin were a diverse lot, but they were united in their pride for the 233rd and their determination to succeed. As in all of America's wars, the soldiers of the 233rd were remarkably young. Most were in their early twenties. As was typical for National Guard units, the 233rd's NCOs tended to be older than their active duty counterparts. Master Sergeant Sam Woods was the unit's elder statesman at fifty-four, but there were also several NCOs well into their forties. Many had logged time on active duty before making the jump to the civilian sector and joining the Guard. Being in the Guard allowed them an opportunity to earn good pay in a part-time job they found rewarding, all the while working toward a military retirement. But serving

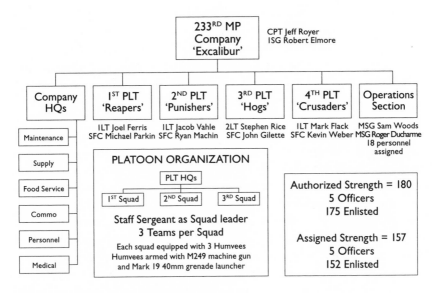

The 233rd MP Company organizational chart

in the Guard wasn't just another job for most of them. They were soldiers, and proud of it.

More than a few of the 233rd's soldiers were full-time college students, a typical feature in the Guard and Reserve where recruiters aggressively courted high school students with the enticement of generous education benefits. Weekend drill was an excellent part-time job, especially since the federal government paid drilling soldiers two days of pay for each day of drill. There were also federal scholarship benefits to be had, and Illinois was especially generous to its guardsmen: the state paid up to four years of tuition to any of the state's many public institutions.

The soldiers of the 233rd possessed a multitude of civilian skills. The unit counted twenty-nine police and corrections officers in its ranks, including ten from the Springfield police department and three more from the local county sheriff's office. Thirteen other police departments were also represented, and Sergeant Jeremiah Fritzsche served as a fireman in Springfield. Many of the unit's college students also aspired to a career in law enforcement. Altogether, the company could draw on a couple of hundred years' worth of experience in police work. It was the kind of experience that their Regular Army counterparts could not match, and that gave the MPs a self-assurance rare among many National Guard units. It didn't hurt that thirteen, soon nicknamed "the dirty baker's dozen," were also veterans of the gulf war in 1991, most as members of the 233rd. It was yet another feature that distinguished the 233rd from the regulars. The typical regular unit could boast of plenty of combat veterans, but none with the longevity in the same unit, as was common in the 233rd.

Because of their many years together, the men and women of the 233rd were a family. They shared a deep bond, a camaraderie difficult to explain to most outsiders. They viewed this as one of their strengths. Many of the regulars saw it differently, claiming that discipline suffered because the guardsmen were overly familiar. Some regulars held their Guard and Reserve counterparts in contempt; others reserved judgment until the citizen-soldiers could prove themselves worthy of their respect.

The MPs knew they would soon encounter such prejudices. Friction between regulars and citizen-soldiers was as old as the nation itself. Indeed, the rivalry was virtually guaranteed when the Founding Fathers wrote both the Regular Army and the state militias into the Constitution. The Founders feared a large standing army, seeing it as a dangerous tool that a despotic president might use to impose tyranny over "the people." As a counterforce, they also wove the state militias into the Constitution—institutions that had existed since the founding of the colonies. Because the militia in principle included all able-bodied adult men, the constitution's authors reasoned that the militia would never act contrary to the interests of "the people" because they were the people. Americans of the era were proud of their militias and proud of their innate ability to rise to any occasion to defend their country, whether that meant expelling a foreign invader, quelling an Indian uprising, or opposing the regulars should a despot ever order them to move against the people.

The logic of the Founding Fathers is largely lost on the regulars and guardsmen of the twenty-first century, but not the old prejudices that linger on as a result of the nation's uniquely dual military structure, one part regular, the other citizen-soldier. Regulars are often quick to challenge the professionalism and skill of their Guard and Reserve counterparts, arguing that they cannot possibly be as proficient as are the regulars in the unforgiving business of war. The guardsmen, for their part, resent the haughty and condescending attitude they too often see from the regulars. For their part, the MPs of the 233rd were confident they would prove the regulars wrong.

The unit's core of experienced law enforcement officers was only one of the advantages the MPs claimed. Also included in their ranks were carpenters, a metalworker, a heating and cooling specialist, a mechanic, a postal worker, and several soldiers with medical training and experience. There were soldiers with retail sales experience, one who worked for the federal government, and others who worked for the state of Illinois—not surprising considering the unit's location in the state capital. The 233rd also included an employee of a local donut shop, another who worked on a gambling boat, a bartender, and a waitress at the Peoria Hooter's, a fact that gained her some notoriety with several journalists eager to give their stories a human interest twist. The diverse set of civilian skills proved to be invaluable once they reached Iraq.

The 233rd included twenty-six women, mostly in the lower ranks. Staff Sergeant Deborah Carter, the unit's mess sergeant, Staff Sergeant Cindy Singley, the administrative NCO, and Staff Sergeant Lisa Morrison, squad leader in 4th Platoon, were the highest-ranking women in the unit. Many of the women were college students, but two served on area police departments, and several had medical backgrounds. As a group, they were capable, ambitious, and aggressive, and they were determined to pull their weight.

Although the unit was based in Springfield, a city of 100,000, a disproportionate number of the unit's members hailed from the small towns that characterized central Illinois, a region blessed with rich soil and abundant rainfall. Indeed, the city was in the heart of some of the richest farmland in the world, and the soldiers reflected the agrarian values of their region. They tended to be more loyal, self-disciplined, and more conservative than many of their contemporaries. They were, by and large, firmly rooted in family and community.

There were only a handful of African Americans, Hispanics, and Asians in the unit, a demographic that was not representative of Springfield itself, but did represent the demographics of central Illinois, and the 233rd cast a wide net when finding its soldiers. This fact was not something that Captain Royer and First Sergeant Elmore reflected on much. It was an old Army adage that soldiers were neither black nor white—they were Army green. The phrase was more than just a bow to political sensitivity. What mattered to Royer and his troops once they got to combat was whether they could count on their buddies to do their job—that the soldier next to them could be trusted in a tight spot. Racial issues mattered little when your life was on the line. So when a battalion staffer asked Royer and Elmore how many African Americans were in the unit, they looked at each other, hoping the other knew the answer. The question seemed irrelevant compared with the overwhelming challenges ahead of them. They faced what was likely the toughest job of their lives. They were headed to war, and were determined to get every one of their soldiers safely back home.[10]

Sixty-seven soldiers in the unit were married, and of those, twenty left both a spouse and children at home. Several soldiers were single parents, and for these, the separation was especially difficult. As part of the military's standard predeployment requirements, they had long ago arranged for their children's care in the event that they were deployed. It was a necessary precaution in an army with so many single parents. A family care plan was also a requirement for Staff Sergeant James Batterson and his wife, Sergeant Jennifer Batterson, both assigned to the 233rd. They left three children from James's previous marriage with his ex-wife, and then scrambled to find a house sitter to look after the house, plus two horses, three dogs, a ferret, and their collection of fish. Jennifer's mother was given power of attorney, which allowed her to pay the couple's bills while they were overseas.

The Battersons were not the only family members who served together in the 233rd. The company also boasted three sets of brothers plus the father-son team of First Sergeant Elmore and Robert Jr. Specialist Blanca Valdez and Sergeant Robert Spence had gotten engaged just before their deployment. Finally, Specialist Ayrielle Singley, assigned to the 233rd's maintenance section, served beside her mother, Staff Sergeant Cindy Singley, the unit's administrations sergeant. The fact that so many of the soldiers had family members in the unit was another feature that differentiated the National Guard from the Regular Army, where such practices were openly discouraged. Guard recruiters had always encouraged young men and women to join up with their hometown buddies. After all, they argued, who did you want beside you in the foxhole when things got tough? To ensure there was no opportunity for favoritism, Royer and Elmore were careful to split up the relatives. As for Elmore's own son, he addressed his father as "First Sergeant," never "Dad." Still, more than a few regulars were baffled by the Guard's tolerance for family members serving in the same unit, insisting that this could only undermine a unit's discipline and cohesiveness in the long run. The difference of opinion on that subject illustrated the cultural divide that often existed between the Army's regulars and its citizen-soldiers. Each group embraced its own paradigm of what it meant to be a soldier.

Fort McCoy

Fort McCoy, Wisconsin, buzzed with activity by the time the 233rd drove through the gates on the evening of February 10. The post, normally a quiet backwater, now hosted units from throughout the Midwest, all mobilizing for war. The place wasn't much to write home about, especially in the winter. Located about 100 miles northwest of Madison, it wasn't too far from Wisconsin's chief resort area, the famed Wisconsin Dells. The state's cranberry region lay northeast of the post. But Fort McCoy itself seemed to validate the old Army legend about an obscure staff officer who long ago had flown over the United States looking for the most desolate terrain he could find on which to build military posts. In Wisconsin, that was Fort McCoy. It consists mostly of a few thousand acres of rolling hills covered by pine and deciduous forests, scrub brush, and plenty of poison ivy.

The post was decidedly spartan, with its streets laid out in a triangular grid. It still boasted more than its share of old World War II–vintage barracks, two-story rectangular buildings thrown together during the early days of that war that had been intended as temporary structures but that stubbornly outlasted everyone's expectations. Many of these buildings had recently been remodeled, but there were also plenty that were condemned. All of the post's buildings were now pressed into service. Fort McCoy was located near several of the state's premier ski resorts, so the MPs were not surprised when they were greeted by cold, a swirling wind, and a dusting of snow as they drove through the front gate. All in all, Fort McCoy was about as different from the deserts of the Middle East as you could get, but such was the Army's logic. For the next two months, the 233rd would call it home.

The Train-up

Royer still knew very little about the 233rd's final destination when he drove through the gates of Fort McCoy, and even less about the unit's ultimate mission. No one seemed to know, least of all the 85th Training Division, a U.S. Army Reserve outfit from Chicago responsible for their training. Royer expected to be at Fort McCoy about ten days—two weeks at the most. But as the days slipped by with no clarification on their mission, the MPs got about the business of training themselves, with assistance from the 85th.

The 233rd possessed a robust organization in order to accomplish its wartime mission. Its 180 personnel were organized into four line platoons, a large operations section, and a company headquarters that contained the company's logistical and administrative assets. Each platoon consisted of three squads, and each squad had three teams of three soldiers each: a sergeant as team leader, a driver, and a gunner. A hard-topped version of the Humvee served as the team's transportation. In the 233rd's case, the Humvees dated from the first gulf war in 1990, when the unit had received them fresh from the assembly line. Thirteen years later, the vehicles had endured plenty of wear and tear, but they were still in decent shape. Unlike the newer models, these Humvees were not armored.

Each Humvee mounted a Mark 19, a 40-millimeter grenade launcher that operated like a chain gun, capable of launching up to sixty grenades per minute to a range of 2,200 meters. The grenades were dual purpose, effective against both light armored vehicles and personnel. That armament alone gave the company an unparalleled amount of firepower for a comparably sized unit, but this was further augmented by an M-249 squad automatic weapon (SAW) for each team, and an M-16 rifle and 9-millimeter pistol for each team member. (Many of the unit's old hands bemoaned the loss of the old M-60 machine gun with a 7.62-caliber round that packed a bigger punch than the SAW's 5.56 round.) The team leader came equipped with an M-203, essentially an M-16 with a grenade launcher attached underneath the rifle barrel. Finally, the company had ten shotguns for close work—weapons that also came supplied with nonlethal rounds. In essence, the 233rd carried the firepower equivalent to a light infantry battalion.

The reason for this impressive array of weaponry was simple. The 233rd was designed to cover a huge piece of terrain. They were expected to operate independently, as part of a squad of three teams, but no more. This meant that team leaders and squad leaders (sergeants and staff sergeants) might find themselves operating independently on a battlefield, expected to face down a determined foe on their own. This put a premium on aggressiveness and initiative, qualities that the 233rd's NCOs had internalized.

The company's ambitious mission called for a robust tactical operations center (TOC) at the company level. Nothing like it could be found in the typical infantry or armor company. The 233rd's TOC was equipped for twenty-four-hour operations, enabling it to monitor the activities of the unit's far-flung squads and teams around the clock. Each twelve-hour shift was supervised by a master sergeant, a seasoned professional with fifteen to twenty years' experience.

Finally, the company included all the assets the unit needed to sustain itself independently for several days. Accordingly, the headquarters platoon included a large maintenance section, plus food service and supply sections, a personnel clerk, and five medics. Organized, staffed, and equipped as it was, the 233rd was relatively self-contained. Over the years, the MPs had trained hard to master their mission, and they could draw on a wealth of practical, real-world experiences. Because of that, the unit had a deep bench—a host of experienced NCOs.

Even with that, Royer was not willing to make any assumptions about his soldiers' fighting edge—not when they were preparing to go into combat, as he had to assume. He and Top decided to go back to the fundamentals and concentrate on the soldiers' basic combat skills, especially survival skills, close-order combat, and convoy operations. Given the paucity of information they were receiving, it was the prudent thing to do.[11]

Royer developed his company's training plan based on the broad outlines of a plan he received from the 85th Training Division, which was required to certify the 233rd when it was deemed ready for combat. Once his plan was developed, Royer relied on the platoon leaders to execute it. He spent a lot of time hammering out his training plan with 85th Division staffers, but as far as he could tell, the army had issued no specific training guidance for the MP companies tailored for the operation in Iraq, and neither did the 85th. Faced with an undefined mission and uncomfortably vague training guidance, Royer and his subordinate leaders turned to the standard MP training manuals, which included a plethora of training tasks covering a wide variety of missions. They assumed that they were headed for Iraq or Afghanistan, and that their mission would be similar to the one that the unit had performed during Desert Storm. That meant they needed to focus on POW handling and rear-area operations. Patrolling the main supply route connecting Kuwait to Baghdad also seemed a safe bet. Given those assumptions, they knew that weapons qualification was a high training priority, especially considering the scarcity of heavy weapons training (especially for the Mark-19) in a typical training year, the result of difficulties associated with acquiring ranges and ammunition. Another logical focus was preparing to operate in a chemically or biologically contaminated environment. Royer also penciled in close-quarter combat drills in the event they were sent to an urban area. And because the unit had replaced its antiquated radio system at Fort McCoy with SINCGARS radios, the army's more secure radio system that regular army units began receiving in the 1980s, mastering this new equipment became a high priority.

Perhaps the most tactically challenging training exercises the platoons received were the simulated combat scenarios ("lanes") run by the 85th Training Division. These lanes came complete with an opposing force—85th Division soldiers trained to fight using enemy tactics. One lane simulated combat operations in a built-up area, a dangerous scenario under the best of circumstances. The Army had increasingly been devoting more attention to that scenario, but Fort McCoy's urban terrain training site was grossly inadequate to the task. The site consisted of a single cement block building surrounded by open meadows and clear fields of fire. There were no streets, no sewers, no cluster of buildings or streets filled with junked cars and other obstructions, the kind of things the MPs knew they might face once in combat. The facility made for a decidedly unsatisfactory training experience, even if the reservists in the training division had been up to the task of running the lane. They were not. Other lane exercises, such as actions on a convoy ambush, were more realistic, but only marginally more beneficial. So except for the basics, most MPs believed the training they received at Fort McCoy was largely ineffective.[12]

Royer stressed physical fitness to his leaders, knowing their success in combat might very well depend on how well they held up to the rigors of combat. In this respect, however, he pushed this responsibility down to his platoon leaders. As a result, the specifics of the PT program varied widely between platoons. Soldiers in a couple of the platoons were given considerable latitude in designing their own individual physical fitness program. Lieutenant Joel Ferris of the 1st Platoon took a decidedly more aggressive approach, insisting that his platoon train as a group, putting them through a rigorous program that included arduous road marches and platoon runs.[13] Much of the MPs' time was also spent in maintaining their equipment and preparing it for shipment overseas. With Fort McCoy inundated with units scrambling to head for combat, replacement parts were particularly hard to come by, a fact that frustrated their maintenance efforts and limited their training time.

As the days slipped by, Royer continually pestered his superiors for information about his mission—anything that would give him some indication of where they were headed and what they might be doing once they got there. Finally, after a couple of weeks at McCoy, he got a call from a staffer with the 16th MP Brigade at Fort Bragg, North Carolina. The 233rd belonged to the 16th, he was told, and was headed to Iraq. Armed with this information, Royer grew concerned that their training matrix included very little cultural training—nothing about the Iraqi people, Arab culture, or Islamic ideology, and no training in the Arabic language. It was quite a contrast to the unit's train-up for Desert Storm. In that war, the Saudi government placed specific limitations on the American soldiers stationed in their country—limitations that necessitated a thorough cultural training program. Ironically, the MPs ended up having very little contact with the Saudi public during Desert Storm. Things looked to be different this time around, yet no one was emphasizing cultural training. So, as was often the case in the 233rd, the officers and NCOs took the initiative and started to do their own research, conducting spur-of-the-moment classes. As often as not, the younger soldiers learned about the Arab world and its culture during a series of impromptu footlocker bull sessions conducted by several of the unit's Desert Storm veterans.[14]

The MPs went after one of their assigned tasks with a relish. They were instructed to come up with code names for the company and for each platoon. The reason for the directive was simple enough: when the unit received the new SINCGARS radios, which included built-in encoding and other security features, the soldiers no longer had to change their radio call signs every day. Their new radios automatically scrambled their messages and could only be deciphered by another secure radio with the same settings. For convenience, each unit came up with its own handle to use throughout the operation. Royer allowed each platoon to develop their own nicknames, a rare case of democracy in an authoritarian world, and the MPs went after the assignment with enthusiasm. Not surprisingly for a culture dominated by young men, the names were inspired more by testosterone and bravado than by political sensitivity. The company headquarters became "Excalibur," while the MPs of 1st Platoon adopted the moniker "Reapers" and those in the 2nd Platoon proudly embraced "Punishers." Those in the 3rd Platoon became "Hogs," and the 4th Platoon MPs unabashedly became the "Crusaders." Because the MPs' cultural education was woefully lacking, they were ignorant of the inflammatory nature of their nicknames. In particular, the 4th Platoon "Crusaders" were oblivious to the Arab world's hatred for the Christian Crusaders of the Middle Ages. As far as the 4th Platoon was concerned, they were "Crusaders," a force for good in America's war on terror. When officers later suggested that their names were inappropriate and unnecessarily provocative, the troops chalked up the comments as just so much political correctness. They weren't politicians; they were soldiers, and such subtleties were irrelevant. The MPs embraced their nicknames. They developed distinctive crests that embodied the names' essence, then proudly stenciled them onto their vehicles.

A month into their training at Fort McCoy, the 233rd loaded most of its equipment onto railroad flatcars destined for Corpus Christi, Texas, one of the military's main ports of embarkation. No one accompanied the equipment as it was moved to the port. First Sergeant Elmore and his son, Robert, flew to Corpus Christi to observe it being loaded onto ships. The 233rd was fortunate—all its vehicles ended up on the same ship, one of the navy's specially designed equipment haulers known in the military as RO-ROs, short for roll on, roll off. The cavernous ship swallowed all of the 233rd's vehicles and Conex containers, plus plenty more.[15] Back at Fort McCoy, the MPs continued their training, now without equipment.

Home Front

While the men and women of the 233rd were preparing for war, their families back in Illinois were struggling to adapt to life without their loved ones. The transition for those left behind was every bit as tough as it was for the soldiers in Wisconsin. Indeed, the Army had long recognized the difficulties that military families faced during long mobilizations, and the separation for the average guardsman's family was especially problematic. When the regulars deployed, those left behind had a built-in support network at the military post. That was not the case in the Guard or Reserve. There was no post exchange, no military hospital, and no family next door with whom to commiserate. Too often, the wives of guardsmen felt abandoned and isolated. They missed their husbands and struggled to cope with little help and few who understood their predicament. For that reason, each deployed unit was required to have a Family Readiness Group (FRG) where the families could find solace, strength, and helpful information.

The 233rd's FRG predated the unit's mobilization by several years. An FRG had long been a unit requirement, but the requirement was typically satisfied by preparing a series of documents stored in a notebook, ready to be displayed for inspections. The 233rd was an exception to this. Laquita Campbell, wife of Sergeant Brian Campbell, approached Captain Livingston and First Sergeant Jerry Calbow in 2000, offering to take on the job of FRG coordinator, and they gratefully accepted. Laquita brought a lot of energy to the position but soon realized the coordinator's position was thankless and time-consuming. The position called for Laquita to be the link between the 233rd's chain of command and the soldiers' family and friends. She organized meetings to generate some interest and conducted fund-raisers on drill weekends by selling snacks to the troops. But few of the other wives or parents showed much interest in the organization. They had their own lives to live. The female soldiers in the unit who were married found their husbands even less supportive. But in February 2003, with the unit now mobilized, the FRG took on a whole new relevance.

Laquita dutifully held several FRG meetings after the unit's departure to Fort McCoy, and attendance was fairly good—certainly much improved from the pre-alert days. But with four children of her own to care for, including two toddlers, and facing the absence of her husband, all while trying to attend nursing school, the duties of the FRG coordinator soon overwhelmed her. She realized she could not do justice to the position and began to look for a replacement. Once again, the 233rd was lucky. One of the attendees at those early meetings was none other than First Sergeant (Retired) Jerry Calbow, who had two nephews deployed with the unit, Staff Sergeant Keith and Sergeant Paul Hildebrandt. Calbow was attending the meetings in order to offer his support to Paul's wife, Monica, who was pregnant with their second child.

As the unit's former first sergeant, no one knew the soldiers of the 233rd better than Jerry Calbow, and no one was more universally respected by soldiers and families alike. He soon found himself thrust into a leadership role, much to the relief of Laquita and the state's FRG officer, Lieutenant

Jennifer Fallert. Faced with eight units deploying, Fallert did what she could to get the group energized, but she knew her success depended largely on the quality of the unit coordinators. She was understandably thrilled when First Sergeant Calbow stepped forward. Calbow soon found that being president of the 233rd's FRG took as much time and energy as he could give it. Fortunately, others stepped forward to help make the organization work. Within a couple of months, the 233rd's FRG was the model on which all others measured their success.[16]

Heading Out

By late March, Captain Royer was in regular contact with the 16th MP Brigade at Fort Bragg, which finally provided a bit of clarity to the 233rd's mission. They were indeed headed to Iraq just as Royer had suspected. They were scheduled to fly to Kuwait by way of Germany, and once in Iraq, they would be assigned to the 503rd MP Battalion, a Regular Army military police unit also from Fort Bragg. Beyond that, they knew little. Were they headed to Baghdad or to a remote desert location? Would they be processing prisoners, securing the military's tenuous supply lines, or conducting police work in Baghdad or elsewhere in Iraq? No one seemed to know. But one thing they did feel certain about. When the invasion of Iraq began on March 20, they knew it was just a matter of days before they would be headed overseas.

In this atmosphere of uncertainty, Royer gave his troops one last weekend off to spend with their families, with the stipulation that his soldiers must stay in the immediate vicinity of Fort McCoy. So on March 22 and 23, wives and children, parents and sweethearts made the long drive up to Wisconsin to say goodbye once again. Several families convoyed up to Wisconsin together, booked into a local motel, and spent this last interlude just relaxing. Paul and Monica Hildebrandt spent the weekend at their aunt's farm just thirty minutes from the fort. It proved to be a great respite from the grind of training and an uncertain future. Paul got an opportunity to play with nine-month-old Caleb and to "walk in the woods . . . to clear his head a bit." Most of the soldiers in the 233rd took advantage of Royer's generosity, but not Jeff himself. "I couldn't stand to say goodbye again," he later recalled.

For Specialist Joshua Holder, there was no joy in the occasion—no one to make the drive north and wish him goodbye. His parents' relationship was strained at the time, and just before he left, Joshua and his mother had traded some harsh words. He consoled himself with the knowledge that his girlfriend was making the long trip up to Fort McCoy. But while he waited impatiently for her to arrive, with a light snow swirling in the air, he placed a call to check on her progress. It was then that he discovered she was in Atlanta, Georgia, and not on her way to see him. The relationship was over, she told him bluntly. He took the news hard but found some consolation from his new family, his buddies in 1st Platoon.[17]

One week later, the FRG and WMAY, a Springfield radio station, sponsored a Support the Troops rally at the state capitol with thousands in attendance. After the rally, Jerry Calbow gathered up a group of family members and headed over to the local Chili's Bar and Grill for a bite to eat. It wasn't long after the group arrived before the parents instinctively gravitated toward each other, while a group of wives and fiancées did the same, sitting on the same side of the extended table. Four young women formed a special relationship that night: Monica Hildebrandt, wife of Paul Hildebrandt, Tammy Hughes, Lawrence Wilson's fiancée, Sarah Mauney, wife of Joel Mauney, and Deanna Victor, the newlywed in the group, married on February 7, just three days before her husband Marc and the rest of the 233rd headed north to Fort McCoy.

The four knew each other before that night, but only casually. By the time they left the restaurant three hours later, after they finished the desserts a sympathetic couple bought for them to mark the occasion, it was obvious to all four that they shared not just the same circumstances but a special bond as well. For the next twelve months, they were always there for each other, serving as each other's confidantes and comforters, through the good times and the bad—friends who could be counted on in the dead of the night when one of them needed to talk, vent, or cry on a friendly shoulder. To hear the women explain it, each developed her own particular role in the relationship. Sarah was dubbed the mom, the steady one the other women could count on to take care of them—to get them out of trouble. Monica, with a young son and another child on the way, was the baby of the group, but also their reality check. Being pregnant, she refused to let herself be enticed by any rumor that their men would be coming home soon. "Deanna kept us in line," explained Tammy. She could be counted on to speak her mind, firmly but diplomatically. Tammy was the group's upbeat spirit and their social coordinator. As the months passed, the four even took to calling themselves the Band of Sisters, and they embraced the full implications of that phrase. They were determined to get through the year—and to do it together.[18]

3
Into Iraq

It was 2:00 A.M. on April 6 when the charter 737 flight carrying the 233rd landed at Kuwait City International Airport. The MPs had boarded the plane some thirty-six hours before, in the midst of a freezing rain. Since then, they crossed nine time zones, touching down in Germany before reaching their destination. As they debarked, they were hit by a wall of heat. Even at 2:00 A.M., Kuwait felt like an oven, and this close to the ocean, the humidity held the heat. The contrast between Fort McCoy and Kuwait could not have been greater.

The MPs quickly loaded onto buses for the short trip to Camp Wolf, adjacent to the airport. They stayed only twelve hours, then boarded another set of buses bound for the interior, feeling all the while "like a can of sardines in a microwave." They soon arrived at Camp Virginia, a desolate camp carved out of barren desert. This would be their home for the next two weeks while they acclimated to the desert heat and waited for their equipment to arrive in port. There was a lot to reflect on while they waited. The tanks of the 3rd Infantry Division were already roaming through Baghdad.

During their first couple of days at Camp Virginia, the MPs did little except sleep, sweat, and lounge on their cots. Their barracks were nothing more than large rectangular tents arrayed in sterile lines. The oppressive heat sapped their energy and made any kind of exertion difficult. The sand seemed to find its way into everything, and a visit to the shower tent every other day offered only temporary relief. They followed the news about the war whenever possible, watching CNN or Fox News in Camp Virginia's Morale, Welfare, and Recreation tent, wondering about what lay ahead. Would they process POWs, pull rear-area security, or perhaps perform police-type duties somewhere in Iraq? No one knew for sure. When their equipment arrived, a team hustled down to the sprawling port facility and convoyed the equipment back north to Camp Virginia, where they spent the next couple of days performing maintenance, packing, rearranging the equipment, checking weapons, and contemplating their future.[1]

The 233rd was fortunate in one respect. All of its equipment arrived in port on the same ship. That was not the case for most units waiting at Camp Virginia. More often, a unit's equipment arrived on several ships that queued up in port, waiting for their chance to offload. That fact led to a change in the unit's mission. They were abruptly shifted from the 503rd, the unit with which Royer had conducted all of his coordination, to the 519th MP Battalion from Fort Polk, Louisiana. The 519th, as well as the 709th MP Battalion out of Germany, were aligned with the 18th MP Brigade, itself based in Mannheim, Germany. The 18th had drawn perhaps the toughest MP assignment of all: establishing security in Baghdad and rebuilding its police force. Finally, after two weeks in Kuwait, the 233rd knew its mission. They were headed for Baghdad, due more to a twist of fate than any carefully devised plan.

At the time, the 233rd was the only company assigned to the 519th MP Battalion. The 519th brought plenty of experience to its new assignment, with tours in Kosovo, Bosnia, and Haiti on its résumé. It was fresh off a tour at Kandahar, Afghanistan, where it provided command and control over all of the confinement facilities in the country. The 204th MP Company, a unit normally aligned with the 519th, was en route to Kuwait from Fort Polk, and several other MP companies were also due to arrive. But for the first few days in Baghdad, the 233rd was it. Once there, the 233rd would help Task Force Baghdad, consisting primarily of the 3rd Infantry Division, to secure the heart of the city. Royer was told nothing about how long they might be in Baghdad. With little else to go on, he still hoped they would head back home in six months. But whenever the troops raised the question, as they often did, he was as vague with them as his higher-ups were with him. No one knew.[2]

The wait at Camp Virginia did give the MPs a chance to get some much-needed cultural training. They scrounged up some handouts and brochures, most of it recycled from Desert Storm. Much of it pertained to the Saudis, and far too little was geared to the Iraqi people or their culture. They also enlisted the help of a soldier who knew a few useful phrases of Arabic, things like "stop," "put your weapon down," and "get down." They were soon practicing the phrases on each other in their best pidgin Arabic. "Show me your hands or I will shoot" was one of the phrases they memorized. Not until later did they discover that the phrase actually translated as "show me your hands *and* I will shoot." The haphazard nature of the cultural training, and especially their difficulty in getting some clarity on their mission, left many to wonder who, if anyone, was planning this show. They joked that Operation Iraqi Freedom was just a typical Army snafu—Situation Normal, All Fouled Up—only on a grand scale. Meanwhile, they waited for the word to head north. The wait afforded them an opportunity to call home, one last intimate conversation with loved ones before moving out. Officially, they could say nothing about where they were headed; the best they could do was hint that they would be out of the loop for a while. Still, a couple MPs were less discreet with their comments, and it didn't take long for the grapevine in Springfield to pass the word around that they were headed to Baghdad. The mood at Camp Virginia was a mixture of eagerness and apprehension, tension and excitement.[3]

North to Baghdad

It was Easter morning, April 20, when the 519th MP Battalion's command element departed Camp Virginia for Baghdad with a detachment from 1st Platoon of the 233rd in the lead. A few minutes later, the rest of the 233rd also hit the hardball, threading its way north along Route Jackson, the Army's main supply route into Iraq. The MPs were headed to Tallil Air Base just outside of An Nasiryah, their stopover for the first night. Tallil was actually an Iraqi air base the U.S. Air Force converted for its own use. Army troops called it "austere." Air Force personnel called it "downright primitive." But at least it provided the MPs some relative safety during their first night in Iraq. They set up their cots next to their vehicles and slept under the stars.[4]

The Iraqi Culture

The drive through southern Iraq brought one point home to the MPs: they had entered a very different world. Although they were growing accustomed to the climate, this was only April. It would only get hotter over the next few months. So they guzzled prodigious qualities of the bottled water that the Army provided with their rations. They passed huge expanses of open terrain interspersed with isolated villages as they wended their way north. Often, curious villagers waved tentatively as they drove by, but the MPs could not help but wonder whether these people were friend or foe. Their impression of the Iraqi people came primarily from watching coverage of the war on Fox and CNN. They understood very little of the complexity of Iraqi culture. They were generally unaware that the area they now drove through consisted primarily of Shi'ite Muslims, but that Baghdad itself was an ethnically diverse city. They understood little about the deep-seated animosities between the minority Sunni population, which had dominated Iraqi government and politics for decades, and the Shi'ia, who comprised roughly 60 percent of the Iraqi population. The Shi'ia shared their religious outlook with the Iranians but were also fiercely proud of their ethnic Arab background and Arabic dialect, in contrast to the Iranians, who were ethnic Persians, with their own distinctive language. They despised Saddam and his Ba'athist (secular) thugs, but fought well during the Iran-Iraq war, defending their most sacred Shi'ia holy sites against the Persians. They identified themselves as Shi'ia first, but Iraqis as well.[5]

The members of the 233rd understood precious little about the Arabs' fierce pride, about how to avoid insulting or degrading them, or how to defuse their latent hostility. They would learn these things the hard way, by making mistakes and then sharing their lessons learned with their fellow Americans.

Convoy North

The unit departed Tallil just after first light on April 21. (The battalion's advance party had already departed for Baghdad the previous day, augmented by a squad from 2nd Platoon.) A battalion element, which included a contingent from 1st Platoon, departed about an hour ahead of the main body. Both elements traveled independently and stuck to the main supply route, passing burned-out Iraqi tanks and armored personnel carriers, twisted guard rails, and junked cars and trucks as they moved north, skirting built-up areas whenever possible. Staff Sergeant Robert Smith, the 1st Platoon's first squad leader, was effectively the point man for the entire convoy. He felt his way north for much of the trip, a necessity because the Army had supplied him with only five of the eight topographic maps he needed for the drive. Fortunately, some resourceful MPs had taken the precaution of downloading satellite maps of southern Iraq while still at Fort McCoy. These, plus a crude strip map provided by the battalion, were all Smith had for the trip north. He placed more faith in his Garmin device, a combination global positioning system (GPS) and radio that he and several others had purchased at Wal-Mart. It proved a wise investment; the military-issue GPSs were sometimes unreliable.

Smith was only a few kilometers north of Tallil when he faced an important decision. He knew to expect a road junction just north of town where routes Jackson and Tampa split. He was told to stay on Jackson. As he approached the junction, he spotted a makeshift sign constructed from an MRE box dangling by a string from a wooden post. The sign, with "Tampa" scrawled across it, swayed in the wind, shifting back and forth between the two routes. Just as Smith closed on the intersection, the wind caught the sign and turned it to the left. He directed his driver to go right, then immediately began to second-guess his decision. He quickly perused his maps, then made several readings with the Garmin device before determining that he was leading the convoy in the wrong direction. They were ten minutes down the road before he turned the entire convoy around and drove back to the intersection. With that glitch behind him, the rest of the trip north was pretty much a straight shot. Smith kept to the hardball, moving along the path of destruction leading north to Baghdad.[6]

That delay allowed the 233rd's main convoy to close the gap a bit, at least until they came upon two of their Humvees from the lead platoon pulled over to the side of the road. One of the Humvees had a flat tire, and as prescribed by the unit's standard operating procedures, the other Humvee stayed with it to provide security. In the distance was an Iraqi village with several women and children milling about. Royer brought the convoy to a stop, and the MPs immediately went into their drill to establish security at a halt, a procedure they had drilled to perfection at Fort McCoy. As he dismounted, he watched the unit's wrecker pull up next to the downed Humvee. Several MPs formed a semicircle around the mechanics to shield them from direct fire.

Staff Sergeant Keith Hildebrandt, the unit's full-time mechanic before the war, was in charge of the maintenance section. Hildebrandt had grown up in the tiny farm town of Illiopolis and signed up with the National Guard right out of high school. For him, joining the 233rd was a no-brainer. His brother Paul was already in the unit, and Uncle Jerry was the first sergeant. Now several years removed from that decision, Hildebrandt found himself risking his life to change a tire in the middle of Iraq. He looked young for his twenty-four years. He kept his dark hair cropped tight to the head, and his facial features projected an air of innocence, a common feature for the sons of the prairie.

Hildebrandt quickly assessed the situation and discovered that all of the bolts on the tire's split rim had sheared off. His maintenance crew was prepared for such a contingency, but they knew that persuading the lug nuts off the tire would take time and considerable muscle. They dove into the job but were soon startled by the sound of gunfire coming from the village, followed immediately by a distinct ping. A bullet ricocheted off the ground just a foot in front of Captain Royer. A second round passed over his head before the shooter ducked for cover. Only a couple of the MPs had caught a fleeting glimpse of the enemy, but with their attacker out of sight and with other Iraqis milling about, they were unable to return fire. The near miss nevertheless gave the maintenance crew an even greater sense of urgency, especially after Royer moved the bulk of the convoy out of the ambush area, leaving the first sergeant at the repair site with a couple of squads for security. "Welcome to Iraq," Royer thought to himself as he led the main body north.[7]

The rest of the drive to Baghdad was uneventful. The MPs approached the city from the west, spending just enough time at the Baghdad International Airport, soon christened BIAP, to take a head count and reorganize the convoy. By the time they departed the relative security of BIAP for the heart of Baghdad, darkness had descended on the city—a city largely without electricity on a night with no moon. They were headed for the government sector located in the heart of the city, an area now known as the Green Zone. The Green Zone, containing government office buildings and elite residential areas, hugged the north shore of the Tigris River, where it made a tight loop through the heart of the city.

The convoy, with its two elements now rejoined, consisted of more than fifty vehicles, with Lieutenant Colonel Keith Warman, the 519th Battalion commander, serving as convoy commander. He conducted a quick briefing to the drivers before heading into Baghdad, giving them a chance to become familiar with the route and destination. But in the rush to get moving, Sergeant Hildebrandt and First Sergeant Elmore never made it to the briefing. "OK, let's go," was all they heard. It was their fate to enter Baghdad in the blind. Fortunately, the Americans had imposed a strict curfew on the citizens of Baghdad, maintained by a handful of 3rd Infantry Division patrols. But in a city of over 5 million, the American presence was insignificant.

Hildebrandt and Elmore hustled back to their vehicles and took their positions at the rear of the convoy, arriving just in time to see the vehicles in front of them depart. Hildebrandt drove the unit's maintenance truck, an ancient two-and-a-half-ton truck (known throughout the Army as a "deuce and a half") pulling a trailer. The truck lacked power steering, and muscling the steering wheel for several hours had taken its toll. Next in the convoy came the unit's wrecker, driven by Sergeant Mike Whited, pulling a crippled Humvee. First Sergeant Elmore brought up the rear, as was the Army's time-honored tradition.[8]

Lieutenant Colonel Warman, positioned near the front, set a fast pace for the rest of the convoy. The lead vehicles soon wove their way north past an infantry checkpoint and through a series of cement dividers laid out in a serpentine pattern. The road Y'ed immediately beyond the checkpoint and

Warman jogged right, just as he'd told everyone to do at the briefing. The convoy stretched out behind him.

The Humvees had little problem negotiating the roadblock, but it was a different story when the maintenance truck reached the cement barriers. Hildebrandt was already tired, having spent the entire day behind the wheel. Specialist Grant Barnes should have been driving that day, but he lay curled up in the passenger seat, suffering from what Hildebrandt guessed were heat cramps. Hildebrandt tugged hard at the steering wheel as he worked his way through the barriers and finally emerged on the other side, only to realize he had lost contact with the rest of the convoy. The two peered into the darkness, hoping to spot a pair of taillights receding into the darkness, but saw nothing. Hildebrandt made a snap decision and went left, stepping on the gas in an attempt to catch up with the rest of the convoy. Sergeant Whited, driving the unit's wrecker with a Humvee in tow, had even more difficulty negotiating the roadblock, jockeying back and forth a couple of times before he made it through. By that time, Hildebrandt's truck was nowhere in sight, so Whited turned right, with First Sergeant Elmore's Humvee following him.

Hildebrandt hadn't gone far before he realized there was no convoy in front of him and no wrecker to his rear. He was lost and alone in the heart of Baghdad. Thankfully, the streets were deserted. Fighting to keep his emotions in check, he eased the truck to a stop at an intersection. With no map and no GPS, a handheld Motorola was his only lifeline to the rest of the world. He managed to raise First Sergeant Elmore, who was racing to catch up with the main convoy. "Where are you?" came Top's curt reply. "I don't know," said Hildebrandt with as much confidence as he could muster. Weighing his options, he decided to double back to the roadblock and catch up with the rest of the convoy. That was his second mistake of the night. He'd been traveling on a one-way street, and Hildebrandt assumed that the adjacent street led back to the intersection. He drove on for several blocks before it veered away from the airport—and more ominously, away from the Y in the road. And the further he drove, the fainter the radio signals became. Soon, Hildebrandt was relying on other American patrols to keep his lifeline with Elmore open, who had doubled back in an attempt to link up with the maintenance truck.

Hildebrandt's next decision was his best of the evening. He pulled to a stop, jogged his truck and trailer back and forth until he was turned around, and then headed back down the one-way street going the wrong direction. He hadn't traveled far before he saw headlights advancing toward him. He experienced a brief moment of anxiety until he realized that they were Humvee headlights—the first sergeant's headlights. His lonely odyssey was finally over. Hildebrandt breathed a sigh of relief. Once he linked up with First Sergeant Elmore, it wasn't long before the entire unit had closed on a residential compound on the banks of the Tigris River, their home for the next twelve months. For the next few days at least, the 519th was alone in the Green Zone.[9]

Viper Base

The MPs spent the next two days settling into their new quarters in a compound along the west bank of the Tigris River. They shared the compound with the battalion headquarters. Because the 519th used "Viper" as its handle, the base was christened Viper Base. Their new residence was plush by Baghdad standards. The compound was the former residence of Izzat Ibrahim al-Duri, the Hussein confidant, regime vice president and deputy chairman of the Revolutionary Command Council. The redheaded al-Duri soon became better known as the King of Clubs—number 6 on the toppled regime's most wanted list.

Viper Base lay in the heart of the Green Zone, the most secure neighborhood of Baghdad, an area that formerly included the Ba'ath Party headquarters, two of Saddam's sprawling presidential palaces, a massive monument to Iraq's Unknown Soldiers, plus most of the government's key offices and residences for many of the regime's highest-ranking members. The Green Zone had been a target-rich environment for the Air Force during the war, but because of its use of precision munitions, most of the area's critical infrastructure remained intact. From now on, it would serve as the headquarters area for the Coalition Provisional Authority.

The MPs' new quarters were just a stone's throw away from the former Ba'ath Party headquarters and within sight of the huge arch of crossed sabers of the Unknown Soldiers monument. Al-Duri's compound consisted of about fifteen buildings and included some landscaped areas and a parade ground, all ringed by a ten-foot-high cement block wall. Several of the buildings were residences for al-Duri's extended family; others served as barracks and office buildings. The front gate opened to the north, toward the Unknown Soldiers monument. The back gate opened onto a road that paralleled the Tigris River, a route that connected some of Baghdad's most desirable real estate before the war. To the west was the new presidential palace, a favorite haunt of Saddam's eldest son Uday. That extensive complex included Uday's private zoo. Two thousand meters upstream was the presidential palace, sometimes referred to as the Iraqi White House, the official capitol of Iraq. A unit of Ghurkas later moved into the compound directly east of Viper Base, and next to them was another compound that included a

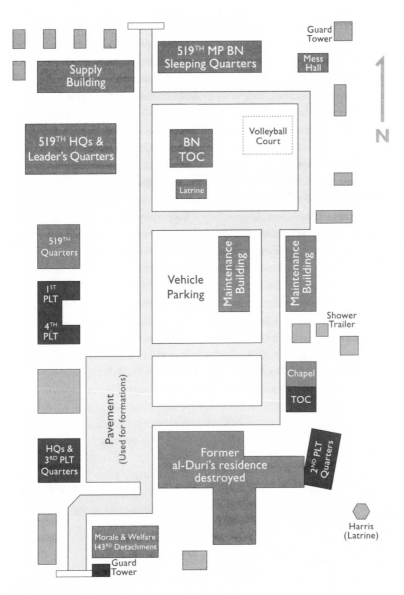

Viper Base

luxurious swimming pool, its water an unenticing green when the Americans first arrived. That compound soon became home to the 32nd MP Company, a National Guard unit from Wisconsin.

Al-Duri's personal residence, featuring bulletproof glass and reinforced walls, had once hosted meetings for Ba'athist bigwigs. A few Air Force bunker busters had reduced it to rubble. The 233rd occupied one of the adjacent buildings that had sustained less damage, converting it into a makeshift barracks. Those quarters proved to be far too cramped, and they soon converted several other residences in the compound for their use. Spacious rooms featuring luxurious chandeliers and lacy curtains were now overtaken by rows of cots, duffel bags, assorted personal gear, and growing mounds of dirty laundry. The pungent odor of sweat hung in the stale air. Throughout the company, men and women shared the same quarters. The women insisted on this arrangement, asserting that they should not be pampered or patronized. The men quickly adapted, looking away at those awkward moments when the women changed clothes. It soon became no big deal.

An office building on al-Duri's compound was adapted to serve a variety of purposes. It housed the company's tactical operations center, the unit's aid station, and a chapel on the main floor. The troops converted the second floor into a barracks for the headquarters section. It didn't take long for the MPs to clear the rubble out of the streets, but getting windows installed and the electricity and plumbing repaired in their work and living quarters was a bigger challenge. The MPs hired local Iraqis to install new windows, but they tackled much of the electrical and air conditioning work themselves. Master Sergeant Roger Ducharme, a heating and cooling contractor by trade, had brought his own tools from the States, and he worked long hours to get the compound's air conditioners operational before the unbearable summer months arrived. With the city's electricity so unreliable, the unit's generators were immediately pressed into service. Thereafter, the roar of generators became the MPs' constant companion.

While the troops settled in under Top's watchful eye, Captain Royer focused most of his attention on two things: establishing security for the compound, and getting some clarification on their mission. Even now, the information he received was sketchy.[10]

The Home Front

As far as the families and friends back in Illinois were concerned, the 233rd had fallen off the map. Maintaining contact with loved ones was hard enough from Kuwait. Once the unit reached Baghdad, it was nearly impossible. There was no mail, nor would there be for over a month. Colonel Warman did have a satellite phone that got passed around, but the opportunities to use it were rare, especially for those in the lower ranks. Occasionally a sympathetic reporter might offer his cell phone to some lucky troop, allowing for a quick call home. But for most of the wives and families, what they knew about their loved ones they learned from the news. And by this time, most of them avoided the news. It only increased their apprehension.

The key to maintaining the families' morale was the Family Readiness Group (FRG). Sergeant Calbow and Lieutenant Fallert worked hard to make the FRG meetings as informative as possible. They brought in finance representatives from the state headquarters to talk about pay issues, corralled representatives from the governor's office to discuss benefit issues, and brought up employees from the Scott Air Force Base commissary, located two hours south of Springfield, to let the families know about those privileges. What Calbow was hard-pressed to provide, however, was information about what was going on in Iraq. In the absence of hard facts, the rumors flew thick. Much of his time was spent dispelling the latest rumor. Calbow was the ideal man for the job. Since he had served as the unit's first sergeant for so many years, and because the unit drilled in the shadow of the state headquarters, he still maintained plenty of useful contacts in the headquarters building. It didn't hurt that Major Wendell Lowry, the unit's former commander who now worked full-time in the Guard's finance office, was also a personal friend.

The FRG meetings started while the unit was still at Fort McCoy. Once Calbow took the reins, they met monthly, most often at the Springfield Northenders' VFW Club. Meetings were well attended, with anywhere from 100 to 150 typically showing up. There were no dues, but several family members willingly stepped forward to organize fund-raisers. Sales of T-shirts and caps became their best money-maker, generating the cash needed for postage and other office expenses. It wasn't long before the FRG had a newsletter editor, a Web site coordinator, and two phone tree coordinators. Laquita Campbell agreed to take charge of notifying those who lived in the 217 telephone area code (Springfield), and Pamela Weber, wife of Sergeant First Class Kevin Weber, covered everyone else. The group also created a new position when Judy Victor, the mother of Sergeant Marc Victor, volunteered to serve as a birthday card coordinator to make sure that no one was forgotten. All of this was in the interest of keeping information flowing between the FRG members and their loved ones overseas. Attendance at their meetings and events grew steadily from month to month. They even started attracting a few parents of active-duty soldiers serving overseas who had no support system of their own. Eventually, girlfriends and fiancées were also brought into the fold.[11]

But all of this was yet to come, developed as the 233rd FRG matured. From April to early June, there were a lot more questions than answers, more frustrations than joy, and no shortage of rumors. The folks in Illinois had lost contact with their soldiers.

4

Early Operations

The coalition's fight from Kuwait to Baghdad had been so fast, and the fall of Saddam's regime so unexpected, that detailed planning for what came after the regime collapsed was sketchy and largely incomplete—at least, that was how it seemed to the few thousand American soldiers on the ground in Baghdad in April 2003. Now, these combat-hardened soldiers were expected to bring order to a city of over 5 million, a city torn by wholesale looting and violence. In short, Baghdad was in the grips of anarchy.

Delirious Iraqis began pulling down Saddam's statues on April 9. Four days later, General Tommy Franks, commander of the United States Central Command (CENTCOM), announced that the Iraqi army had been destroyed. Most Iraqi soldiers never surrendered to coalition forces; they simply discarded their uniforms and melted back into the civilian population. The same could be said for the city's police force, something the war planners had not anticipated. As a result, the American military was forced to fill the vacuum.

The American presence in Baghdad consisted of the 3rd Infantry Division, using Baghdad International Airport (BIAP) as a base of operation, and elements of the 1st Marine Division patrolling the volatile eastern portions of the city. (The Marines departed on April 20, the day the 233rd departed Kuwait, and turned over their portion of the city to the 3rd Infantry Division.) The Americans, spread dangerously thin, concentrated their efforts on securing the governmental areas, a few palaces, and critical infrastructure assets. For such a huge and sprawling city, the force was miniscule, totally inadequate to the job it now faced. Baghdad spun into violence and chaos.

Mobs of looters roamed freely through the streets. There was no shortage of Iraqis who despised Saddam, eager to lash out against the symbols of the toppled regime. Further complicating matters, Saddam had released thousands of hardened criminals in the months leading up to war, and now they swelled the ranks of those bent on revenge, giving the mob a particularly brutal dimension. There were also tens of thousands of opportunistic Iraqis, desperate to get something of value to help them survive the days and weeks to come. Finally, more than a few former police officers and soldiers joined in the mayhem.

Nothing was safe from looters. They started with official government offices and presidential palaces, then moved to the police stations, schools, museums, hospitals, power plants, shops, and stores. They took everything of value, plus much worth nothing. Once a building was stripped, it was often put to the torch. The violence subsided only marginally at night, in part because of a citywide curfew imposed by the Americans, but also because the city, desperately short of electricity, turned an inky black. Before the war, the city's power supply was never reliable, but Saddam made sure that the citizens of Baghdad got more than their share while he slighted the rest of Iraq. American planners had meticulously avoided attacking the city's infrastructure during the bombing campaign, but Baghdad's mobs were merciless and brutally efficient in destroying everything in their path. As a result, most of the city fell dark at night, and its streets were largely deserted.[1]

It wasn't just looting that plagued Baghdad, however. The city was also swept by a wave of revenge killings as aggrieved Iraqis settled grudges, some decades old. "It was 'get back' time in Baghdad," explained Lieutenant Joel Ferris of the 1st Platoon. The sound of gunfire was constant. Some of it had malicious intent, but celebratory fire was even more common, for Iraqis had a long history of celebrating by firing their rifles (overwhelmingly the Soviet-manufactured AK-47) into the air. They did so for weddings and for graduations, and now they did it to commemorate the joy of liberation. It was an emotional catharsis that inevitably accompanied the fall of every statue, the defiling of every portrait of Saddam, or the looting of any despised symbol of the old regime. The Iraqis "shoot when they are happy, when they are mad, and when the power goes out," observed Royer. "Everyone has a weapon." Put bluntly, Baghdad in April 2003 was a city in anarchy. The MPs aptly labeled it "cowboyland."[2]

The Mission Clarifies

The 233rd served at the tip of the spear in April 2003, the first MP unit to operate within the city. Its mission guidance was succinct: it was their job to restore order for a huge slice of Baghdad, and to do so against overwhelming odds. They had no real blueprint to work from, little understanding of Iraqi culture, and no one in the company who spoke Arabic.[3]

The 3rd Infantry Division commander served as the land manager for Baghdad, and he divided the city into sectors of responsibility. The division had its own organic MP company, but that unit concentrated its efforts on BIAP. The 519th MP Battalion, with only the 233rd under its control, was assigned to the 3rd Infantry Division and given the daunting task of establishing a police presence in the city. The 233rd drew a variety of missions during those early days. Several teams were assigned each day to escort the 519th commander, sergeant major, and the other key staff officers as they made their rounds through the city. Other teams escorted other coalition elements. About half of the teams were given reconnaissance missions. In essence, their job was to locate and assess key assets throughout the city, with special emphasis on the city's police stations. By the time the mission orders filtered down to the MPs, however, the instructions were a bit vague. "Go out there and see what you find" was about as specific as their instructions got. The reconnaissance patrols felt their way through Baghdad using what maps they had, but relied mostly on their Garmins to keep track of their location. Once back at Viper Base, they submitted their reports to the company tactical operations center (TOC).

Of course, the MPs were by no means the only ones patrolling the city. The 3rd Division had already established checkpoints at key locations scattered throughout Baghdad, and its infantry and armor units aggressively patrolled the city, seeking pockets of armed resistance and thwarting some of the worst cases of looting when they encountered it. Even while they conducted mop-up operations, 3rd Infantry Division units also relocated their bases of operation to sites throughout the city. It was a good way, planners asserted, to establish an American presence.[4]

When the MPs ventured into Baghdad, they did so in unarmored Humvees, in contrast to the armored versions many in the infantry and armor units used. They soon removed the Humvee doors to allow for a quick exit. From the beginning, the MPs stood out, driving through town with crossed pistols, the symbol of the MP branch, stenciled prominently onto their Humvees. Their rules of engagement were pretty straightforward. They were placed on amber status, which meant they could keep magazines in their weapons but could not chamber a round. If a crowd looked hostile but otherwise posed no direct threat, they were instructed to keep their weapons at the ready and to avoid any provocative gesture. If they perceived a direct threat or actually came under fire, they could return fire. Most importantly, they were told to minimize "collateral damage," the military's euphemism for civilian casualties. The trick was identifying friend from foe. Their potential enemies—and there were still plenty of them in Baghdad—had discarded their uniforms, but not their weapons. Because of that, they could choose the time and the place to fight. Not surprisingly, the MPs considered their rules of engagement to be too restrictive for what they knew was still a war zone.[5]

Life on their early reconnaissance patrols was a disconcerting mixture of experiences. On the one hand, enthusiastic Iraqis often mobbed the MPs as they passed through the neighborhoods. But occasionally, they came under fire from the remnants of the old regime. Thankfully, it was rarely effective. The MPs patrolled Baghdad in two-vehicle convoys. Each turtle-shell Humvee carried three or four personnel, including the driver, an assistant driver, the senior MP in the vehicle riding shotgun, and the gunner, who manned a Mark-19 in the turret. (Increasingly, the MPs swapped out their Mark-19s, which proved ineffective because of their excessive arming range, for the more versatile M-249 squad automatic weapon [SAW].) They had no interpreters, and they knew precious little about the Iraqi people's culture or the Arabic language. Drivers were instructed to keep moving and to avoid traffic jams in order to minimize the target they presented. They routinely disregarded the speed limit, not that it mattered much. Most of the traffic signs were in Arabic (and occasionally in English as well), but as Captain Royer observed, "traffic control laws were merely suggestions to these people."

By the time the 233rd began active patrolling on April 23, the roads and side streets were jammed with traffic. That fact, plus the occasional destroyed Iraqi tank or armored personnel carrier, junked vehicles, donkey carts, and the ever-present piles of garbage that spilled into the streets, made driving a challenge. Patrols often encountered long lines of Iraqis waiting patiently outside a gas station for fuel, further clogging the roadways. In a nation awash with oil, the gasoline shortage was one of the nation's most painful ironies. And even by late April, it was already uncomfortably hot, a harbinger of the oppressive heat that would soon arrive. Finally, the pungent smell of rotting garbage and decomposing animal carcasses hung heavy in the air.[6]

The reception the MPs received varied from neighborhood to neighborhood. In some, the tension and hostility were palpable. In most, they were treated like conquering heroes, instantly mobbed if they slowed or stopped. In these neighborhoods, crowds lined the streets, waving and cheering excitedly, flashing wide smiles and an occasional thumbs-up or V-for-victory sign as the MPs drove by. Cheers of "Go Bush," "Thank you, America," or "Good Bush" were common. Whenever the MPs stopped, they were quickly mobbed, despite their best efforts to keep the Iraqis at arms' length. Newly liberated Iraqis were determined to press forward to shake their liberators' hands, to give them a customary embrace, or to offer up cigarettes or a cup of hot tea. Lieutenant Mark Flack was struck by how many Iraqis thanked him for leaving his family to help them, and by several who apologized if the patrol happened to come under random fire. "I've never been kissed so much by a man as I was in Baghdad," recalled Royer.[7]

The MPs were earnest students, absorbing the nuances of the Iraqi culture as quickly as possible, knowing that their lives might soon depend on that knowledge. They were struck by Iraqi men's habit of holding hands and exchanging kisses, and also by their treatment of women. Women were clearly second-class citizens, yet they were fiercely protected by the men, who guarded them against any slight and insisted they be put at the head of a line. The MPs preconceived notion about heavily veiled women quickly evaporated. There were plenty of burkas to be seen, but none of the women was completely covered. Instead, some wore the traditional black head covering; others sported more colorful versions. Just as often, women wore blue jeans, flattering blouses, and high heels, looking elegant in their western garb. Regardless, the MPs quickly learned that the Iraqi men would tolerate no fraternization with the women. Searching the women proved especially problematic. It was better to relegate that job to the female MPs.[8]

The sight of the female MPs in military uniform performing the same tasks as their male counterparts was quite a shock to the Iraqi men, especially when the women performed their duties with assertiveness and obvious confidence. The female MPs got so much unwanted attention that Royer stopped worrying about how they would handle themselves on the street. Instead, he worried about "how many Iraqi men I was going to have to beat off because they wanted to marry them, or . . . touch them, or talk to them." Women with blue eyes and blonde hair were a special novelty for Baghdad's men. Despite their efforts to disguise those features behind sunglasses and Kevlar helmets, they drew more than their share of attention. Sergeant Shauna Cashion found that some of the older men were openly hostile, occasionally shouting obscenities her direction or making lewd gestures toward her. In contrast, the younger men were more likely to blow kisses. Several called out marriage proposals. "Will you marry me?" or "I love you" were phrases she heard frequently, especially during her first few months in Iraq. One particularly ardent Iraqi offered to trade his prized goat for her hand. As a defensive measure against the more persistent ones, she often flashed her engagement ring, indicating she was already spoken for. Specialist Sarah Schmidt got two questions repeatedly fired her direction. "Married?" was the most common question, and when she lied by stating that indeed she was, the Iraqis invariably followed up by asking, "Babies?" Specialist Laura Thomason found herself speechless after one exchange with an ardent suitor. When she told the young man she was married and that her husband was back in the States, he was undeterred. "I'll kill your husband so you can marry me. I go to America and take care of that."[9]

Children were ubiquitous during these patrols, and like kids everywhere, they had fewer inhibitions than their elders. They pressed in on the MPs with curiosity and enthusiasm, hoping to get a closer look, to shake hands or practice their English. More than anything, they hoped to get a handout of candy or trinkets. As far as the MPs were concerned, the kids were irresistible. Like their fathers and grandfathers before them, they gladly distributed candy and items from their MREs, and they offered gestures of friendship and goodwill. It wasn't long before they grabbed as much hard candy as they could before departing on patrol, cramming it into their commodious uniform pockets.[10]

Firefight Near the Rail Yard

Despite the outpouring of enthusiastic support the MPs received in most neighborhoods, the city was by no means pacified. That fact was driven home on April 28, after only a week of active patrolling in Baghdad. Second Lieutenant Stephen Rice commanded a patrol from 3rd Platoon that was driving through the rail yards west of Viper Base, with Sergeant First Class John Gillette, the Hog's hard-nosed platoon sergeant, serving as his driver. Gillette was more than just the platoon sergeant; he was also Lieutenant Rice's mentor, the seasoned noncommissioned officer (NCO) whose job it was to teach young lieutenants the ropes, and he carried himself with an air of authority befitting that responsibility. Specialist Quntrell Crayton completed the lead Humvee's crew. He hailed from Fairview Heights, Illinois, but now manned the turret machine gun, a world away from the quiet life of suburban St. Louis. Behind them was the patrol's second Humvee, this one commanded by Sergeant Dana Hodges and driven by Specialist Lucas Jockisch. The Hogs' mission was to conduct a reconnaissance of an area north of their compound on the west side of the Tigris River, a commercial and residential area that bordered the city's railroad terminals. Scattered throughout the neighborhood at six-block intervals were Third Division checkpoints. Many of the checkpoints featured armor support, a stark contrast to the thin-skinned Humvees the MPs drove. Other 3rd Infantry Division elements conducted armored patrols of their own.

The patrol was heading north on a crowded four-lane highway when it became sandwiched behind a red double-decker bus, boxed in by traffic to its right and a center median to its left. The road was flanked on both sides by commercial buildings and high-rise apartments. As the Hogs continued north, they entered an area that Rice knew from intelligence briefings to be a hotbed of Saddam fedayeen resistance, the regime's elite and fanatical paramilitary organized to wage guerrilla war on the Americans. As the bus to their front began to slow, then stopped altogether, Sergeant Gillette spotted a ten-story apartment building to his left, and immediately experienced a wave of foreboding. They were trapped, and he knew it.[11]

Suddenly, the air was torn by the sounds of rifle and machine gun fire coming from their left. A dozen fedayeen poured out of an apartment building and were now laying down murderous fire in their direction. Other fedayeen fired toward the convoy from second- and third-story windows. Bullets struck ominously near them, some ricocheting off the ground, others thudding into palm trees in the center median. One machine gun burst tore into the bus, blowing out a window and tearing into several passengers, whose bodies twisted in agony. Sergeant Gillette watched in horror as the head of one man exploded. All the while, he kept his left hand on the steering wheel while holding his M-16 with his right hand, cradling the rifle barrel across his arm, firing at a black-clad fedayeen who was shooting at the convoy from a second-story window. Gillette sprayed the area until he found his mark, even as the other fedayeen continued their deadly barrage. The convoy's two gunners laid down withering fire with their SAWs as several fedayeen came tumbling out the front door before a couple of them fell to the ground in agony. Meanwhile, Gillette continued his firing, then discovered he had rammed into the back of the bus, the Humvee's tires spinning wildly in a losing battle to push the bus out of the way. He eased off the accelerator, then forced the steering wheel to the left, found an opening in the median, and steered around the bus, plowing over a tree in the process. All the while, he continued firing toward the fedayeen, changing magazines and tossing the empty into the back of the cab. Specialist Jockisch followed close on the heels of the lead Humvee until both vehicles pulled to a stop at the end of the block. There, Lieutenant Rice contacted Excalibur TOC while Gillette quickly assessed the damage. Amazingly, they had sustained no casualties, and the vehicles had taken no hits. Within moments, the patrol once again came under fire, although ineffectively. Even so, Rice knew this was no place to stop, and he motioned the convoy to move out. They drove on for several blocks, stopping only when they came upon a 3rd Infantry Division checkpoint that included an M-1 tank for fire support. As Rice completed transmitting his situation report to the TOC, he watched two tanks rumble past, headed for the ambush site.[12]

With the spot report in and the 3rd Infantry Division armor element headed for the action, the Hogs returned to Viper Base. It was the first time the group had fired their weapons in Baghdad. It would not be their last.

Within days of the incident, the coalition authorities changed the rules of engagement. The MPs could thereafter patrol the streets of Baghdad with a round chambered in their M-16s. Days later, Sergeant Gillette heard that the incident near the rail yard had resulted in eleven fedayeen killed and nine wounded, plus an unknown number of civilians killed and wounded. It was a bloody baptism to a turbulent year.[13]

A Shortage of MPs

The Army in Baghdad was stretched precariously thin during the early days of the occupation. This was due in part to the Army's dramatic downsizing during the previous decade—a downsizing that cut heavily into the Regular Army's MP strength. Some of the shortage resulted because of the military's remarkable speed and precision during the war itself, coupled with the regime's sudden collapse. But fundamentally, the Defense Department made a conscious decision during the buildup to war to fight it with a much smaller force than many war planners previously thought prudent. Advocates for a small invasion force had proven to be right about the fight to Baghdad, but the size of the force the coalition needed to keep the peace was still an open and hotly debated question. Nevertheless, units of all types were now unloading in Kuwait, then quickly reorganized before heading north. Those units included several MP companies earmarked to reinforce the 519th. But these units were not scheduled to arrive in Baghdad for days or weeks.

One fact soon became obvious to the war planners: the Army needed a lot more MPs than were currently in the force. By July 2003, fully 90 percent of the Army's MP units were deployed somewhere in the world. War planners wanted fifty MP companies in Iraq; they had only a handful available.[14]

Prewar Assumptions

The security problems of May 2003 were born of several flawed assumptions made by the Department of Defense and CENTCOM planners in the months leading up to war, and resulted in part from the military's stunning success during the war itself. CENTCOM staffers had assumed the combat phase would last for 125 days. Instead, it was much shorter and less intense than even they anticipated. That gave CENTCOM's overworked staffers much less time to work out the details for phase 4 of General Tommy Frank's plan, the phase he called "stability operations." Planners were thrilled when some of their assumptions proved wrong. There was no epidemic or humanitarian crisis after the war, as many planners had feared, and no starving and emaciated Iraqis flooding refugee camps and soup kitchens. Nor did they face any environmental disasters, such as burning oil wells that filled the air with dense clouds of acrid smoke, or mammoth oil slicks in the Persian Gulf. The speed of the assault had preempted all of that. And perhaps most surprising of all, Saddam unleashed no weapons of mass destruction on either coalition formations or his own people. That fact would have important political implications in the future, but it came as a huge relief to troops and Iraqi civilians alike.

The planners were also wrong about some assumptions that made governing Iraq much tougher than anyone had anticipated. One reason coalition forces advanced so quickly was that Iraqi conscripts, when faced by the overwhelming power of the American military, deserted en masse, discarding their uniforms and disappearing into the population. As a result, the ranks of Iraq's unemployed expanded greatly, compounding the Americans' challenge of restoring the economy. This fact also swelled the ranks of the looters, as did Saddam's decision during the days preceding the war to release tens of thousands of criminals from his prisons. These elements only exacerbated the intensity and duration of the looting, which contributed immeasurably to the destruction of the nation's infrastructure and the challenges the coalition thereafter faced. There simply were not enough Americans on the ground to keep the looters in check. For many, both in and out of the military, this was the worst flaw in the invasion plan—the paucity of forces available for the occupation.[15]

It was no secret that some Army planners argued for a much larger force when the war plans were first discussed. This was the view of the Army's chief of staff, Eric Shinseki, the secretary of the Army, Thomas White, and initially General Tommy Franks as well. Based on the troop model used for the Balkans, which in turn was based on conventional military wisdom for counterinsurgency operations, it would take half a million troops to provide security for Iraq. Secretary of Defense Donald Rumsfeld, anxious to wrench the military into the post–cold war world—a world where masses of heavy armor, artillery, and high-performance aircraft had less relevance—insisted that a much smaller force armed with smart bombs and the tools of the information age could do a better job. Rumsfeld's opinion won the day, and as it turned out, he had been right for the combat phase: slimmer was better.

As for postwar Iraq, CENTCOM planners anticipated that the Iraqis themselves would step forward and take charge of their own security, that the old government agencies would continue to function at some level, and that Iraqis would hasten to establish a new government. "Our planning assumption," wrote Tommy Franks, "was that we would guide the Iraqi interim government in building a military and a paramilitary security force drawn from the better units of the defeated regular army. These units would serve side-by-side with Coalition forces to restore order and prevent clashes among the religious and ethnic factions."[16] Unfortunately, by May 2003, these units ceased to exist. They were not available to reestablish security or to help rebuild Iraq, in part because of a decision made in May by L. Paul Bremer, the administration's senior official in Iraq, to disband the entire Iraqi army. In making the call, he essentially ignored the advice of several prewar studies advocating the retention of a smaller, de-Bathified army rather than expelling tens of thousands of ex-soldiers into a nonfunctioning economy.[17]

Planning for the Posthostility Phase

When the combat phase abruptly ended in late April, the plan for the occupation, infinitely more challenging and multidimensional than the war itself, was only beginning to come together.[18] CENTCOM's occupation plan was nearly as extensive as the war plan, but that fact revealed something of the administration's myopia on the subject of occupation. What the coalition forces needed was an infinitely more detailed plan, one that addressed the multifaceted challenges they would face after the war. First and foremost, they needed a plan for reestablishing security, a task that grew exponentially when the nation's own police and security force essentially disappeared. That meant American troops had to restore law and order in the streets while the Coalition Provisional Authority (CPA) simultaneously created an ethical and humane judicial and prison system. The occupying army had to accomplish all this while also guarding a long list of critical infrastructure assets from the looters they knew would come. And only after security was reestablished could the CPA begin to rebuild Iraq.[19]

But developing a security plan was just the start. CENTCOM war planners needed detailed plans for cleaning up the streets, rebuilding the electrical grid, fixing sewers, supplying clean water, getting oil flowing to generate revenue, distributing food, opening hospitals, guarding against disease, restoring the telephone grid, reopening banks, preserving historical artifacts, getting millions of unemployed back to work, issuing a new currency, rebuilding and reopening schools, writing and printing new textbooks, kickstarting a free press, and on and on. Of course, there was also the critical need to secure the thousands of ammunition caches scattered throughout the country, even while searching for the elusive weapons of mass destruction. Indeed, the list was endless, and each task seemed monumental in its own right. Alas, the plan was inadequate. "All the A team guys wanted to be in on phase 3," recalled one staffer, "and the B team guys were put on phase 4 (post hostilities)." As a result, CENTCOM planners developed only the broadest framework for administering Iraq after the war; they planned to fill in the details as the situation on the ground developed. When Congress members grilled Jay Garner in late May about the continued chaos in Iraq, he fired back, "This is an ad hoc operation, glued together over about four or five weeks' time. [We] didn't really have enough time to plan."[20] One 233rd NCO summed up the posthostility plan more succinctly. "The plan sucked," he stated bluntly. Those in the 233rd were inclined to agree.[21]

The 233rd Mission

With so few units on the ground in April, and because the 233rd was the only MP company working in the heart of Baghdad for the first few days, the unit was overloaded. The MPs got both mundane missions, jobs like escorting supply runs, and high-profile missions. No job was more high profile than the one they received for April 28, when they provided security for a meeting of some 300 prominent Iraqis to discuss the creation of an interim government. The CPA chose a location adjacent to the al-Rashid Hotel in the heart of the Green Zone as the site for the two-day event. Captain Royer assigned one platoon to control access to the building. It established a perimeter that extended a couple of blocks out from the hotel and directed attendees to park their vehicles near Iraq's tomb of the Unknown Soldier, where the MPs searched both the vehicles and all the participants before they proceeded to the meeting. A second platoon was posted inside the hotel for internal security, and another platoon stood at the ready as a quick reaction force. The event went off without a hitch, a fact that added to the unit's growing reputation for efficiency and professionalism.[22]

The mission guidance Royer received for the next day illustrated the scope of the unit's challenge. "The 233rd MP Company [will] conduct joint military operations with the Iraqi Police in the vicinity of Baghdad . . . to facilitate in providing a safe and secure environment to enable transition to the office of Reconstruction and Humanitarian Assistance . . . led efforts in establishing a legitimate Iraqi governing authority." Put another way, it was the 233rd's job, all 156 of them, to restore and then maintain order in a city of roughly 5.6 million Iraqis. The order went on to provide this guidance: the "unit will conduct mounted and dismounted joint patrols, while maintaining a well protected yet highly visible posture."[23]

By late April, the looting began to subside, having run its course. But even by then, coalition planners must have known that the Baghdad police, armed only with pistols, would be seriously outgunned. Still, a handful of Iraqi police had already returned to duty, many reporting to the city's police academy on the east side of the Tigris River near the Olympic stadium. The police academy was located within the perimeter of a hastily established American compound, which was actually nothing more than a cluster of buildings and facilities that included the 519th's headquarters element and its TOC. The decision to locate the 519th's forward operating base at the academy while the troops slept in Viper Base made little sense to Captain Royer, but in the scheme of things, he had far more important things to worry about. The 233rd patrols were instructed to report to the police academy, where they would pick up Iraqi police and interpreters for joint patrols. As often as not, the Iraqis failed to show, and the MPs conducted these "joint" patrols on their own.[24]

It was during this time that Royer received another mission crucial to the city's future. He was directed to identify the location of all of the city's police stations plus the police academy jail, also known as Tas Ferrat. To accomplish the mission, Royer had only a 1:100,000 scale map of Baghdad that, when folded, fit neatly into his cargo pocket. Otherwise, the map proved useless for the task at hand. It showed the city's major thoroughfares but none of the side streets or other details he needed to navigate through the city. Fortunately, he also had a global positioning system (GPS) device, which proved indispensable as the MPs made their way around the sprawling city. And for this exercise, Royer also had an Iraqi guide, a mysterious character who went by the name of Ahmed Kadhim Ibrahhim. He spoke in broken English when he presented himself to Captain Royer, stating that he was a captain in the Baghdad police force and an authority on the city's police stations. Thus, Captain Kadhim, Captain Royer, and two escort teams drove from neighborhood to neighborhood, with Kadhim pointing out the otherwise nondescript police stations to Royer as he glanced at the GPS display and scribbled down the ten-digit grid. As the two toured the city's police stations, Royer noticed that Kadhim kept promoting himself as he introduced himself to other Iraqis. By the end of the day, he was a colonel, and the other Iraqis were in no position to challenge him, escorted as he was by the Americans. Over the next few weeks, Kadhim moved steadily higher up the chain in the newly organized provisional government until he reached the exalted position of general, chief of the Iraqi national police, and the deputy interior minister. Weeks later, Royer heard a rumor that Kadhim had been arrested because of his former Ba'athist ties, then later discovered Kadhim still retained his position in the interior ministry. In the long run, Kadhim proved himself to be an agile survivor.[25]

Whatever Royer felt about Kadhim, at least he ended the day with a series of grid locations for the city's police stations. He didn't have a lot of confidence in the quality of the information, but it was a start. Armed with this information, on May 4, Lieutenant Colonel Warman directed the

233rd to assess ten stations on the eastern side of Baghdad, while the newly arrived 204th MP Company was given seventeen stations on the city's west side. Royer passed the assignment onto his platoon leaders, instructing them to report on their condition and on the status of the Iraqi police who they found at each station.

At the same time, the coalition provisional authorities put out an appeal to all Iraqi police officers, asking them to return to work on May 4 to begin the job of restoring "law and order among the people of Baghdad." The message included instructions for a new uniform. "The police officer uniform will be a white shirt (with no rank epaulette), trousers (no beret), and a crest on shirt pocket and only sidearm," the order specified. The Iraqis were also expected to provide some form of identification when questioned by the Americans.[26]

What the lieutenants discovered when they arrived at their designated stations was anything but encouraging. Under Saddam, the police had been the regime's brutal enforcers. They were grossly underpaid, so they supplemented their meager pay by extorting it from the public. They took to this task with relish. As a result, police corruption was not just endemic—it was accepted and encouraged by the senior Ba'athist leadership. When the old regime collapsed, the people of Baghdad lashed out at the police stations. The policemen, fearing for their lives, discarded their uniforms—the same as those worn by those in the Iraqi army. When the looters hit police stations, their first target was invariably the extensive personnel files the police had maintained on common criminals and political prisoners alike. Gone were the hated mug shots and fingerprint cards. Every scrap of paper in every filing cabinet was fed to the fires. Furniture was carted away, electrical wires and plumbing stripped out. Windows were broken and the frames torn out, and then the buildings were torched. The fires destroyed whatever was left. Thus, what the lieutenants found on their initial assessment tours were nothing more than empty shells. There were no personnel files, no weapons, no police cars, and no prisoners held in the detention cells. In many cases, even the cells' bars were gone, sold as scrap metal. All had been lost to the mob's fury.

Lieutenant Joel Ferris of the 1st Platoon followed his GPS into a neighborhood just east of the Tigris River in search of the al-Mesbah police station. When he reached the grid, he found no signs of a station. "We had to ask off the street," he later recalled. He was forced to trust an Iraqi who was willing to help. Ferris was unable to understand the young man's limited English, but he fared better in understanding his creative hand and arm signals, and they eventually found the station on a back street. As the patrol drove up, the lieutenant noticed thirty or forty men milling around in front of a burned-out building, as if they were waiting for someone. Ferris assigned a couple of MPs to guard the vehicles, then walked into the throng of Iraqis, who immediately pressed in around him. To his surprise and dismay, this was the police force, and they were waiting for him. Finally, these Iraqis hoped, here was someone who knew what was going on.

When Sergeant First Class Ryan Machin pulled up in front of the al-Karadah police station, he found nothing but a gutted building. Not one window had survived the violence. There was no running water, no electricity, and no telephone service. The hallways were littered with burned papers and a heavy dusting of ashes. Only one policeman was present for duty. He was cleaning up the mess, "out of loyalty to his police station, his city and his country," he explained to Machin.[27]

Lieutenant Mark Flack started his day early, awakened in the middle of the night by a member of the TOC's night shift. There was a change of mission, he was told. In addition to his platoon's other duties, they were now tasked to perform assessments on three police stations. Because he had already tasked four of his MP teams to conduct escort missions at BIAP that day, only the 1st Squad, led by Staff Sergeant Lisa Morrison, was left to accompany him on his hunt for the elusive police stations. Flack, an Illinois state trooper before the war, had seen plenty in his two years on the force. Combined with eight years in the 233rd, he had an abundance of experience to draw on. But as he stumbled out of bed that morning, he wondered whether any of that experience and training would be of any use.[28]

The four-vehicle convoy, with Flack's Humvee in the lead, departed Viper Base shortly after breakfast, heading for the first grid coordinate, where, they hoped, Flack's Crusaders would find the al-Jadriya police station. When the patrol found nothing, the convoy drove to the next station on his list, only a couple of hundred meters away. There, Flack hoped to discover the al-Jadrya station, with a spelling remarkably similar to the first station. He found nothing that even vaguely resembled a police station, and he concluded that wherever the station was, al-Jadriya and al-Jadrya were merely two spellings for the same station. As he scanned the neighborhood, he noticed police motorcycles parked in front of a restaurant. The motorcycles obviously belonged to two uniform-clad Iraqi customers seated at a sidewalk table. Flack concluded they were traffic police, and after approaching them, he asked where he could find al-Jadriya. Neither man spoke English, but Flack persisted, repeatedly asking where he could find the elusive station. The two finally relented and led the patrol to the outskirts of Baghdad University, but nowhere near a station house. Once again, Flack, his frustration growing with each dead end, stressed that he was looking for a police station, not the university. The Iraqis then flagged down a passing motorist who spoke some English, and after a short conversation, the traffic police finally led Flack to the al-Jadriya police station. What he found was hardly promising—only a gutted building, and no Iraqi policemen.

The patrol wasted little time at al-Jadriya, but as the MPs drove away, an Iraqi man rushed across the street as the convoy's last vehicle passed by, obviously fleeing a 3rd Infantry Division infantryman who was in hot pursuit. The infantryman called out a warning, then shot the Iraqi in the leg when he failed to stop. At this, Flack turned the convoy around and sped back to the incident. Specialist Kristina Ward and Sergeant Kurt Glosser quickly dismounted and rushed to the injured Iraqi to administer first aid. The drama soon caught the attention of several television crews who were lingering outside their nearby hotel, and they too came rushing to the scene. With the street now clogged with an MP convoy, infantry Humvees, an injured Iraqi, and several news crews, traffic slowed to a crawl. The next incident took the whole scene from comical to surreal. Two trucks collided, and the drivers squared off in the street. When one of the men flashed a knife, Sergeant Jim Kollins ordered him to drop the knife, then took him to the ground. That altercation was all the probable cause the MPs needed to search both vehicles, and by the time they were done, they discovered two AK-47s and four magazines of ammunition in the knifeman's truck. That triggered an argument between Flack and an infantry sergeant about who should take the injured Iraqi into custody. Flack had his mission to perform, and escorting prisoners was not part of it. That, he insisted, was the infantry's job. As he returned to his Humvee, he shook his head in amazement. "It's going to be an interesting year," he thought to himself.

The Crusaders' visit to the second police station on their list was much less eventful than the first. They found several Iraqis clustered outside the al-Karadah headquarters when the convoy pulled to a stop outside the station. Thankfully, a few of them spoke a smattering of English—enough, at least, for Flack to determine that no one at the station had been paid since March. He soon located the station commander and patiently filled out a simple assessment form, taking note of the commander's irritation as he worked his way through the questions. With the assessment form completed, the Crusaders headed back to Viper Base.

By the end of the day, Lieutenant Flack was able to make a couple of broad conclusions about the state of the Baghdad police force. The city effectively had no police—no one who could even begin to challenge the looters and criminals, no one who could bring order out of chaos. His day marked an inauspicious beginning to the 233rd's most important mission: rebuilding the Baghdad police force. "I would hate to be a cop here," Flack wrote in his journal that evening. Then, as an afterthought, he added, "Well, I guess I am already."[29]

May 4 went much the same for the other platoons as well. Once a patrol arrived at a station, it did not take long before disheveled men, most dressed in civvies, began to wander in. The MPs had no way of verifying which of them had been police before the war, and who were now masquerading as police officers in hopes of getting paid. They also had no way to identify the Ba'athist flunkies from those who had no blood on their hands. They usually found Iraqis who were eager to help them sort such things out, but it was up to them to decide whom they could trust. And complicating it all was the language barrier; they had no interpreters. Fortunately, it typically did not take long for volunteers to emerge, eager to serve as interpreters in exchange for a few dollars. Five dollars was the going rate during those first chaotic days. The lieutenants often paid their new assistants out of their own pockets.[30]

Lieutenant Flack returned to the al-Karadah headquarters later in the week, this time equipped with a much more detailed police station assessment form and instructions to report on the station's general condition and on the status of the police force then working at the station. (Flack later discovered that al-Karadah was also known as the al-Mesbah police station, the station initially visited by Lieutenant Ferris.) The questions and his comments revealed the extent of the problem the MPs now inherited. "What was the amount of the [police station's] operating budget?" read one entry, followed by this question: "When were [the Iraqi police] last paid?" The answers Flack received were hardly promising, but not surprising. The stations had no operating budget, an Iraqi policeman explained. How could it be otherwise when their government no longer existed? More to the point, the officers who stepped forward had received no pay since March, before the war began. In fact, most had only returned because the coalition provisional authorities had broadcast messages throughout the city promising $20 if they came back to work. When the MPs arrived, the Iraqis naturally assumed that the MPs were there to pay them.

For the question, "What type and number of weapons are issued to the police officers?" Flack wrote, "Previously, officers and commissioners had various types of pistols—guards had machine guns and rifles. Nobody currently has any weapons." These "presumably" had disappeared during the wholesale looting; most were hidden safely in the policemen's homes, and some no doubt ended up on the booming black market. Flack concluded his assessment of the station with this comment. "Due to a lack of weapons, the [Iraqi] officers fear coming to work." As he moved from station to station later that day, he made the same comments for each station he inspected.

Flack amended his comments when he later returned to the stations. "These people have been promised that they would receive guns, money (initially $20.00), and uniforms. So far not a single promise has been addressed. They keep asking when they will get these things. The MPs assisting these police stations are not given direction on when these things will arrive or through what channels. The police officers are growing impatient toward the MPs." He concluded with this: "If progress is not made quickly, then future joint efforts could be hindered."[31]

While Flack's patrol tracked down its designated stations, Staff Sergeant Jay Fritzsche of the 3rd Platoon led another patrol in search of the Diyala Bridge police station located next to a tributary of the Tigris in the southeast quadrant of the city. Fritzsche had plenty of company that day, with both First Sergeant Elmore and Sergeant First Class Gillette tagging along for the ride. They found the station easily enough: they discovered it next to the bridge, which was guarded by a 3rd Infantry Division Bradley fighting vehicle. The station looked more like a medieval castle, complete with turrets and firing holes, than a modern police facility. By the looks of the scorched chunks of a greenish metal twisted beyond recognition littering the ground, the place had obviously been targeted by the Air Force. The team dismounted and proceeded inside. A few curious Iraqis, clearly former police officers, showed up as they began their formal inspection. What made this visit so memorable, however, was what they found in the building's courtyard. There, lying on top of a pile of blocks underneath a tree, was an old Soviet-style radiacmeter, a device used to alert the presence of radioactive contamination. More disturbing was the sight of the radiac needle pegging well inside the yellow range of the exposure scale. "That piqued our interest," Sergeant Dan Hinds noted laconically.[32]

A Full Plate

After the initial assessment of the police stations, the platoons were directed to visit each of their assigned police stations twice a day. Beyond that, the lieutenants received only vague guidance about their missions—little more than a requirement to report in occasionally to the company's TOC back at Viper Base. At this stage of the occupation, CPA officials hoped that the Iraqi people would resurrect their police force on their own, free from CPA involvement.[33]

With the twice-daily visits to the police stations now a permanent part of their mission, the 233rd settled into something of a routine that left the troops with precious little personal time. Every morning, the platoon leaders received their mission brief for the day. Besides the police station visits, they routinely split off several teams to escort 519th staff officers, assigning others to provide security for the base or to serve as a quick reaction force.

The missions on May 9 were typical. The 1st Platoon sent two teams to escort an engineer brigade commander and command sergeant major, and two more teams to protect a coalition payment team. The daily mobile patrol was directed to check in at the platoon's police stations. Additionally, the mobile patrol was tasked to link up with Iraqi police at the city's police academy to conduct a joint patrol in the morning. The missions for the 2nd and 3rd Platoons were much the same. The 4th Platoon was tapped as the duty platoon, which meant they belonged to the 519th sergeant major, pulling duties at Viper Base.[34]

Sometimes, the missions they drew didn't make much sense to the MPs, trained as they were to be cops in a city in desperate need of cops. Staff Sergeant Roman Waldron spent four successive days at a link-up site waiting for fuel trucks that never showed, practicing his golf swing with his Humvee's antenna to pass the time. Lieutenant Flack spent a couple of particularly hot and frustrating days escorting a transportation company in and around Baghdad. The Crusaders started the mission by meeting the truckers south of Baghdad and escorting them north to BIAP, where they picked up a crane. From BIAP, they headed to a weapons cache located in northeastern Baghdad. The truckers loaded two Soviet-era FROG (Free Rocket Over Ground) missiles per trailer, and then the convoy was on the road again, this time threading its way north to Taji and the designated drop-off site.

At Taji, their instructions unraveled. An ordnance sergeant in charge of an unexploded ordnance detachment insisted that the transportation lieutenant could not drop the missiles off with him. Instead, he provided Lieutenant Flack with two different grids even farther north. Flack guided the convoy to each of the new grids only to be turned away at both locations. He finally decided to take the missiles back to the original location and force the issue. "Either you let us drop the missiles off inside, or we'll just leave them on the street," Flack stated bluntly. By this time, the mission was well into its second day, and as they headed back toward Baghdad, the truckers were "dropping like flies" from the 130-degree heat, with Flack's medics pumping IVs into them. The worst was a trucker with a full-blown case of heat exhaustion. The MPs discovered him curled tightly into a ball, no longer able to sweat or even shiver. They were only five minutes from Viper Base, so they decided the best course of action was to rush him to the compound. That night, the entire convoy stayed in the Green Zone, and the next morning, Flack led the truckers back to their own base south of Baghdad. By the end of the patrol, his hands were so red and tender he pulled on his gloves for protection. In retrospect, he realized that for this mission, at least, his worst enemies weren't insurgents; they were confusion and the unrelenting heat.

On the drive back to Viper Base, Flack struggled to understand why the MPs were stuck doing this job instead of helping reestablish the police force. Here they were in the middle of a city where the police force was in a shambles, and yet someone decided to use them, the troops most able of helping the Iraqis, to escort some trucks around town. Why couldn't the infantry escort the convoy? He couldn't make any sense out of it. Who was in charge of this mess, anyway?[35] But on another level, however, Flack understood why. Not since World War II had the American Army been given such an ambitious mission—nothing short of building a nation of 27 million from scratch. It was the coalition's job to forge a nation where the infrastructure had totally collapsed, to bring security and stability to a society torn by religious and political turmoil, and to set the conditions for democracy in a region that had seldom known it. It was a tall order, especially considering they were so shorthanded and possessed precious few resources. Finally, both the Iraqi people and the American public were impatient to see progress. By virtue of their presence in Baghdad, the soldiers on the ground were now committed to try. It was as Secretary of State Colin Powell had stated: "If you break it, you own it." Meanwhile, as far as the MPs could tell, it seemed like much of the world was rooting for them to fail.

The one commodity American soldiers in Baghdad possessed in abundance was their resourcefulness and resilience. And in this, the men and women of the 233rd were no exception. They coupled their innate confidence and an unshakable belief in their mission with a resolve to do the job well and get everyone back home alive. Through sheer luck, the Army had gotten one thing right. They had stumbled across the ideal unit to perform one of the coalition's most important missions—that of rebuilding the Baghdad police force.[36]

By mid-May, the 519th MP Battalion had grown with the arrival of the 204th MP Company from Fort Polk and the 549th MP Company from Fort Stewart, Georgia, both active duty units, plus the 307th MP Company, a National Reserve unit from Pennsylvania. More companies were on the way, including two National Guard MP companies scheduled to arrive in June: the 32nd from Wisconsin and the 812th from New York. As the battalion's strength grew, the pressure on the 233rd lessened, but one fact remained the same. There was still a lot more to do than there were MPs to do it.[37]

Keeping in Touch

During this period, the MPs in the 233rd effectively lost touch with their loved ones at home. The break in contact was tough on them, but because they worked around the clock seven days a week, they had little time to reflect on it. That was not the case for those they left behind. The spouses and parents knew only that their loved ones were in the heart of Baghdad, and they found little succor from the frequent reports of violence they saw on the evening news and on the front page of the morning newspaper. Most of the MPs did find an occasional moment to jot down a letter and get it mailed, and those at home were especially good about writing, but it made little difference since the mail system was in complete disarray. Incoming mail was piling up somewhere in theater, but as far as the MPs were concerned, their precious letters and packages could just as well have been on the moon. They yearned for their mail, but they had no illusions about getting it soon.[38]

First Sergeant Elmore took the break in contact personally. As the unit's top NCO, maintaining the troops' morale was one of his highest priorities. He understood his soldiers' needed to know things were all right at home in order to maintain their fighting edge. But their only contact, regrettably, was the battalion's satellite phone. Back in Illinois, Jerry Calbow understood Elmore's concern, and he kept busy staying on top of the rumors that inevitably arose as the wives and parents passed around what little information they gleaned from sporadic phone calls and from the media. Jerry dealt with the rumors by firing off e-mails to everyone on his growing address list. He worked hard to keep everyone informed with the best, most accurate information he had. He got his facts from a variety of sources—from the parents and wives, from officials at Camp Lincoln, and, as communication from Iraq became more reliable, from the soldiers themselves. But he especially relied on "Top" Elmore to keep him informed.

By early June, Elmore began sending e-mails to First Sergeant Calbow whenever he could, relying on Calbow to pass them on. Elmore told the families about their soldiers' mission (being careful to avoid anything that might cause alarm) and about their living conditions, and he even offered advice on what to send and what not to send through the mail. In one of his very first e-mails, he addressed the one question that everyone wanted answered. "There is still no news about when we get to come home," he began. "I am not going to make any guesses. I know a lot of people have their hopes set on August, but that is highly unlikely. . . . I am telling the soldiers to prepare for the long haul and not to mentally set themselves up for a disappointment. Family members need to do the same."[39]

A New Commander

By mid-June, the troops were working grueling twelve-hour shifts, seven days a week. Although the vast majority of Iraqis seemed thrilled to have them there, those who still resisted the occupation were becoming more sophisticated. Random potshots became less common as the MPs cruised through the streets of Baghdad, but the insurgents were now employing car bombs, what the Army called "vehicle-borne improvised explosive devices" (VBIED), the kind of overly precise acronym on which the military thrived. Even more feared by the MPs were the roadside bombs, or IEDs. They could be disguised in the most inconspicuous ways, ingeniously hidden on the side of the road in a heavily traveled area, then detonated remotely with a cell phone or garage door opener whenever the Americans drove by. The MPs were taking a crash course on how to survive in an often hostile city. Little of their training back at Fort McCoy seemed relevant to their lives now. As one sergeant later reflected, "Everything we learned, we learned on our own. We learned by being out there every single day and interacting and asking questions and staying alert."[40]

By June, the heat was oppressive, often reaching into the 110s and 120s. That fact alone sapped their energy, as did the nerve-wracking drives through Baghdad and the grueling pace they maintained. When they were at Viper Base, they spent their time on work details, attending briefings, cleaning weapons, and maintaining equipment. In their spare moments, they worked on improving their living areas. They converted slit trenches into outdoor latrines, cleared up the rubble left over from the war, and scrounged for materials to improve their sleeping quarters. Electricity was still a scarce commodity; what they milked from their generators kept the all-important communications equipment going. They took their meals in the battalion's mess hall on the north end of the compound, staffed primarily by the 233rd's own cooks. They learned that the best time to take their showers, using a chemical decontamination sprayer converted for that purpose, was at the end of the day—that they slept best if they washed off the sweat and salt and grime of Baghdad before collapsing into the sack. Their routine left them precious little personal time, and never enough time to sleep. Most of them could count on little more than four to five hours of sleep a night. And in the early days, before they had scrounged for air conditioning in their living quarters, even that much sleep was hard to come by as they lay in the sweltering heat.

The joke in Baghdad by June was that every day was Groundhog Day, a term derived from the Bill Murray movie of the same name about an endlessly repeated day—an acknowledgment that there was no way to distinguish one day from the next. Every day had the same monotonous weather forecast: sunny and hot, with no clouds. There were no weekdays, no Sundays, no rhythm to break up a week. One day flowed into another in a seamless procession until they all became a blur. That rhythm was only occasionally disrupted when something significant occurred to alter their routine.

June 11 was one of those days. That was the day the 519th MP Battalion changed command. In a simple ceremony held on a makeshift parade ground on Viper Base, Lieutenant Colonel Paul Warman handed the battalion's flag over to Lieutenant Colonel David Glaser, symbolizing the change of command. Glaser had arrived in Baghdad on June 3, flying in directly from Fort Polk. During the next few days, Glaser shadowed Warman as he made his rounds, learning firsthand about the mission that lay before him. Most importantly, he got a feel for the soldiers in his new command, and from the outset, he liked what he saw. He was particularly impressed by the 233rd's command team of Captain Royer and First Sergeant Elmore, and by the obvious knowledge and competence of their troops.

The 519th's change of command occurred roughly at the same time the 3rd Infantry Division handed over control of the city to the 1st Armored Division. The 3rd Infantry Division had borne the burden of fighting the war and had made the difficult transition from liberators to occupiers. It now fell to the troops of the 1st Armored Division, newly arrived from Germany, to administer the troubled city.[41]

Lieutenant Colonel Dave Glaser hailed from the Midwest, growing up in a small town near Cincinnati, Ohio, embracing small-town values in the process. He received his college degree and an officer's commission from Xavier University in Cincinnati before heading off to a career in the Regular Army. He possessed the bearing and confidence the Army expected of its commanders, with pale blue eyes and a high and tight that revealed a slightly receding hairline and hints of gray. Everything about the man spoke of confidence and professionalism, and Captain Royer took an instant liking to him.

Glaser wasted little time before making a couple of significant changes. First, he relocated his forward operating base from its location near the Baghdad police academy to Viper Base, where security was much better. His other significant change raised his stock with everyone in the battalion. During Glaser's initial inspection of the command, he couldn't help but notice the troops' haggard appearance. They were near the ragged edge of their endurance. "You could just see it in their eyes," he later recalled. "They were just worn out, tired, sometimes making some bad decisions." During the first few chaotic weeks in Baghdad, Warman had little choice but to work his MPs around the clock. The few MPs in Baghdad could not possibly do everything the coalition authority needed to have done. By the time Glaser got there, they'd been working for fifty days straight, twelve to eighteen hours every day. If they were going to stay the course for the long haul, he reasoned, then a day off here or there was crucial. The troops needed time to catch up on maintaining their vehicles and weapons and on cleaning their uniforms. But most importantly, they needed a break from the unrelenting mental and physical toll. Accordingly, shortly after he assumed command, Glaser called his company commanders together and laid down the law. They would develop a work plan where their soldiers got a day off every week to ten days, he informed them, even if that meant that they manned fewer police stations. Few commands had ever been so enthusiastically received.[42]

5
Forging a New
Baghdad Police Force

The fight from Kuwait to Baghdad was an infantry and armor war. As always, it was the grunts—GI slang for infantrymen—and tankers who shouldered the greatest burden and took on Saddam's military in close combat. By May 2003, however, that fight was over, and Captain Royer had no illusions about what lay ahead for his soldiers. From here on out it would be an MP war, where success depended more on the MPs' particular talents and expertise than on the skills of the infantryman. Success and failure would no longer be measured by a line advancing on a map or by a body count, but by a much more elusive and fragile objective: winning the hearts and minds of the Iraqi people. At one level, Royer recoiled from that catchphrase of the Vietnam war. That was much too touchy-feely for him. But at another level, he knew it was true. The job his MPs drew was to bring order and security to a society that had been run as a brutal police state for decades, where the police had long been feared and despised. His MPs were the new cops in town.

Their job was greatly complicated by a handful of Iraqis who still saw the Americans as the enemy and dedicated themselves to killing the foreigners every chance they got. There were just enough of these—a combination of former Ba'athist holdouts, foreign insurgents, and radical Islamic fundamentalists—for Royer's soldiers to view all Iraqis with suspicion. Although he understood that their main job was to serve as the city's police force, he also knew they would still have plenty of opportunities to play grunt as well.

The Prewar Police

Perhaps no Iraqi institution needed a more thorough restructuring than the nation's security forces. Saddam's regime, after all, had been a totalitarian police state, a society where even the hint of opposition was ruthlessly crushed. The Iraqi police (IP) force was initially formed in 1920, then was dramatically restructured in the 1970s when the Ba'athists seized power. The Ba'athists essentially militarized the police, and after Saddam Hussein's assumption of power in 1979, the police became increasingly brutal. Saddam looked to Joseph Stalin for his inspiration, emulating that dictator's tactics, complete with mysterious midnight disappearances, children informants, and a population that lived in constant fear. He proved himself to be every bit as cunning and paranoid as Stalin.

The Baghdad police force was structured both to combat common crime and to crush political dissent and religious activism. Noncommissioned officers were on the lowest rung of the city's police force, most of them possessing only a primary school education plus two to three months of poorly conceived police training. These were the police that the Iraqis knew, the ones they encountered on the street every day. One rung up were the "assistant officers," who generally had a secondary education, many being graduates of the police high school. They typically performed administrative functions. On the top of the ladder stood the "officers," high school graduates who then attended the police professional college in Baghdad (the same police academy the Americans now occupied) before becoming a member of the force. The school's curriculum was heavily weighted toward military subjects.[1]

Before the city's liberation, the U.S. Army estimated that the Baghdad police force numbered some 16,491 police working out of fifty-seven different police facilities. Unlike in the United States, those police assigned to neighborhood police stations did not patrol the neighborhoods. Rather, they functioned more like firemen, waiting in the station until a call came in for help, whereupon they piled into a pickup truck and drove to the action. The patrol police, in contrast, did just that: they drove through the neighborhoods. Their primary focus, however, was traffic control. Of course, the boundaries of the two forces overlapped, making for a confusing and inefficient system. The whole arrangement confounded the MPs when they took the reins, resulting in plenty of misunderstandings.[2]

The Saddam-era police force was an institution fueled by corruption. That fact was hardly unique in a society that was riddled with it, but during Saddam's rule, policy decisions were made that only accentuated the corruption. The police were grossly underpaid, generally about $20 a month, far below a living wage for an average family. To supplement their pay, the police extorted money from the citizens they supposedly served. Most cops expected a tip when they returned a stolen car. Dishonest ones might work behind the scenes to steal a car, then demand a ransom if and when they returned it to the rightful owner. Kickbacks from brothels and other illicit activities provided many police with a lucrative source of income. If a citizen wanted to make a complaint, he had to purchase the necessary forms from a vendor. If an Iraqi was arrested, his family would have to pay a bribe to get him released. The police didn't worry about the formality of a search warrant, and a search often became a convenient time to grab some booty to line their pockets. There were honest cops, of course. They usually held down a second job on the side, and they dared not complain about their brethren on the take.

Not surprisingly, the police were despised for their corruption, but they were also despised because they were Saddam's enforcers. For that reason especially, when Saddam went into hiding, the police force essentially evaporated. Within days, every one of Baghdad's fifty-seven police stations had been gutted by wave after wave of looters, and the police were nowhere in sight.[3]

Creating a New Police Force

Transitioning from war to occupation is always dicey, but this was especially true for Baghdad in 2003. During the war, Air Force staffers at Central Command (CENTCOM) meticulously avoided hitting any of the city's infrastructure. Unfortunately, Saddam's neglect and years of sanctions had otherwise left it in sorry shape. Looters destroyed most of what was left. This was the situation in Baghdad when the 233rd arrived on April 21. The 3rd Infantry Division had established a strict curfew but could do little to quell the wholesale looting. Only a handful of police had gone back to work in their gutted police stations, and they did nothing to challenge the looters. Within a week of the 233rd's arrival, the Americans and Iraqis were conducting joint patrols, linking up at the police academy when Iraqis bothered to report.

After Royer's reconnaissance of the Baghdad police stations and his lieutenants' initial assessment of the same, the MPs stopped by their assigned stations two or three times a day. What they found on those stops was not encouraging. The IPs who did show up made no effort, as far as the MPs could tell, to take back control of the streets. Instead, they often spent their time cowering in the stations. With so little help from the IPs, the Americans were unable to restore order, and looters continued to ravage the country's infrastructure. Looters hit Baghdad's telephone communication center on May 11. Two days later, Bremer authorized the soldiers to shoot looters. Even with this, looters hit Baghdad's power system hard on May 17. On May 20, authorities announced that Iraqis must turn in their automatic weapons. That directive illustrated yet another miscalculation made by the war planners, who were surprised by the flood of weapons available to the average Iraqi. Under Saddam's regime, all reservists were expected to keep an AK-47 in their homes. And in the months leading up to war, Saddam went to great lengths to disperse his arsenal throughout the country. Iraq was essentially one gigantic weapons cache. With the Baghdad police a non-factor, it was time, the authorities concluded, to step in more forcefully.[4]

The Americans Take Charge

In many respects, the MPs who patrolled the streets of Baghdad and encountered the Iraqi people every day were way ahead of the planners. They saw what needed to be done, and they often took the initiative to make it work. On May 17, the 204th MP Company, the 233rd's sister company from Fort Polk, Louisiana, became the first unit to begin around-the-clock operations at the chief of police headquarters. Battalion instructed them to

> set up a 24-hour joint MP/IPS [Iraqi Police Service] desk . . . The desk will be manned by at least two MPs and two IPFs at all times. An interpreter will be on shift 24-hours. A journal will be kept for all complaints/issues that are handled/received. The narrative regarding each raid, arrest, complaint, crime committed, and weapons/equipment seized must include: Who, What, When, Where, Why, How, Disposition, and all notifications.

Two days later, elements of the 233rd also began twenty-four-hour operations at the al-Alawyah police station, located a couple miles south of the police headquarters. But these were essentially ad hoc experiments. The rest of the city's police stations operated without such assistance.[5]

By early June, it was painfully obvious that the Baghdad police force was not capable of resurrecting itself. Only about 9,500 police out of a prewar strength of 16,500 had returned to work, and most of these were afraid to venture out from their stations—afraid to challenge the looters and criminals, who were often better armed and totally ruthless. That was essentially the situation when Lieutenant Colonel Glaser arrived in Baghdad. His arrival coincided with an important shift in strategy for the Coalition Provisional Authority. The time had arrived for the Americans to step in and take charge.

The order came down from the 18th MP Brigade, dividing the rebuilding of the city's police force into phases, with phase 1, the invasion and initial occupation, just completed. Phase 2 would be the reconstitution of the IP, with the MPs in the lead. Glaser directed his company commanders to keep a detailed log at each station to record how the IPs were progressing toward a series of tasks and objectives. When station commanders declared that the IPs were ready to take over, phase 3 could begin, which they hoped would occur around the end of August. Glaser knew that he'd have to keep things flexible, that the transition date would vary from station to station, and that he might have to push the MPs back in the lead if things did not work out.

By this time, the 519th MP Battalion had grown to six companies. Three of those, the 233rd, the 204th, and the 307th MP Companies, were assigned the critical job of staffing the police stations twenty-four hours a day while also training and monitoring the performance of the IPs. Glaser's other three companies—the 32nd, from Wisconsin; the 549th, a Regular Army unit from Fort Stewart, Georgia; and the 812th, a National Guard unit from New York—were detailed to work directly for the infantry brigades that also patrolled the city.

Colonel Glaser's most important mission was to rebuild the IPs. For that mission, he leaned heavily on his National Guard and Reserve units, America's citizen-soldiers. With so many civilian police and corrections officers in their ranks, they possessed the prerequisite of knowledge and experience.[6] He initially directed the 233rd to concentrate on five police stations plus the police academy jail, also known as Tas Ferrat, which was located next to the police headquarters and the academy—the same place the MPs had reported to before joint patrols. Royer's MPs continued to staff the al-Alawyah station, and they also gained responsibility for the al-Kerrada patrol headquarters, the New Baghdad police headquarters (also known as al-Muthana), the al-Mesbah police station, and the al-Sa'adoun police station. Each station went by a plethora of names, as if the Arabic language, with its distinctive alphabet, wasn't confusing enough. There was, for example, a New Baghdad patrol headquarters, a New Baghdad police headquarters (aka al-Muthana), plus a New Baghdad police station (aka al-Jadeda), all located in the New Baghdad district of town. Adding to the confusion were the various ways Americans translated the Arabic names into English. For a month or more, it seemed that a station's name, spelling, or grid location changed from day to day, causing the 233rd's tactical operations center (TOC) personnel an inordinate amount of confusion as they sorted it all out with the battalion TOC. To help keep things straight, the MPs gave the stations nicknames, just as they had adopted names for their platoons. Al-Sa'adoun became Boondocks. The New Baghdad police headquarters became Grayskull. And because al-Alawyah was named Camelot and their company went by Excalibur, the 1st Platoon "Reapers" thought "White Castle" was a fitting name for al-Mesbah. They considered themselves pretty clever.[7]

The inability of the IPs to take back the streets masked a larger problem. Many of those who had returned to duty were part of the corrupt old system. The MPs insisted that all of the IPs they worked with must sign a form forswearing any allegiance to the old Ba'athist regime, but everyone knew that was just a formality. The Americans not only had to build the police force from the ground up; they also needed to radically remake the police culture. The problem wasn't isolated with the police force. The Iraqi judicial system relied on confessions instead of evidence. If a person witnessed a crime and told the police, he was often locked up to ensure he was available when it came time for the trial—unless, of course, a relative paid a bribe to have him released. The brutal practices of the prewar days had to be purged, but the MPs harbored no illusions about how difficult it would be to convince Iraqis to change the habits and procedures of a lifetime. It was a tall order, made that much harder by the scarcity of MP companies then working in the city. "The MP teams will operate jointly with the IPS [Iraqi Police Service] at each police station," read Fragmentary Order 29, dated June 10, which implemented the change. "The MPs will continue to train and monitor the performance of the IPS." It sounded so simple on paper.[8]

The Reapers Reopen al-Mesbah

At midmorning on June 11, Lieutenant Joel Ferris, the 1st Platoon "Reapers" platoon leader, pulled up in front of the al-Mesbah police station, deep in the heart of the al-Karradah district of Baghdad. Al-Karradah was an upscale neighborhood of government employees, white-collar workers, TV stations, and foreign embassies. By some estimates, it contained nearly 100,000 residents, an eclectic mixture of Iraq's religions and ethnicities.

Ferris, at twenty-seven, was the oldest lieutenant in the company. He looked like a lot of GIs in Baghdad, with short-cropped brown hair, a medium build, a serious yet friendly demeanor, and a ready smile. He hailed originally from Mount Olive, Illinois, a small farming town about 50 miles south of Springfield. Ferris earned his bachelor's degree and an ROTC commission from Southern Illinois University at Edwardsville in 1997, then headed off for a three-year hitch as a Regular Army MP. He resigned his Regular Army commission in 2000 and transferred into the Inactive Ready Reserve (IRR) to serve out the rest of his commitment. He returned to Edwardsville, where he split his time between a job with the Social Security

Administration and graduate school at the local campus. Ferris was content with his life as a civilian, but when the military's operations tempo increased dramatically after 9/11, the Army needed experienced officers. He wasn't surprised when he received a letter from the Army in late 2002 directing him to return to active service.[9] Army officials backed up the letter with two voice messages on his answering machine. With the situation in Iraq steadily escalating, Ferris decided he needed to find a Guard or Reserve unit with which to serve before the Army found one for him. In early January 2003, he called a National Guard recruiter and discovered an MP company just up the road in Springfield.

His next call was to the 233rd Orderly Room, where the voice on the other end told him that the company was seriously over strength, but getting into the unit was up to the company commander, who might have an officer slot coming open. Ferris immediately faxed his officer evaluation reports to the unit, and he was soon informed that Captain Royer would meet with him on the Friday evening before the unit's January drill. Ferris got his hair cut, shaved off his goatee (a relic from the fall deer season), and reported to Springfield in his best suit. A short conversation with Captain Royer sealed the deal: he would serve as a platoon leader in the 233rd. It was a fateful decision because the unit was soon mobilized. He spent his first drill with the company at Marseilles, going through the in-processing procedure with the rest of the company.[10]

Accompanying Ferris to al-Mesbah was the 2nd Squad, led by Staff Sergeant Jimmie Mayes, plus a team from 1st Squad—nine soldiers in all, traveling in three Humvees. Sergeant Mayes, a game warden with the Illinois Department of Conservation, was pretty easy to spot, solidly built, with blue eyes, bright red hair, and a moustache to match. His squad had earned the assignment to rebuild al-Mesbah by virtue of its depth of civilian police experience; they counted three police officers among its ranks. Besides, Ferris thought that he and Mayes made a good team, with one man's strengths complementing the other's weaknesses.

The convoy pulled up in front of a burned-out shell of a building that they had visited several times before. Milling around outside were twenty to thirty Iraqis in civilian attire, former police officers who had heard about the MPs' mission to reopen the police stations on the radio and from flyers posted around town. Ferris, Mayes, and Sam, a local Iraqi who served as their interpreter for the day, dismounted and waded into the crowd of IPs. They were immediately inundated with a barrage of questions: Would they be retained as police officers despite their status as policemen under the old regime? asked the IPs as they pressed in around Ferris and Mayes. How about weapons? they queried. When would they get paid? All of these things were coming, explained Ferris lamely. In the midst of this commotion, he found out that the station commander had already gone home for the day.

Ferris wasn't given much guidance that day. He was told little more than to use his judgment and initiative to get things organized. The lieutenant had no doubt about what his first priority must be: security. He knew that the quicker he could convert the desolate, two-story building into a fortress, the better. Sergeant Mayes posted one soldier with the vehicles and sent two more to the roof with a squad automatic weapon (SAW), giving them instructions to find a position where they could observe the streets leading into the station. Once on the roof, the SAW crew manhandled a burned-out filing cabinet and disheveled desk in front of their position for protection, a stopgap until they could get their hands on some sandbags. Because the station opened directly onto the street, protected only by a 3-foot wall, Ferris posted one of his soldiers at the police station door, and he sent a couple of IPs to the end of the street leading into the station.

With security established, Ferris's next order of business was to get a rough head count of the IPs who had reported for duty. He wondered if these men would defend the station if it came under attack. Did he have enough MPs if they suddenly turned on the Americans? That eventuality seemed unlikely, but Ferris was taking nothing for granted. His noncommissioned officers gathered up the IPs as best as they could in the dusty courtyard in front of the station house. It turned very quickly into an exercise in frustration as the IPs had little interest in cooperating and constantly bombarded both Ferris and Mayes with questions. They counted heads as best they could, then moved to other tasks.

While Mayes conducted the head count outside, Sergeants Dennison, Getz, and Denagel were inside cleaning up the station. Even a month and a half after the place had been looted, it was still a mess. They swept up the trash and the thin layer of ash left over from the fire, yanked out loose wiring, picked up garbage that still cluttered the floor, and took it all out behind the station to a burn pit they dug in the sandy soil. Once Mayes completed his impromptu roll call, the MPs concentrated on setting up an operations room. They scrounged a desk, hauled in radios from the Humvee, and hung chemical lights for night operations.

By this time, Ferris was back with the befuddled Iraqi policeman who claimed to be in charge that day, firing off a series of questions in rapid succession. Where were their weapons? he asked the man. Did they have uniforms? How many IPs worked at the station? Because the station commander had left for the day, the questioning went nowhere. But Ferris stayed at it, spending the rest of the day trying to make some sense of how the Iraqis did business at al-Mesbah. By the time the MPs' night shift arrived at 1700 hours, he was tired and frustrated. He was ready to turn the station over to Sergeant First Class Mike Parkin, the Reapers' platoon sergeant. Parkin reported for duty with 3rd Squad in tow, augmented by a team from 1st Squad. The first day at al-Mesbah had been hectic and frustrating for all concerned. But it constituted the first step in rebuilding the station, and by extension, the Baghdad police force. Variations of this scenario were being played out at police stations throughout the city.[11]

Lieutenant Steve Rice and the 3rd Platoon drew al-Sa'adoun for their assignment, and he also turned first to security. Rice's platoon sandbagged the station windows, strung coils of concertina wire along the courtyard wall, and emplaced a machine gun position on the roof of the building. A few days later, an engineering unit arrived to help position barricades around the perimeter of the stations. Eventually, the station was ringed by Jersey barriers, the kind of cement barriers American road crews so often used back in the States. The Americans in Baghdad increasingly used the more imposing Texas barriers, similar to the Jersey barriers but standing 12 to 15 feet high. Hesco barriers, basically a locally fabricated wire box filled with sand and gravel, was a cheap and prevalent substitute. Over time, al-Sa'adoun and every other station in town increasingly resembled fortresses.[12]

Day 2 and Beyond

Day 2 at al-Mesbah wasn't much different from day 1, except that Ferris finally met the station commander. Colonel Norman was a holdover from the Saddam era, which was to say that he had been a reliable lackey for the Ba'athist thugs who formerly ran Iraq. As far as Ferris was concerned, Norman had few redeeming qualities. He also held little sway over the rest of the IPs at the station. Ferris had a litany of questions for the colonel. Unfortunately, the station commander gave few clear answers. What was the history of the station? Ferris asked. Who did he report to? How many IPs were stationed at al-Mesbah? How was the station organized—how many shifts, and using what as a chain of command? Were they actively patrolling now? What was the neighborhood like? Colonel Norman's responses were consistently vague, especially when it came to the station's organization and intel about the surrounding neighborhood. But Ferris had a plan.

The citizens of al-Karradah, he decided, were his best source of intelligence, and their support and cooperation were crucial to the station's security. So on day 2, after his fruitless grilling of Colonel Norman, Ferris gathered up a small patrol and took to the streets, going door to door and introducing himself to the neighbors. No doubt the sight of a young American soldier with an M-203 slung over his shoulder knocking at their doors startled many in the neighborhood. But they were invariably cordial, and some even invited Ferris inside for a cup of tea, a time-honored Arab custom. Occasionally, he accepted their offers, and he found his hosts to be both gracious and receptive to his offers of friendship. He explained that the Americans were there to reopen the police station, to offer them some protection, and to fight crime. He asked for their help in bringing security to the neighborhood. He listened as much as he talked, and he discovered that many Iraqis were willing to tell him much of what he wanted to know—the religious, ethnic, and economic profile of the neighborhood, their problems and frustrations, their hopes for the future. There was one message that came through loud and clear as he toured the neighborhood. These people did not trust the IPs, and many were more than happy to name names and provide incriminating details. They were ready to cooperate in order to rid their streets of thugs and thieves.

With the neighbors' cooperation and support, al-Mesbah gradually became more secure. It was their neighborhood, and they knew when someone did not belong. Ferris was even able to cobble together an ad hoc neighborhood watch group. A hotel owner north of the station kept an eye out for trouble on his side of the street, and soon news reporters found lodging in his hotel. Bank security guards helped secure the area west of the station house, and east of the station, Ferris got support from Iraqis who worked at a UNICEF building and as employees at a couple of major newspaper outlets. Finally, located just south of the station was a large vacant building and another structure where a local madam operated a lucrative business. The IPs seemed unfazed by her enterprise, and Ferris tolerated it in exchange for the madam's help with security.[13]

Day 3 for the Reapers was much like their first two days, but on day 4, a Friday, the Americans were in for a shock. Friday was the weekly day of prayer, and to honor the occasion, only a couple of IPs reported to work.

During the next couple of weeks, Ferris conducted guard mount each day at 0800 hours. This was often poorly attended because the IPs had only a relative sense of time and decidedly little sense of urgency. As often as not, IPs straggled in throughout the morning, but Ferris continued pulling the guard mount. He needed some kind of mark on the wall, some way to determine not just who was there, but who he could rely on and who he could not. As it was, sorting out the good police from the bad would take months. It went beyond identifying who was a Ba'athist. Many had joined the party because that was the only way to get a job under the old regime.

The big breakthrough with guard mount came the day Staff Sergeant Roman Waldron, who worked the night shift, and Sergeant Mayes struck on the idea to move roll call to the roof. Once there, Waldron argued convincingly, the IPs couldn't wander off so easily or otherwise be distracted. The idea achieved the desired result. One by one, they filed past Sergeant Mayes, who stood with clipboard in hand. Each Iraqi stated his name to Farouq, their interpreter for the day, who then patiently spelled the name in English as Mayes scribbled it down. (The Reapers hired Farouq off the street. He was something of a shady character, but he knew the neighborhood and proved himself an adept scrounger as well.)

Ferris continued his neighborhood tours whenever possible, usually accompanied by Specialists Ater, Street, and Holder, Private Carmody, and an interpreter. His escorts weren't entirely enthusiastic about his excursions, but Ferris was convinced they paid dividends, encouraged by the fact that the neighbors increasingly made their way to al-Mesbah with intelligence and especially with a flood of complaints.[14]

Almost everyone in the 233rd found community relations to be their trickiest challenge, one filled with pitfalls but also with the potential for rich rewards. Having received very little cultural or language training, the MPs struggled to overcome the language barrier. Thankfully, many Iraqis knew some English, and a few knew enough to be truly conversant. The 519th did have one interpreter of their own, an Iraqi émigré named Manhal "Mike" Jijika, who had fled to Michigan after the first gulf war and who agreed to accompany the Army into Iraq during this war. But the battalion needed scores of interpreters, so selecting one from the many Iraqis who eagerly showed up for work became an imperative for the lieutenants. Five dollars a day soon became the going rate, at first paid by the MPs themselves. Even that low rate drew plenty of volunteers, and the lieutenants soon held impromptu tryouts for the positions. As with all things in Iraq, they relied on their instincts when deciding whom to trust.[15]

A Botched Investigation

Sergeant First Class Ryan Machin, the Punishers' platoon sergeant, had the look of authority you wanted for a cop—short-cropped hair and an air of self-assurance. Like many cops, he didn't have much patience for incompetence, and his first patrol with the IPs pushed his patience to the limit. Machin was at the al-Karradah patrol headquarters when the call came in from the police academy. Apparently, an Iraqi had gone to the academy to report a murder in the al-Karradah neighborhood. It was Machin's job to go and investigate the crime. He took eleven MPs in three Humvees, plus two more sedans loaded with IPs. After racing through the streets for a few minutes, they pulled to a stop in front of a newspaper printing shop. There were already twenty or more Iraqis milling around outside the building, and Machin, a policeman back in Springfield, immediately knew what that meant. He had already lost some evidence. He quickly posted his security force, a combination of MPs and IPs, then waded into the crowd, taking with him a medic, the interpreter, and a couple of IPs. It didn't take long for an MP to follow a path of blood down a flight of stairs. At the base of the stairs lay the victim, face down in a pool of blood. He was dead, shot in the head at close range. By the time Machin reached the victim, the dead man's family had already handed the IPs two shell casings. Machin could do little but shake his head: they had lost valuable evidence. There would be no fingerprints and no location of the spent shells to help piece the story together.

The family members now gathered around the IPs, excitedly telling their story. It seemed that an Iraqi man and woman had struck up a conversation with the witness's uncle, who worked as a guard at the shop, then left for a bit. They soon came back, with the man toting an AK-47. The two forced their way inside and shot the man in the entryway, then dragged him through a hallway and tossed him down a flight of stairs into the shop's basement. The IPs heard the story, then passed their findings to Machin. They had reached their conclusion after just a few minutes of work. They mentioned nothing about a motive.

The story just didn't add up for Machin, who had performed plenty of investigations as a civilian police officer. He noted that there was no blood in the entryway, so he doubted their uncle was shot there. He grabbed the interpreter, who then helped him talk the "witnesses" through the crime step by step. After that, Machin thoroughly examined the entryway, and he soon found what he was looking for: two more bullet casings and two rounds lodged in the wall. By the time he was done with his investigation, he determined that the assailants had fired at the guard in the entryway and missed, then ran up to him in the hallway, where they stabbed him in the back with a knife. Finally, they carried him down the stairs and shot him, execution style, in the back of the head. With his investigation complete, the suspects were transported to the Abu Ghraib prison on the southwest side of town. "I'll never forget that patrol as long as I live," Machin recalled months later. "After that day, I knew that we had a long haul ahead of us."[16]

Sergeant Machin's frustration with the IPs' sloppy police procedure was indicative of the condition of the entire Baghdad police force. As the IPs began accompanying the Americans on patrols, the monumental scale of the task that lay before the MPs became clear. Somehow, they had to transform a totally corrupt and incompetent police force into a modern and professional force that treated the public humanely. For starters, the MPs refused to allow the IPs to go anywhere until they had established procedures for issuing weapons from the newly established arms room, for dispatching vehicles, and for logging the patrols. Most of this was as foreign to the IPs as Baghdad was foreign to the MPs. So was the MPs' insistence that any evidence they collected be tagged and meticulously managed in order to establish the chain of custody, thus preserving it for future legal actions.

Much of the MPs' time during the first few weeks was spent helping the IPs establish administrative procedures. There were no personnel files and no criminal records, and from what the MPs could tell, there was not much interest in keeping records in the first place. Even something as basic as personnel accountability seemed alien to the Iraqis, and in some cases, resented by them. Often, IPs didn't report for work because they were moonlighting. The reasons were simple enough: the IPs still were not getting paid, a problem that infuriated MPs and IPs alike. Still, the MPs persisted. They explained that without a personnel file and a procedure to keep track of an officer's comings and goings, the IPs would never get paid. And because computers were nonexistent, it was entirely a stubby pencil drill.[17]

Training the IPs

About a week into LT Ferris's operations at al-Mesbah, the Reapers started teaching the IPs proper police techniques. No one told them to do so; it just seemed like the logical thing to do, especially when they discovered that many of the IPs had never received any training to speak of—at least not the kind of formal training that American police took for granted. It was, perhaps, the lieutenant's greatest challenge—training the IPs in proper policing techniques and in the process, instilling in them a sense of professionalism. Not until they truly embraced those values could the public begin to respect these men or the police department in general. After all, these were the same officers who the public previously feared and despised. Ferris insisted that his MPs model the behavior he expected the IPs to emulate: "I gave my word [to those in the neighborhood] that as long as I was the American commander and my sergeants ran the police station, we would be fair and just, meaning no one would be held without due process or evidence to the contrary."

Sergeant Mayes usually headed the training sessions. He conducted them after the morning guard mount and deliberately kept them short. Sergeant Christopher Dennison, an experienced police officer, and Sergeant Ryan Getz, a law enforcement major in college, often aided Mayes, and together, they taught the Iraqis things like the proper use of Flex-Cufs, treatment of civilians, how to use the appropriate level of force, and proper search techniques. For the most part, the IPs were eager to receive the training and were usually receptive to the spot corrections the sergeants made, at least on the surface.[18]

Eventually, Ferris and his fellow lieutenants started receiving more explicit training guidance from higher headquarters. These instructions largely validated what they had already begun on their own. They were told to place a heavy emphasis on weapons training (the Iraqis were notoriously bad shots) and on "training in discipline and ethics." Captain Royer, intent on making the biggest impact, stressed a train-the-trainer program, Army jargon for developing a cadre of Iraqi trainers who could then pass their knowledge on to others.[19]

Recruiting New Police

One of the MPs' toughest and most important challenges was recruiting new policemen. In one sense, the process was fairly easy, because once they established a permanent presence in a station, a steady stream of Iraqis began arriving to volunteer their services. In most cases, the Iraqis responded to the flyers that civil affairs officers had posted around town, or to the announcements made on the American-run radio and TV stations. The men who showed up were desperate for work. Staff Sergeant Jim Nayonis could attest to that. While using the company's minesweeper outside his station, hundreds of men suddenly arrived, anxious to join the police force.

The hard part about this flood of recruits was determining who could be trusted. Most Iraqis readily produced crudely made ID cards, but those were easily purchased on the black market. In fact, you could get just about anything in Baghdad's booming black market, from weapons of all types to police badges to MP brassards. So it was left up to the discretion of the MP sergeants and lieutenants to decide whom to hire.[20]

An equally thorny problem for the MPs was equipping the police. The IPs provided much of what they needed themselves, especially when it came to vehicles. It was not uncommon for them to simply seize a vehicle they needed, offering little in the way of compensation. Only rarely did the Americans step in. They suspected that many of the vehicles the IPs procured had indeed been police vehicles before the war. Soon the city's police academy served as a clearinghouse for vehicles, usually issuing white Nissan Altimas, Maximas, Volkswagen Passats, or the small white pickups favored by the patrol police. Procuring firearms was a tougher problem to solve. It wasn't that the IPs had none. Most had sidearms. The problem was that practically everyone on the street was better armed, a carryover from the Saddam regime when all able-bodied men were required to serve in the national militia and therefore were expected to keep their AK-47s at the ready in their homes or shops. AK-47 automatic rifles were the most common, but you could get just about anything on the gun market: handguns, rocket-propelled grenades, hand grenades, small mortar systems, and artillery shells—lots of artillery shells.

In reality, the Iraqis' persistent plea for more and better weapons illustrated another problem: lack of weapons accountability. When the Americans arrived, they discovered that IPs routinely took their weapons home after their shift. The MPs insisted that they turn their weapons in to an arms room attendant at the end of their shift, a fact the IPs resented. Where was the logic in that, they argued, if the citizen they just angered was waiting outside with his own AK-47? It was a valid point.[21]

While the MPs concentrated their efforts on training the existing police force, a small team of American police officers hired by the Department of Defense arrived in the country. That group, aided by a cadre of MPs, reopened the police academy in late June and began training the next generation of police. Jerry Burke, a retired Massachusetts state trooper, headed the team. John Meiklejohn, who specialized in setting up police academies in hot spots around the world, threw together a curriculum that including subjects like "Probable Cause," "What Are Human Rights," "Domestic Violence," and "Prohibition Against Torture," along with a heavy dose of small arms training and search procedures. The first class was tiny, graduating a mere ninety-six students on July 16 after a three-week crash course. Burke and his people hoped these graduates would become disciples of the new way of policing. The MPs shared their hopes, but they feared that the new graduates would soon be corrupted by the old hands on the street. Still, at least these graduates would know there was a better way, and gradually, the MPs hoped, the new ways would win out. It would take years, but it could be done.[22]

The Daily Routine

A couple of weeks into the Reapers' operation at al-Mesbah, things began to settle into a routine. Shift change occurred at 0700 hours and 1900 hours daily, with the 2nd Squad pulling the day shift and Staff Sergeant Roman Waldron's 3rd Squad pulling the quieter night shift. Lieutenant Ferris typically accompanied the day shift. Sergeant First Class Parkin, as the Reapers' platoon sergeant, was Ferris's night-shift counterpart.

By early morning, the station was abuzz with activity. Sergeant Mayes's first order of business each morning was to swap out the MPs pulling security, followed by the 0800 roll call for the IPs. Ferris started his day by coordinating with Colonel Norman, running down a list of tasks for the day.

For weeks, he followed this with another attempt to sort out the station's organization with the colonel. More often than not, Ferris was frustrated on both accounts. Colonel Norman was always cordial and deferential during their conversations, and when asked to do something, he always agreed. But Ferris's instructions only got implemented if and when he cornered Norman later in the day and insisted on action. As for Ferris's attempts at discerning the station organization, it wasn't that Norman didn't answer his questions, but that his answers changed with maddening regularity. Not until the lieutenant discovered that the station had an administrative section did he finally get a sense of how the station was really organized. The truth was, Colonel Norman was nothing more than a relic of the old regime—inefficient, corrupt, and distrusted by his own men. Unfortunately, he was all Ferris had to work with. He was stuck with him, at least for the moment.

Conditions at al-Mesbah were primitive at best. For light, the MPs used chemical sticks, and they slaved power into the station from their parked Humvees. (A few weeks into their occupation, they traded with a local Special Forces unit for a generator.) For water, Ferris hounded Colonel Norman to get the local fire department to fill the cistern located on the station's roof. Only when the cistern was full could they flush out the raw sewage that built up inside the station's two detention cells; the whole operation was gravity fed. Without enough water, the raw sewage would get lodged in the sewer canals that led into the street's main sewage system. When that happened—and it often did—they lived not only with the stench, but also with swarms of flies.

The detention cells were one of Ferris's biggest concerns, filled to overflowing with a hodgepodge of prisoners. The rooms had no cots and no chairs, and for obvious reasons, no air conditioning. The prisoners' only window to the outside world was a tiny one in the door, which was barred and covered as often as not. The detainees survived on the food, clothing, and sleeping mats that relatives brought in each day. The MPs supplemented the prisoners' meager rations as best as they could, supplying them with excess MREs and as much cleaning supplies as they could scrounge. A visit from the water truck meant the prisoners could also wash themselves. Meanwhile, the detainees could do little but wait for the day they would appear before the judge some 15 miles across town. Only the judge could determine whether the detainees would be released or sent to prison.[23]

Indeed, handling prisoners was a constant point of friction between the Americans and their Iraqi counterparts. The IPs paid little attention to the number of prisoners they crammed into the police station holding cells, often filling them to the point where it was impossible for prisoners to sit down. The 3rd Infantry Division commander soon directed that common criminals be taken to Tas Ferrat, reserving Abu Ghraib, on the southwest side of town, for suspected insurgents and terrorists. On at least one occasion, when an Iraqi officer was ordered to move the overflow prisoners to Tas Ferrat, he obliged by walking into the street, commandeering a passing bus, then loading it full of prisoners for the trip across town.[24]

Ferris spent the bulk of his day meeting with a steady procession of visitors, usually with Azad, the platoon interpreter, close at hand.[25] The volume of visitors was a tribute to his early trips through the neighborhoods and to the faith the Iraqis now put in Ferris and the MPs. Citizens came in with intelligence on a suspicious neighbor, or complaints about a particular Iraqi policeman, or to report a crime. By mid-July, Ferris also could look forward to daily visits with a local contractor hired by civil affairs personnel to rebuild the station. The contractor was like businessmen everywhere, interested in the bottom line but also in making sure the job was done right. He subcontracted most of the work, including the plumbing, electrical work, and basic carpentry. He was Ferris's most welcome visitor, and not just because he spoke excellent English. With the lieutenant's help, he was transforming al-Mesbah into a functioning station. For that, he earned the Americans' lasting respect.

Red Cross inspectors began making frequent visits to the station in late July to check on the detainees. Despite the MPs' best efforts, the Red Cross found plenty to take issue with, including overcrowding, poor sanitation, and a shortage of food. But the attention wasn't all bad. Shortly after the Red Cross visits began, local contractors were hired to provide meals for the prisoners.[26]

As far as interrogations went, since the Iraqi judicial system formerly relied on confessions more than physical evidence, the IPs were justifiably notorious for their brutal interrogation techniques. It went well beyond slapping a suspect around. More sinister techniques, like wiring genitalia to a car battery, were commonplace under Saddam's old regime. The older IPs were reluctant to give up techniques that worked. On this point especially the MPs insisted on a higher standard, and more than once, they stepped in to stop IPs from roughing up a prisoner. If the IPs were ever to gain the public's trust, this practice had to change, but it was a tough sell.[27]

Attack on the al-Mesbah Police Station

By July, the MPs had fallen into a routine. They conducted daily patrols through the surrounding neighborhoods, sometimes on their own but often with IPs accompanying them. They conducted raids on suspected insurgent safehouses, patrolled the streets for crime, and handled the daily flood of complaints from Iraqi citizens. Most importantly, they spent long hours training the IPs in basic police tactics and the fundamentals of police administration, all the while supervising the rebuilding of the five police stations that they monitored 24–7.

The grueling pace left the MPs precious little time for sleep—maybe four or five hours a day. That made pulling the midnight shift on al-Mesbah's rooftop machine gun post a real test of willpower and endurance, a constant fight against fatigue. That was nineteen-year-old Josh Holder's destiny during the midnight hours of July 3. He found his mind wandering as he hunkered down behind the SAW on the roof of White Castle, drifting back to the ironic quirk of fate that had brought him here. He and twin brother Jason had both attempted to join the marines while in their senior year in high school in Carbondale, Illinois. His brother made it, but because of a minor head injury, Josh did not. He joined the Illinois National Guard instead, and in an ironic twist of fate, he now served with the 1st Platoon in Baghdad, at the center of the world's attention, while Jason was stationed in Hawaii.

By 0130 hours, with the heat of the day dissipating and with only four or five hours of sleep the night before, Holder's main concern was staying awake and alert. He tinkered with the machine gun's belt of 5.56-millimeter ammunition, twisting it until the links separated, then snapped them back into place. His thoughts drifted back to that day in basic training when he first laid hands on the SAW. He'd taken an immediate liking to it, despite its tendency to jam. He took pride in his mastery of the weapon. Now he noticed that the gun's rear sight was turned all the way to the left, indicating its previous owner had a "lazy eye." If only he could use his own weapon, thought Holder, as he adjusted the sight.

Thankfully, there was enough light from the neighborhood streetlamps to see his surroundings clearly. As he peered into the street, Holder absent-mindedly tugged at a couple of sandbags that ringed his position. The machine gun sat on a metal table that allowed the muzzle to clear the short retaining wall, the kind that rimmed almost every roof in Baghdad. He sat behind the SAW on a rickety old chair, which in turn rested on a filing cabinet, an arrangement that gave him enough elevation to cover the street below. Holder kept his Motorola radio close by—his link to Sergeant Ryan Getz and the rest of his 2nd Squad mates downstairs. Next to him lay a water bottle, an MRE, a set of night-vision goggles, and an additional container of SAW ammunition.

Because Baghdad was under curfew, scanning the street got old fast. Down the street to Holder's left were a couple of UN security guards pro-

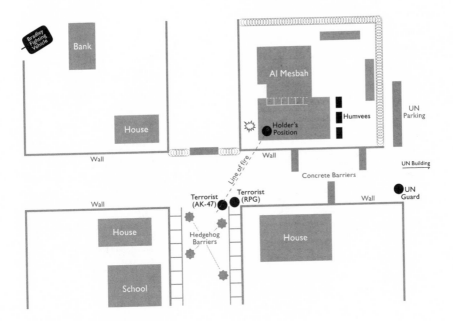

Raid on Al-Mesbah

tecting a building that housed several UN officials. That street was protected by a cross-hashed pattern of Jersey barriers. Directly below him was another barricade that blocked the street adjacent to the police station. IPs were often stationed there, but not tonight. Farther down the street to his right and around the corner, beyond his view, was a Bradley fighting vehicle that belonged to the regulars of 1st Battalion, 6th Infantry Regiment. Directly across the street to the south was an Iraqi home. There wasn't much to watch. Nothing held his attention, so he lit a cigarette and broke open an MRE, all the while scanning the streets below.

At 2:00 A.M., the lights suddenly flickered out, a depressingly common occurrence in a city plagued by power shortages. Holder marveled at how dark everything became once the streetlights went out, especially on a night with no moon. For a couple of minutes, his eyes followed the lights of a high-flying aircraft as it circled the sky; then he donned the night-vision goggles for a look into the street below. NVGs turned everything a shade of translucent green, but Holder was always amazed at how much detail he could make out. The fact that there were a few lights on, powered by small generators, added to the ambient light that the NVG relied on. The generators also put out enough noise for Holder to safely place a call to his buddies downstairs—a quick wisecrack, just enough to reassure him that there were friends just a few steps away.

Then he caught some movement out of the corner of his eye—nothing more than a shadow next to the house across the street. He brought the NVGs quickly to his eyes, scanning left, then right, then back to the center again. Suddenly, two figures appeared from around the corner of the house. "Hey, we've got two subjects that are coming up," Holder whispered excitedly into the Motorola. Just as he finished his message, he caught another glimpse of them through his NVGs, this time more clearly. On the street corner directly across from the station stood a man dressed entirely in black, holding a rocket-propelled grenade (RPG) pointing toward the ground. And then a second man appeared, this one armed with an AK-47 and carrying a large black bag on his back. "F***, RPG, RPG, RPG," Holder screamed into the inky night as he simultaneously trained the SAW on the man with the RPG and pulled the trigger. Nothing happened. The weapon had jammed. Without thinking, he automatically went into the misfire procedures, pulling back on the bolt, lifting the weapon's feed tray, ripping out the ammunition belt before reinserting it, then slamming down the tray and pulling the trigger once again. This time he felt the SAW jump in response as he fired a short burst into the street below. The whole thing had taken only a couple of seconds, but in the intensity of the moment, time slowed to a crawl. Holder watched as the tracer rounds coursed their way to the street below. He watched the rounds hit the pavement, then ricochet down the streets. In the midst of it all, he spotted a muzzle flash.

By the time Holder looked up, his ears ringing, Sergeant Getz had burst into action downstairs, barking out orders. He sent several IPs to the roof, called the company TOC to request a quick reaction force, then issued AK-47s to a squad of IPs and directed them into the street to investigate. They found nothing—no blood, and no sign of the enemy. Not until 0320 hours did the quick reaction force finally arrive, a full seventy-five minutes after the incident.

Holder wasn't relieved from his rooftop post until 0700 hours, and he remained on duty the rest of the day. When morning dawned, several MPs went out to examine the site more thoroughly. They found a rusty rifle shell casing near some trees where Holder thought he had seen the muzzle flash, but otherwise there was no sign of the incident at all.

The 2nd Squad pulled the night shift again the next evening, the Fourth of July. To celebrate, they launched a couple of signal flares into the night sky. The Bradley that was posted just around the corner arrived in fifteen seconds.[28]

The Long Haul

The Reapers were pretty much on their own during their first couple of months at al-Mesbah. Save for the Iraqi contractors who worked on rehabbing the stationhouse, they relied on their knowledge of police work and their abundant ingenuity. All of that changed in early August. Suddenly, the IPs began receiving uniforms, Glock pistols, and ammunition. Most importantly, the IPs finally received a paycheck. That money flowed through Iraqi channels, passed down from the police headquarters to Colonel Norman, who personally decided which IPs received pay that day. This function, Ferris concluded, was the man's only real source of power, but it was necessary to use him because the IPs were known to move from station to station in an attempt to extort money in all the confusion.

Within days, one more change occurred at al-Mesbah, the most welcome change Ferris had experienced in months. The Iraqi police headquarters decided to relieve Colonel Norman and replace him with Colonel Salmon, who appeared one day with no orders but with a deep desire to get the station working. Salmon, an educated man, boasted a degree in law. He was smart, and he listened. Even more refreshing for Ferris, Salmon sometimes disagreed with the lieutenant, and when he did, he made compelling arguments on why they should do things differently. That was a far cry from Norman, a "yes man" to the core and entirely untrustworthy. Within days, Salmon and Ferris forged a relationship based on mutual respect. After Salmon's arrival, the situation at al-Mesbah steadily improved.[29]

Things were still touch and go in Baghdad by the end of August. IED attacks were on the rise, and there were plenty of insurgents making life difficult for Americans and Iraqis alike. But Colonel Glaser was justifiably proud of what his MPs and their Iraqi counterparts had accomplished. When he arrived in early June, the Baghdad police force was a shambles. Now, the day was approaching when the Americans could back away from their twenty-four-hour presence and turn the police stations over to the IPs. Even more encouraging, the Baghdad police academy had already graduated its first couple of classes. Slowly but surely, the lessons the MPs taught their Iraqi counterparts were taking root. The IPs' pride grew as their competence grew.

Most of the IPs trusted the Americans implicitly, although some still resisted the new methods that the Americans insisted they follow. They gradually earned the MPs' respect as well. Part of that resulted from the weeding-out process—the purging of the most corrupt among them, those most tainted by their former association with the Ba'athists. Glaser knew that process was crucial to Iraq's future, and to make sure they went about it right, he directed Royer and his lieutenants to develop a "Duds and Studs" evaluation form, which was basically a list of good cops, bad cops, and potential leaders. Over time, they moved the "duds" to marginal positions or into retirement, and they offered encouragement and chances for advancement to the studs. The good cops weren't the ones who slobbered over the MPs. As far as Glaser and Royer were concerned, the mark of a good IP was a community-oriented cop, and one who was willing to go out and arrest criminals.[30]

By August, the MPs believed that they were also building trust with the communities surrounding the stations. It wasn't just the constant offers of cigarettes or the frequent invitations to share a cup of stout tea. Those were manifestations of the Arab culture, where one was always hospitable to a guest. By August, they also frequently received important intelligence from Iraqi citizens. And several times, especially after a successful police operation, grateful neighbors would bring the MPs a meal to the station. Those simple and sincere gestures meant a lot to Royer's troops. It meant they were making a difference in Baghdad, despite the small percentage of Iraqis still bent on their destruction.[31]

On September 1, in part as a result of the growing number of companies assigned to the 519th, Glaser realigned his MP companies. Thereafter, the 233rd monitored only two stations, the New Baghdad police station (Tombstone), and the New Baghdad police headquarters (Grayskull). More importantly, the time to put the Iraqis in the lead had arrived. The MPs no longer manned the stations twenty-four hours a day. Instead, they checked on the stations several times a day and continued to conduct joint patrols. Increasingly, however, policing of Baghdad became an Iraqi show.[32]

In retrospect, Colonel Glaser, Regular Army to the core, was glad he had assigned some of his National Guard and Reserve companies to the crucial job of rebuilding the Iraqi police. His regular companies performed wonderfully, but his guardsmen not only brought a wealth of knowledge and experience to their job, but also a measure of steady maturity. "When you look back at the police stations that . . . got rebuilt . . . correctly," he later reflected, "it was those National Guard companies, the 32nd MP Company (Wisconsin National Guard), the 233rd, and the 812th out of New York that set the standard. They had the experience. They were the cops and DEA agents that had been serving in those positions for 10, 15, 20 years . . . They were as good [as] or better [than] any company I'd ever been around."[33]

6
Anything but Routine

"Greetings to all 233rd families and friends," began a June 15 e-mail that First Sergeant Elmore fired off to Jerry Calbow. Calbow immediately forwarded it to everyone on his growing e-mail address list. Elmore knew that keeping the families back home informed was critical to keeping his soldiers focused on their mission in Baghdad. He knew that intuitively, but he also knew it because First Sergeant Calbow had thoroughly groomed him for his job.

"EVERYONE is still OK!!!" continued Elmore.

Not much has changed here in Baghdad except that it is steadily getting hotter. Temperatures on top of our police stations have been around 140. Our soldiers are adjusting well, but it is extremely hot. Living conditions here steadily improve with the addition of more air conditioners and glass in the windows. We are still able to shower every day. We have two hot meals a day, often with fresh fruit. . . . We now have a volleyball court, a horseshoe pit and Frisbees.

We are grateful that the mail is now coming through for the Battalion . . . delivering our mail within five to nine days, . . . including our care packages. Our soldiers are working hard every day to make things happen for the company, often with little or no logistical support. Each MP platoon is assigned a police station and is tasked to assist the Iraqi Police Service in re-establishing themselves and train the IPS. Our maintenance section struggles daily to keep our vehicles fully mission capable with what little replacement parts they have available.

"Top" Elmore closed with this: "Thanks for all the support that we are getting back home. Keep praying for us and keep sending letters and packages."[1]

It was the kind of blunt, matter-of-fact report one would expect from a first sergeant, but a message that reassured everyone who received it. The families found it comforting to hear that things were going pretty well in Baghdad. They were also reassured that Top was there to make sure the troops kept their minds in the game. Soldiers tended to get sloppy when things became routine, and the heat and the constant stress of Baghdad inevitably took their toll. It was Elmore's job to make sure his soldiers did not get sloppy.

He certainly did not exaggerate the oppressive heat, but this far into their rotation, the MPs had learned to cope with it. What they couldn't get used to was the infestation of flies, which multiplied at a prodigious rate, feasting on the massive piles of garbage that now lined the streets. The dump sites were pungent reminders that the Americans still had not won the security battle, a fact that hampered their efforts to rebuild the city's infrastructure. At least mosquitoes didn't plague them—the heat cooked them.

Maxed Out

Helping the Iraqi police (IP) get back on their feet was the 233rd's most important mission, but by no means its only job. Battalion also expected Captain Royer to maintain a quick reaction force (QRF) every day, and a squad or two was needed to help with compound security. There was also no shortage of escort missions to perform, just a shortage of MPs to pull them. MP teams were often detailed to accompany unit supply, maintenance, or mail runs, as well as numerous escort missions for civil affairs officers or engineer units. Sometimes the unit was tasked to provide escorts for visiting VIPs, or for news reporters who wanted to tell their story. Occasionally, a more interesting mission came down the pike—a raid conducted jointly with an infantry or cavalry unit, or a POW transfer.

Almost every day, the 233rd provided several escort teams for the 519th Battalion Commander and staff, tasked not only because they shared the compound with Colonel Glaser's headquarters, but also because Glaser trusted the Illinoisans' abilities. On the rare occasion when Royer told him that the 233rd was maxed out, Glaser didn't question him. He trusted Royer, seeing him as the kind of commander who could effectively balance his concern for the troops with the needs of the mission.

For their part, Royer's soldiers sometimes thought he was a bit too willing to take on so many missions and that the battalion tapped them for more than their share of the tough ones. There was an element of truth to their suspicions. Glaser respected Royer's competence and knew the 233rd could get the job done. Royer, for his part, trusted his soldiers implicitly, knowing these were some of the best MPs in Baghdad. He could be moody at times, but he was also fiercely protective of his MPs, and Glaser respected that. That explained why Royer insisted that his soldiers keep their Kevlar helmets and flak vests on whenever they were on patrol. Those were the kind of things that kept people alive, he figured, and that was his highest priority. The MPs might grumble, but they always did their job. Even if given a choice, they would have served with no other unit. As far as they were concerned, the 233rd was the "best damn MP company in Iraq."[2]

Patrolling

Whether pulling escort duty or on roving patrols, the MPs spent many of their waking hours on the streets of Baghdad, coping with the heat, the crowds, the Iraqi traffic, an occasional sandstorm, and the constant threat of violence. It didn't matter that most of the Iraqis they saw every day were either friendly or indifferent; it only took one individual and one moment for their lives to change forever. So they maintained constant vigilance and did their best to keep the public at arm's length.

As far as Royer was concerned, the 233rd was fighting a guerrilla war. Although the number of active insurgents was miniscule, there were just enough to prevent them from letting down their guard. By the middle of 2003, the insurgents consisted of a hodgepodge of largely unrelated groups, each with their own set of motivations, organization (or lack thereof), and even tactics. There were thousands of common criminals to deal with. There was also a committed core of old Ba'athist loyalists. They fought simply to regain power and proved just as ruthless in war as they had been in peace. But increasingly, foreign jihadists (overwhelmingly fundamentalist Sunni radicals) were popping up around the country. This group included Syrians, Saudis, Jordanians, Yemenis, Egyptians—disaffected young Muslim men from throughout the Islamic world. Their goal, as much as they understood it themselves, was to drive out the Americans and then to establish an Islamic fundamentalist state. To achieve victory, they were willing to wage war not just on the American occupiers, but increasingly on the nation's civilian population as well, especially the Shi'ites. Finally, there were Shia radicals, representing the nation's long-suppressed Shia Muslim majority, a group that was deeply suspicious of the Americans' motives.

This volatile mix of enemies shared very little in common except a hatred for the Americans and a willingness to resort to terrorism. The tactics they used included random gunshots fired at passing convoys, the equally random rocket and mortar attacks, an occasional suicide bomber, and, increasingly, improvised explosive devices (IED), typically used on the sides of heavily traveled roads. Unfortunately, there was no shortage of materials from which to construct IEDs. Old artillery and mortar shells were especially popular, in part because they were so prevalent. For a trigger device, the insurgents preferred cell phones and garage door openers. There was also no shortage of these. Finally, the terrorists proved to be remarkably ingenious in hiding their bombs. They used everything from innocuous burlap bags and cardboard boxes to rotting dog carcasses.

The MPs faced a delicate balancing act: they were expected to be part policeman and part diplomat. Their lives depended on maintaining a constant vigilance against terrorists even as they were lectured about treating the Iraqi public with respect and dignity. They were increasingly bombarded in their daily briefings with information on the Iraqi culture, including facts about the Muslim religion, restrictions on their access to mosques, or tips on negotiating with local Sunni or Shia leaders. But like everything else in Baghdad, the MPs learned most of their lessons about the Iraqi culture the hard way. They discovered that showing someone the bottom of your feet was considered the ultimate insult, a sign of utter contempt. They also learned that Iraqis despised lying prone, the technique the MPs preferred when taking a suspect into custody. The Iraqis would kneel, but they invariably resisted when the MPs tried to get them to lie face down on the ground.

They learned to be especially careful when searching Iraqi women, a job the female MPs performed whenever possible. It also helped to search the Iraqi women out of sight of other Iraqis. Better yet, they learned to allow a respected elder to be present when a woman was searched. Before entering a home or business, the MPs gave the women time to cover themselves. Best of all was to let IPs conduct vehicle or personal searches, giving an Iraqi face to policing the city.[3]

The Springfield Connection

Sergeant Chris Cunningham always enjoyed his afternoon jogs at Viper Base. It was a great way to sweat out the day's frustrations, and since it was the middle of June, it didn't take long to break a sweat, even at night. Cunningham and his running partner, Matt Himpelmann, were just finishing a lap when Specialist Abraham Bain, Cunningham's gunner, flagged him down. "Hey, we've got to go!" Bain called out. "I thought he was kidding," recalled Cunningham later. He had already spent a long day escorting Captain Royer around Baghdad, and Bain was known for his wry sense of humor. He wasn't the kind of guy you always took seriously, so Cunningham pushed himself through another lap, only to find Bain still waiting for him when he finished. "Seriously, Sarge, we have to go!"

With that, Cunningham raced to his room and suited up, still drenched in sweat. Within minutes, Captain Royer led a convoy out the gate, heading into the early evening twilight toward the al-Sa'adoun police station. The station had just experienced another mortar attack, and this time Royer was determined to find the insurgents launching the attacks.[4]

The tiny patrol made good time for the first few blocks, then slowed to a crawl as it reached a bustling marketplace along Karada Boulevard. The marketplace hummed with activity, its sidewalks and shops packed with customers. Jacob English, from his vantage point as Captain Royer's gunner, had a bird's-eye view of the entire shopping district. He also had a keen eye for detail, and he zoomed in on something suspicious to his front: a young Iraqi man sitting in a purple station wagon parked next to the market area. As the convoy continued forward, English focused on the meticulously dressed man as he slipped out of the station wagon, then watched the man furtively tuck a pistol into the back of his waistband before walking to the front of the car, heading toward the crowded marketplace. He was immediately joined by an attractive young woman dressed in dark slacks, blouse, and headscarf. It was at this moment, with the convoy now even with the station wagon, that English reacted instinctively. "Gun," he roared, and with that, the Humvee screeched to a halt and Captain Royer launched himself into the street, followed closely by Staff Sergeant Eugene Sielagowski, an active Army dog handler attached to the company, sans dog. That was Cunningham's cue in the second Humvee to do the same, and First Sergeant Elmore followed close on his heels. Elmore and "Ski" immediately went into crowd control mode, cajoling the bystanders to back up while Royer and Cunningham pushed their way through the crowd, stealing glances over their shoulders as English continued to gesture toward the gunman. The crowd immediately engulfed Royer and Cunningham as they pressed on. "There's a guy with a gun up there," Royer yelled over his shoulder. Cunningham had no idea who, but it was obvious Royer did. They continued to plow their way through a sea of people, which parted just enough to let them pass, then immediately closed in behind them. Top and Ski forced their way forward a short distance behind.

Royer was entirely focused on his quarry, pressing the pursuit until the man was finally cornered against the wall of a shop. One step behind Royer's right shoulder stood Sergeant Cunningham. Both men, breathing heavily from the exertions of the chase, had their M-16s raised and pointed directly at their quarry. Cunningham felt the crowd pressing ominously in around them. "Raise your hands, drop to your knees," the two bellowed in broken Arabic. Instead, the man raised his gun hand, "coming up in Jeff's direction." Seeing that, thoughts raced through Cunningham's mind. He felt his finger tighten on the trigger, his selector switch already set on "fire." With the crowd pressing in, he realized that gunning down the man might prove disastrous. More than likely, he would also hit an innocent bystander, and this was by no means a friendly crowd. Instead, Cunningham brought his weapon down to port, then thrust his body forward until he slammed into the man, hitting his left side with so much force that the dazed Iraqi struck the wall hard, with the pistol tumbling to the ground. Royer immediately stepped on the pistol while Cunningham did his best to subdue the Iraqi, who resisted his best efforts to lie face down on the ground. It had all happened in a split second.[5]

In the background, Cunningham heard a young woman screeching in protest as Elmore and Ski fought to keep the crowd under control. While Cunningham pressed the Iraqi into the ground, Ski handed his weapon to Top, then stooped down to cuff the Iraqi. Once secured, they pulled the man to his feet, and then the group began working their way back through the crowd, with the angry young woman following close behind. The trek to the Humvees took much longer than Cunningham calculated. They'd obviously run a long way before cornering their prey. Once there, they wasted no time in saddling up and speeding to the police station, where they dropped off their suspect for interrogation. Only then did they discover that the irate young woman was the man's sister. The streets were dangerous, the man protested, and he carried the gun to protect her from unruly thugs and kidnappers.

Cunningham was exhausted and soaked with sweat by the time the patrol left al-Sa'adoun, but his day was still not over. Royer led the group through several raids on suspected apartment complexes in a vain attempt to find the source of the mortar fire. By the time they finally returned to Viper Base, Cunningham headed for the showers, more than ready to scrub off the grit of a very long day. When he later heard that Royer credited him with saving his life, Cunningham just shrugged it off. "Jeff did just as much as I did," he later insisted. "I had the backup side, and Jeff had the . . . contact side. It was just two cops working together."[6]

A Summary Execution

By July, with temperatures routinely in the 130s, the MPs felt like they lived in a pressure cooker. It was a constant battle to stay hydrated, and the U.S. Army was big on keeping its soldiers hydrated. But that posed a problem, for the Army was not able to issue enough bottled water to the troops who worked the streets. They were rationed two 1.5-liter bottles of water per day, not the four to six they needed to deal with the scorching heat. When things got desperate, the MPs drew water from the unit's water buffalo (the water trailer normally hauled behind the unit's mess truck), but the heat nearly cooked the stuff, leading to some peculiar chemical reactions that made the water nearly undrinkable.[7]

On July 5, a team from the 4th Platoon "Crusaders" served as the unit's QRF. Specialist Kristine Ward, a twenty-one-year-old airline employee from Springfield who now worked as the Crusaders' medic, made sure to stuff several IV bags into her aid bag. Heat casualties were par for the course. Ward liked the National Guard and the satisfaction she got from doing something important. She was only nine when the Guard came to her tiny community of Timewell to fight the great flood of '93. She had a blast helping the guardsmen fill sandbags. When she turned seventeen, Kristine pestered her mother until she finally consented to sign the enlistment papers. Kristine certainly found life in Baghdad challenging, but the situation back home was really no better. Shortly after she deployed, she got word that one of her closest friends had committed suicide. On top of that, her aunt had recently been diagnosed with cancer, and a great-grandmother was also ailing. It was a lot to digest, especially so far from home.

Ward was eating lunch with the rest of the QRF at Viper Base when a call came in to head to Baghdad University ASAP. The team immediately headed for the university campus, which was located just across the Tigris River. The information they received as they drove was sobering: a young Guardsman had just been gunned down in the university's cafeteria. Specialist Jeffrey Wershow of Charlie Company of the 2nd Battalion, 124th Infantry Regiment, Florida National Guard, had been escorting several civil affairs officers as they met with university officials. Thinking the cafeteria was secure, he took off his body armor and Kevlar helmet, slung his M-16 over his shoulder, grabbed a 7-Up, and then headed toward a shaded terrace. That's when a man walked up behind the young American, pulled out a pistol, and shot him in the base of the head. The man, a stranger to the students in the cafeteria, slipped away in the ensuing confusion. Specialist Ward was the first medic to reach Wershow.

She did what she could, but it was obvious that Wershow was in a bad way. Ward dove into her bag, bandaged his wounds as best as she could, and struggled to find a vein that wasn't collapsed so she could administer an IV. She worked without surgical gloves and was soon covered with Wershow's blood, but she was determined to keep him alive. It seemed like an eternity before a physician arrived and hastily checked her work. He reassured Ward she had done her job well, but he also confirmed what she already knew: Wershow could not possibly survive such a serious wound. Through it all, Wershow's best friend hovered close by, inconsolable. By the time the medevac arrived, Ward was physically and emotionally exhausted.

After Wershow was loaded into the helicopter, Ward washed the blood off her hands as best as she could, gulped down some water, then went back to work, this time helping the other female MPs search the women in the cafeteria in a vain attempt to find the assassin. After fifteen minutes of this, the heat and stress finally caught up with her. "I looked over at Sergeant Johnson and said, 'I don't feel so good. I feel like I'm going to pass out.'" "Take fifteen," he told her while the rest of the QRF continued work, but within moments, she started hearing people call out for medics. Iraqis were passing out from the heat, and Ward had no choice but to go back to work, administering IVs to the cafeteria's patrons. It wasn't long before some Americans succumbed to the heat as well. When several 1st Armored Division medics finally arrived, Ward was all in—near shock, and in need of an IV herself. It took seven attempts before a medic found her vein. She started hyperventilating, then passed out. The medics drenched her with water from head to toe, put her on oxygen, and rushed her back to the hospital in the Green Zone.

Ward spent the next two days in the hospital recovering from her heat injuries, then returned to the company area and to her friends in the 4th Platoon. She had recovered physically, but her nerves were worn thin. It wasn't just the events of the past few days that had ground her down, or even her worries about home. Working and living with the same people—people she loved and respected—took its toll as well. She worked, ate, and relaxed (in those rare moments of free time) with the same people 24–7.

Ward reached her breaking point over the most innocent of circumstances. She was standing near the doorway to their sleeping quarters when a roommate jokingly bumped into her as he walked by, declaring in an exaggerated voice, "Get out of my way." At one level, Ward understood he meant nothing by it, that it was nothing more than soldierly horseplay. But this was "a really bad day and I just snapped," she later recalled. A torrent of invectives spewed out, including a couple of not-so-veiled threats about committing suicide. When Captain Royer and First Sergeant Elmore found out about the incident, they were in no mood to take chances. They directed

Ward to turn in her M-16 to the supply sergeant, then transferred her from 4th Platoon to the operations section in the headquarters platoon. Most importantly, they decided to ship her to the 785th Combat Stress Company, where Ward spent the next three days decompressing.

The whole concept of dealing with battlefield fatigue so close to the front was fairly new to the military. The 785th did yeoman's work, and in most cases, they released their patients back to their units within seventy-two hours. The way the Army saw it, soldiers like Ward were casualties every bit as much as those with physical injuries. The whole process was carefully designed to help them recover and return to duty as quickly as possible, with their self-esteem and mental health intact. While there, Ward participated in both group and individual counseling sessions. She did PT with the rest of the patients, cleaned her room, helped prepare meals, and attended classes. In the evening, she caught up on some reading, watched TV, and joined a couple of card games. The therapy and time away from the 233rd definitely worked, and after three days, Ward was ready to go back to work. Still, returning to the unit was tough. Some of her buddies made a point of giving her a reassuring word and welcoming her back. Some kept their distance. She felt like an outsider, separated as she was from 4th Platoon. She couldn't deny that living and working with the same people around the clock had taken its toll, but they were her family, and she missed the old, easygoing camaraderie they had once shared.

The Home Front

Kristine Ward was by no means the only member of the 233rd who found her separation from family and friends difficult. Almost everyone felt the pain of separation, on both sides of the Atlantic. For Monica Hildebrandt, now approaching her third trimester of pregnancy, time passed in a blur. She continued to work as a paramedic at the Effingham County ambulance service, and when not at work, she struggled to keep things going at home. She felt herself shutting down emotionally. "The worst was driving somewhere in the car and a happy song would come on the radio," she later recalled, "and I'd just lose it." Most of the time, however, she toughed it out and surprised herself with how well she was coping.[8]

Pamela Weber, wife of the Crusaders' platoon sergeant, Sergeant First Class Kevin Weber, faced adjustments of her own. Kevin's parents had just sold their home in Jacksonville and purchased an RV. They planned to spend the winter in Texas before building a new home near Murrayville the following spring. They were in Texas when Kevin was mobilized, but they immediately made their way north to offer any support they could to Pamela and her two children, three-year-old Alexandra and baby Ethan. After a quick family meeting, they reached a decision. The best for all concerned was for Kevin's parents to move in. They took over Ethan's room and their cat got the run of the basement, as far away from Pamela and her allergies as possible.[9]

Perhaps no one dealt with more change than did Lisa Conner, Sergeant Ed Higginson's fiancée. Ed worked the night shift in the company's tactical operations center. Technically, his hitch in the Guard should have been up in May 2003, but Ed was one of many in the 233rd who were involuntarily extended when the unit was activated. Like most of those in the same circumstances, he took the extension in stride. Ed and Lisa first met at Rantoul, Illinois, where Lisa worked for Cingular and Ed for Lincoln's Challenge, an Illinois National Guard program that steered high school dropouts toward a GED and a brighter future. When Ed landed a job with the Springfield police department, the two kept their relationship going by making frequent jaunts along the 100-mile I-72 corridor. Meanwhile, Lisa pestered Cingular to move her and her five-year-old daughter to Springfield. Only then, the two agreed, would they get married. Lisa was finally relocated to Springfield—the same week Ed shipped to Kuwait. They decided that the wedding would have to wait.

"I was completely alone in a brand-new town," recalled Lisa, "just me and my daughter. That was scary." Ed's family helped Lisa move into a small apartment and did all they could to make her feel welcome. Even so, Lisa felt isolated. As an Air Force brat, she was used to moving a lot, but now she found herself alone in a new town, with a new job, cut off from the man she loved. The separation was agonizing. Ed got a chance to call Lisa while in Kuwait, waiting in line for three hours only to miss her. It was daughter Amber's first day in kindergarten, a rare day when Lisa left her cell phone at home. So Ed ended up talking to his folks, and they relayed what little Ed was able to tell them to Lisa. He was headed to Iraq, they told Lisa, but Ed wasn't able to tell them anything else—not where in Iraq he was headed, or what he would be doing once there.

Lisa became obsessed with the news during the military's initial push north, but when the bad news did not stop after the Americans occupied Baghdad, she became disgusted with the coverage. "I didn't want to hear [the bad news]," she later recalled. "It just made me sick to my stomach. I couldn't breathe until the next time I talked to him." But that was the problem, because she heard nothing from Ed for the next five weeks—no letters, no e-mails, no phone calls. It wasn't that Ed wasn't trying. He wrote to her often after his shift in the company tactical operations center, and he fired letters off regularly. But the mail system had essentially broken down, and his work schedule gave him no opportunity to call home. When Lisa finally started receiving mail from Iraq in late May, she got it in bunches.

Those five weeks of silence felt like an eternity for Lisa. As far as she was concerned, she was living through the old adage about bad things happening in threes. There was the traumatic move to Springfield followed by the death of her much-loved grandmother. Worst of all, Ed was somewhere overseas, and the only thing Lisa knew was that he was in the middle of the most dangerous place in the world. When she got no news from him, she invariably thought the worst. So did Pamela Weber, who made a point to avoid the news.

The breakdown of communication between Iraq and Illinois was exactly why the unit's Family Readiness Group (FRG) was so important. It provided people like Lisa with a support group, linking her with others who were going through the same kind of problems and who understood what she was coping with. But because Lisa was a fiancée and not a wife, she was not initially included in the organization's network. Not until Ed's folks told her about a FRG picnic in July did she officially get plugged into the net. By that time, Lisa had already seen a counselor to help her cope with the stress.[10]

Ed didn't receive his first letter from Lisa until June. It wasn't that mail wasn't arriving in Iraq. The problem was distributing it because the handful of postal personnel in-country were swamped. Like so much of what happened in Baghdad, Top took the initiative. He went looking for the unit's mail and discovered a conex container filled with mail at Baghdad International Airport (BIAP). He rounded up several soldiers and spent a week sorting through the backlog. Once the trickle of mail started, it soon became a flood. By late June, the MPs weren't just receiving letters, but also a steady supply of care packages containing everything imaginable. They received athletic gear, soccer balls, books, CDs and DVDs, electronic equipment of all types, even air conditioners and computers. Pamela Weber sent Kevin balsa wood airplanes to pass out to the kids he met on patrols. The planes never made it to the streets because Kevin's soldiers had a blast with them in the barracks. Kevin also got a letter or package every day from his State Farm insurance agent. It was the agent's way to show he cared, but Kevin took his share of ribbing from the guys in the platoon, amazed that an insurance salesman should take such an intense interest in his welfare. Finally, the MPs received tons of food and candy, much of it destined for the streets of Baghdad, plus lots of beverage powder and a bounty of toiletry items. They learned early on not to mix food with toiletries because the heat made the entire contents unpalatable. Thankfully, by July, not only was the mail getting through, but the MPs also had regular access to telephones.[11]

Judy Victor dove into the FRG activities, and especially her self-appointed job as birthday card coordinator, a position she suggested to Jerry Calbow so that no soldier would be forgotten on his birthday. As a grade school teacher at Springfield's Wilcox Elementary School, she had no trouble finding willing supporters. She convinced her students to adopt the 233rd, and they took to the task with a passion. A steady stream of letters, posters, and pictures soon was making its way to the MPs in Iraq. It seemed like a small gesture to Judy, but the feedback she got from Iraq was heartwarming.[12]

The real communications breakthrough occurred on July 16. That was the day the 233rd finally got regular Internet access. Before that date, it was a rare event when someone got access to a computer with an Internet connection. Kevin Weber got his first chance on May 25, when he accompanied one of his soldiers to an Army hospital outside the city. He excitedly logged on and immediately checked his e-mail account, where he found a message from Pamela dated April 27, a message wishing him a happy anniversary. The next time he got online was July 16, the day an enterprising Iraqi set up a bank of nine computers for the unit. The bitrate was good, and the chance to surf the Internet, order things online, and especially send e-mail messages home was well worth the fee of $3 an hour. Best of all, they now had a chance to instant-message their loved ones, the next best thing to a telephone call. Within a couple of weeks, the Army set up its own version of an Internet café. The price was right, but their new terminals lacked the speed of their Iraqi Internet café. Still, with about twenty computers available, they rarely had to wait. [13]

Logistics Challenges

Of all the serious logistical challenges the 233rd faced in their first couple of months, none was more serious than the lack of potable water. But the logistical challenges hardly stopped there. The root of the Army's supply problems stemmed from the fact that the logistical units the Army needed to sustain the force were late in arriving. The Pentagon, faced with a temporary shipping shortage, had elected to push the combat forces into the theater first. When the combat phase abruptly ended, the logistical assets that sustained the military in the long term were only just arriving. For the next several months, the military played catch-up, and the soldiers improvised.[14]

Some of the shortages stemmed from the harsh realities the convoys faced on the run from Kuwait to Baghdad—convoys that presented a tempting target to the growing insurgency. Staff Sergeant Randy Camden, the company's easygoing supply sergeant who greeted everyone with a ready smile, felt especially vulnerable when he made his daily ten-minute run from Viper Base to BIAP for rations and water. He typically made the run at fifty to sixty miles an hour, keeping his foot on the accelerator as he raced along the route. For the next several months, the 233rd's supply personnel felt like they were in perpetual motion, shuttling daily from Viper Base to BIAP, and logging many more miles to a growing list of Baghdad outposts. They also made several trips from Baghdad to Kuwait, but perhaps their least favorite mission was transferring Iraqi prisoners from one of the company's police stations to either Tas Ferrat or Abu Ghraib. As much as they disliked the mission, it was undoubtedly tougher on the prisoners, who bounced around in the back of the supply deuce and a half, their hands bound behind their backs with Flex-Cufs, seated either on the side benches or in the bed of the truck. MP teams accompanied the trucks in front and back as an escort.

Flex-Cufs were in critically short supply throughout the supply system, but ironically, it was toilet paper that soon topped the MPs' shopping list. The 233rd had it good as far as their living quarters were concerned. Al-Duri's estate was lavish by Baghdad standards, but it took a while to get running water, and even once it was restored, the MPs had a hard time adjusting to the smaller diameter of Iraqi plumbing. The system simply could not accommodate things like baby wipes, feminine hygiene items, and small rags, and clogs became the depressing norm. An edict was soon declared: no flushing allowed. The MPs relied instead on a burn barrel for their business.

Like so much else about their year in Baghdad, a trip to the latrine took on a character of its own. Part of the unit's standard gear was a 55-gallon drum cut in half. The base was cut out, and the unit's carpenter then fashioned a wooden lid for the drum, attaching a standard toilet seat to the top. This contraption was then placed over a hole dug into the sand and declared open for business. Whenever this makeshift latrine became full, a detail of unfortunate MPs poured diesel fuel on top of the excrement, then burned the whole foul mixture. The hole would then be filled with sand, another hole dug, and the contraption placed on top of it. Next to the 55-gallon drum, the troops also buried a couple of PVC pipes into the sand, slanted at an angle, and in this way created "piss tubes" for the men. That innovation relieved the congestion around the "shitter."

It didn't take long before the MPs began to crave a little privacy when attending to business, and Sergeant Matt Harris, the unit's Nuclear, Biological, and Chemical Materials NCO, soon rose to the task. He scrounged up a discarded closet door along with some lumber and nails from a scrap heap, then fashioned a portable screen for their "field expedient" latrine with help from a few able assistants. The whole arrangement immediately became known as "the Harris," and thereafter the MPs never spoke about going to the latrine or the john or the can. One went to "the Harris," and no one thought it unusual that it should have a name of its own.

While Staff Sergeant Camden struggled to keep the unit supplied, Staff Sergeant Keith Hildebrandt and the maintenance section fought to keep the unit's vehicles and generators running. It was a monumental struggle. The unit's problems started stateside during their two months at Fort McCoy. With the post jammed with Guard and Reserve units all clamoring to get their vehicles into top-notch condition before shipment overseas, there simply were not enough parts to go around. Still, Hildebrandt was confident that his vehicles were in decent shape by the time they were rail-loaded for Texas. Once the troops linked up with their equipment in Kuwait, the shortage of repair parts became more severe. Hildebrandt's mechanics replaced a lot of seals and tuned up the unit's forty-seven Humvees as much as possible, but no one in Kuwait was getting the parts they really needed. As a result, the unit's ancient wrecker towed one Humvee deadlined for a bad engine during the move from Kuwait to Baghdad, while another Humvee towed one deadlined for a bad transmission.

Once at Viper Base, the maintenance section settled into a large maintenance and storage building on the compound and declared themselves open for business. They had plenty of business, and soon they were cannibalizing both of the Humvees they hauled into town, combining the good engine from one with the good transmission from the other to get one back into operation. The unit wasn't authorized to perform such complex maintenance tasks, but like everyone else in Baghdad, Hildebrandt and his crew learned to make do.

For the next couple of months, the Army's repair-parts system strained under the demand. Humvee tires became the American Army's proverbial nail on which the whole operation depended. Because of the intense heat, the unit burned through tires at a prodigious rate. With no tires in the supply system, the MPs continued to ride them until they were slick. When they were close to threadbare, Hildebrandt's mechanics swapped out tires from deadlined trucks, then made sure there were no more than two slick tires on each Humvee. When the tires blew in the middle of a patrol, Hidebrandt would saddle up and drive into the heart of Baghdad with the wrecker and a couple of escort Humvees to rescue the downed vehicle.

The unit's generators, designed to run for a few hours at a time, soon burned out from the constant use. Oil and lubricants also broke down much more quickly in the intense heat. On this too, Hildebrandt ignored the scheduled oil changes dictated in the maintenance manuals and kept the vehicles on the road long after he should have deadlined them. When the oil absolutely had to be replaced, they purchased it locally. In this way, the mechanics managed to keep the unit's vehicles running, maintaining an acceptable 10 to 15 percent deadline rate. It took a Herculean effort, plenty of scrounging, and some creative reporting, but they kept the 233rd on the road.[15]

Keeping up with the basic repairs was not the only task the maintenance section took on. Almost immediately, the MPs started to modify the unit's Humvees. They started by removing the Humvees' fiberglass doors to allow for better visibility and a quicker exit. When random ambushes and roadside bombs became a problem, the word soon came down to put the doors back on. The MPs scrounged sets of body armor and hung these on the doors for extra armor, but they kept the windows rolled down.

It wasn't long before the MPs looked for more substantial ways to armor the Humvees. They contracted with local Iraqis to weld quarter-inch diamond-pointed steel onto the doors at $150 per vehicle, then lined the floors of their Humvees and trucks with sandbags. The sandbag could absorb quite a blast, transferring the energy from a piece of shrapnel to the sand, which filled the cab with flying sand but left the chunk of metal lying harmlessly on the floor.[16]

From MP to Medic

Sergeant Dana Hodges was taking a rare moment to relax after finishing lunch on July 7, when a call came in to the New Baghdad police station. The IPs received a garbled message, something about a possible robbery or carjacking at a nearby highway overpass. Dana Hodges was something of a rarity in the 233rd. As B Team leader for 1st Squad, 3rd Platoon, she was one of the few women who served in a leadership position in a line platoon. Hodges, blonde with a slim build and of average height, nevertheless carried herself with an air of confidence. She commanded Specialists Quntrell Crayton and Steven Keith, and together, the team had seen more than its share of action. That's the way Hodges liked it—a line platoon was where the action was. These were the MPs who patrolled the streets every day, made the arrests, and conducted the raids, and as a team leader, Hodges was often in the thick of it. She was unique in another respect as well. As a certified medic, she often pulled double duty.

Second Lieutenant Stephen Rice quickly rounded up his response team, which included a van full of IPs and two MP teams, then headed for the action on the southbound lane of a divided highway where a dusty white pickup truck was cornered. The incident began when four Iraqi men robbed a gas station attendant of several million dinars (roughly $12,750), then casually went to a nearby restaurant for lunch. After lunch, they drove their truck onto the divided highway, deliberately going against the flow of traffic so they could precipitate a traffic jam and carjack a vehicle. Unknown to them, their victim had tailed them, and when they stopped on the road, he went to a nearby police station to report the incident. The MPs knew nothing of this as they raced to the action. Arriving on the scene, Rice pulled his two Humvees to a stop on a frontage road opposite the white pickup, allowing the IP van to continue toward the scene, thus letting the Iraqis take the lead.

Hodges watched as an IP dismounted, approached the truck, and ordered the three subjects in the cab to exit with their hands up—standard procedure for such encounters. This request was met with gunfire from the truck cab at the same instant a fourth suspect rose up from the bed of the truck. "Fire!" Lieutenant Rice barked. MPs responded in unison, immediately laying down a withering volley of rifle and machine gun fire directed at the pickup. Not until Rice saw a nearby fuel truck take a hit did he call for a cease-fire. By then, all four suspects had been hit. Rice directed Sergeant Dan Hinds and Specialist Lucas Jockisch to cordon off the area from the growing throng of curious Iraqis, then cautiously approached the truck, now riddled with bullet holes. That was Sergeant Hodges's signal to grab her aid bag and race to the injured Iraqis.[17]

It did not take her long to determine that two of the Iraqis were dead and the other two seriously wounded—and obviously intoxicated to boot. Hodges went to work while other MPs kept a wary eye on her patients. She set up an IV for each man, then patched them up as best she could. It was no small task. Hodges counted eight bullet holes in one victim, and the other man wasn't much better. She was soon joined by another medic from the 210th MP Company QRF, just arrived on the scene. Over her shoulder, she could see several Iraqi civilians watching, enjoying the show as she fought to save their lives. The crowd lingered until all four victims were crammed into the back of the Iraqi Police Service van for the trip to the nearby al-Kindi hospital. The two medics stayed with their patients as they headed to the hospital, struggling to keep them alive.

Staff Sergeant Fritzsche, Hodges's squad leader, sweated out the whole incident at his post at the New Baghdad station, following the action as best he could on the radio. When his soldiers returned, he met them at the back door cradling a case of water in his arms. Sergeant James Batterson, who had arrived late to the action, was the first through the door, tossing off a casual comment about finding only one weapon on the scene as he passed Fritzsche. "So what?" Fritzsche responded tersely. As the rest of the patrol filed by, Fritzsche handed each a bottle of water, then told him to head upstairs to separate rooms. He wanted them segregated until he could debrief each one individually. Batterson's comment had triggered a disturbing thought. Fritzsche knew instantly the kind of rumors Batterson's information might generate in certain circles—that the IPs or even an American had dropped a weapon at the scene after the incident was over, that the criminals had been unarmed, that the IPs and his soldiers had been trigger-happy, that they had indiscriminately blasted away at unarmed Iraqis. Fritzsche knew better than to believe that, having followed the entire incident on the radio. He knew that Hodges, Crayton, and Keith had seen far too much action to respond unprovoked. Fritzsche remembered how Crayton, devoutly religious, had struggled with his emotions after the incident at the rail yard—the first time Crayton fired his weapon in combat. When Sergeant Hinds caught up with Crayton at the station, finding him alone at the rooftop security position, Crayton was still trying to make sense of the day's events. "I don't understand why they shot," Crayton muttered in disbelief. "Why would they do that? I'm tired of all the killing. I'm tired of it!"

Fritzsche knew that his people were seasoned veterans, calm in a crisis and competent in the performance of their duties. He also knew the prudent thing to do was to rigorously follow their standard operating procedure and segregate everyone involved until they had completed their incident reports and been properly debriefed. Fritzsche questioned each soldier separately, including Lieutenant Rice, and got the same story from each. The only discrepancy was who in the pickup had started the whole thing by firing on the IPs—just the kind of detail that usually got lost in the rush of adrenaline. Some thought it was the driver who leaned across one of the passengers to fire; others believed that the driver handed a pistol to his buddy, who then fired.[18]

At Viper Base the next day, rumors began swirling that someone had dropped a weapon at the scene. Fritzsche chalked the talk up to jealousy among some soldiers in another platoon. But when the rumors reached Captain Royer's ears, he felt obligated to interview all of the participants again. Royer conducted his investigation at the police station, talking to each participant separately, just as Frtizsche had done the day before. Royer didn't dance around the issue; his questions were blunt and to the point, including whether there was a dropped weapon involved. Once again, the conclusion was the same. The criminals had precipitated the exchange by firing on the IP, everyone had done his job well, and the rumors were unsubstantiated. At one level, Fritzsche understood that Captain Royer, upon hearing the rumors, had to follow up with his own investigation. But at a deeper level, the whole thing ate at him. The next time they were in a tough spot, Fritzsche feared, his troops might second-guess themselves, leading to a split second of doubt that could prove disastrous. "The day of the incident they had no doubt what they had to do," he recalled later. "After the commander came and questioned [them], they had doubts." For the rest of the day, his troops "had their heads in their ass."

That night, immediately after the squad arrived at Viper Base, Fritzsche strode across the compound, determined to vent to Top about the incident. Captain Royer, anticipating as much, intercepted Fritzsche before he made it to the first sergeant. Fritzsche was tired and clearly angry, but he managed to keep his emotions under control. For his part, Royer understood why Fritzsche was upset, and immediately after their talk, he headed to the barracks and aired things out with the squad members, explaining why he had to question them on the incident, in essence apologizing for having to do it.[19]

There was one more unexpected consequence to the whole affair. In the days after the incident, the Hogs noticed that relations with the local Iraqis started to improve. Hodges chalked it up to the simple act of patching up a couple of criminals. "They saw that we had gone over there and given them care," she later reflected. "I think that actually helped with a lot of our relations in the community." Slowly but surely, the citizens of Baghdad were beginning to respect the Americans who rode in the Humvees with crossed-pistols stenciled on their sides.

July 7 wasn't Hodges's and Hinds's last encounter with the two Iraqis whose lives Hodges had saved. Months later, while sitting in a police station, two IPs walked in with an Iraqi in custody—the same man who had miraculously survived eight gunshot wounds. Hodges was taken aback. Sergeant Hinds took the opportunity to clear up some things that had bothered all of them about the incident. The man admitted they had fired at the IPs that day, and he also confessed to being drunk, thanks to some home brew purchased at a roadside stand. They liked the Americans, he told Hinds matter-of-factly. It's just that they had run across the Americans on a bad day, a stupid day.[20]

Wire Across the Road

July 22 was a good day for the Americans in Iraq. That was the day Uday and Quasai Hussein, Saddam's brutal sons, died in a firefight in Mosul. Once again, the Iraqi people had reason to celebrate. They fired their AK-47s into the night sky.[21] The insurgency, as the media increasingly called the disjointed resistance, had steadily increased since the American occupation in April. Even more disturbing, the insurgents were increasingly targeting their fellow Iraqis, including seven police cadets who died along with seventy injured in an attack in Ramadi on July 6. Still, despite the attack, the Baghdad police were on the rebound.[22]

Neither side had illusions about the immediate future. It was bound to be bloody. The insurgents grew steadily more creative and ruthless in their tactics. The 233rd encountered one of their new tactics in the early morning of August 7. Specialist Bradley Marcy, assigned to the Punishers' 2nd Squad, was riding in the turret of X-ray 17, watching the rear to provide security for a two vehicle patrol en route to the al-Alawyah police station. Suddenly, a wire mysteriously dropped down into the street, catching Marcy on the back of the neck below his helmet. The Humvee's momentum caused the wire to slide up Marcy's neck before snagging the rim of his Kevlar helmet. In an instant, his head was slammed into the machine gun stock. The convoy screeched to a halt, and teammates attended to Marcy while others retrieved a single strand of copper wire with white insulation. He was lucky: he escaped the incident with only a friction burn on his cheek and a swollen lip.

Captain Royer couldn't determine whether the attack was intentional or merely another of the many bizarre incidents they so often encountered, but he was in no mood to take chances. The maintenance section welded metal angle irons onto the front bumper of every Humvee in the unit. These were designed to catch and cut any wires they might encounter while on patrol. Colonel Glaser liked the idea so much that he directed all of his companies to adopt the modification. The change didn't last, however. The division sergeant major frowned on the unauthorized modification, and the pickets soon came off, but not without considerable grumbling from the MPs.[23]

By early August, the MPs' lives had settled into a predictable routine. Their days were long and exhausting, and the heat was unrelenting. They maintained a constant state of vigilance, knowing that at any moment something might happen—a sniper, an IED going off, or an accident, something that could change a life forever. Still, conditions in Baghdad were much improved over their first two months. They lived in some of the best barracks in Baghdad, and they now enjoyed an occasional day off. Their quarters were air conditioned, and the plumbing worked most of the time. They could count on a couple of hot meals a day, and they looked forward to their daily shower. Mail was arriving regularly, and even when it didn't, they could always reach home on the Internet or by phone.

Ed Higginson sugarcoated their existence whenever he wrote or e-mailed Lisa, but not by much. He smiled whenever he thought about one of his first calls to Lisa, when an interpreter let him use his cell phone. Ed climbed to the roof of his barracks, enjoying the cool morning breeze and a beautiful sunrise. From his vantage point, he could take in the Tigris River as it flowed nearby and the 14th of July Bridge a kilometer to the east. It was about

10:00 P.M. in Illinois when he finally got through to Lisa. Both relished the rare chance to hear each other's voice. Then Lisa heard the unmistakable sound of gunfire. "What's that?" she asked with an obvious note of alarm. "Nothing," said Ed in reassuring tones. "Just some guys shooting." What Lisa heard was a 50-caliber machine gun firing at a boat drifting ominously toward the 14th of July Bridge, where boat traffic was prohibited. "How close?" Lisa asked impatiently. "Pretty far away," came Ed's terse reply. Lisa was unconvinced, and the rare phone call home was spoiled. Even Ed's news that they might be home by December, early 2004 at the latest, did little to console her that night.[24]

LT Joel Ferris and MSG Roger Ducharme relax amid the rubble at Viper Base on April 21, 2003, their first morning in Baghdad.

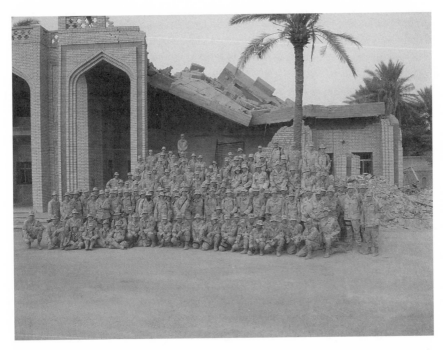

This 233rd MP Company portrait was taken in front of the destroyed residence of Izzat Ibrahim al-Duri, the former Ba'athist official, who was later designated the King of Clubs.

CPT Jeff Royer takes a break in front of his residence on Viper Base. Photo by Nelvin C. Cepeda / San Diego Union-Tribune. Copyright 2007 San Diego Union-Tribune.

1SG Robert Elmore, the 233rd's top NCO. Photo by Nelvin C. Cepeda / San Diego Union-Tribune. Copyright 2007 San Diego Union-Tribune.

LTC Dave Glaser was the 519th MP Battalion commander during most of the 233rd's time in Baghdad. Photo by Nelvin C. Cepeda / San Diego Union-Tribune. Copyright 2007 San Diego Union-Tribune.

Unit humvees are parked in front of the former residence of an al-Duri family member. The building served as home for 1st and 4th Platoons.

SGT Kurtis Glosser and SGT Tim Tolbert find a moment to relax in their makeshift barracks. Photo by Nelvin C. Cepeda / San Diego Union-Tribune. Copyright 2007 San Diego Union-Tribune.

SSG Roman Waldron of the 1st Platoon "Reapers" draws a crowd of curious Iraqis on April 30, only a week into their time in Baghdad. SPC Joshua Holder and SSG Robert Smith are in the background.

Iraqis enthusiastically greet SSG Jimmie Mayes on April 30.

SGT Jameson Denagel and SPC Zachary Street settle in at the al-Mesbah Police Station in mid-June. Repair of the police station is still a month away.

SPC Joshua Holder stands in front of the al-Muthana police station during a lighter moment in October 2003.

Several "Crusaders" join their Iraqi Police counterparts in front of the al-Muthana police station, including SPC Raine Vonnida, SPC Cynthia Hilliard, SGT Kurtis Glosser (in the back with sunglasses), SFC Kevin Weber, 1LT Mark Flack, and SGT Phillip Holt. Courtesy Washington *Post*.

1st Platoon "Reapers" proudly pose with several Iraqi police in front of al-Karadah. From left to right are SPC Mike Ravenscraft, SGT Christopher Turner, SPC Jason Brown, SGT George Martin, SSG Robert Smith, and SPC Shawna Keith.

SGT Jennifer Batterson of the "Punishers" supervises an Iraqi being taken into custody. Photo by Nelvin C. Cepeda / San Diego Union-Tribune. Copyright 2007 San Diego Union-Tribune.

SGT Dan Hinds and SFC John Gillette working the neighborhood. Photo by Nelvin C. Cepeda / San Diego Union-Tribune. Copyright 2007 San Diego Union-Tribune.

SSG Roman Waldron mans the Humvee's M-249 squad automatic weapon at a fly dump location in October. Note the crossed pistols stenciled on the hull, the plates of diamond-plated armor attached to the doors, and the ubiquitous flies, the bane of their existence in Baghdad.

This photo of a very pregnant Monica Hildebrandt with son Caleb made the front page of the Springfield *State Journal-Register* in July.

The self-proclaimed "Band of Sisters" included Monica Hildebrandt, Tammy Wilson, Sarah Mauney, and in front, Deanna Victor. The strong bond they formed got them through the absence of their husbands and fiancé.

BAND OF SISTERS

The 1st Platoon "Reapers" leadership team at the al-Sa'ad school pose with the headmistress. From left to right are SSG Robert Smith, SSG Roman Waldron, SSG Jimmie Smith (kneeling), SGT George Martin, and 1LT Joel Ferris.

Al-Sa'ad schoolgirls enthusiastically greet members of the 1st Platoon in December.

December 15 was a big day for both the "Reapers" and the students at al-Sa'ad primary school. SGT Shauna Cashion helps distribute school supplies to a line of well-behaved students.

SSG Roman Waldron passes out supplies to the school's impatient teachers.

SPC Zachary Smith enjoys a game of soccer with several boys at the al-Sa'ad school. The members of the 233rd passed out scores of soccer balls during their year in Baghdad.

SPC Adam Moma takes time to play with the children of the Dar al-Mahabha (House of Love) Orphanage, an institution founded by Mother Teresa. The orphanage cared for some of Baghdad's most severely handicapped children.

The TOC night shift included MSG Sam Woods, SPC Joshua Waters, SGT Ed Higginson, and (kneeling) SSG Lawrence Wilson.

The MPs' contraband storage room held only a small part of the weapons they eventually collected while in Baghdad. The stack of money to the left is counterfeit.

1LT Joel Ferris made a special friend of these young girls during his frequent visits to their Baghdad neighborhood.

Elmer Fudd, created by SPC Abraham Bain, the company's artist in residence, offers friendly advice to the MPs as they departed Viper Base.

SPC Jacob "Jake" English and SPC Sarah Schmidt found romance while working in Baghdad, and were married within a month of their return.

The 3rd Platoon "Hogs" leadership team in Kuwait: SFC John Gillette and 2LT Stephen Rice.

SGT Richard Carroll received an up-armored Humvee ten months into the mission. On the vehicle's maiden voyage, the windshield stopped a chunk of shrapnel headed Carroll's direction.

Several 4th Platoon "Crusaders" gather for a group photo during some down time. From left to right are SSG James Nayonis, SPC Paul Woolsey, SGT Mark Johnson, SPC Naythan Stewart, SGT Phillip Holt, SPC Blake Mays, and SGT Sean Wright. Photo by Nelvin C. Cepeda / San Diego Union-Tribune. Copyright 2007 San Diego Union-Tribune.

The convoy of buses bearing the 233rd home, joined by a huge fleet of police vehicles, was greeted by enthusiastic crowds when it reached the city limits of Springfield. Courtesy Springfield *State Journal-Register*.

SSG Randy Camden, the unit's supply sergeant, receives a heartfelt greeting from his wife and daughters. Courtesy Springfield *State Journal Register*.

7
Bombing at the UN

In the vernacular of postwar Baghdad, the United Nations headquarters in eastern Baghdad was a soft target. After the fall of Saddam, the UN set up shop in the Canal Hotel, named for the canal just south of the hotel that sliced through eastern Baghdad, now filled with fetid water. There were no military personnel controlling access to the UN compound, no tanks covering the entrance, and no strands of concertina wire surrounding the building. Only the Iraqi security guards hired by UN officials screened the comings and goings at the UN. Sergio Vieira de Mello, the fifty-five-year-old career diplomat from Brazil who served as the UN's point man in Baghdad, insisted it be that way. But everyone knew this was a risky proposition, especially with violence on the upswing in Baghdad. Seventeen people had died at the Jordanian embassy on August 7 when a massive car bomb exploded outside. And then there was the mortar attack on the Abu Ghraib prison on August 16, where nine prisoners died and scores more were injured. Nationwide, insurgents staged an average of fifteen to twenty attacks a day.[1]

Despite the upswing in violence, the military police (MPs) felt good about the progress they were making in the neighborhoods they patrolled—neighborhoods that included the UN headquarters. Citizens often flagged down MPs as they drove through the neighborhoods, tipping them off about the locations of hidden improvised explosive devices (IEDs) or weapons caches. Still, no one would argue that Baghdad was a dangerous place. That fact was driven home on the afternoon of August 19.[2]

It all started with what appeared to be a run-of-the-mill delivery. A Russian-made flatbed truck driven by a clean-shaven young man in a white

T-shirt turned off Canal Road into the UN compound at about 4:30 P.M. Those who saw the truck, with its cargo concealed under a tarp, gave it little thought. Delivery trucks made frequent visits to the compound, and nothing about this truck raised any suspicions. But the truck suddenly veered to the right, crashing into the building directly below Vieira de Mello's office. Seconds later, the truck disintegrated in a horrific explosion, bringing most of the building down with it. The hidden cargo was a deadly payload of mortar and artillery shells scavenged from the nation's ubiquitous ammunition bunkers.[3]

Staff Sergeant Fritzsche was the senior American on duty at the New Baghdad police station, aka Tombstone, that afternoon. Fritzsche was a firefighter in the Springfield fire department back in the States and a ten-year veteran of the Illinois National Guard, almost all of that time spent with the 233rd. He was also newly married; he'd tied the knot in a hasty ceremony just nine days before his deployment. The wedding had been planned for the summer, but when he discovered his deployment was imminent, his fiancée, Amy, accelerated their plans. He wanted to make sure Amy was taken care of in case anything happened to him.

Fritzsche was sitting in Tombstone's main office when the force of the massive explosion rattled the station. Moments later, he heard his telephone jangling. It was Specialist Dustin Ruyle calling in from his rooftop observation post, reporting on an explosion and an immense cloud of dust and debris billowing skyward north of Tombstone. Fritzsche raced upstairs, thinking about the previous day's IED explosion only a few hundred yards from the station. That came from an attack on an American supply convoy, triggered when a 5-ton truck passed nearby, resulting in one American death and another injured. But this explosion was much louder, and from the way it rattled the entire station, Fritzsche guessed it was just down the street. He crested the top of the stairs and peered at the enormous plume of smoke nearly 3 kilometers to the north. This explosion, he realized, was far worse. He couldn't determine the exact location—only that he needed to head there immediately.

Fritzsche ran back downstairs, barking out orders to Iraqis and Americans alike. He quickly organized his response, including two MP teams plus a van full of Iraqi police (IPs), leaving Sergeant Jason Haworth's team to staff Tombstone along with an M-1A1 tank crew assigned to the station. Within minutes, they were racing toward the growing cloud of smoke, with Fritzsche flipping through radio channels hoping to find out anything he could about the blast. Every channel was filled with chatter, all carrying the same traffic: "What was that? Where was the explosion?" It was the most disturbing radio traffic he had ever heard.

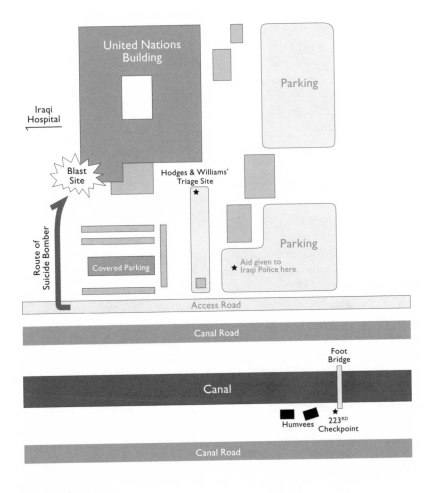

UN Bombing

Only when the convoy pulled to a stop next to a pedestrian bridge on Canal Road did Fritzsche discover the site of the explosion: the UN headquarters building located on the other side of the canal, about a hundred yards and a few buildings to his north. Fritzsche's first thoughts were to establish a security perimeter in order to control access to the UN building itself. He stationed Sergeant Dan Hinds and Specialist Stephanie Stretch near the entrance to the pedestrian bridge spanning the canal, issuing blunt instructions to allow only Coalition Provisional Authority forces and IPs across. He ordered Specialists Steve Keith and Dustin Ruyle, the Humvee gunners, to stay with the vehicles. Then Fritzsche, Sergeant Hodges, and Specialist Richard Williams, the medic attached to the platoon, raced across the pedestrian bridge into the chaos.[4]

The three were the right team for the grisly job that awaited them. Fritzsche was a career firefighter and a trained emergency medical technician, and both Hodges and Williams were experienced medics. Every company in the Army had one person whom the troops called "Doc," and twenty-six-year-old Williams was it for the 233rd. He had a youthful face but a receding hairline that suggested he was much older. For the next hour, Williams had no time to worry about that, or even his wife and son back home in Springfield. He jogged into the compound and immediately went to work amidst the carnage.

When the trio reached a parking lot, they encountered a small group of IPs and an Iraqi woman, two of whom were seriously wounded. Williams and Hodges bandaged their wounds, hooked them up to IVs, and flagged down a civilian pickup truck. They grabbed their aid bags and headed toward the building still obscured from their view, toward the cries for help emanating from around the corner. None of the trio was prepared for what they saw. The UN building had sustained massive damage, with cement and steel jutting out from the wreckage at menacing angles. In front of the rubble was a small grassy area, now covered with scores of casualties who had somehow managed to stumble and crawl their way to the tiny oasis of green. Fritzsche figured there must be at least six dead and somewhere between fifty to a hundred wounded on the grass. In the background, survivors were crawling over the wreckage, desperately looking for those still trapped in the rubble. It was clear that several who lay on the grass could not possibly survive. One woman, still alive, had a huge gash in her back near her shoulder blade. Another man's face was pierced by a chunk of rebar, the metal extending 6 feet beyond his sinus cavity. The sounds of breaking concrete, the screams of pain, and the wails of sirens were like nothing they had ever heard before. A sickening stench of blood and death already lingered in the air.

As Fritzsche led them forward, Williams and Hodges realized they were among the first medical personnel at the site. The two went to work immediately, setting up a makeshift triage, moving from patient to patient in a frantic attempt to help as many victims as possible. It did not take long for Hodges to determine that her first patient, an attractive Iraqi woman, was dead. Hodges's next patient was a man suffering from massive head trauma. Her hands shook as she dug into her aid bag. She took a deep breath and put her mind to the task at hand. For the next half hour, the two worked on their patients. Many had massive head injuries, and most suffered from deep lacerations. Some required leg or arm splints, and almost all needed an IV to keep them hydrated. All suffered from some level of trauma, and the intense heat of the August afternoon only hastened the onset of shock.[5]

Williams and Hodges moved quickly from patient to patient. They caught fleeting glimpses of Fritzsche, who often directed them to their next patient. After a few minutes, they were joined by more medical personnel, along with several others who wanted to do something—anything—to help. One senior noncommissioned officer managed to catch Hodges's attention, asking her, "What do you need—do you need any help?" She gave him only a fleeting glance, catching the look of absolute fear and disbelief in his eyes; his hands shook uncontrollably. Midway through their labors, Williams grabbed his water bottle and quickly gulped down a few swallows before tossing it to Hodges with instructions to finish it off. They immediately returned to their grisly labors, working in intense heat, swirling dust, and a growing din. By the time they exhausted their medical supplies, both had worked their way through twelve patients.[6]

Through it all, Sergeant Fritzsche focused on securing the area where Doc and Hodges worked, even as people streamed into the area. He helped load a couple of Humvee ambulances that arrived on scene, and when a box of bandages and surgical gloves arrived, he tossed some of each to Hodges and Williams and handed them out to the walking wounded. When he saw several American officers who were billeted nearby standing in the carnage, he barked out instructions to grab a litter and transport the wounded to trucks waiting outside the perimeter. When the call went up that someone was still trapped in the building, he helped dig into the rubble, and when there was a lull, he grabbed his Motorola and sent in a progress report to Tombstone.

Back at the pedestrian bridge, Sergeant Hinds and Specialist Stretch struggled to control the flow of rescue personnel into the area, and especially to prevent people from leaving the scene before they could be properly debriefed by the authorities. Hinds patted down the men while Stretch did the same with women. They turned away the curious, crews from the BBC and al-Jazeera, and those they suspected of mischief. Hinds blocked one especially persistent Iraqi from leaving the area, a contractor who spoke very good English and who badly wanted to leave the area. "He was acting strange," recalled Hinds. Only afterward, when Hinds discovered the bomb vehicle was a concrete truck, did he have reason to wonder about this frantic contractor.

When military 5-ton trucks lined up on Canal Road next to the pedestrian bridge to transport the casualties, Hinds went down the line to make sure the drivers had their tailgates down and the seats up in order to expedite the loading. One by one, the truck beds filled with stretchers carrying the injured. The stretchers were placed lengthwise to maximize the load.[7]

By 5:30 P.M., both Williams and Hodges had used up their medical supplies. Thankfully, enough UN World Health Organization physicians and coalition forces medics had arrived to handle the few casualties that remained in the area. Williams then noticed a young American soldier slumped against the rubble, looking dazed and overwhelmed. "You all right?" Williams asked. "It's just my second day here," came his pained reply. "I wish I could say that it gets better," Williams thought to himself. To the soldier, he could only offer a few lame words of encouragement and a bottle of water. As the trio departed the site, Hodges looked back one more time at the place where they had fought to save lives. What caught her eye was the grass, so saturated with blood that it pooled on the thirsty ground.

The walk to the Humvees and ride back to Tombstone took only fifteen minutes. They finished their shift at the police station, and when they were duly relieved, they headed back to Viper Base. As exhausted as they were, sleep was hard to come by that night. Williams found himself wide awake at 2:00 A.M., reliving the events of the day. His brain simply refused to shut down. For the trio that went into the UN compound, August 19 was their worst day in Baghdad—indeed, the worst day of their young lives. Hodges was thankful that most of 1st Squad did not have to see what she had seen that day.[8]

The Sanchez Letter

Most in the 233rd ranked September 8 as one of their worst days in Baghdad. That was the day a letter arrived at the company tactical operations center (TOC) signed by the commander of the American forces in Iraq, Lieutenant General Ricardo Sanchez. The letter, written in a precise military style, stated, "Reserve Component units will remain in theater for one year unless the command determines that the unit's capability is no longer needed. Mobilization orders for these units will be extended to reflect one year boots on the ground." Sanchez followed this with a vain attempt to assuage the anger he knew the message would generate:

> I realize that many of our Reserve Component soldiers are anxious to return to their families and jobs. I understand the impact this decision has on our great volunteer citizen-soldiers. However, the Army, our nation and the coalition still need the critical skills these units provide as we continue to fight. This undertaking is difficult and dangerous, yet worthy of our country and critical to the security not only of Iraq but the entire world.[9]

Most in the company agreed with Sanchez's sentiments, but the words carried little weight to soldiers who had already sacrificed so much and were impatient to get on with their lives back home. The day before, they were hoping to return home by the end of the year. When they read Sanchez's letter, they knew they were stuck in Baghdad until April, maybe even later. For many in the company, September 8 was the day their morale hit rock bottom.

Before the 8th, speculation on when they'd be going home was everyone's favorite topic of discussion and the source of endless speculation. When the unit was first mobilized, many MPs assumed they would be gone for six months, the same as during Desert Storm. That put their return date somewhere in August 2003. By the time they reached Baghdad in April and discovered a city in chaos, they realized an August date was far too optimistic.

As the weeks and months passed, the unit's return date kept moving further and further out. Most soldiers clung to the hope that the Army would honor the terms of the unit's activation order—that they would remain on active duty for no more than one year. That meant they'd be heading back home in January so they could be released by February 6, their 365th day. Others were enticed by more optimistic rumors, especially ones that sent them home before Christmas. Those who subscribed to this theory were reassured when a couple of units rotated back home in the summer.

In late summer, Lieutenant Colonel Glaser gave Royer a bit of welcome news. They'd be heading home by December 7, Glaser said, patting Royer on the back. "Jeff, things change, but remember this," he said with a wink. "We're being told right now that the 10-month mark is when you're leaving." That meant they'd be home for Christmas! It was a wonderful thought, and more than a few of the MPs and their loved ones in Illinois circled December 7 on their calendars.

The optimistic mood held until the day the Sanchez letter arrived. Now, they discovered, their 365 days did not start with the day they mobilized, but rather, with the first day they were "boots on the ground" in Kuwait. That pushed their projected departure date all the way out to April 6, 2004. The news crushed their hopes, and the mood in the 233rd was ugly for the next several days. Sanchez became the most unpopular person in Baghdad, and his memo soon met a variety of fates. It was burned, used as a dartboard, and even tossed down the Harris. Gradually, the soldiers came out of their funk. As Top put it, "You can't be miserable all the time."

Even before the Sanchez letter, the Hogs had maintained a "days" calendar in their hallway, with someone crossing off each day as it passed. Afterward, days calendars proliferated. There was something very satisfying about crossing out each day that passed. Master Sergeant Woods did the honors for the TOC where Higginson and Sergeant Jim Kollins started an End of Tour pool, their way to make light of a lousy situation. It cost $10 to purchase a stake in the pool. Those who were optimistic picked dates in December; the unit's pessimists laid their money on late April or May.[10]

The Sanchez letter elicited a similar reception back in the states. Wives, sweethearts, and parents experienced anger, disgust, and disillusionment upon hearing the news. Most felt powerless; a few fired off angry letters and phone calls to their congressmen and to the governor. Pamela Weber remembers the day well. She was balancing the books at her father's seed grain business in Jerseyville when she decided to check her e-mail account. She was always excited to find messages from Kevin in her mailbox, and so she naturally opened his message first. It was very brief that day, and got right to the point. He'd be in Baghdad until April, he wrote matter-of-factly. Up to that point, Pamela had held up well each time Kevin called or wrote with news that his return date had been moved back. But after hearing of Colonel Glaser's optimistic prediction, she had allowed herself to dream about Kevin making it home by the end of the year, maybe even by Christmas. That would be great for the kids, three-year-old Alexandra and baby Ethan. Now that dream was crushed, and the news of Sanchez's edict hit her on a bad day. "I took off my glasses," she later recalled, "put my head down on my desk, and just started bawling." It was then that Pamela's father walked into the office and spotted his daughter. He desperately wanted to know why she was crying, but he was equally afraid to ask. When he did muster up the courage, all Pamela could say between her sobs was, "I just found out that he's going to be there till April."[11]

Raid on the Chop Shop

For Sergeant First Class John Gillette, the raid the battalion was planning against a Baghdad "chop shop" was nothing special. The shop was one of scores in Baghdad that dismantled carjacked vehicles for sale as individual parts, one of Baghdad's most prevalent crimes. Raids broke up the routine of the daily patrols and endless reports, but Gillette would have preferred tracking down insurgents rather than wasting their police skills on raiding a chop shop. In his mind, insurgents should have been the unit's priority, not petty crime. But he didn't get to pick their missions. His job was to execute the orders written by some staffer far above his pay scale.

Captain Royer selected the 3rd Platoon "Hogs" to be the assault force for the raid, a mission that involved elements from every platoon in the company, because the intelligence that led to the raid originated in the Hogs' police station. An Iraqi citizen reported that he observed something resembling a missile being unloaded at the shop. No one was surprised when Sergeant Gillette got the nod to lead the assault force. He was one of the unit's main go-to guys, and for the best of reasons. He was technically competent, professional, and cool under pressure. He was the guy you wanted with you when things got tough.

The chop shop was located in the upscale al-Muthana neighborhood of eastern Baghdad, not far from the city's Olympic stadium and the technical university. It was larger than most of the city's chop shops. This one had three bays and abutted a two-story house. The shop was also unusual because it sported a parking area in front, with the shop separated from the street by a small gatehouse and metal fence. Across the street from the shop was a three-story building that the Hogs now used as their staging area.

The plan called for Sergeant Gillette's assault force to rush the chop shop, and once inside, to detain all of the occupants for questioning, then thoroughly search the premises for evidence. Although each platoon still had its usual slate of missions for the day, all were expected to contribute forces to the operation. Captain Royer, working with a detachment from the unit's operations section, was in overall command. A crew from 1st Platoon served as a quick reaction force in the event of trouble, and the 4th Platoon drew the job of sealing off the rear of the shop. The 2nd Platoon was assigned the important job of establishing a series of roadblocks on all streets leading into the neighborhood. It also provided a team of snipers who were stationed on the roof of the building across the street from the shop. The operation even included an OH-58 observation helicopter flying over the neighborhood, ready to alert Captain Royer in the event of an attack from the outside, or to track any suspects attempting to flee the area. And as always, the plan incorporated Iraqis. IPs would reinforce the 2nd Platoon in their cordon operations, and others were incorporated into the assault force, which also included interpreters. Finally, agents from the Iraqi special crimes unit would be on hand to help.

The raiding party rallied at the New Baghdad police station on the morning of September 18, a typically stifling and cloudless day for Baghdad. Twenty-four hours before, four trusted IPs had been briefed on the operation and sworn to secrecy. Anyone more, and the chop shop owners would certainly have been tipped off. No one was surprised when the IPs involved in the operation arrived at the police station a few minutes late that day—that was par for the course. But Captain Royer grew agitated when they reached their departure time and the special crimes personnel had still not arrived.

Royer was still waiting at H-hour, when the Punishers cordoned off the streets right on schedule. Simultaneously, the snipers set up their overwatch position, and Sergeant Gillette's assault force positioned itself inside the building directly across from the gatehouse. Overhead, the OH-58 flew wide circles over the neighborhood. But Royer had strict instructions to wait for the special crimes personnel, so they waited. And because they waited, they lost the element of surprise. Employees of the chop shop watched much of the action unfold before them. At first, they assumed the target for the operation was the building across the street, the same one where Gillette's team now huddled. Meanwhile, the roadblocks were drawing a crowd of curious bystanders. The entire neighborhood was now on edge with antici-pation. Still the MPs waited, growing more furious as each minute slipped by. Gillette's assault crew could do nothing but wait in the shadows in full "battle rattle" and sweat it out. Each minute felt like an eternity. With the element of surprise gone, Royer considered scrubbing the whole operation. He was ready to do so when the special crimes unit showed up, forty-five minutes late. They were finally ready to trigger the raid.

The operation began when the assault force, in a stack-on-line formation, made a full-out run across the street, weapons at the ready. They rushed past the metal gate and burst into the parking area, where they encountered a couple of startled Iraqis. Two assault team members peeled off to guard them while the rest of the team moved toward the bay area itself. None of the building's occupants offered resistance, and they were soon rounded up as other members of the team began a thorough search of the building and grounds. They didn't find much. There were a couple of AK-47 assault rifles plus some automobiles in various stages of disassembly and a couple of car parts believed to be from IP vehicles. The MPs also found a 1950s-vintage unmanned Russian surveillance aircraft—obviously the item their informant had told them about, the item that justified the raid in the first place. But there was no camera mounted in the plane's fuselage and no way it could carry a warhead, and it was in a serious state of disrepair. It was essentially a nonfunctional antique. Other than the discovery of 2 million di-nars and some documents that eventually justified other raids, the operation was pretty much a bust. As for the occupants of the chop shop, most were questioned on the spot and then released. Two of the occupants, the chief target of the raid and another Iraqi, both named Mohammad, were taken into custody and transported back to the police station for interrogation.[12]

Conducting interrogations was nothing new for the Hogs. They supple-mented their experiences as civilian police with plenty of official guidance received since arriving in Baghdad. Their guidance included warnings to "treat all coalition forces with personal dignity and in accordance with inter-national humanitarian law." The policy went on to state that "commanders are responsible for continuously training their units in the soldier's code of conduct and its strict enforcement." The soldiers of the 233rd were no strangers to the provisions of Geneva-Hague as they pertained to the treatment of prisoners. The subject was briefed annually and reinforced during their mobilization training. They were thoroughly trained in the appropriate interrogation techniques, both for enemy prisoners of war and in the performance of a police investigation. (Technically, terrorists and insurgents were not subject to the provisions of Geneva-Hague, but troops were generally instructed to adhere to its provisions regardless.) Segregating prisoners before interrogation was routine. So were prolonged interrogations designed to disorient or confuse a suspect, to play on his emotions, and to use his pride or fear against him. Essentially, it was just a matter of wearing them down without resorting to physical violence. It was acceptable to lie to the subject and threaten to beat them. Just the threat of violence often achieved results.

The MPs often got the information they sought, even while strictly following the rules. And by September, they had picked up a couple of new tricks that often worked to their advantage. Because the prisoners neither trusted nor respected the IPs, the MPs made it a point to exclude IPs from the room during questioning. If the suspect proved especially uncooperative, the interrogator often feigned disgust and began to walk away while suggesting the IPs would now take over. That threat tended to loosen tongues pretty quickly, especially because the IPs' reputation for brutality was so well deserved. Ironically, the MPs now worked hard to convince their IP counterparts to abandon the old techniques, even as they found that the mere threat of an IP interrogation worked wonders. More than a few of the IPs found the Americans' logic on this issue incomprehensible.[13]

The raid on the chop shop turned up very little, but there was still one act left to play out in the drama. That occurred two days later, when Sergeant Gillette and Staff Sergeant Jim Batterson were at an east Baghdad checkpoint talking to several gregarious Iraqis. Suddenly, a 1980s-vintage Lincoln town car, brown in color, pulled to an abrupt stop across the street from the pair, halting just long enough for a passenger to lean out and spray the area with a burst from an AK-47. Gillette and Batterson lunged for cover, then immediately returned fire as the car raced away from the scene. They jumped into their Humvee and gave chase as best as they could, aided along the way by several excited Iraqis who gladly pointed toward the direction the town car now headed. Their chase petered out when they discovered some skid marks on the pavement, but no town car in sight.

The car, as it turned out, belonged to the cousin of the chop shop owner. For the rest of their time in Baghdad, Gillette and Batterson kept an eye out for that brown Lincoln town car, the only one amidst a sea of Passats and Nissans. They never spotted it again.[14]

8
Midtour Leaves

By late September, almost everyone in the 233rd hoped for a chance to take leave, especially after rumors about a midtour leave program began circulating. For Ed Higginson, the possibility of taking leave took on a greater urgency. He had just received a message from the Red Cross that Lisa was facing surgery to repair a heart murmur, something the doctors called toximal atrial tachycardia, a condition that often occurred in young women, especially those dealing with stress. Lisa tried to keep it from Ed, but when she discovered Ed's mother had included the news in a letter, she immediately e-mailed Ed. She told him about her condition matter-of-factly, mentioning that she was scheduled for an operation on October 2. The operation called for threading an arthroscopy probe through a vein up one leg all the way into a chamber of the heart, and a surgical laser through the vein in the other leg. Once there, surgeons could cauterize the damaged portions of the heart. The doctors told Lisa it was a routine operation, but it sounded pretty serious to Ed, who felt powerless so far from Illinois. Armed with Lisa's e-mail and a letter from the Red Cross confirming the condition, Higginson approached Staff Sergeant Wilson, hoping for some consideration. Neither of them was optimistic. Ed had seen plenty of people in the battalion turned down for leave, even in the case of a pending birth or to go home for a family emergency. Besides, Lisa was only a fiancée, not his wife. The Army did not recognize her as family.[1]

Ed got lucky however, because Lisa's news roughly corresponded with the announcement of an official leave policy for the entire force, something the military in typically equivocal fashion designated "environmental leaves," as in a change of environment for those sent stateside. The program was announced on September 23, just two weeks after the infamous Sanchez letter, and was set to start immediately. The program's design was pretty basic. Commanders were directed to develop an order of merit list (OML) to prioritize those in their units most deserving of leave. Those selected for leave would receive fifteen days at home, with the clock starting one day after they arrived stateside, and ending one day before departing the States. The Army's largesse only went so far, however: soldiers were expected to pay for their flight from Germany to their final destination. Within a week, Senate Bill 1670 fixed that problem. A grateful nation would cover their full travel expenses.[2]

Captain Royer wasted no time in directing the troops to submit a request for leave based on their particular needs and circumstances, then told First Sergeant Elmore to develop the OML. Top went to work immediately, soliciting input from the platoon leaders who, together with their platoon sergeants, developed their own OML. On the basis of the leave matrix generated by the battalion, only a limited number of slots were allocated to each time period, and not everyone would be able to get a leave. Invariably, the lieutenants and senior noncommissioned officers (NCOs) put themselves at the bottom of the list. They already knew which of their soldiers faced hardships at home. Beyond that, married soldiers and those with young children were placed on the top of the list. Lieutenants Ferris and Flack kept their names off the list altogether, as did several senior NCOs. Even before he deployed, Flack told his wife he wouldn't see her until the entire tour was over. He wasn't the only one.[3]

The MPs did have other options for a break from duty. One was the Fighter Management Pass Program, an unnecessarily complex name for a four-day pass to a U.S. Air Force base in Qatar. The base boasted a swimming pool, a movie theater, a fully equipped gymnasium, shops, and a well-stocked post exchange. There were also excursions available to a sprawling mall or to a local beach for a day of swimming and jet skiing. Best of all, those who took advantage of the program spent four luxurious days away from the constant roar of generators, lounging in air-conditioned quarters with easy access to telephones and the Internet. Finally, there was the Freedom Rest Hotel in the Green Zone itself, offering a short respite from the rigors of life on patrol.[4]

Sergeant Higginson ended up topping the 233rd's OML, and a few names down was Paul Hildebrandt, who on September 1 became a new father with the birth of his daughter, Julia. Higginson felt especially blessed to be sent home first. Because he wasn't married, Captain Royer would have been justified in placing him farther down the list. But Royer didn't hesitate to pencil in his name at the top of the OML, confident that no one would begrudge Higginson the chance to be with Lisa when she underwent heart surgery. Higginson repaid the favor by writing an e-mail to Top as soon as he got home, offering up pointers to all those who would follow.[5]

Higginson found out his leave was approved on September 24. He spent the rest of the day packing and writing a coy e-mail to Lisa. "What are you doing on Saturday?" it read. "Are you free about 5:00?" Lisa interpreted Ed's message just as he intended, as an instant message rendezvous. Later that day, he rethought his plan to surprise her. "If I just show up and the apartment is a mess she'll kick my ass," he thought to himself. Ed placed a call that night while pulling his normal midnight shift in the tactical operations center (TOC). He was flying out the next day, he told her, and would be with her for the operation.

Immediately after his shift, Ed grabbed a quick shower, donned a clean uniform, and headed to the battalion, where the chaplain gave a briefing to the lucky few heading home. They flew into Kuwait late that afternoon. Once there, Higginson waited eight hours before he finally got his chance to talk to the government-contracted travel agent and arrange for a flight home. Exhausted and filthy, the group of GIs, all dressed in their gritty desert camouflage uniforms (DCUs), finally boarded a commercial flight to Germany en route to Bangor, Maine. It was there that they went through customs before boarding a commercial flight to Baltimore, where they would scatter to the four corners of the country.

By the time Ed reached Baltimore-Washington International Airport, he was famished. He felt the Kuwaiti sand grate against his feet as he strode down the airport's long corridors, and worried about raising a cloud of dust wherever he walked. After grabbing a quick bite to eat, he spotted a phone bank and got in line to call home. Within moments, an airline employee was offering up her cell phone, thanking him for his service and explaining that the airline had authorized soldiers to use their phones. Wherever he went, people were gracious and supportive. Thankfully, for the most part, they respected his privacy. Ed made sure to avoid the reporters that were looking for soldiers to interview at the USO club, relishing a few moments of peace before boarding a flight home.

As Ed boarded his flight to St. Louis, he looked forward to catching some sleep. He quickly settled into his seat and had just closed his eyes when an airline attendant woke him up with the news that he had to move. He didn't appreciate the interruption but was too tired to argue, and he followed her without complaint. They walked to the front of the plane, where she gestured toward a vacant seat in first class. Two other GIs, also dressed in DCUs, were already there.

Lisa, five-year-old Amber, and Ed's parents met him at Lambert International Airport in St. Louis. During the two-hour drive back to Springfield, Ed soaked in the lush, green prairie landscape, brightly lit by a beautiful September sun. He marveled at the incredible bounty of rural Illinois, with its ripened fields of corn extending as far as he could see. He was home! It hardly seemed real.

Ed and Lisa packed a lot into his two weeks at home. Back in Baghdad, the chaplain had told the group to decide what they wanted to do when they got home—what was a priority for them. "I wanted to enjoy eating again," Ed decided, so Ed, Lisa, and Amber went out to eat for almost every meal. When Monday morning came, he got up early and took Amber to school, just as if he had never left home. "I fit like a round peg," he thought to himself.

Lisa went in for her operation on October 2, six days into Ed's leave. She was scared, but having Ed home for the operation made all the difference. For the next two days, Ed played nursemaid, and by Sunday, October 5, Lisa was on her feet again. That same day, Ed gave her a lesson in Army protocol, explaining that had it not been for the timely advent of the environmental leave program, he would never have been sent home—that fiancées did not rate an emergency leave. That piece of news didn't sit well with Lisa, and it helped precipitate an important decision for both. They would get married immediately, and not wait until Ed returned home for good. The next day they finalized their marriage plans, such as they were, and by Tuesday they were at the Sangamon County courthouse to get the license. Two days later, they were married in a simple courthouse ceremony with both sets of parents present. Steve Bridges, Ed's best friend and a former 233rd member himself, served as his best man.

Ed headed back to Iraq a few days later. Lisa made a half-hearted attempt to talk him into staying, even though she knew he had to go. "Canada is not an option—they extradite," Ed joked, and with that, the two parted, after being inseparable for two weeks.[6]

A Newborn

Sergeant Paul Hildebrandt was the next to come home. He was eager to see Julia, who had been born, ironically, on Monday, September 1—Labor Day. Wife Monica had become something of a celebrity while Paul was in Iraq. A reporter from the Springfield *State Journal-Register* had been on hand for the unit's send-off to Fort McCoy and discovered Monica among the throng of relatives and well-wishers. She was not only a good interview subject, providing him with some quotable quotes, but was also a couple months pregnant at the time. It was just the kind of human-interest story worth following up.

Monica made the front page of the *State Journal-Register* on July 12, with her picture appearing above an article entitled "Families still wait." She was seated at her kitchen table, appearing very pregnant as she cradled her stomach and gazed lovingly at one-year-old Caleb. "I instantly became the local sob story by virtue of the Springfield *State Journal-Register*," she later recalled. She could have lived without the notoriety, however. Paul was a Moultrie County deputy sheriff in his civilian life. Now the entire community knew that Paul was overseas and that she lived alone in rural Bethany, Illinois. Seven months into the pregnancy, she could have done without the publicity and the accompanying stress.[7]

Paul originally hailed from tiny Illiopolis, just east of Springfield, and joined the National Guard while still in high school. Because he wanted to be a police officer, it made sense to join the 233rd. It didn't hurt that his uncle Jerry Calbow also happened to be the first sergeant. Several years later, he made his way to Western Illinois University to take advantage of the Illinois National Guard's generous tuition benefits. The school boasted one of the largest ROTC departments in the region, but Paul, already a sergeant in the National Guard, knew that being an officer was not for him. He skipped the program, preferring to mock the ROTC cadets rather than become one himself.

Paul met Monica at Western. She hailed from suburban Elgin, Illinois, and was also drawn to the university because of its excellent law enforcement program. The two became engaged three months later and were married the next year. Both dropped out of college, and when Paul landed a job with the Moultrie County sheriff's department, they moved to Bethany, a town of only 1,300 some twenty miles south of Decatur. It was a far cry from the Chicago suburbs, but less than an hour's drive from Paul's parents in Illiopolis.

By the end of August, Monica was on a leave of absence from her job as an Effingham County paramedic. By this time, a growing list of friends and relatives were impatiently awaiting the birth. Paul called every morning, Illinois time, to get the latest progress report, using the unit's cell phone provided by Captain Royer. Because the baby was due at the end of August, Monica's sister Rachel came down from Elgin to spend the Labor Day weekend with her, telling Monica, only half in jest, to please have her baby before she left on Monday. The plan called for Monica's mother, who had taken two days off from her job as a school administrator, to then replace Rachel. On Labor Day morning, Monica received her customary call from

Paul. There was nothing to report, she told him in matter-of-fact tones. Apparently this baby had its own schedule.

An hour later, Monica's water broke, and fifteen minutes after that, Monica's mother arrived, feeling a bit like the proverbial cavalry riding to the rescue. The three women quickly devised a plan. Mom stayed with Caleb, who was napping at the time, and Rachel drove Monica to the hospital in Decatur. During the drive, Monica convinced her sister that she had plenty of time—enough, in fact, to grab a salad from a local fast food restaurant. Meanwhile, she called Paul's mom, who then called Uncle Jerry so he could e-mail First Sergeant Elmore in Baghdad. Rachel and Monica arrived at St. Mary's Hospital with time to spare. At 11:49 P.M. on September 1, Labor Day, Julia Hildebrandt made her way into the world. She weighed 8 pounds, 15 ounces and measured 21 inches long.

Paul called Monica the next day at the usual time, both excited and apprehensive after Top gave him the news that Monica was in labor. "Well, congratulations, Dad," Paul heard Monica begin, then the line went silent. Things got frantic in Baghdad as Paul struggled to get another call through. Finally, after a few minutes of frustration—minutes that felt more like hours—he headed over to battalion, where Colonel Glaser allowed him to use the unit's satellite phone to place another call. As far as Glaser was concerned, Sergeant Hildebrandt's predicament definitely constituted an emergency.

Sargeant Hildebrandt's Leave

Paul flew home exactly one month after Julia was born. Monica could barely contain her excitement as she waited for him at Springfield's Capital Airport. With her were Caleb, Julia, and Paul's parents. Paul had called earlier that day. "I want to wake up next to you," he told her, "give you a kiss, go make bacon and eggs, and watch Caleb play." She could think of nothing better; the simple pleasures were the sweetest.

Abbey Brown, a reporter from the *State Journal-Register,* was also there with the Hildebrandts, ready to capture the emotional reunion. Paul's flight from O'Hare Airport was due to arrive at 5:45 P.M. Then came the word that the flight was canceled, that he wouldn't arrive in Springfield for another three hours. So Monica, along with Mike and Micki Hildebrandt, restarted their countdown, watching the minutes crawl by. Finally, she found the courage to announce, "Four minutes until he's supposed to land," then had her hopes dashed moments later when Micki returned from the ticket counter, fighting back tears. The flight was delayed again, she reported, and wouldn't arrive until 11 P.M. Deanna Victor arrived a few minutes later with a pillow and blanket for Caleb, hot coffee for the adults, and some words of encouragement. "I've been waiting eight months," Monica told the others. "I can wait another hour and a half." Thankfully, Paul finally arrived late that night.[8]

It was well past midnight when Paul and Monica pulled into the newly paved driveway. Paul was struck by how natural it felt to finally be home. "You're building up all these thoughts about coming home and how great it's going to be," he reflected later. "But when I got out of the car, it was just a normal feeling"—but a very good feeling.

The next morning, Paul woke up, kissed Monica, and headed to the kitchen to whip up a batch of bacon and eggs. Monica and Caleb soon joined him at the breakfast table, and he proudly soaked up the scene. "Oh my God," he said while watching Caleb. "I've never seen him eat with a fork before." Paul's two weeks at home flew by. There were a lot of things he wanted to do and plenty of people to see. There were more demands on his time than he could possibly accommodate. He spent a lot of time visiting with friends and relatives, and managed to knock out a couple of odd jobs around the house, but best of all were the times he spent just relaxing with Monica and the kids.

When the day came to head back to Iraq, Paul and Monica went alone to the Decatur Airport. Monica's dream of spending their last few minutes together cuddling in the waiting room was soon dashed, however. Paul was the victim of the random search that was now required because of the war on terror. The Transportation Safety Authority worker matter-of-factly instructed Paul to unpack his bag for a thorough inspection. Monica resented that it was Paul, of all of the passengers going through security, who got the run-around that day. Paul unceremoniously dumped the contents of his duffel bag onto the floor, then spent thirty precious minutes repacking. So much for her romantic interlude, thought Monica resentfully. She did find time to urge Paul to keep writing, despite the fact that e-mailing and instant messaging were so much more immediate. "I want to hold something you recently held," she told him. "I still wanted something in . . . the mail . . . where you feel the envelope and there was dust all lining it [and the] paper was gritty when I pulled it out. That's what I wanted."

After Paul boarded the plane, Monica stayed in the lobby, gazing out the window until the plane bearing her husband disappeared over the horizon. When she walked outside, she saw her mother standing by the car waiting for her. She had taken two days off from work to be with Monica and was waiting in the parking lot rather than intrude on Paul and Monica's last few moments together. Now she was there for Monica, who let down her guard and cried.[9]

A Break from Action

Sergeants Higginson and Hildebrandt were the first of many to travel home over the next several months. A steady procession of 233rd soldiers headed home even while others in the unit took advantage of R&R in Qatar. Most who returned to the States were pleasantly surprised by the outpouring of enthusiastic support they experienced as they passed through the nation's airports. Everywhere they went, people went out of their way to thank them, to offer their seats on outgoing flights, or to insist on buying them drinks, which they invariably declined because Army regulations prohibited them from drinking in uniform. There were even occasional cheers from the crowds as they passed through a terminal. In general, the MPs would have preferred some anonymity. They appreciated the accolades but couldn't help but feel embarrassed by all of the attention. Paul Hildebrandt's experience while standing in line at an O'Hare Airport McDonalds, hungrily anticipating a Big Mac, was typical. Like all of the returning MPs, it was impossible to go unnoticed, dressed as he was in DCUs. Soon, a curious traveler strode up. "Hey, are you one of those guys from Iraq who just got leave?" "Yes," came the subdued reply. "Well, what are you doing here?" the man loudly exclaimed. "I'm just waiting for a Big Mac." With that, the traveler turned to a McDonalds employee and asked in a booming voice, "Hey, where's this guy's Big Mac?" Paul was mortified at the time, but he later found humor in the man's exuberance.[10]

Most would have preferred to just quietly pass through the airport unnoticed, but that rarely happened. A grateful nation wanted to show its support, and to a certain extent, atone for the horrendous treatment sometimes leveled against Vietnam veterans a generation before. During that war, the soldiers too often became a scapegoat for those in America who protested the nation's involvement in the war. For the conflict in Iraq, even those who strongly opposed the war were careful to make the distinction that they supported the troops. Overall, the MPs who came home on leave were treated like conquering heroes in scenes reminiscent of those seen by their grandfathers after World War II.

Homecomings

Staff Sergeant Jim Nayonis's homecoming was especially memorable. One of the toughest parts about duty in Baghdad was not getting to see his two children, twelve-year-old Thomas and nine-year-old Chloe. He missed watching them at baseball games, dance classes, swimming back in Tuscola, Illinois, and knew that those opportunities were lost forever. When he discovered he was coming home, he arranged with wife Tracey to surprise Tom and Chloe. Both kids were spending the night with friends when he arrived home. Tom was just across the street, so Tracey called the neighbor with a message for Tom to come home and get his contact lenses. Tom walked into the living room where his smiling dad was waiting for him. The next morning, Jim drove over to the house where Chloe was staying. "I just walked in and said, 'Hey, where's my daughter?'" All Chloe could muster in reply was an excited "Dad!" Seconds later, she was in her father's arms, and she "wouldn't let go . . . for about an hour."

Staff Sergeant Jay Fritzsche arrived at Lambert International Airport in St. Louis on January 31, his wedding anniversary. He and wife Amy engineered a similar surprise, this one for Jay's entire extended family, who were gathered at his grandfather's house in Ramsey, a town of 1,050 located in rural Fayette County, to celebrate Grandpa's ninetieth birthday. Jay and Amy left the airport and headed straight to the family reunion, Jay still in his DCUs. When they pulled up outside the house, Amy went inside, tracked down one of Jay's uncles, and asked him to get everyone's attention because she had a surprise. Moments later, Jay walked in, and the house erupted with screams, cheers, and clapping.[11]

Once the MPs got home, most quickly reverted back to the familiar and comfortable routines of their lives. Even so, some found it difficult to readjust to life at home. Staff Sergeant Lawrence Wilson, who worked the TOC night shift back in Baghdad, struggled to tone down his heightened senses. He was surprised at how clean everything was—no piles of rotting garbage cluttering the streets, no stench permeating everything. He marveled at how civilly everyone treated each other, how the traffic actually obeyed the street signs and traffic lights, how life was able to effortlessly flow around him. Wilson had difficulty falling asleep at night. He was unsettled by the eerie silence, almost missing the roar of the generator that lulled him to sleep in Baghdad. Instead, he substituted a good night's sleep with catnaps during the day. He was surprised at how uncomfortable he felt because of the sudden lack of structure in his life, the absence of a clearly defined chain of command and the imperatives the daily mission imposed on his life. Wilson's fiancée, Tammy Hughes, found his difficulties to adjust disconcerting.[12]

Sergeant Wilson was not the only MP who found it difficult to readjust to life in the states after so many months at a heightened state of alertness. All of the MPs struggled to adapt to life back home. Joel Mauney described it as feeling like a fish out of water. Once, when pulling his car out of the driveway with wife Sarah sitting by his side, he unconsciously patted the side of his leg and then immediately pulled the car back into the driveway. He was halfway out the car door when Sarah, bewildered, asked, "Where are you going?" "I need my weapon," he replied. "Joel, you're in Springfield," Sarah responded. "You don't need your weapon."

The MPs were troubled by another discovery upon returning home: as far as they were concerned, the American media was seriously distorting the situation in Iraq. Yes, things were tough in Baghdad and violent incidents were far too common, but the MPs were amazed and perturbed by how much the media focused only on the bad while excluding most of the good that was happening in Iraq. In fact, they hardly recognized the Baghdad they saw in the nightly reports. They understood why the media was presenting the war this way: bad news sells, and otherwise mundane things in life, like reopened schools, humanitarian efforts, and improving security, did not. But they resented the distortions nonetheless. Captain Royer summed it up succinctly: "The American media didn't have a clue about what was going on in Iraq except when something blew up."[13]

Returning to War

When the inevitable day arrived for the MPs to return to Iraq, soldiers and families once again experienced an emotional roller coaster. A handful found this departure even harder than the first; most did not. The uncertainty that clouded their initial departure was largely gone. This time, the MPs knew what to expect, and everyone knew when he would be returning home for good. And now something else pulled them back to Iraq. Try as they might, many felt a nagging sense of guilt knowing that while they were relaxing in the States, their buddies were putting their lives on the line in Iraq. "It didn't hurt as much as the first time," explained Sergeant Mauney, "I think because I was leaving one family to get back to another family." He was anxious to get back to his squad, to make sure they were all right, to start pulling his load once again.[14]

9
Hearts and Minds

If Americans believed the news coming out of Iraq in late 2003, they would soon conclude that the nation was spinning out of control. Suicide bombings and roadside bombs were on the increase, and Iraq's many factions were arming themselves for the sectarian struggles to come. Sunnis and Shi'ites alike decried the presence of the American military. It was just a matter of time, the talking heads suggested, before the nation slid into a full-fledged civil war, destroyed by its own internal contradictions unleashed by an un-witting American administration and an inept occupation force. The MPs were inclined to disagree. They would not deny the nation was riddled with problems, not the least of which were ethnic tensions and rampant corruption. They wondered whether there were enough Iraqis who were committed to stand up to the insurgents and build a new and democratic society. Still, they were guardedly optimistic about Iraq's future, largely because they knew there were a lot of good things happening in Baghdad—that not all was violence and dissent. There was much the American media left out of the story.

By late summer, security was slowly improving. Additionally, electricity and other basic services were starting to come online, although at a frustrat-ingly slow pace. The nation's hospitals had suffered terribly from looting, but most recovered quickly and served the Iraqi people once again. The nation's Shi'ites were returning to their most sacred shrines after years of brutal repression. The streets of Baghdad were flooded with traffic because the Iraqis' pent-up demand for cars could finally be satisfied. Even more im-portant, Iraqi citizens finally gained access to the outside world. Cell phones and satellite dishes, both banned under Saddam, were ubiquitous. Scores of independent newspapers emerged to replace the propaganda the Ba'athists formerly published. And July 22, the day Uday and Quasai were killed, was unquestionably a good day. There was no widespread epidemic, nor was there a devastating food crisis as prewar naysayers had predicted, and finally, the long-feared civil war, clearly the goal of many of Iraq's insurgents, had not happened. The Coalition Provisional Authority (CPA) trumpeted all of these as successes even while a growing list of critics, including the international media, pointed to a long list of failures.

A lot of the good things happening in Baghdad had little to do with official CPA planning or directives. As often as not, they resulted from the initiative and compassion of individual American soldiers. The soldiers of the 233rd epitomized that spirit. The MPs extended a hand of friendship almost from the first moment they entered the city. Each act of kindness, every piece of candy and every soccer ball they handed out helped contradict decades of propaganda spewed by Saddam's Ba'athists. But the MPs harbored no illusions. They knew it would take years to change attitudes that had been decades in the making. Most also understood that any act of cruelty or an unintended insult could undo the good they were trying to achieve. There were also things about the way the MPs conducted business that undoubtedly angered the average Iraqi: their excessive speed when driving through the streets, the occasional fender-benders that resulted, a perceived insult, however unintended, and their quintessentially American pride and confidence, traits that were often interpreted as signs of arrogance and disrespect. Try as they might, the MPs were guilty of all of these. However well intentioned, they were uninvited foreigners in an alien world. As far as Iraqi Muslims were concerned, they were interlopers and infidels, albeit more benign than Saddam's Ba'athists. Most Iraqis waited impatiently for the Americans to deliver on what they promised, reserving judgment for the time being, staying noncommittal.

The MPs understood they were ambassadors for America. What made that job so challenging, however, was their inability to differentiate the insurgents, a tiny minority of the public, from the thousands of Iraqis they saw every day. As far as Captain Royer was concerned, the only prudent thing to do was to assume an Iraqi was an enemy until proven otherwise. His priority was getting everyone home alive.[1]

The Schools

When the American Army fought its way into Baghdad in April 2003, the city's schools closed down. Some reopened briefly in mid-May but soon closed again for the annual summer break. It was just as well, for the nation's educators had much to do to in the wake of the overthrow of Ba'athist rule. The day Saddam's statues fell, almost every textbook, peppered as they were with images of Saddam, became obsolete. The most immediate challenge Baghdad's educators now faced, however, was rebuilding the schools, which had been destroyed in the looting.[2]

Adopting al-Sa'ad

Staff Sergeant Roman Waldron, the 3rd Squad Leader for the 1st Platoon "Reapers," was one of the 233rd's more colorful characters. Solidly built, with a quick smile and a square jaw, Waldron worked for the federal government before the war. In Baghdad, he was known for his pragmatic, hard-nosed approach to his duties, and also for his flair for creative vulgarity. Waldron's blunt talk was part of his persona, his way of expressing his convictions, a mask for his cynicism. More than anything, it disguised a compassionate heart.

Waldron was also known for his work with the al-Sa'ad school. He was leading a mobile patrol in eastern Baghdad on a typically oppressive late summer day when he spotted the school. "Let's check it out," he told his driver, directing him to a stop outside the school's gate. That spontaneous decision was the start of the Reapers' long relationship with the al-Sa'ad school. It was the kind of thing that was happening all over Baghdad—individual soldiers motivated by compassion and good sense to take it upon themselves to do something to help Iraqis get back on their feet.

The al-Sa'ad school was a total wreck. From the schoolyard's numerous foxholes and the discarded military gear strewn about, it was clear that the school had doubled as an Iraqi antiaircraft battery site during the war—a callous attempt by the Iraqi Army to stave off American air attacks. Looters destroyed whatever Saddam's soldiers left behind. Wires dangled from the ceiling, hinting at former lights or ceiling fans. The walls were pockmarked, streaked with grime, and sported holes where light switches and electrical boxes had once been. Broken desks, chairs, filing cabinets, and other furniture littered the compound, most of it beyond repair. Trash filled the school's courtyard, now overgrown with weeds. Scattered about were a few old textbooks. It was a depressing scene, made even more so when the MPs found human waste among the trash.

No one came to greet the MPs that first day, and it was obvious that the neighbors had done little to clean up the school since the looting in the spring. As the squad pulled away, Waldron resolved to get the school back in operation. It seemed like the least they could do for the kids—the same kids who flocked to them whenever they passed through the neighborhoods, the boys and girls who invariably greeted their patrols with a smile. Opening the schools was also a good way to counter the wave of kidnappings that now plagued Baghdad. Children were brazenly snatched right off the street, then ransomed back to desperate parents for a handsome profit. Kidnapping was one of Baghdad's new cottage industries. The MPs actively patrolled the streets to curb that kind of crime.

Waldron cornered Lieutenant Ferris that night and suggested that the platoon could adopt the school and do whatever it took to get it operational again. "This [will be] a good way for us to get involved with the community and show them that the soldiers aren't just here for . . . oppression," Waldron explained, "that we were here to try and help them . . . as well." It was an easy sell. It fit into the lieutenant's notion of security: help the community, and the community will help you.

A couple of days later, Waldron led a group of volunteers, including most of the Reapers not then on a mission, back to al-Sa'ad. They came armed with shovels, axes, brooms, and plenty of plastic garbage bags, and they were soon at work sweeping out classrooms, picking up broken glass, filling in foxholes, and chopping down brush. The textbooks they discovered, featuring pictures of Saddam, were discarded with the rest of the garbage.

The Reapers hadn't been at their task long before curious teachers and a school administrator started arriving, excited to see someone cleaning up the place. Soon they were gesturing to the MPs, indicating what needed to be done. As far as Waldron was concerned, their sudden interest was more than a little irritating. The school had languished for months, but now that the Americans had arrived, they were boldly offering suggestions. He wondered if the teachers' lack of initiative, the same trait that so irked him about the Iraqi police, was the result of some inborn trait, a part of their culture, or merely a survival skill learned over decades of harsh repression.[3]

As Waldron dug through the piles of rubble, he also made an unexpected discovery: three emaciated kittens hiding in a pile of trash. He soon found willing hands to scoop them up and carry them to a nearby classroom. The MPs poured water into a saucer and fed the ravenous kittens some mushed-up food from an MRE. By the end of the day, with the kittens' mother nowhere in sight, the inevitable occurred. The Reapers adopted three kittens, one calico, one brown, and one black. It was the beginning of the company's growing menagerie of pets.

Rebuilding al-Sa'ad

Over the next couple of months, the Reapers repeatedly returned to the school, while the other platoons followed the Reapers' lead and adopted schools in their own neighborhoods. With October 4 marking the official beginning of the school year, another imperative bore down on them. The al-Sa'ad school needed serious repairs before it could be used again, and the students needed school supplies. Waldron was delighted when the headmistress told him that al-Sa'ad was selected to be one of the first schools rebuilt. It was part of the coalition's effort throughout the city, with San Francisco–based Bechtel Corporation overseeing the rehabilitation of scores of schools. Bechtel relied, whenever possible, on local Iraqi contractors to do the work. It might take several weeks, the headmistress explained to Waldron, well past the official beginning of the school year on October 4. In the meantime, the students would attend a nearby middle school. As for school supplies, the Reapers decided to appeal to their friends and relatives back home to donate supplies and ship them through the mail. By the end of August, things were looking up for the al-Sa'ad school.[4]

Al-Sa'ad wasn't the only school that caught the Reapers' attention. They discovered the al-Yarmuk school in September when an Iraqi man frantically flagged down a passing patrol. Officials, the man explained in an agitated state, were distributing books displaying Saddam's pictures in preparation for the upcoming school year. Waldron promised the parent he would take care of the matter.

The patrol soon arrived at al-Yarmuk, a girls' middle school in a serious state of disrepair. Waldron wasted no time in telling the headmistress to get rid of the offending books. The CPA decreed that such books were propaganda, he explained, and were offensive to the parents in the community. But the headmistress protested, explaining that these were the only textbooks they had. Waldron was unsympathetic to the woman's plight. For him, it was personal. He had not come all the way to Iraq to allow Ba'athist propaganda in the schools. "If you continue to pass out the books, I'll have to arrest you," he replied bluntly, allowing his interpreter enough time to translate. He was bluffing, of course, and she said as much. "I'm serious," he shot back, retaining his stern expression. "Before you give out any more books, you'll remove all of his pictures." It was an inauspicious beginning to what eventually developed into a relationship of mutual friendship and respect.[5]

Lieutenant Ferris and Sergeant Waldron encountered similar difficulties when working with the Iraqi contractor selected to rehab the al-Sa'ad school. Officially, the task of supervising the project belonged to a young cavalry lieutenant who oversaw a multitude of such projects—far more than he could possibly handle. Sergeant Waldron once again stepped into the vacuum and acted as de facto supervisor.

Al-Sa'ad served roughly 550 grade school girls and the same number of boys every day, six days a week. The girls attended school in the morning and the boys in the afternoon on one day, and then they switched for the next. That meant over 1,100 students flowed through the school every day. Waldron made it a point to watch the contractor closely, and he soon noticed that the man was willing to settle for grossly inadequate standards. A dispute over the school's only bathroom was typical. The bathroom was primitive to start with, featuring only five stalls plus a trough for the boys, all fed by water supplied from a 250-gallon tank located on the school's roof. The tank, in turn, was filled by a pump that no longer existed; it had fallen victim to the looters. As far as the contractor was concerned, that was not his problem. "You bid the contract," Waldron insisted before telling the contractor he needed to get a pump and get the bathroom operational. "In Shallah (God willing)," came the impertinent reply. His indifference only infuriated Waldron. "That's not acceptable—you need to get a pump!"

"I wasn't contracted to do that!" the contractor again asserted.

"Well, you contracted to fix the bathroom, and the bathroom obviously doesn't work if there's no pump to move the water from point A to point B!" Their conversation was going nowhere, but Waldron was adamant, determined to get the bathroom operational.

Ever resourceful, he located a brand-new pump at Viper Base that evening, a pump that looked tailor-made for the job. But even that wasn't good enough for the contractor. The pump won't work, he now insisted—it was too big, and it was the wrong type. It was at this point that Waldron's interpreter, a trained engineer, grew impatient with the contractor's obstinacy. The contractor could exchange the pump, he suggested, for the right model. In fact, such a fine pump could fetch two or more pumps that would work just fine. Waldron saw his opportunity, and he immediately instructed the contractor to trade this pump for one that worked, and while he was at it, barter for an additional 250-gallon tank for the roof as well. Finally, Waldron stated firmly, he would tolerate no more delays on the project—the school needed a functioning bathroom. Within days, the al-Sa'ad bathroom was fully operational.[6]

The Schools Reopen

The bathroom crisis unfolded even as the school year began, with al-Sa'ad's students attending a nearby school that was bursting at the seams. The MPs continued to visit al-Sa'ad to check on its progress, spending time with the school's two administrators (a headmistress for the girls, a headmaster for the boys) and teachers, often over a cup of tea or potent Arabic coffee. Back at Viper Base, the mail clerks received a growing stack of school supplies. What started as a trickle soon grew into a deluge, arriving at the rate of a box or two every day. The MPs decided that delivering just a box or two of pens and pencils at the school would never do—they faced a major logistical challenge. So they stockpiled the school supplies, sorting and counting the items as they arrived, anticipating the day they would have enough to give every child something worth having.

The effort to gather up enough school supplies soon took on a life of its own. The Reapers tapped into their extensive list of contacts back home, and aided by the power of the telephone and the Internet, word spread exponentially. Waldron's father reached out to his old school buddies. Churches, schools, and businesses throughout central Illinois also picked up on the appeal. It seemed like everyone wanted to get involved, to do something to help the children of Iraq. When the initial shipments arrived with an overabundance of pens and pencils, the Reapers tweaked their appeals and were soon rewarded with boxes filled with notebooks and notepads, reams of paper, art supplies and construction paper, scissors, glue, erasers, marking pens, and crayons. Since they intended to give each teacher something as well, they also asked for three-ring binders, chalk, erasers, flashcards, workbooks, and glue—anything a grade school teacher might need. Often the contributions came in the form of cash. Sergeant Waldron's father collected up the cash he received and purchased whatever supplies were mentioned in Roman's last e-mail. Much of the money went for postage, an expensive proposition.

When an Army postal worker in the Middle East found a busted-up box of school supplies passing through, he took note of Waldron's Baghdad address and started his own campaign. He contacted his wife, who was soon collecting money and supplies from her neighbors and friends, including a professional football player. Meanwhile, Lieutenant Ferris took on the daunting task of writing personal thank-you notes to their growing list of benefactors.[7]

First Sergeant Elmore acted as liaison between the 233rd's network of supporters, who shipped a veritable cornucopia of merchandise to Iraq, and the platoons. He made sure the school supplies were separated from the generous assortment of candy, toys, and stuffed animals that also arrived. One box from a Springfield businessman contained forty deflated soccer balls and, thankfully, one hand pump. Indeed, soccer balls were one of the most common items received, often tucked in with school supplies. The packages arrived from individuals, churches, grade school classes, Girl Scout troops, and corporations, and they came at a rate that amazed Elmore. But he understood what lay behind the flood of packages. It wasn't just compassion. It was also the families' way to show their support to their soldiers in Baghdad. Through these shipments, they could help their loved one succeed in Baghdad.[8]

When the al-Sa'ad school finally opened in November, Sergeant Waldron and a contingent of Reapers wasted no time in paying the students a visit. The girls "went crazy," the MPs recalled. They lined the balcony, smiling and waving enthusiastically, calling out "hello, hello" in their best English. Others spilled out of their classrooms and into the school's dusty courtyard. They "loved to come up and shake our hands and touch us," recalled Sergeant Mayes. Waldron likened the scene to a "mini-riot, with me standing in the middle of it." The MPs dug into their pockets and handed out whatever candy and trinkets they could find, but they soon ran out. The kids didn't mind; they were thrilled to meet their benefactors. The response from the Iraqi parents when they arrived later that day was mixed. Many kept their distance, but others expressed their thanks, not just because the MPs' frequent visits eased their concerns for their children's safety, but also because of their efforts to rehab the school.

The Reapers loved visiting when the girls were in class. Arriving when the boys were there was a dicier proposition. Where the girls were invariably pleasant, well-mannered, and generally passive, the boys were decidedly aggressive in their enthusiasm, not at all hesitant as they pressed in around the MPs, grabbing at their gear, brazenly begging for candy, rambunctious to the point of being obnoxious. To keep the boys under control, their teachers, mostly women, freely meted out corporal punishment, slapping an out-of-control boy on the cheek or the back of the head—"whatever was available," as Waldron put it. Still, there was nothing malicious about the boys' behavior, and the MPs invariably enjoyed their visits. They were also surprised at how much the kids knew about western culture. "We love America, we love Bush, we love Michael Jackson," the boys called out. Mayes was struck by their adoration for Jackson, as he took a decidedly more jaded view of the superstar. He sometimes teased the boys about their pop hero, their cue to break into a moonwalk or other Jacksonesque dance moves. School visits quickly became part of the MPs' daily routine. After a while, however, they learned to keep their visits short because instruction stopped whenever they arrived. By winter, they showed up late in the school day to minimize the disruption that they caused.[9]

Distributing the School Supplies

It was the middle of December before the Reapers collected enough supplies to make a delivery, enough for 500 complete school kits. Because it might be many weeks before they received enough for all 1,000 children, they decided to deliver the kits to the girls first. That decision was a no-brainer given the girls' more restrained behavior. They hoped the boys would understand that their day would come.

When the MPs pulled up to al-Sa'ad on the morning of December 15 with their truckload of supplies, Waldron marveled at the school's transformation. He recalled their first day at the school, with its building and grounds in a shambles. Now al-Sa'ad was the pride of the neighborhood, its walls gleaming white with light blue trim, the interior equipped with new plumbing, brightly lit classrooms, and functioning telephones, its classrooms filled with eager girls excited about coming to school.

The MPs wasted no time in unloading the supplies. Waldron had already worked out the logistics for the distribution with the school's headmistress. The Reapers quickly formed a line, each one handing out a different item. When the MPs were ready, the signal was given, and all the girls—more than 500—came streaming down into the courtyard, forming a long queue that snaked through the courtyard. The girls filed past a line of MPs one by one, receiving pens, pencils, crayons, notebooks, and other supplies. The girls thanked each MP in turn, their faces beaming with excitement and pride. Sergeant Mayes marveled at how polite and gracious they were.

Once the last girl passed through the line, the MPs quickly retooled their operations, laying out a packet of supplies for each teacher, who soon clustered tightly around them. The MPs couldn't help but compare the students' polite demeanor with the teachers' more assertive conduct. The teachers needed these things in order to teach their students, Waldron decided, and they were not bashful about getting as much as they could. It wasn't until later that he realized that the boys had their own set of teachers, and those teachers got nothing that day.

It would take two full months before the Reapers stocked up enough supplies to deliver kits to the boys. Even then, the MPs fretted about the task at hand. When the date finally arrived, they altered their distribution plan based on the headmaster's recommendations. The boys were sent to the courtyard one class at a time. In that way, the headmaster, a security guard, and the teacher for each class were on hand to ensure that the boys behaved themselves. "Much to our surprise," Waldron recalled later, "they were very cooperative and . . . very pleasant." Still, "[I] didn't regret changing my tactics with the boys."[10]

The Orphanage

Captain Brian Reck, the 519th's MP Battalion's chaplain, had traveled the world with the unit, including a tour in Afghanistan. Reck began his career in 1985 as a private in the infantry, then switched to a mental health specialty after four and a half years as a grunt. All the while, he plugged away at his college degree. He received an officer's commission in 1997 and simultaneously was accepted into the Army's chaplain corps. As a member of the Church of Jesus Christ of the Latter-Day Saints (Mormon), Reck was something of a rarity in the Army's chaplain's corps.[11]

Reck's duties in Baghdad kept him busy. Given that the unit had over a thousand soldiers who lived and worked in an inherently dangerous environment, there was no shortage of young men and women to counsel. There was also an ambitious schedule of religious services to conduct. Still, like so many Americans, Reck was eager to find some way to help the Iraqi people. He soon discovered an orphanage located nearby, directly across the river from the Green Zone. The Dar al-Mahabha (House of Love) Orphanage was run by four nuns from India and Bangladesh, disciples of Mother Teresa and her Sisters of Mercy. Mother Teresa founded the orphanage in the days after the gulf war, personally traveling to Baghdad in 1991. Ironically, Sister Beth Murphy, the same sister who Captain Royer had joined in prayer on the steps of the old capitol in Springfield, had visited the orphanage several times before the war.[12]

In March 2003, when the city became a target for American bombers and cruise missiles, the sisters at the House Of Love Orphanage stubbornly refused to leave. Their charges, twenty-two severely handicapped Iraqi children, had nowhere else to go. The sisters were no strangers to hardship, and they were still at the orphanage when the Americans arrived in April. In the months that followed, every orphanage in Baghdad was adopted by American units. Reck had no illusions about what motivated this outpouring of altruism. The commanders in Baghdad knew that working with an orphanage would impress their superiors. It was the kind of thing that looked good on an officer evaluation report.

Still, whatever the motives, the Army accomplished much good in adopting the city's orphanages, and none was more challenging than Mother Teresa's orphanage. The children at the House of Love were some of the most severely handicapped children in Baghdad. Many had been abandoned by their parents at birth. Several had cerebral palsy. One had no arms or legs. Others were blind, or suffered from speech impediments, or were severely retarded. Many were so severely handicapped that they were permanently confined to their cribs, liberated only when someone lifted them out. The youngest were infants; the oldest were nearing their teens.[13]

Chaplain Reck visited the orphanage twice a week, typically on Monday and Thursday afternoons. He always took soldiers from the 519th with him, in part because he needed an escort, but also because he needed the help.

Often they came bearing gifts: candy, toys, or oversized crayons suitable for handicapped children. He knew that the kids loved their visits, and that they were just the kind of thing good Christians should be doing. Just as important, it was good therapy for the MPs, and it gave them a chance to forget about their own missions and feel good about themselves. They always left the orphanage with their spirits lifted.

The nuns, for their part, expressed apprehension about the Americans' first few visits to the orphanage, fearing the soldiers' presence would elicit the insurgents' wrath. (It was a fear that Sister Beth shared as well.) But by September, the nuns welcomed the Americans with open arms. Their visits gave the sisters a respite from their grueling labors. More importantly, the children were thrilled when the soldiers came to call.[14]

MPs from the 32nd MP Company, a National Guard unit from Milwaukee, usually accompanied Chaplain Reck. On September 29, Specialists Abraham Bain, Adam Moma, and Laura Thomason from the 233rd accompanied him. Their visit represented a rare break from their normal duties escorting Captain Royer. The three-vehicle convoy arrived late in the afternoon, pulling up outside the metal gate that separated the orphanage's courtyard from the world outside. The Humvees quickly formed a circle, sealing off the street. Reck dismounted, walked over to the gate, and pulled on a string attached to an old metal bell. The clanging bell summoned a young sister neatly dressed in a white habit trimmed in blue. She welcomed the chaplain and his party into a tiny courtyard featuring a modest statue of the Virgin Mary. The sound of the bell also signaled the children that the soldiers had arrived. Confined to their cribs, they nonetheless squealed with delight. Several rocked rhythmically in their beds, and those who could manage it struggled to their feet, calling out to the soldiers to pick them up and play with them.

The chaplain usually timed his visits to correspond with supper. That allowed the soldiers time to play with the children for a bit, then help the sisters serve the children supper. This Monday was no different, with Bain, Moma, and Thomason lifting the younger children out of their cribs and helping feed those who were unable to feed themselves.

"Fatma's dad is here," a couple of the children called out excitedly upon seeing the young chaplain. Moments later, a nun laid a tiny three-year-old girl into Reck's outstretched arms. Fatma was severely disabled from cerebral palsy, unable to see or swallow. Reck took to her from the start. During his first few visits, Fatma's body was rigid whenever he held her in his arms. Gradually, over many trips, she began to respond, relaxing in his arms as he fed her formula from a baby bottle, signaling her contentment by cooing softly.

After supper, the MPs spent a few more minutes in the courtyard playing with the orphans, then bid their farewells and headed back to the Humvees. They felt good about helping these children, but their joy was mixed with considerable anguish. Laura Thomason experienced that peculiar mix of emotions. "It hurt my heart," she explained later. The children's handicaps were so severe, their future so bleak, that she found the experience tough to bear. "I just couldn't stand to see the kids like that." It was one of the hardest things she encountered during her entire year in Baghdad, but she was glad she accompanied Chaplain Reck that day. She felt a twinge of guilt as she left the orphanage, as well as admiration for the nuns who devoted their entire lives to these children.[15]

10

An Embedded Reporter

As the unit's first sergeant, it was "Top" Elmore's job to take care of the soldiers of the 233rd, to deal with their complaints and address their concerns, to make sure their morale was good and that their heads were in the game. His job was all about maintaining the unit's fighting edge, and Elmore worked hard at it.

In light of that, nothing frustrated him more during the unit's first few months in country than the total breakdown of mail delivery and the soldiers' almost complete inability to keep in touch with their loved ones back home. The way Top looked at things, it was his responsibility to keep the folks at home informed, even when the troops weren't able to get through themselves. So when he got temporary access to the Internet in mid-May, he wrote an e-mail to Jerry Calbow with instructions to forward it to everyone in the Family Readiness Group (FRG). In the e-mail, Top detailed the troops' living conditions in Baghdad and also provided a thumbnail sketch of their duties and mission in Iraq—at least the unclassified version. More than anything, Elmore wanted to reassure family members that their soldiers were doing well and were in good spirits. Calbow used Top's e-mail to good effect, forwarding the e-mail to those on his Internet address list. He also distributed it at an FRG meeting, where a reporter from the *State Journal-Register* was in attendance. That's how Top's e-mail made its way to the front page of the newspaper.[1]

As the weeks passed with little improvement in mail delivery, Elmore sought every opportunity to get the unit's message back home. His e-mail in May was the first of a series sent to Jerry, always with the intent that they be transmitted to the FRG members. If things got hairy in Baghdad, Elmore saw it as his personal responsibility to write an e-mail to reassure the families. "You may see an explosion on TV," a typical message might state, but "we're all OK; we weren't involved."

Even after communications between Iraq and the States improved, Elmore looked for ways to get the unit's story out and to keep the families informed. That led him to the Springfield *State Journal-Register.* "If there is some specific stuff you'd like to know about the unit," he wrote the editors, "feel free to ask me, and I'll give you the straight scoop, or [at least] what I'm authorized to tell you." The editors jumped at Elmore's offer. From the earliest days of the unit's mobilization, editor Mike Kienzler recognized that the 233rd's mobilization had great human interest potential. As metro editor, his beat was the local community, but here was that rare story which could link his readers with "the big stuff that's going on in the world." After the success of the paper's first feature story on the 233rd describing its emotional departure from Camp Lincoln, Kienzler looked for ways to keep the unit in the public eye. "I was frustrated right after the 233rd got sent," he later recalled. "There was a story there that we didn't have a . . . good way to get a handle on." Their front page story in July featuring a pregnant and photogenic Monica Hildebrandt was a natural—just the kind of thing the public liked to read. Now Elmore was offering Kienzler an insider's view, and he jumped at the chance.

On Sunday, August 10, a story on the 233rd dominated the front page of the paper, complete with a letter from First Sergeant Elmore, printed verbatim, his response to a series of questions from Kienzler. The article also included a photo of Elmore, a portrait that suggested both compassion and professionalism. In the days that followed, the *Journal-Register* received several complimentary letters thanking the paper for running the story. As far as the families were concerned, the article was a welcome respite from the images they saw on TV about the war—the reason that many of the wives and parents went to such great pains to avoid the news.[2]

The positive responses the cover story received only whetted Kienzler's appetite for more. If only the paper could get a reporter on the ground with the 233rd! He recalled that Marcus Stern, a reporter for Copley News Service, had done some excellent coverage of the war's northern front during the invasion. Copley, headquartered in San Diego, was the *State Journal-Register*'s parent company. Stern worked out of Copley's Washington bureau. Kienzler wrote an e-mail to a friend in the Washington office. He wasted no time in getting to the point. "Do you suppose anybody out there with the initials Marcus Stern would be interested in going to Iraq if we got something together here?" The response was more than encouraging.

"Wow! He's been really looking for an excuse to go back there." Armed with that encouragement, Kienzler then approached Barry Locher, the *State Journal-Register*'s editor, suggesting that they could pull it off if only "we are willing to spend a little money."[3]

Marcus Stern was indeed looking for an excuse to get back to Iraq. As a third-generation reporter with almost twenty-five years of experience, reporting was in his blood. Indeed, his father was a war correspondent during the Vietnam war for the *Washington Post*. Stern's own work covered the gamut from politics, to award-winning reportage on immigration, to work as a foreign correspondent, and lately as a war correspondent. Now he had an opportunity to return to Iraq, this time to get the individual soldier's perspective of the conflict. He also wanted to see how the occupation was going for the Iraqi people, and he was intrigued by the chance to spend some time with an American unit—a new experience for him. He jumped at the chance.

Getting the Story

Stern had spent his first tour in Iraq chronicling the invasion. He crossed the Turkish border into northern Iraq before hostilities began, traveling as an independent reporter. With him was Nelvin Cepeda, a Copley photographer. Unlike many of his peers who had accepted the military's offer to embed with American units, Stern steered clear of the military, preferring to work independently. He wanted to see the human side of war and chronicle the war's impact on the people of Iraq. He and Cepeda hired an Iraqi who owned an SUV, then drove through Iraq, spending a month in the north before the war began, then following in the American Army's wake as it liberated city after city. After Baghdad fell, the two headed to Kirkuk, then Mosul, then Tikrit before they arrived in Baghdad at about the same time the 233rd was settling in at Viper Base. Stern and Cepeda finally headed home in late April, after ten weeks in the country.[4]

The logistics for Stern's return to Iraq came together quickly. Copley's San Diego affiliate offered to split the travel expenses with the *State Journal-Register* in exchange for a feature on the situation in Iraq. Cepeda soon signed up for the trip as well, and Kienzler helped Stern link up with First Sergeant Elmore, who cleared the way for the team from his end. Stern considered himself fortunate that he did not have to work with any military middleman for the trip. Instead, he corresponded directly with Elmore—the beginning of a relationship that largely freed him from government oversight, just the way he liked it.

In early October, after a six-month absence, Stern and Cepeda were once again flying to Baghdad, the center of the world's attention. Their plan was to spend a week with the 233rd, but instead of living with the unit 24–7 as did the embedded reporters, Stern reserved a room at a hotel in the heart of Baghdad, and the two shuttled back and forth from the hotel to the Green Zone.[5] From the idea's inception, Stern and Kienzler agreed on the focus of the project. Kienzler recommended not just one or two stories but a whole series, enough to give his readers a real sense of "what it was like to be a citizen-soldier in Baghdad." That suited Stern just fine. He wanted to capture the MPs' perspective of a typical mission, but beyond that, he had no definite ideas, and Kienzler's proposal appealed to him.

On Stern and Cepeda's first day with the unit, Top Elmore served as escort, walking them around the compound, showing them the unit's several barracks, the motor pool, exercise equipment, and a room packed with computer terminals, each one hooked up to the Internet. In the process, Elmore also introduced the journalists to as many soldiers as possible. By the end of the day, Stern's plan for the rest of the series took shape. "I saw immediately that there were a lot of family members [in the unit]," Stern later recalled, including the first sergeant and his son, three pairs of brothers, a mother and daughter, and even a husband and wife. He hadn't expected that, but he knew it would make for great copy. He was surprised to see the unit's Internet café and was impressed by the soldiers' ingenuity in staying in touch with family and friends back home. The Internet was obviously something new to this war—something worthy of a story. Stern decided to develop eight different story lines that together would paint an accurate picture of the unit's life in Baghdad. Just as important, he also decided the unit was worthy of the coverage. He recognized a great story when he saw it.[6]

Back in Springfield, Mike Kienzler and editor Barry Locher agreed to give the 233rd unprecedented coverage. The unit was by no means the only one from the area currently overseas. Several other units, both National Guard and Reserve outfits, were also deployed, most serving in Iraq and Afghanistan. More units were in the pipeline preparing to deploy. The city's Air National Guard wing, the 183rd Fighter Wing, had been shuttling detachments to the theater ever since Desert Storm, flying missions over Iraq's no-fly zone. Central Illinois also had its share of sons and daughters serving on active duty. But few units were more accessible and more entwined with the community than the 233rd, and not just because it was the area's largest unit then serving overseas, or the fact that ten Springfield police officers served with the unit. What made the 233rd's story especially compelling for Kienzler and Locher was its mission. They worked in Baghdad and were charged with performing what was arguably the Army's most important and difficult mission in Iraq: restoring order out of chaos all while rebuilding the Iraqi police (IP) force. Because they served at the center of the president's efforts to transform Iraq and the Arab world, the paper's decision to feature the 233rd on the front page for eight days running was an easy one. And each day, Nelvin Cepeda's dramatic color photographs, combined with Stern's colorful narrative, would help readers identify with the soldiers overseas.

The series kicked off on Sunday, October 19. Stern introduced the unit with a dramatic flourish, giving a thumbnail sketch of daily operations in the streets of Baghdad. A photograph of Sergeant Daniel Hinds dressed in full "battle rattle" while cradling his M-16 dominated the front page. "In the real world," began Stern, "Jeff Royer is a four-year veteran of the Springfield Police Department. John Gillette is with the Sangamon County Sheriff's Office. But this isn't the real world. It's Baghdad. It's hot. And it's night." That was enough of a teaser to capture most readers' attention, and for the next eight days, they eagerly awaited the next installment.[7]

Stern minced no words in painting a picture of duty in Baghdad. He wrote graphically about the MPs' response to a distress call. Several armed men had just forced their way inside a local hospital, he explained in his first installment, and a patrol led by Sergeant First Class Gillette was dispatched to the scene.

> The unit sped toward the hospital, driving their wide Humvees the wrong way up one-way streets and the wrong way around traffic circles. . . . When one car was slow pulling out of their way, Gillette ordered his driver to plow through the offending Volkswagen. His driver complied, ramming the rear end of the car until their Humvee could pass. The second Humvee also plowed into the Volkswagen, ripping off its trunk. But the jagged metal of the car punched a hole in one of the Humvee's tires.
>
> With the flat tire shredded, smoking and flapping, the convoy continued on to the hospital.
>
> Once there, they found it had been a wild goose chase.

By describing the MPs' experiences in such visceral terms, Stern intended to help his readers understand what it was really like in Baghdad, and to whet their appetite for the rest of the series.[8]

On day 2, Stern highlighted the MPs' life in Viper Base. Sprinkled throughout the article were shots of the soldiers in their natural surroundings—the unit's barber in action, soldiers hanging out laundry, an impromptu church service, even a shot of Top Elmore strumming his guitar amidst a pile of rubble and MRE boxes. One photo showed Roman Waldron and Shauna Cashion sitting on their bunks, a scene that highlighted the fact that men and women shared the same sleeping quarters. Stern's text and Cepeda's photos gave a clear impression of their lives in Baghdad: things were far from plush, but their living conditions were bearable. After six months in country, they had most of the amenities of home—stereos, TVs, computers, sleeping quarters decorated with pictures, and air conditioning.

On day 3, Stern turned his focus to the unit's female soldiers. Wednesday's article featured the Internet café and how it had changed the way soldiers in combat kept in touch with the rest of the world. On Thursday, Stern wrote about the surprising number of relatives serving in the 233rd, the thing that so surprised him on his first day with the unit. Friday's article was devoted to Captain Royer, and on Saturday, Stern featured First Sergeant Elmore. He wrapped up the series on Sunday, October 26, with a story about the unit's efforts to build relations with the citizens of Baghdad, an article that inevitably focused on the vast cultural differences the MPs encountered every day in Baghdad. Inside Sunday's paper was a full page of "Portraits of Area Soldiers," a collection of some of Cepeda's best photos of Springfield's soldiers. By the end of the series, Kienzler and Locher accomplished what they set out to do. They helped their readers to connect with their soldiers overseas, to identify with their challenges and triumphs. By the end of the series, thousands of central Illinois readers not only knew who these soldiers were, they rooted for them and prayed for them. The war had become more personal.[9]

In many respects, Stern's series presented a very different view of the conflict in Iraq than that being presented by the mainstream media. "I haven't read any of this kind of stuff anywhere else," Kienzler's publisher excitedly told him, not "in the [New York] *Times* or anywhere." "We knew this was going to be the chance to do something unique," said Kienzler. "And the readers told us it was the right thing to do." That point was validated when a representative from the city's police department came in to personally thank Kienzler for the articles. The visit was surprising, especially considering the paper's usually contentious relationship with the city's police force.[10]

The Community Response

Despite Stern's long experience as a war reporter, his coverage of the 233rd marked a departure for him. It was the first time he worked directly with the military. He preferred to report on the other side of war, on its impact on the civilians who were caught in the vortex of violence. "I don't think war should be glamorized," he later reflected, or even that "service should be glamorized. But I did find [the 233rd's story] very compelling." The story he wrote was not the one he had anticipated. What he expected was to see indifference or worse from the Iraqi people—angry Iraqis shaking their fists at the Americans, spitting and tossing invectives toward them as they drove by. But while accompanying a patrol led by Staff Sergeant Mark Walden, Stern was struck by the friendly greeting the MPs received from all quarters. Instead of icy stares and expressions of defiance, they were met with friendly waves, thumbs-up, and smiles, often attracting groups of young boys as if the soldiers were the Pied Piper. It was quite a contrast to what Stern had expected to see, and he admitted as much to Sergeant Walden.

Stern later returned to Iraq, this time working closely with several other units. But of all the units that he saw, "the 233rd . . . stands out as a unit that had strong morale and cohesiveness." He attributed that to the unit's solid leadership team, and at least in part to their better-than-average living conditions. The MPs performed admirably under some very trying circumstances. In conclusion, Stern decided that the MPs were much more relevant to the situation in Iraq than were the infantry. By the end of his stay with the 233rd, he had come to admire these citizen-soldiers.

The War Through the Media's Eyes

Stern offered a more critical assessment of his own profession. Citing the old journalist maxim that "if it bleeds, it leads," he understood his colleagues' (or more accurately, their corporate executives') fascination with car bombs and improvised explosive device (IED) explosions. "But there should be a point in time," he stressed, "when journalists stand back, take a look, and try to do a broader assessment and focus on some other things that might be crucial." Not much of that story was making it into the coverage of the war, to the great consternation of almost everyone in uniform in Baghdad and a growing number of their loved ones back home. That reality explained the often distrustful and contentious relationship that characterized relations between the soldiers in Baghdad and the journalists who covered the war.[11]

Relations between the military and the press had started well enough in the early days of the occupation, in part because of the rapport many embedded reporters forged with soldiers. But that relationship changed over time. By late summer, many in the 233rd viewed the reporters they encountered in Baghdad as nuisances, and increasingly with suspicion. Relations with the Arab media soured first, especially after the Americans noticed a disturbing trend: Arab journalists often managed to get to the site of an IED attack even before coalition forces arrived. More than a few concluded that al-Jazeera reporters were being tipped off about impending attacks and arrived on site early to capture the event. By October, the MPs were instructed to sever all communication with al-Jazeera and al-Arabi reporters.[12]

In Colonel Glaser's view, the regional media—folks like Stern and others who wrote for the smaller markets in the States—took the time to get the story right. But he had little use for the larger outlets. When he expressed his disappointment with press coverage to an Associated Press reporter, the journalist was quick to respond: "I can write 50 stories on the things you guys are doing right, but nobody's going to pay me a dime." Not surprisingly, the military soon limited the media's access to the police stations, a step taken ostensibly to improve security.

In some respects, media relations in Baghdad became something of a game, with the military as the prey. The soldiers could always count on reporters pressing for more and freer access at the scene of any incident. "[The media] are everywhere, and seem to know when things are going to happen," Royer wrote in an after action report. "Make sure your soldiers have the proper guidance on how to deal with the media. . . . They will do everything they can to get inside a cordon. The stock answer is for them to contact the Corps Public Affairs Officer. They won't like the answer, but they know it well."

The official guidance from the coalition headquarters on public relations was consistent. The Americans were waging a war not just against the insurgents, but also for the support of the Iraqi people. "Each member of the coalition is an ambassador for the new freedoms the Iraqi people enjoy," wrote General Sanchez in a letter to his command. "Our proper treatment of the Iraqi people and the media will ensure our success and the success of a free Iraq." To the MPs, it was a statement of the obvious, and as far as Captain Royer was concerned, his soldiers were doing their part as good ambassadors. How else to explain the lack of attacks on unit patrols? As for the media, Royer was convinced they cared more about a good story—one with lots of blood and gore—than they did about winning the war.[13]

Insurgents on the Attack

Given the level of antipathy that normally existed between the military and the media, Stern's experience with the 233rd and the nature of his coverage of the MPs was refreshingly candid and upbeat. Both he and the MPs came away with greater respect for each other. On October 27, however, the day after Stern's expose concluded, an event occurred that reverted the MPs' perception of the international media back to form.

October 27 marked the first day of Ramadan in the Islamic world, commemorating the month that the Qur'an was revealed to Muhammad. For Muslims, it began their holy month; they were obligated to observe it as one of the five pillars of their faith. During Ramadan, the city's Muslims would fast during the day and also abstain from other worldly vices. At dusk, they broke their fast, enjoyed an evening meal, and often visited with family and friends. The devout among them spent their evenings in prayer and reflection, and read the Qur'an. Not all residents of Baghdad were Muslims, and many of those who claimed to be Muslims did not rigorously adhere to the precepts of Ramadan. But the majority observed the fast, and the MPs hoped that that meant life would slow down.

A tiny core of Islamic radicals, however, viewed Ramadan not as a time of peace but as Allah's ordained time to destroy the "infidels." They chose October 27 to unleash a coordinated series of suicide attacks on five Baghdad police stations and the Baghdad headquarters of the International Red Cross. At 8:30 A.M. local time, two suicide bombers, both driving vehicles disguised as police cars, crashed into two separate targets, the Saidiya police station in southwest Baghdad and the Baya police station just west of the Green Zone. Five minutes later, a terrorist plowed an ambulance through a barricade of sand-filled 55-gallon drums protecting the Red Cross headquarters, then detonated his deadly cargo, instantly killing more than a dozen and injuring scores more, the vast majority being civilians. At 8:55 A.M., another police station was hit in northern Baghdad. At roughly 9:15, two more bombers struck. One was at the Khudra police station in western Baghdad. The other was intended for the New Baghdad police station, staffed by a contingent of IPs trained by the 233rd MPs. It was the only attempt all day that was successfully foiled.[14]

Moments before the attack at New Baghdad, an Iraqi policeman stood guard outside the station's south gate while another IP armed with an AK-47 manned a fighting position on the roof. It had taken a lot of cajoling on the MPs' part to convince the Iraqis to man these positions, but those arguments were now several months behind them. Gone were the days when the MPs called the shots at the stations. It was the IPs' show now. In front of the gate was a cluster of Hesco and Jersey barriers arrayed like a funnel pointing toward the gate. At 9:15, the gate guard spotted a white 1988 Toyota Land Cruiser entering the barrier system. He immediately ordered the driver to stop. But it was obvious that the driver had no intention of stopping as he continued to weave his way through the barriers. Both the IP on the roof and the gate guard instantly opened fire on the Land Cruiser, which careened forward before crashing into the compound wall, one turn short of the gate, barely missing the guard. Wounded in the hail of gunfire and unable to detonate his deadly cargo, the suicide bomber bailed out of the SUV, tossing a hand grenade over the compound wall as he did so. He ran back through the barrier system. The grenade exploded harmlessly in the compound while several IPs pursued the driver, catching up with him only 100 meters from the station. They took him into custody and transported him to al-Kindie, the neighborhood hospital, for treatment. The incident was over in minutes.[15]

Half an hour passed before a patrol led by Sergeant First Class Kevin Weber received a call from Excalibur's TOC. Weber was ordered to head to the New Baghdad police station to investigate why a large crowd was gathering outside the station. The MPs knew little about the series of terrorist attacks or the foiled attack at New Baghdad. Their instructions were both brief and vague: report to New Baghdad and send up a situation report. Ten minutes later, the patrol pulled to a stop about 100 meters from the station. Weber dismounted and waded into the crowd, looking for some IPs so he could find out what had happened. It took several minutes before he was able to piece together the incident. By that time, an Iraqi explosive ordnance demolition (EOD) team had already completed its work on the SUV, discovering a deadly cargo on board: three 130-millimeter mortar rounds wired to a detonator, and tucked away in the truck's side panels, another 1,500 kilograms of PE-4 explosives. The EOD team carefully disarmed and removed the explosives, then reported their findings to the station commander before departing the scene. With that, Sergeant Joshua Hubbard called in a situation report to the Excalibur TOC. Weber then spotted a group of IPs hauling the Land Rover into the compound. He instantly began frantically waving his arms in a vain attempt to stop them. They did, but only after the SUV sat in the middle of the police station's compound. In the IPs' haste to get the vehicle off the road, they had just destroyed the crime scene, and no amount of cajoling could make them understand. Still, the IPs had performed well that day. They alone had thwarted an attack on a day of deadly and demoralizing attacks. All told, thirty-four innocent Iraqis died that day—Baghdad's bloodiest day since the end of August.

Lieutenant Flack arrived at the station later that morning and soon pressed the IPs about the status of the injured bomber, who was now being treated at a local hospital. When Flack discovered this fact, he immediately dispatched a patrol to retrieve him, telling the team to move the suspect to the 28th Combat Support Hospital, where he could both be cared for and interrogated. Days later, the Coalition Provisional Authority announced that the insurgent was a Syrian national, as evidenced by his Syrian passport.[16]

Admittedly, October 27 was not one of the coalition's better days—five successful attacks and only one thwarted. The *New York Times* called it "45 minutes of mayhem," declaring that "the bombings contributed to a general sense that the security situation was deteriorating." Farther down in the report, the paper stated that the "violence has helped turn many Iraqis against the Americans." The soldiers in Baghdad were struck by such statements. Wouldn't the attacks also sour Iraqis on the insurgency, they asked? They cynically concluded that the *Times* statement was just another example of the media's liberal bias.

Two months later, Lieutenant Colonel Glaser watched a news report filed by CNN reporter Christiana Amanpour. She stood in front of the wreckage of one of the police stations bombed that day, yet to be rebuilt. The Americans had let the Iraqis down, she explained to her viewers, backing up her statement with a quote from a police officer who was happy to oblige with a comment critical of the Americans. Amanpour's presentation of "reality" in Baghdad infuriated him. "Go look at the other forty-nine [police stations] that are rebuilt," Glaser yelled at the screen. All their months of hard work, all the sacrifices his soldiers made every day, all the impressive progress they achieved—it didn't seem to matter to these journalists. Only the failures got reported. To file her report, Amanpour deliberately passed by several functioning police stations within a mile of CNN's base of operation at the Palestine Hotel to find a police station in a Sunni dominated pro-Saddam area in west Baghdad. "You would think we'd . . . done nothing [in Baghdad]," Glaser bitterly complained. The blatant disinformation and bias made him furious. For Glaser's escort team, it was a rare show of emotion from their commander.[17]

11

A Typical Day

There were three clocks in the 233rd MP Company's tactical operations center (TOC), two with a simple black frame, a model ubiquitous throughout the military, the third a remnant of Saddam's defeated regime. Only the labels underneath each clock distinguished the three. One read "Springfield," the place of the MPs' daydreams. Another read "ZOOLU," a deliberate corruption of the term "Zulu," or Greenwich mean time, a modification that served as a conversation piece for visitors to their world. When the clock labeled "Baghdad" indicated midnight, Specialist Joshua Waters of tiny Scottville, Illinois, performed the first official act of November 22, 2003. He scrawled "0001" across the top of the duty log, indicating the time in proper military parlance, and wrote "Log Opened." Thus began another day for the 233rd MP Company in Baghdad. There would be little to distinguish November 22 from most other days in Baghdad. In most respects, it was a pretty typical day—a typical day in the middle of the most extraordinary year of their lives.

Joshua joined the Illinois National Guard in 2001 while still in high school, signing up to take advantage of the Guard's generous educational benefits. The state would pay for four years of tuition at any state college, the recruiter told him, in exchange for Josh serving six years in the Guard, nominally one weekend a month plus two weeks each summer. It sounded like a great idea at the time, but the war on terror interrupted Waters's school plans. Still, he was nothing if not upbeat about his current situation. Now twenty, he routinely flashed an infectious smile that revealed a mischievous streak. As the lowest-ranking soldier on the TOC's night shift, he served as the radio-telephone operator, a position known throughout the Army as the RTO, one acronym in a world rich with acronyms. His was the "voice in the darkness," the familiar voice that reassured his fellow MPs while they were on patrol.[1]

Waters performed another key function on the night shift, for his good nature and mischievous spirit brought levity to the TOC. Master Sergeant Sam Woods, the company's elder statesman at age fifty-four, headed the shift. He provided experience and stability to the team, serving as the sage father figure to many of the company's younger soldiers. Woods also served as the occasional foil for Waters's good-natured pranks.

Woods supervised a capable crew of four that also included the section's battlefield circulation control noncommissioned officer (NCO), Staff Sergeant Lawrence Wilson, a serious-minded former Regular Army MP who joined the Springfield company in November 1990, just in time to accompany the unit to Saudi Arabia for Operation Desert Storm. He had spent his first drill in the Illinois National Guard with the 933rd MP Company in Chicago. That unit conducted its drills at the Chicago Avenue armory, a decrepit old structure just one block east of Michigan Avenue, in the heart of some of Chicago's priciest real estate. Wilson, fresh off active duty, was unprepared for the easygoing atmosphere of many National Guard units. He arrived early Saturday morning and waited ten minutes until he was introduced to his platoon sergeant, a disheveled looking NCO who wasted no time with pleasantries. "I've got a job for you," he told Wilson before taking him to the armory's main entrance, actually an industrial-sized metal garage door that opened onto Chicago Avenue. Behind him was the armory's cavernous drill floor, which in its glory days had once doubled as an indoor polo field for Chicago's social elite, but now provided cheap parking for the troops.

Wilson stood by the open door, occasionally catching a glimpse of Lake Michigan to his left, and soon found himself correcting soldiers who arrived for drill grossly out of uniform, needing haircuts, and sporting jewelry. "I was an MP just . . . off active duty," he later recalled. "That's my job. I walked my post making uniform corrections." When Wilson asked those arriving for their ID cards, he became even more disgusted—most had none. Forty minutes expired before Wilson's platoon sergeant, growing tired of the complaints he kept hearing, approached Wilson. Soldiers were upset about being challenged on their uniform and appearance, he explained, and some had left with no intention of returning. It was an inauspicious beginning to a long and boring drill weekend. On Sunday afternoon, Wilson turned his gear in, bluntly telling his sergeant, "I don't want to be a part of this." Wilson's next drill was with the 233rd in Springfield, where he encountered a completely different mentality. The move south had an added benefit. He was now reunited with his best friend, Jim Batterson. The two had known each other since the third grade in tiny Franklin, Illinois.[2]

Rounding out the night shift was Sergeant Edward Higginson, who had long ago returned from leave. As he watched Master Sergeant Woods cross off November 21 on the TOC's "days" calendar, he found his mind wandering; "105 and a wake-up," he realized. Only 105 more days until he went home to Lisa for good.[3]

Operations Planning

By November 22, the 233rd no longer staffed their two police stations around the clock. The platoons stopped by the stations periodically during the day, but otherwise, they let the IPs take the lead, which allowed the entire company to spend the night at Viper Base.

With no patrols to monitor, the nights in the TOC were usually long and monotonous. That left plenty of time for other distractions. The conversation often turned to the events of the previous day, or to the latest wrinkle in insurgent tactics, or to the latest news from home. Much of Wilson's and Higginson's time was spent finalizing the previous day's reports. They maintained an impressive array of documents and reports, many of them of their own design—a synthesis of civilian police documents and combat reports. A large-scale topographic map of Baghdad showing the city's infantry and cavalry sectors dominated one wall of the TOC. An overlay for the map also divided the city into MP company areas of responsibilities, a fact that illustrated why the 233rd's patrols so often encountered infantry and cavalry units during their own operations. Technically, the infantry and cavalry units owned the terrain while MPs were in charge of the police stations, but it was not uncommon for the MPs to take over aspects of the infantry mission, and vice versa. This reality was precisely the reason that the TOC was so important. It existed to sort out the harsh realities of war, to keep everyone working on the same page.

The night shift's chief responsibility was to plan for the next day's missions on the basis of daily orders received from the 519th. It was Sergeant Woods's job to convert the battalion order into a company-level FRAGO (Fragmentary Order), an abbreviated version of the battalion's mission guidance tailored for the 233rd. Like most days, he delegated this task to the capable hands of Staff Sergeant Wilson, who had a passion for detail and a thorough understanding of both MP tactics and the strengths and weaknesses of the company. Meanwhile, Sergeant Higginson worked on the daily mission matrix, a document that allowed the commander to scan the day's assignments at a glance. The final products in the daily planning cycle were the platoon FRAGOs.

The battalion FRAGO for the 22nd was pretty typical. The company had monitored the same two police stations since the beginning of September. The 3rd Platoon typically checked in at the New Baghdad patrol station, better known as Tombstone. The name was more than fitting, conjuring up images of America's own rough-and-tumble roots. The 4th Platoon's mission included oversight of the New Baghdad police headquarters, aka Grayskull, a station that provided police protection for the southeast side of Baghdad.[4]

Monitoring the police stations was an important mission, but it was only one of many tasks the unit was typically assigned. For November 22, the 233rd was also charged with providing one team of MPs to accompany Colonel Glaser as he traveled the streets of Baghdad, while the battalion S-3 (operations officer) accompanied one of the unit's roving patrols. Other teams were assigned to accompany a maintenance run, and three teams were earmarked for a run to Baghdad International Airport (BIAP) to drop off the battalion's personnel heading home for leave before picking up several soldiers returning from the States.

Woods and Wilson determined that they would need six MP elements to make roving patrols in Baghdad that day, patrols that would also check in on Tombstone and Grayskull. Finally, four teams were designated to remain on the compound, some to staff the front and back gates and a couple to provide a quick reaction force in the event of any incident. This duty often fell to teams from the 2nd Platoon, and today was no different. All of this was incorporated into the platoon FRAGOs, typed up, and placed into the platoon leaders' mailboxes for them to retrieve in the morning. If the day's missions were more complex, such as when the unit was involved in a raid or special mission, Woods woke the platoon leaders up early to give them more time to plan. Sergeant Wilson concluded that the unit's missions were manageable that day, but he had learned to expect the unexpected in Baghdad.[5]

Filling the Quiet Time

Woods's crew usually managed to keep busy, but boredom was also part of their experience, and they found inventive ways to keep themselves alert. Specialist Waters, while manning the unit's radios, was known to drop down to a side frequency and "get a little chit-chat going," swapping jokes and inanities with distant stations. Sergeant Woods used the time to catch up on some reading (the Civil War was a favorite subject), or to scratch out a letter to the folks back home. Higginson often turned to his wartime diary, finding it therapeutic—a good way to vent the frustrations of the day.

Occasionally, the TOC became the haven for off-duty MPs in search of a spirited game of poker, which Master Sergeant Woods tolerated, but only until it interfered with their mission. It was low-stakes poker. Hard candy, which had arrived in abundance in their care packages, subbed for poker chips. There were several regulars in these poker games, including Sergeant First Class Jim Hobbs, who otherwise worked the day shift in the TOC, plus the Hildebrandt brothers and Staff Sergeant Bob Smith, who hailed from the St. Louis suburb of Hazelwood. Others merely passed through the game. The regulars invented countless variations of poker in an attempt to keep things fresh. A favorite was a seven card–no peek variety, something they christened Calvin Ball after the old *Calvin and Hobbes* comic strip, where the precocious Calvin played spirited games of baseball with Hobbes, a stuffed tiger who was his best friend. Anytime Sergeant Hobbs thought he might be winning, "Calvin," usually Higginson, frustrated him by tweaking the rules when his turn came to deal. So it was that the TOC's poker games continually evolved.

Specialist Waters found that scheming about practical jokes was a good way to keep his brain functioning late at night. Even Master Sergeant Woods occasionally served as a victim. One memorable incident involved a trip to "the Harris," the compound's latrine, still frequented because of the compound's faulty plumbing. As Specialist Waters made his way to the piss tube on one dark Baghdad night, he struggled to make out the cement path that led away from the TOC. By the time Waters headed back, however, his eyes had adjusted to the darkness, and he could clearly see Master Sergeant Woods exiting the TOC. Excited about his good fortune, Waters quickly hid behind a tree along the path and waited for his opportunity. When Woods was nearly upon him, he stepped onto the path and loudly reported, "Good evening, Sergeant Woods." Woods was more than a little startled, and Waters took delight in telling the story to the rest of the night shift. Waters added another wrinkle a few days later after discovering Sergeant Woods had a distinct dislike for snakes. He once again slipped out ahead of Sergeant Woods, then lay a menacing-looking stick across the cement path. He was elated when Woods gave it a wide berth. Sergeant Woods was thankful that Ordnance, one of the cats the Reapers had rescued at the al-Sa'ad school, treated him more respectfully.[6]

By 0530 hours, Waters began changing the TOC's several radios over to their new frequencies, and he began another ritual: calling around for information from other stations, asking for the latest on roadside bomb reports, any suspicious activity, and the current weather outlook for the upcoming day. The daily weather report was included in the intelligence summaries the 233rd received from the battalion. By November, the temperatures had finally moderated from the searing heat of the summer, when the mercury routinely reached 120 to 130 degrees. Back then, the road dogs (the affectionate term the TOC crew used for their brethren on the streets) would contact Waters for a weather update. That was his signal to go into his National Weather Service routine, adopting his best radio-announcer voice and issuing a fictitious weather report where the temperatures were always hot and the skies invariably cloudless. Officially, Saturday November 22, looked to be a good day weatherwise, with highs in the 70s and lows in the mid-40s.[7]

Prepping for Missions

Sergeant Phillip Berriman was one of the first to awaken that morning. His team was scheduled for an early morning patrol. Berriman, who looked younger than his twenty-four years, always set his alarm to go off an hour and a half before a patrol briefing, and because the team was scheduled to depart no later than 0630 hours, that meant he was up well before 0500. He shared a large room in 4th Platoon's barracks with team members Brad Clark, Phillip Shipley, and nine other soldiers. During the first couple of months in Baghdad, the twelve had slept on cots arranged around the perimeter of the room, but in October, they were able to scrounge some lumber from the local economy, and with this material, they built individual cubicles inside the room, complete with ceilings. When several soldiers moved their cots to the upper level, they effectively doubled their living space.

Compared with many Americans in Iraq, Berriman and his squadmates lived in relative luxury. He had his own eight-by-eight-foot room inside a building that featured air conditioning (as long as the unit's generators held out), electricity, running water, showers, and even toilets (when they weren't clogged). Berriman's room was equipped with a narrow bed and mattress obtained from local contractors, plus a small nightstand and some plastic shelving. The accommodations were spartan, but more than adequate. The infantrymen Berriman encountered every day would have considered it extravagant.

After a visit to the latrine and a shave, Berriman grabbed an obligatory cup of coffee, then headed out to check on the team's Humvee, making sure the vehicle's gas was topped off, the windshields were clean, and the radios worked properly. He grabbed a quick breakfast at the battalion's mess hall, located on the north end of the compound, and then headed to the TOC for his morning patrol brief. There he linked up with First Lieutenant Flack, his platoon leader and the man in charge of that day's patrol.

Flack was paying particular attention to the daily intelligence report, making a mental note of any suspected trouble areas, suspicious vehicles, and the latest in the insurgents' improvised explosive device (IED) tactics. Specifically, his mission for the day was to conduct a mobile patrol, a task that would require him to stop by the New Baghdad police headquarters before spending several hours driving the dangerous streets of east Baghdad. With seven months of experience under his belt, Flack had a good sense of what he could expect: almost anything. Still, it was rare that an Iraqi actually took a shot at the patrols as they moved through the neighborhoods, and even rarer when he or one of his soldiers fired back. Flack had one more reason to be optimistic about November 22. The city's Muslims were still celebrating Ramadan.[8]

Captain Royer also rose early that morning. Like most days, he was scheduled to start his day with an early morning brief at the battalion TOC, something that required him to drive through the heart of Baghdad to Mule Skinner, an American compound on the southeast side of town. Royer had celebrated his thirty-fifth birthday just two days before; his soldiers had surprised him with a cake and a small celebration. The cake, festooned with gummy bears, looked much better than it tasted, but it was the thought that counted. Royer also had a surprise visit from Colonel Glaser, which counted for a lot.

On the morning of November 22, First Sergeant Elmore could count on the services of 131 soldiers out of the unit's actual strength of five officers and 151 enlisted men and women. They had arrived in Baghdad with 156 enlisted personnel on the rolls, but as in all wars, slowly but surely, the unit's numbers had been whittled down. They had sustained no casualties, but the 233rd lost a couple of people back in Wisconsin for medical reasons during their initial month of training. Others had departed the company for similar reasons after the unit arrived in Baghdad. The heat, the unrelenting workload, and the stresses of daily life in a strange and austere environment had taken their inevitable toll. Five soldiers who arrived in Baghdad with the unit in April were now on medical leave in the continental United States and no longer appeared on the unit's roster. Two soldiers who were still on the books were actually in Germany, one having been medically evacuated for a heart condition aggravated by high blood pressure, the other with a knee injury. (Neither would return to the company.) Two more were on emergency leave in the States, both because a grandparent had passed away. Such compassionate leaves had long been standard procedure for the military, routinely approved after the American Red Cross verified the legitimacy of the incident. What was unprecedented, however, was the number of soldiers now on environmental leave. Elmore counted twenty-two currently on leave or pass. Eighteen were in the States, and four were in Kuwait for a three-day R&R, including the Battersons, the unit's married couple.

As for the unit's equipment, Royer and Elmore could count on forty of the forty-four Humvees assigned to the unit, thanks to the efforts of Sergeant Hildebrandt's maintenance section. The only significant glitch was the wrecker, which was deadlined for a clutch.[9]

The Morning Missions

On this day, as on most, Royer and Elmore went their separate ways, a practice that allowed them to cover the maximum amount of territory. At 0650 hours, Royer departed the Green Zone and headed for Mule Skinner and his meeting with the tankers of the 2nd Battalion, 37th Armored Task Force. He dreaded the drive: the route took him past one of Baghdad's most notorious spots for IED attacks, a cloverleaf on the south side of the sprawling city. But he trusted Sergeant Harris, his driver, implicitly. Harris was the unit's Nuclear, Biological and Chemical (NBC) NCO. He had also earned the distinction of being the best driver in the company, someone who knew the streets of Baghdad like the back of his hand. The daily trip to Mule Skinner was necessary because it allowed Royer to attend a daily briefing conducted with his armored unit counterpart. It was there that the commanders of the units patrolling Baghdad had the opportunity to compare notes, with the intent to avoid unnecessary friction between the American elements as they worked in the city's neighborhoods.[10]

Royer wasn't the first in the 233rd to depart the Green Zone this morning. Both Hog-6 and Crusader-6 beat him out the gate. Hog-6 was actually Lieutenant Stephen Rice, platoon leader for the 3rd Platoon, and Crusader-6 was Lieutenant Flack's handle. Royer went by Excalibur-6, the number 6 being the Armywide designation for a unit's leader.

Lieutenant Rice led a two-vehicle patrol charged with checking on the status of the New Baghdad police station located in a predominantly Shi'ite neighborhood in southeast Baghdad. The station straddled the border between a more upscale neighborhood and an open-air market. The market area was pretty rough, but not nearly as dangerous as Sadr City, a poverty-stricken neighborhood named after a Shi'ite cleric murdered by Saddam's brutal regime, whose son now led a radical Shia group. The 549th MP Company, an active-duty unit out of Fort Stewart, Georgia, had the dubious distinction of managing that part of town. Still, Lieutenant Rice's mission had its share of dangers. Rice's patrol crossed the Tigris River at 0605 hours.

Lieutenant Flack's mission that day was to check on the IPs who manned the New Baghdad police headquarters before conducting a roving patrol of the adjacent neighborhood, keeping a close eye out for any suspicious activity. As Flack leaned against the hood of his Humvee, the other team members gathered around. They scrutinized the topographic map of Baghdad spread across the hood as they listened to the lieutenant review their mission for the day. Flack followed this with a standard list of topics: actions on contact, actions in the event of an IED, the nearest evacuation point, and other key issues. After returning to their own vehicles, the MPs conducted their standard precombat checks and inspections almost by rote.[11]

The uniform of the day was full "battle rattle," the military jargon for a battle-ready soldier. They kept their desert camouflage uniform (DCU) sleeves down to minimize the amount of skin exposed, and over that was a cumbersome flack vest. Next came their web gear, on which almost everything imaginable was attached: ammo pouches, two canteens, a red-lens flashlight, first aid kit, smoke grenades, flares, perhaps a handheld radio, plus a butt pack that rode uncomfortably low on their backs. The soldiers crammed all manner of things inside the butt pack, including wet wipes, which were ideal for wiping away dust and sweat, insect repellant, toilet paper, a change of socks, and, depending on the weather, perhaps a poncho or light blanket. The basic load of ammunition included 210 rounds of M-16 ammunition, 30 rounds for the 9-millimeter pistol, and between 600 and 800 rounds for the M-249 5.56-millimeter machine gun. Each team chief also carried twelve rounds for the M-203, plus smoke grenades and various colored flares. On their hip, the MPs carried a gas mask, an item that was always a nuisance and fortunately almost never used. But every soldier carried one in the event that the insurgents might use chemical or biological weapons. Finally, the commodious DCU pockets were crammed with pens and pencils, more ammunition, personal items, often a global positioning system device, and a generous amount of hard candy to dispense along the way. The large leg pocket was a convenient place to store a Meal Ready to Eat, or MRE. Topping it all off were goggles and a Kevlar helmet, the culmination of 100 years of design, yet the first item removed when out of harm's way. All told, the MPs' standard gear added up to approximately 40 pounds, a fact that contributed to the high rate of heat casualties during their early months in Baghdad. Thankfully, by November, their bulky gear was almost tolerable.[12]

Crusader-6, aka Lieutenant Flack, made a radio check at 0613, then crossed the start point as the patrol headed due south over the 14th of July

Bridge. They drove quickly through the upscale Karada district, also referred to as "the thumb" because of its location inside an elongated loop of the Tigris River. The area included an electronics market, and at the thumb's tip, the University of Baghdad. The patrol soon crossed the Tigris again over the aptly named Double-Decker Bridge and sped on toward Grayskull.

At precisely 0700 hours, the last of the morning's patrols departed Viper Base, this one led by Sergeant Kurtis Glosser of 4th Platoon. It was his team's job to escort those in the battalion heading to the airport for environmental leave. The 233rd had no one departing for leave that day, nor anyone waiting at BIAP to return to the company. But five had returned to the company on the 21st, including Specialist Stephanie Stretch, one of the unit's youngest soldiers at twenty. Stretch had spent two weeks at home with her family in Chatham, a suburb of Springfield, and found it hard to say goodbye all over again as she boarded a commercial flight at Springfield's municipal airport. Her flight into BIAP in the back of a C-130 helped jolt Stephanie back to the realities of life in Baghdad. She was a bit apprehensive about returning to Iraq, but the feeling was nothing like the knot in her gut during the initial drive into Baghdad seven months earlier. She never felt quite right while on leave. It was great to see her family, but they seemed unable to relate to what she was experiencing in Iraq. "If you're not there," she later reflected, "you don't completely understand." Now she was heading home to her other family, the members of the 233rd, back to where she belonged. When members of her own squad met her at BIAP, she was both excited and relieved to see them again, knowing they were OK.[13]

Back in the TOC, Specialist Waters dutifully recorded all of these comings and goings in the daily log. After logging in Sergeant Glosser's mission to BIAP, Waters turned over the log to Sergeant Shannon Clarkson, a capable and articulate twenty-three-year-old from the small farm town of Tuscola, Illinois. It was 0700 hours—time for the TOC shift change.

Into the Heart of Baghdad

By that time, both Hog-6 and Crusader-6 were in the heart of eastern Baghdad, making a beeline for their respective police stations. The streets were already packed with traffic, an eclectic mixture dominated by sedans, plus plenty of trucks, buses, bicycles, and motorbikes. Donkey carts loaded with vegetables, ice, propane tanks, and other essentials also elbowed for space on the main thoroughfares and back streets. The congestion was one of the consequences of the American victory: car sales exploded after the statues of Saddam came tumbling down.

The sidewalks were usually packed with pedestrians by this time. The devout Muslims among them had been up before sunrise, grabbing a bite to eat before the daylight fast began, and then responding to the early morning calls to prayer emanating from the city's many minarets. The city had a surprising mix of ethnic groups and religions. The patrols passed through neighborhoods that were predominantly Christian and others that reflected the mix of ethnic and religious diversity that characterized Iraq. Some neighborhoods were upscale; others displayed the signs of abject poverty and unemployment that plagued postwar Iraq. Rice and Flack knew not to tarry in these neighborhoods.

Lieutenant Rice and Sergeant Larry Hundsdorfer, the Alpha Team leader for the Hogs' 3rd Squad, rode shotgun for their respective Humvees. From that perspective, they continually scanned the streets during their drive to the New Baghdad police station, being careful to check pedestrians' hands for weapons or any sudden movements, ever watchful for roadside bombs or suspicious activity. They searched for anything out of place—a burlap bag left in the center median, an unattended piece of luggage, a pile of rubble, a suspiciously parked car—anything that might harbor an IED. Rice cautioned his troops to be "situationally aware"—in other words, they were to be aware of their surroundings at all times. "Without it, you are basically a mark waiting to be taken down," Rice asserted.

The insurgents had grown increasingly inventive over the past months. In the early days after liberation, the remnants of Saddam's military brazenly took to the streets and fired AK-47 rifles or rocket-propelled grenades at the Americans in plain sight. Now IEDs were their preferred method of attack. While Rice and Hundsdorfer watched for IEDs and suspicious behavior, the gunners, from their vantage point in the turret, swept their eyes back and forth in regular patterns, from street to sidewalks, to buildings on either side, then to the streets again, always with their machine guns at the ready. Specialist Ben Lynch, as the gunner in the lead vehicle, scanned to his front in regular patterns. Specialist Jacob Blome did the same to his rear. It was this constant vigilance, the fact that they never could let their guard down, that wore the MPs down.

A few blocks from their destination, Lieutenant Rice caught sight of a blue Mercedes in the middle of the street, blocking traffic. He directed the patrol to stop, and the team quickly and efficiently established a ring of security around their vehicles while simultaneously halting the oncoming traffic. That action took no commands—everyone knew the drill. Rice and Hundsdorfer then approached the Mercedes and found two Iraqi men seated inside. They motioned the two to get out, then systematically searched the vehicle. Rice discovered a Browning automatic pistol on the passenger during the search, and immediately took the passenger into custody. He then sent the driver on his way. By this time, as was typical, a small crowd of curious bystanders had gathered near the vehicles, the gunners being careful to keep them at arms' length. Within minutes, the patrol was back on the road, and by 0750, the Hogs pulled up in front of the New Baghdad police station and notified the TOC that they had arrived at Tombstone.[14]

The Police Station

The police station differed little from the rest of the structures in the neighborhood, but the concrete barriers, sandbags, and concertina wire that surrounded the building marked it as an obvious terrorist target. So too did the presence of two Iraqi policemen who stood guard at the front gate, as did a sandbagged machine gun fighting position on the roof. The station was a large two-story brick-and-mortar structure located approximately 40 feet from the street. It was surrounded by a dirt compound, and that was separated from the neighborhood by a cement block wall roughly 8 feet high, itself only 10 feet from the street. If possible, the MPs preferred to park inside the compound, but when they couldn't, Rice left the drivers and gunners with their vehicles as security. Lieutenant Rice and Sergeant Hundsdorfer quickly dismounted and walked toward the front steps, past the security guards who screened and patted down any unknown Iraqis entering the compound. Rice strode up a small flight of stairs and into a large outer office, where he was immediately greeted by several IPs, all eager to shake hands and talk over the events of the previous day. Considering the condition of the station when the Americans first arrived, the structure had undergone an amazing transformation. The walls had been patched and painted, the windows replaced, electricity and plumbing reinstalled. A generator was set up in the courtyard to provide backup electricity. The furniture was basic but functional. Ringing this main office was a cluster of smaller offices, one serving as the weapons room, another as the evidence room. These were features that the MPs had worked hard to help the Iraqis develop. Something as basic as weapons accountability and a chain of custody for evidence were new concepts for the Iraqis, and the troops suspected that the Iraqis returned to their old habits whenever they were not around. It was worth Rice's time to check on their compliance to the new standards. Located on the station's bottom floor was the detention facility, a barred room that could officially house as many as thirty prisoners.[15]

Rice found twenty-seven IPs on duty that morning, plus thirty-two detainees. Whenever the Americans spent any time at the station, they manned the rooftop machine gun position. But on this day, he stopped just long enough to hand over his prisoner and the confiscated weapon to the IPs. He picked up an interpreter before heading back out to patrol the neighborhood. He was hoping for a quiet day.

A frequent stop for the Hog patrols was the market district that bordered Tombstone. By this time of day, the narrow streets were crowded with vendor stands where Iraqi merchants sold everything from vegetables and canned goods to clothing, cigarettes, electronics, appliances, and even alcohol and weapons. One enterprising Iraqi even sold counterfeit police ID tags and brassards until the IPs shut him down. Alcohol sales were authorized only from licensed storefronts; weapons sales were illegal. That meant little to Baghdad's merchants, who brazenly sold handguns and rifles, hand grenades, rocket-propelled grenades, and mortars. There was even a lively market for prescription drugs, much of which had been looted from the city's hospitals and clinics. The trade in Viagra was especially brisk.

Some Iraqis set up their stands on the sidewalk, but many others spilled into the street, usually restricting traffic to one lane. Driving through the area was always a challenge, requiring the Humvees to slow to a crawl and weave back and forth between the stands. The IPs, accompanied by their Hog counterparts, often got out at a street corner and meticulously worked their way down one of the market's crowded streets. The MPs were always careful to keep their vehicles in sight. On this occasion, Specialists Lynch and Blome, the patrol's two gunners, stayed with their vehicles while the rest of the patrol conducted their sweep, looking for illegal alcohol or weapons sales, or for anything suspicious. The two kept a keen eye on everything, paying particular attention to the buildings and rooftops that rimmed the narrow streets. The market area made them nervous, crammed as it was with merchants and shoppers, and plenty of distractions. They couldn't recall ever taking direct fire in the market, but not a day went by when they did not hear gunshots. Much of the firing could be attributed to celebratory fire, but just as often, it was connected with common crime or vendetta shootings. Too often, they could neither identify the source of the firing nor the intended target. It paid to be vigilant—and safe.

Lieutenant Rice split the rest of his MPs into two teams, with each group working its way down opposite sides of the street, serving as escorts for the IPs who took the lead. The MPs walked with their M-16s at the ready, weaving their way through the maze of stands, merchants, and shoppers, who usually gave them a wide berth. While the IPs searched for contraband, they also focused on petty crimes like drunkenness and other infractions whose significance escaped the MPs. Within minutes, the patrol was on its way again.

The Rasheed Bank Demonstration

Lieutenant Flack was running through his daily checks at the New Baghdad police headquarters when a call came in from the al-Rashad police station, one of the four substations that answered to New Baghdad. The caller reported on a possible demonstration—specifically, an angry crowd of 900 to 1,000 Iraqi men gathering outside a branch of the Rasheed bank. Flack quickly rounded up his team, including two translators, and four Iraqi squad cars with two IPs each, then headed for the bank. The initial information was sketchy. He never knew what to expect for calls like this, except to expect almost anything. "You could show up and it could be ten people," he later recalled, or "you could show up and it could be 100,000." When the bank came into sight, Flack brought the tiny convoy to a stop at their prescribed standoff distance, close enough to observe the crowd and make an initial assessment, but far enough away to allow themselves sufficient reaction time. The initial reports appeared to be accurate. A large crowd of men was milling about in the street in front of the bank. They had completely stopped traffic. They were obviously agitated about something, but they were not yet violent, and Flack could see no weapons. He ordered his vehicles to move closer while calling for additional help.

The patrol pulled to within 50 feet of the crowd before Flack once again brought his vehicle to a stop. He quickly put out security, then walked to the perimeter of the crowd accompanied by his interpreters and several IPs. They were immediately encircled by angry Iraqis, most of whom were shouting and gesturing dramatically, each one trying to be heard above the din. It took a while for the interpreters to make some sense out of the chaos, but gradually the incident came into perspective. The bank was responsible for paying former Iraqi military personnel, and on that day, bank officials had planned to pay those whose names began with A through D. Only last month the bank officials had begun the monumental task of exchanging the old regime's currency, dominated with portraits of Saddam, with newly minted money. A month later, they were still struggling to complete the exchange, and now they were saddled with this new task. Low on cash, they paid about forty ex-soldiers before another 100 men, desperate to receive their pay, crammed into the small bank, with hundreds more milling outside trying to push their way in. The bank officials, fearing the mob's wrath, locked up their remaining cash. It did not take long before ugly allegations of corruption began circulating through the crowd. Many in the mob claimed that bank officials were demanding cash before the ex-soldiers could enter the bank. It was a credible charge, considering the corruption that plagued all aspects of Iraqi life. Others in the crowd insisted that the bank guards had fired on them, yet no injuries were reported. The reports of gunfire were eventually discounted.

It took only a couple of minutes before U.S. and Iraqi reinforcements started to arrive. Eventually, a patrol from the 1st Squadron, 2nd Armored Cavalry Regiment (using the handle "Dogtroop"), showed up, escorting several American civil affairs officers and interpreters. Lieutenant Flack, a diligent student of the Iraqi culture who had also earned a reputation both for his rapport with Iraqis and for aggressiveness, watched as this tiny group calmly waded into the crowd and headed toward the bank. He was surprised by their bravado in the face of so much anger, and he feared that they underestimated the danger.

The civil affairs officers spent a few minutes inside the bank before emerging to address the crowd. Major Gafrey, the senior civil affairs officer present, took the lead, allowing time for the interpreters to pass his message onto the agitated throng of Iraqis. Because the bank was only open daily from 8:00 to 12:00, Gafrey explained, they should go home and return tomorrow. An American patrol, he continued, would escort an Iraqi civil defense corps official to the bank to supervise the bank officials as they paid the soldiers. Many Iraqis then pressed forward to make their case to the civil affairs officers, but the crowd gradually dissipated as most of the protesters became resigned to their fate.

It took a long time for the remnants of the crowd to melt back into the streets of Baghdad. Even after most of the crowd departed, a line of disgruntled ex-soldiers queued up in front of Lieutenant Flack, all insisting on telling him their story before they returned to their homes empty-handed. Just the act of complaining to someone in an official capacity seemed to satisfy most of them.

Before it was all over, four more teams from the 233rd had arrived on the scene, plus approximately fifty IPs, twenty bank guards, and an infantry patrol. But Lieutenant Flack's patrol was among the first on the scene and was the last to depart. When the last of the protesters finally left, his patrol headed back to the relative security of the Green Zone, dropping off the IPs en route. By 1344 hours, the Crusaders were back at Viper Base. The Hogs had beaten them in by half an hour.[16]

The Afternoon Missions

By that time, the afternoon patrols were already deep into Baghdad. One patrol consisted of nothing more than a Humvee accompanying the battalion's mail run to BIAP. There were also two mobile patrols, one each from the 1st and 2nd Platoons. Their missions mirrored those performed by the Hogs and Crusaders: check on the police stations, and otherwise conduct random patrols of their assigned neighborhoods. They were also tasked to check on the World Food Programme, a UN-sponsored humanitarian organization.

Lieutenant Ferris commanded the 1st Platoon patrol. With him were Staff Sergeant Jimmie Mayes and four other soldiers, including Sergeant Shauna Cashion, a petite blue-eyed blonde who was one of four women assigned to the 1st Platoon "Reapers." She served both as a team leader and as driver that day. As they drove through the crowded neighborhoods, she kept her focus on the streets and the crowds, letting Specialist Christopher Ater, who manned the turret machine gun, take in the larger vista. Female soldiers were still a curiosity for Iraqis, especially the men, who were not used to encountering young women in a man's world, particularly ones who were both assertive and attractive. Cashion tried to be as inconspicuous as possible while on patrol, hiding her hair beneath her Kevlar helmet, but her feminine features often gave her away.

The Workday at Viper Base

By the time the Reaper and Punisher patrols were driving through the heart of Baghdad, the soldiers from the morning patrols were busy going through their recovery procedures. Drivers and gunners wasted little time attending to their equipment. They cleaned out the vehicles and refueled them before performing the daily maintenance checks. The patrol leaders, meanwhile, made their way to the TOC to begin the required paperwork. Lieutenant Flack, as the first officer to arrive at the bank, had the unenviable duty of writing the incident report for that event. There were also logs to complete, charts to update, and, for the leadership, the inevitable meetings to attend. But to the chagrin of many soldiers, the unit was also expected to meet the same training requirements as if they were back home.

Back in October, the MPs spent several days in riot control training, having been selected by battalion for this dangerous duty. Royer and Elmore made sure they took the training seriously, but they were thankful that they were never called on to perform this dangerous mission.[17] Rifle marksmanship was one of the most important training task the MPs were required to complete each year. The company conducted their marksmanship training at a range southwest of Baghdad, qualifying on both the M-16 rifle and the 9-millimeter pistol.

By far the year's most dreaded training event was the annual physical training (PT) test, followed by the weigh-in. The standards for each were reasonable, but more than a few MPs struggled with one or the other, or both. Many derisively pointed out that failing either the PT test or weigh-in could get you booted out of the Army during peacetime, but the Army ignored that rule once they were mobilized. But Royer and Elmore reasoned there would never be a better time to give their soldiers a PT test, precisely because the harsh conditions and rigorous schedule had hardened them. More to the point, most had lost considerable weight—as much as thirty pounds for some. And since the test was required both by regulation and by an edict from higher headquarters, it made sense to do it during the winter months when the temperatures were moderate. So by late November, each MP pursued his or her own exercise regimen, many preparing themselves by cranking out push-ups and sit-ups, then running along a road outside the back gate of Viper Base that paralleled the Tigris River.

Night Patrols

Just as the morning and afternoon patrols overlapped, so too did the afternoon and evening patrols. By 1800, elements of the 3rd and 4th Platoons were now coursing their way through eastern Baghdad. Staff Sergeant Jeremiah Fritzsche led the Hogs that night, departing Viper Base with three Humvees and nine personnel. The lead Humvee, bumper number X-ray 24, carried Fritzsche, Sergeant Jason Haworth as the driver, and Specialist Lucas Jockisch in the gunner's hatch. The Hogs drove in a random pattern through congested neighborhoods on the east side of the Tigris, stopping only once to check on several Iraqis struggling with a crane that they had loaded onto the back of a battered blue pickup. Fritzsche's crew soon pulled up for chow at Provider, another of the dining facilities run by Kellogg, Brown, and Root, this one located on a small American compound adjacent to the Olympic stadium. Provider was their favorite spot to grab chow, so the Hogs weren't surprised when several Crusaders led by Sergeant Jamie Kollins, also walked into the crowded dining facility. It didn't look like much, consisting of nothing more than a set of semi trailers linked together, but the folks at Provider served some of the best American chow in Baghdad. They featured a full menu, including a short-order line, a salad bar, and a buffet-style table of hot food. Several TVs hung from the ceiling, tuned to CNN and Fox News. Specialist Lucas Jockisch, a husky young college student before the war, headed for the salad bar. Like many others, he had already lost 25 pounds since arriving in Iraq.

Within 45 minutes, the Hogs were back on the streets and headed for Tombstone. They arrived there in good time, with Fritzsche planning to stay just long enough to make a quick count of the IPs on duty and the detainees in the holding cell. But as he linked up with his interpreter, Colonel Glaser also pulled up to the station. His tour of Baghdad had started shortly after lunch, accompanied by Sergeant First Class Ryan Machin, the Provider's seasoned platoon sergeant. For Glaser, making the rounds through the battalion area was the best way to measure the pulse of his command. He had no intention of interfering when things were running smoothly.

Fifteen minutes after they arrived at Tombstone, the Hogs were once again on the road, now accompanied by a team of IPs who followed them in the IPs' favorite mode of transportation, a white Nissan pickup with blue doors. It was dark by the time they left the station, but between the streetlights, a crescent moon, and clear skies, there was plenty of illumination. After conducting scores of patrols through Baghdad, every member of the patrol knew what was expected of them. Teamwork was the key, and the Hogs had the drill down pat.[18]

The neighborhoods were busy with traffic and pedestrians that evening, many in a festive mood because of the Ramadan season. The architecture the Hogs drove by was the type seen throughout residential Baghdad: one- or two-story brick or cement-block houses, shops, and office buildings. Their flat roofs doubled as verandas on these cool evenings, a place to find some relief from the heat of the day. And typical of the region's structures, most of the roofs were rimmed by a short retaining wall, providing a perfect hiding place for anyone who wanted to take potshots at the passing convoys. Still, Specialist Jockisch liked the night patrols. Not only was it much cooler, but the darkness made it easier to spot a muzzle flash if someone took a shot at the convoy—not that this was common. In fact, by November, the night patrols tended to be pretty quiet. If they did hear gunfire, it was invariably of the celebratory variety, usually some exuberant Iraqis celebrating a wedding. The possibility of sporadic gunfire kept them all on edge, but what the MPs dreaded most were the roadside bombs, and "IED time" usually occurred after the early morning prayers, and rarely were planted in the neighborhoods. The insurgents preferred to hide them on entrance ramps and other high-traffic areas.

The Hogs had patrolled for forty minutes when they pulled to a halt at a nondescript street corner and dismounted. Part of their daily routine was to set up traffic control points (TCPs) at road intersections, where they would stop all traffic and search both passengers and vehicles for hidden weapons, excessive cash, or anything out of the ordinary. Fritzsche positioned his three Humvees on three corners of the intersection while the IPs parked on the remaining corner. From there, Specialist Steve Keith, from his gunner's position, kept a close eye on the action in the street, as well as the rooftops that encircled him. He remained vigilant despite the fact he'd never taken fire during a TCP. It was yet another example where the news reports back home conflicted with the reality of life in Baghdad.[19]

Fritzsche, accompanying a couple of IPs, walked into the middle of the street and waved down a passing car. For the citizens of Baghdad, TCPs had become part of the tolerated routine, and they submitted to the searches passively. Those who spoke English usually had a few friendly words for the MPs, who otherwise ignored them as they went about their duties. Once a car pulled to a stop, the passengers were waved out of the vehicle, then told to open both hoods. The Hogs were thorough in their searches, rummaging through bags of groceries and merchandise, lifting papers and bundles of clothing, and peering under seats as they inspected the interior. Meanwhile, the passengers were patted down, even while they watched the MPs work methodically through their vehicles. Sergeant Dana Hodges, as the patrol's lone female soldier, got the job of searching the women that evening. Her mere presence made quite a statement in a society where women were taught to keep a low profile. But Hodges was nothing if not confident as she systematically conducted the pat downs.

One hour and five vehicle searches later, the patrol remounted. Their searches had turned up nothing, just the way the MPs liked it. They soon were heading back to Tombstone, although they made one last diversion to check on the World Food Programme building. After dropping off their interpreter and the IPs, they sped toward Viper Base.[20]

Sergeant Jamie Kollins, one of the unit's many Springfield cops, commanded the 4th Platoon "Crusaders" that night and was accompanied by the 519th Battalion operations officer, Major Zane Jones. Jones, confident in Kollins's ability to lead his patrol, pulled his Humvee in behind Kollins's, content to let the sergeant take the lead. Kollins's patrol mirrored that of the Hogs, except that the Hogs picked up no IPs when checking in at Grayskull. After chow at Provider, where they also encountered Colonel Glaser, they roamed the streets of Baghdad for three hours, making six stops during the course of the night. Those stops included the Rasheed bank, site of the day's demonstration, plus the Iraqi Ministry of Culture, the UN building, and a check at the Olympic stadium, where they discovered several Iraqis burning brush. At 2130 hours, they heard two explosions and spent the next half-hour trying to track down the source. They hit all the usual locations. They drove by the Martyr's Monument, the Ministry of Oil building, the UN compound, and both Grayskull and Tombstone. All was quiet. All patrols were required to return to Viper Base not later than 2200 hours. They missed that time by four minutes. When they arrived, they found the Hogs already well into their postpatrol routine. The entire unit was now secure behind the gates of the compound.[21]

TOC Operations

By that time, the TOC night shift had already been on duty for several hours, once again prepping for future missions. One mission seemed especially promising. Higher headquarters was planning a raid on the house of a former Ba'ath Party member. The IPs had been performing surveillance on his residence for several days, and they had observed a parade of suspicious characters coming and going from the house, most of whom were well armed. The IPs suspected they were Syrians, but as yet, there was no date planned for the raid.

Woods's team was also anticipating the arrival of the Comics on Duty World Tour, a group headlined by Drew Carey and including costars Ryan Stiles and Kathy Kinney, better known as Mimi on Carey's show. The comics were scheduled to perform the next day in the Green Zone's convention center, and Captain Royer hoped to send as many of his troops as possible.[22]

End of a Day

As the clock tolled midnight in the 233rd TOC, one day ended and another one began. Item 131 for the 22nd read, "Log Closes." On the next line, Specialist Waters scribbled "Log Opens."

November 22 was part of a seamless blur, one of 369 days in Iraq for the men and women of the 233rd MP Company. It was a good day, but not an atypical one. They conducted no raids; they took no fire and returned no fire. They had arrested two Iraqis, both for possession of illegal weapons, but otherwise, the streets of Baghdad were quiet. The incident at the Rasheed bank provided some excitement for the day, but nothing serious. Most importantly, the unit had survived another day with no casualties, and they were one day closer to home.

12
Down Time

We MPs love our family and friends back home and miss you. . . . Unlike a postcard from a wonderful vacation, you will probably not see written ANY-WHERE—*Wish you were here*. But, if you're curious, here is a way you too can feel like you're an MP in Baghdad . . .

You will need:

Two friends and about 14 hours

A 12+ year old vehicle with over 100,000 miles, with sunroof

GPS/Map

Handheld radios for you and your friends

Tool belt with D cell Mag-lite

Weighted vest—45 lbs

4 ft metal pipe—9 lbs

Helmet—or large metal pot

Boots and long sleeve shirt, long pants of neutral color, brown t-shirt

Goggles or sunglasses

Cooler with ice

Bottled water—I recommend five 1.5 liter bottles per person

Now . . . Choose the hottest day of the year with no cloud cover.

Get dressed in your above mentioned clothing to include tool belt with Mag-lite worn on your hip (i.e. 9 millimeter pistol), your helmet, goggles, and weighted vest (i.e. flack vest and LBV). You will be wearing this gear until you return from your mission. Sleeves must stay down, helmets on . . . no questions . . . do it . . . hooah. (Remember that phrase and use it throughout the day, just because you can.)

So started a tongue-in-cheek portrait of life in Baghdad as written by Staff Sergeant Lisa Morrison. It was her way to cope with duty in Baghdad—a painless diversion to fill her limited down time. When First Sergeant Elmore got wind of her missive, he forwarded it to the Family Readiness Group (FRG) for general consumption.[1]

Off-Duty Distractions

Those on the TOC night shift were the first MPs each day to get some free time—what little they had of it. After being relieved at 0700 hours, Master Sergeant Woods typically headed for breakfast at the compound's dining facility, now run by civilian contractors employed by Kellogg, Brown, and Root, a subsidiary of Halliburton. After breakfast, Woods often hit the unit's well-equipped weight room, and he sometimes followed this with a scenic run on a road that hugged the Tigris River's shoreline. The Karada District was clearly visible on the opposite shore of the Tigris, and the runners presented a tempting target to any would-be terrorist. Woods scouted for places to dive for cover as he ran. It paid to be cautious, even if no one had ever taken a potshot at those who ran along the riverfront.

Woods, who enjoyed lighting up an occasional cigar after his workout, replenished his supply from one of the many Iraqi shops that ringed the outskirts of the Green Zone. He liked bartering with the enterprising shopkeepers, who conducted a brisk trade in a diverse inventory of goods, from Coca-Cola (with Arabic lettering) to wet wipes, cigars, T-shirts, cameras, and electronic goods—basically anything the Americans needed. By 11:30 A.M., Woods was headed for bed. Since he shared a room with Sergeant First Class Jim Hobbs, who worked the day shift in the TOC, he could usually count on a good six to seven hours of uninterrupted sleep.

Getting enough sleep was a dicier proposition for Sergeant Higginson. He shared a room with several others, a room that saw a lot of commotion during the day. In the days before air conditioning, Higginson would collapse on his bunk at day's end, only to wake up a couple hours later in a pool of sweat. Not until he downed a bottle of water and patted himself dry could he drift back to sleep. By November, the conditions for Higginson and his roommates had improved considerably. Although the roar of a generator constantly serenaded them, they relished their air-conditioned quarters.

By the time the night shift had bedded down, the morning patrols began returning to Viper Base. Specialist Laura Thomason was one of those, back from her duties on Captain Royer's escort team. She made a beeline to her barracks, a room she shared with eleven others, six men and five other women. Cots were arrayed against two of the room's walls, the men on one side, and women on the other. Three cots turned lengthwise ran down the center. Thomason's cot was in the middle. Her space was affectionately christened the "laundry basket," the place where much of the squad's paraphernalia invariably ended up. Not just clothing found its way there; footballs and baseballs were common discoveries, and on at least one occasion, Thomason found pellets embedded in her personal belongings, the remnants of pellet gun wars waged between the guys in the room.

One of the pellet gun warriors was Specialist Abraham Bain, who, after his hitch in Baghdad, planned to return to Southern Illinois University and work on a degree in industrial design. Ever since joining the National Guard in 1998, Bain found his schooling repeatedly interrupted by military service. Baghdad, he resolved, would be the last military diversion of his life. For now, he found artwork to be a pleasant diversion from the war. The wall behind his bunk was plastered with his art, mostly drawings of Warner Brothers' Loony Toon characters, including Tweety Bird and Sylvester, Bugs Bunny, Daffy, and Pepe Le Pew. He drew directly on the plaster wall with pencil, black magic marker, and Crayola crayons. He was soon commissioned to do a mural for the operations sections' TV room, then a wall mural for the 4th Platoon. From there, the demands on his time and talent steadily increased. He painted a road sign pointing toward "Saddam's International House of Cheese," otherwise known as the 32nd MP Company, their sister unit from Wisconsin. Next to the squad automatic weapon (SAW) machine gun position near the compound's back gate stood Elmer Fudd in DCUs, with his arm extended and bearing an MP's brassard. The sign next to Elmer proclaimed, "You must be this tall to ride this ride." Sergeant Kollins referred to Bain's artistry as the "Keep Bain Sane Campaign," and it was true. The artwork was his release from the strains of life in Baghdad.

Bain spent his time on duty as a gunner on Captain Royer's escort team. When the sun scorched his nose red on one patrol, Royer issued stern instructions for Bain to report to the medic. That order gave rise to Bain's most famous stunt. The next day, he slathered his nose with the sunblock he received from the medic, then prepared a sign to complete his new look. During the next day's patrol, Bain grabbed his homemade sign and held it out next to the cupola whenever the patrol halted outside a police station. "Lifeguard on duty," the sign stated, held by a stoic Bain, complete with Kevlar helmet, sunglasses, and a bright white nose. His buddies reveled in the gag, and cavalry troops who passed the scene cheered. Iraqi passers-by, however, were usually perplexed by the spectacle, and Bain's attempts to explain the sight gag were in vain. Captain Royer merely shook his head and rolled his eyes whenever he reemerged from a station.[2]

The unit's co-ed living conditions surprised many visitors to Viper Base, especially those more accustomed to the all-male units. Visitors were often curious about whether fraternization was a problem, something that was strictly prohibited. For the MPs, who had adjusted to their co-ed accommodations with minimal fuss or friction, such questions got tiresome. As far as Thomason was concerned, the men who shared her room were "like my brothers." They spent all day with each other and inevitably got on each other's nerves, but living with the guys also helped keep things fun, especially when some of her female roommates got moody. Thomason shared the viewpoint of most of the women in the company. They insisted on being treated like soldiers, not women. And for the most part, the men obliged, discreetly turning their heads whenever the women had to change their clothes, for example. "After a while, it was really no big deal," Thomason said. Of course, makeshift curtains—sometimes nothing more than towels on a clothesline—helped create the illusion of privacy.[3]

It wasn't that the MPs were saints, but their schedule left them little time or energy for relationships. Captain Royer and the unit's leadership kept a close eye on any budding romances and stepped in whenever they saw a problem brewing. The ultimate taboo was a relationship between a supervisor and subordinate. More importantly, the soldiers knew that relationships between unit members were discouraged and understood that such relationships could lead to serious morale problems. Discretion and professionalism were crucial.

A Baghdad Romance

The 233rd did have one romance that, discreet though they tried to be, became a favorite topic of gossip and speculation throughout the unit. It involved Specialists Jacob English and Sarah Schmidt, both members of Captain Royer's escort team. Sarah noticed Jacob at her first drill back in Springfield. He was helping to process newly enlisted soldiers into the unit that day as Private Schmidt and several other recruits stood in front of a table awaiting instructions. A noncommissioned officer handed Sarah and the other recruits a form, then gave instructions in such rapid-fire succession that everyone was baffled, including Sarah and her high school buddy, Jennifer Weiss. Sarah's face revealed her confusion and a bit of apprehension—an expression that Jacob English spotted. "Can you help me?" she asked him shyly, and he obliged, tossing off a quick joke that put her at ease without making her feel stupid. It was hard not to notice Sarah, with her bubbly personality and girl-next-door appeal. She looked more like Reese Witherspoon in DCUs than a no-nonsense MP. She was blessed with naturally blonde hair, ruddy cheeks, and bright blue eyes that sparkled when she smiled. She had the kind of looks and personality that had inspired a lot of guys to hit on her over the years. That, plus a bit of youthful naiveté, helped explain her reserve when she first met people, especially soldiers from other units. Sarah had heard her share of pick-up lines.

But Jacob made a stronger impression on Sarah that first meeting than the other way around. As she and Jennifer walked away from the table, Jennifer turned to her friend and said, "Oh my gosh, he is so your type!" And he was, for Sarah was already smitten. Jacob English was solidly built—muscular, definitely not fat, with a well-sculptured face and dark hair. He conducted himself professionally, yet was also friendly and approachable. And most importantly, he made Sarah laugh. From then on, every time Sarah came to drill, she kept her eye out for Specialist English, but always from a distance. She soon shipped out for several months of basic training and advanced individual training.

Sarah returned to the unit only months before their mobilization, a time when Jacob's attention was focused on that. He was an easygoing guy, someone who knew how to relax and have a good time when not in uniform, much more of a "Jake" than a "Jacob." But when he was on duty, he strove to be the best MP possible. Like most military policemen, he was a "hoo-ah" kind of soldier, the type who took pride in how he looked and in doing things right. As a third-generation GI, the last thing Jake wanted was to let his family down. He often thought of his grandfather, an Iwo Jima veteran, and his father and four uncles, all Vietnam veterans. Whenever the family visited their cabin, located on a point jutting into Lake Jacksonville, Jake admired a wooden post painted red, white, and blue, with planks attached to honor each veteran in the family. At the pinnacle was one for his grandfather, Don English, with the tip pointing toward Iwo Jima, where he piloted a landing craft onto the beach. Below his plank were ones for his father and uncles. Uncle Bruce and Aunt Marcelle were both career Navy and nearing retirement, and each had a plank. Jake wanted his name added to that post. He could only imagine the reaction his father and uncles would have if they discovered he was dating a soldier from his own unit—something they would surely frown on. Jake kept his distance from Sarah, determined that theirs would be strictly a professional relationship.

Jake even managed to keep things professional when he served as the First Sergeant's driver on the trip up to Fort McCoy, with Sarah as a passenger. Only once did the two strike up a conversation, and that was at a gas station when Top stepped out to check on the rest of the convoy. It was nothing more than a polite chat, something to fill the silence. Sarah was especially struck by one comment Jake made: he mentioned that he had a young daughter. She took it as a signal that he was not interested in a relationship.

Once at McCoy, Jake focused on training. Sarah nevertheless kept an eye out for him and invariably felt a twinge of excitement whenever he walked by. Only once did they really talk during the two months in Wisconsin: on the day the unit loaded their duffel bags for Iraq. It was a little after 4:00 A.M. when Jake spotted Sarah sitting alone on the barracks stoop with her head buried in her hands. He was surprised to find her alone—she was rarely alone. He, in contrast, liked to keep to himself at breakfast, the one time each day he preferred some private time. But after seeing Sarah down, he acted on impulse. He walked up, asked if she was worried, and invited her to breakfast.

The two shared few words as they ate their breakfasts, sharing a table in the busy mess hall. When Jake asked her a question, she answered quietly, fearing that the quiver in her voice would reveal her nervousness. She was anxious about loading up for war and apprehensive about how she would perform in Iraq, but most of all, she was nervous about being with Jake. Was he interested, she wondered, or just being nice? After breakfast, they went their separate ways.

After arriving in Kuwait, their paths crossed more frequently, especially because both were assigned to the headquarters operations section. Most of the MPs shared a tent at Camp Virginia, with the cots arranged by section, men and women intermixed. Sarah couldn't help but notice that Jake often joked around with her friends, Specialists Laura Thomason and Nicole Hammack, but never with her. Even so, whenever "he would be by my bunk, . . . my heart was just pounding," she later recalled. Once, when she walked in on her girlfriends recounting a conversation they just had with Jake and several other men, Sarah quickly zeroed in. The boys had just discussed who they thought were the prettiest girls in the 233rd, the other women told Sarah. What about Specialist English, she asked persistently. "Who all is on the list? . . . What did he say?" "Why do you care so much?" they replied. "Because I have a crush on English," she heard herself say. "Oh my God," they squealed with delight. From that moment on, they were Sarah's most trusted confidants.

Only once in Kuwait did Sarah and Jake have any private time together. That happened as Sarah was hand-scrubbing her laundry in a large tub outside the tent. When Jake came out to retrieve his own laundry from the tent lines, he tossed a throwaway line her direction. "What are you doing?" he asked. Sarah chuckled to herself at such an inane comment. "I'll never take doing laundry for granted again," she replied. For the next couple of minutes, they had their first real conversation. She told him about her grandmother, who often scolded her for throwing clothes in the wash pile when they weren't really dirty. "I'll see you later," Jake said in a nonchalant tone after he finished gathering up his clothes. With that, he headed back to the tent and thought little about the incident. For Sarah, however, it was a breakthrough. At last she had a real conversation with Jake.[4]

Once in Baghdad, the relationship blossomed, in no small part because Jacob and Sarah ended up bunking next to each other at Viper Base. They shared their barracks room (a large room above the unit's TOC and battalion chapel) with ten other operations personnel. "Oh, great, I've got to sleep next to you for the next six months," Jake said sarcastically when he discovered the sleeping arrangements. Sarah laughed, and for Jake, the ice was broken. For the next year, they went on patrols together, ate together, and slept in the same room together, along with ten other soldiers. They were hardly ever apart, and even more rarely were they alone together, privacy being the scarcest commodity at Viper Base.

Sarah started her tour in Baghdad as the radio operator on the TOC day shift. That's where she worked on the day the 233rd pulled security for the first meeting of the interim Iraqi government, monitoring the unit's command frequency and maintaining the radio log. When she recognized Jake's voice coming through the speaker, she once again felt her face flush and her heart pound faster, even as she struggled to concentrate on his message. A few days later, she was reassigned to the commander's escort team as the driver for the second Humvee. Because Jake served as the gunner in Royer's Humvee, from that time on, they were rarely apart.

The relationship finally blossomed about three weeks later. Captain Royer's escorts were gathered around their Humvees one afternoon while waiting for their boss to take care of business at a Baghdad police station. Jake grabbed a water bottle and tilted it up for a swig. As he swallowed, he caught Sarah watching him intently. "Are you staring at my lips?" he kidded as he lowered the bottle. "I'm just seeing if you're going to backwash," she replied. "I'm going to take a drink after you." "Whatever," he responded, and with that, he handed her the bottle. That night, Jake caught up with Sarah in the section's tiny foyer area adjacent to their TV room and sleeping quarters. He struck up a conversation, casually tossing her a soccer ball as they talked. Then he abruptly changed the topic and threw out a comment about kissing, intimating that he wanted to kiss her right there. The comment threw her off-balance. Where did this come from?

Later that same night, with the lights off and their squadmates fast asleep, Sarah heard Jake, in the adjacent bunk, trying to discreetly catch her attention. "What!" she whispered back. "Do you want to write notes?"

With that, they began scribbling messages with the aid of a flashlight, then passed the scraps of paper back and forth like two high school kids. After a few rounds of this, Jake scribbled down "thanks for blowing me off earlier," an obvious reference to their encounter in the foyer. Sarah's brain went several directions at once. Did he really like her? Did he want a meaningful relationship? Was he just looking for a Baghdad fling? She was interested, but she wanted no part of a temporary affair. Her emotions ruled the day, however, and with that, she leaned toward him and whispered, "Do you need a smoke?" That phrase was the universally understood code for going to the roof. With that, they headed to the stairway, first Jake, and Sarah a couple of minutes later. The two shared their first kiss, and they also resolved to keep their relationship as discreet as possible.

As the relationship developed, they worked hard to keep it under wraps, whispering in the darkness, passing notes to each other in the middle of the night, stealing private moments in the middle of the day. Laura Thomason was the first to notice the change in the two, picking up on their body language and on the way they gazed at each other. "What is going on?" she challenged Jake and Sarah when she finally cornered the two alone. They admitted nothing at the time, but Sarah confessed later that night, feeling better when she no longer had to pretend around her friend. And because Laura knew, that meant Sarah also had to tell Nicole Hammack, the other person in the company to whom she confided everything.

Jake and Sarah's relationship was anything but conventional. They never had a date—not in any normal sense of the word—and there were very few moments they shared with just each other. The roof was usually the best place to meet, but it was also a popular refuge for others seeking a cool evening breeze and a peaceful retreat from life on the compound. Some time in June, during a rare moment when they were alone together, Sarah suddenly shifted the conversation from the events of the day to something she'd been brooding over for some time. "What are we doing?" she asked bluntly. "Is this going anywhere?" Taken aback, Jake found himself struggling to find the right thing to say. "I'm more than happy to be involved," he heard himself say lamely. The conversation then shifted to how they should manage their relationship under such restrictive circumstances. On one issue especially, Sarah agreed with Jake. "We're never going to let this interfere with our duties," he stated emphatically.[5]

A couple of weeks later, Jake made a statement that once again caught Sarah by surprise. He didn't want to have any more children, he said. His daughter was enough, he continued, and furthermore, he did not intend to marry again. Sarah definitely wanted both of those things, and she told him as much. What she did not say was that she wanted those things with him.

Her old doubts now came rushing back. What did he expect out of their relationship? Should she call it quits? She decided not to, once again letting her heart rule the day.

Jake and Sarah's romance didn't stay secret for long. It didn't help that Sarah hid her emotions so poorly whenever the two quarreled. Like any small community, everyone knew everything about everybody at Viper Base. Jake and Sarah often found themselves arguing over the small things—not surprising given the amount of time they spent together and the stress they both coped with. And the intense heat could make anyone irritable. Sarah commiserated with Laura and Nicole during the relationship's rough spots. For Jake's part, he sorted things out with Sergeant Matt Harris and Specialist Adam Moma.

There was one issue Jake and Sarah discussed a lot but never argued over. Jake was reluctant to tell his family about Sarah. "It was very hard for me to say, hey, I've got a girlfriend over here," he later explained. He kept imagining the reaction from his dad and uncles if they discovered he had time in a war zone for romance, and often revealed his apprehension to Sarah. Finally, he mustered up enough courage to tell his sister. He left it to her to tell the rest of the family.

When they went on patrol, Jake worked hard to concentrate on the mission. The lives of the six people depended on him staying alert as he sat behind the lead Humvee's SAW. It was much the same for Sarah. As a driver, speeding through the streets and alleys of Baghdad was hardly the time to lose concentration. On occasions when the convoy parked inside a police station compound, the whole escort detail could relax while Captain Royer went about his duties. Because everyone in the escort detail knew about their romance, Jake and Sarah dropped any pretense. Still, the group downplayed the relationship. They shot the bull just like every other tightly knit team in combat. It was in this environment, in fact, that Jake started smoking again. In Baghdad, just about everyone smoked. Even Sarah eventually succumbed.

There was one feature of their relationship that Jake especially struggled with. Wherever they went, Sarah drew a lot of attention. Trips to the dining facility at Mule Skinner were the worst for him. The KBR mess hall was often packed with several hundred loud and rowdy soldiers. After the two grabbed chow, Jacob usually walked behind Sarah as they maneuvered through the mess hall tables in search of a place to sit. It was the perfect vantage point to see GIs give Sarah the once-over as she walked by, and to hear the occasional wolf whistle or off-color comment. All that attention was the inevitable consequence of being a woman in an environment with an overabundance of testosterone, but Jake found it hard to deal with nonetheless. On one memorable occasion, the team was eating their lunch when a wiry young infantryman, caked with the dust of Baghdad and looking to be no more than eighteen years old, walked up to Sarah with his tray in hand and stared at her in wide-eyed amazement. The best he could muster was an awkward "how ya doing." Jake almost felt sorry for the kid.[6]

Free Time

Many MPs found an outlet in sports during their free time. Their options included lifting weights, running, or a pickup game of basketball. There was even a decent swimming pool located a couple of compounds over—one of the benefits of living where Saddam's old cronies once lived. Still others tried their hand at less rigorous sports. Sergeant Harris scrounged up some golf clubs and managed to get in some practice with his sand wedge, occasionally launching a ball into the Tigris.

For those looking for less strenuous activities, the Armed Forces Network provided a decent selection of television channels and radio stations. And there was no shortage of TVs, DVD and CD players, and other electronic devices, often purchased from the local economy. Several MPs assembled a sizable DVD and CD library, covering pretty much the entire range of genres.

But the troops were most passionate about keeping in touch with their loved ones back home. Everyone looked forward to receiving mail—not just letters from their loved ones, but also the birthday cards and bundles of letters that arrived from schoolkids and church groups, compliments of Judy Victor and other members of the FRG. By August, the Internet café became the MPs' favorite off-time destination. Once online, barring occasional frustrations with connections, they could e-mail family and friends, play chess or card games, check on the news from home, and shop. The troops became prodigious Internet shoppers and made good use of the military's mail system to have merchandise shipped overseas. Web sites like Rangerjoes.com, Amazon.com, eBay, and Wal-Mart became unit favorites. Their purchases normally arrived in about ten days. Their hands-down favorite Web site, however, was Dialpad.com, which allowed the soldiers to talk directly with family and friends in the states for three cents a minute. Around the clock, the Internet café was one of the busiest places in the compound.[7]

Religion

On Saturday evening, November 22, First Sergeant Elmore grabbed his acoustic guitar and headed over to the unit's sparsely furnished chapel, picking up his son on the way. They found about twenty-five others already gathered for the battalion's weekly "Praise and Worship" service, a service where Command Sergeant Major Richard Schnitker, the battalion's senior noncommissioned officer and also a licensed minister, presided. Most of the attendees were 233rd soldiers. Back in Winchester, Top Elmore occasionally played his guitar in the Cornerstone Baptist Church. Now he headed a small ensemble that provided music for Schnitker's services, with son Robert joining in on a set of bongo drums. The group was christened "Beyond the Surface," so named to encourage their audience to value people for who they were, and not by how they appeared.

Captain Reck, the 519th's chaplain, held the week's main religious service on Sunday morning. He conducted a nondenominational service for the battalion's Protestants, downplaying his own Mormon faith during the traditional service. Schnitker's service was more contemporary, weaving in plenty of music and singing along with a solid gospel message. It generally drew a larger crowd. As for the unit's Catholics, the brigade chaplain made occasional trips to Viper Base to deliver services and the sacraments. Between the three services, no unit had more faithful attendees than the 233rd—not that most soldiers in the unit attended. Missions, after all, came first. Reck estimated that on average, twenty-five usually showed up for either his or Schnitker's service. There were plenty of foxhole Christians in the 519th—those who turned to God when things got tough—but most otherwise stayed away from services. Still, of all the units in the battalion, he could always count on the 233rd to turn out their share. He chalked up the unit's success and their lack of casualties to their good church attendance.

The highlight of the religious year for those at Viper Base was the day Specialist Ayrielle Singley, a 233rd mechanic, was baptized. She and Schnitker waded into the Tigris River, and he then spoke the ancient words of the baptismal ceremony before lowering her body into the Tigris. The symbolism of Singley's baptism in the waters of the Tigris in the heart of the old Babylonian empire escaped no one. Chaplain Reck was proud of Ayrielle and honored to be a part of it.[8]

Grousing

When the men and women of the 233rd exhausted other distractions, they found plenty to gossip about. Just as often, they launched into a litany of complaints, just like their grandfathers during World War II and Korea, and their fathers in Vietnam. It was their right as soldiers, and there was no shortage of material. They groused about petty annoyances, about lousy mail service and bland food, and very often about how the idiots at higher headquarters were so adept at fouling things up. The higher up the chain they worked, the more pointed their comments became. They complained about some of the regulars they worked with (although they held the folks in the 519th, especially Colonel Glaser, in high regard) and especially about the 1st Cavalry Division troops they frequently encountered. The Coalition Provisional Authority came in for special attention, especially Lieutenant General Sanchez, the author of that infamous letter. Occasionally, Secretary of Defense Rumsfeld and Deputy Secretary Wolfowitz also became targets. Ironically, the MPs had served as escorts for both during their visits to Baghdad.

But for the most part, the MPs' complaints were the natural consequence of doing a hard and dangerous job—a release for soldiers whose morale was otherwise high. Although they enjoyed venting about higher headquarters, they believed in what they were doing and were convinced that Iraq was better off without Saddam. More than anything, they were intensely proud of the 233rd. As far as they were concerned, it was the best unit in Baghdad, a sentiment often shared by their chain of command.

13

"The LT's Hit!"

For the soldiers of the 233rd, there was little about November 22 to distinguish it from any other day in Baghdad. November 23 proved to be different. On that day, a group of 1st Platoon "Reapers" became firefighters. It happened while a patrol led by Lieutenant Joel Ferris was taking the platoon's interpreter home for the evening, cruising through the al-Jadidah neighborhood, a predominantly working-class neighborhood midway between Tombstone and Grayskull. The patrol was driving along the main boulevard when the Reapers spotted an orange glow and smoke off to their left. Ferris immediately directed his driver to make a U-turn and head toward the action. The patrol soon pulled to a stop at an intersection. Down the street was a four-story apartment complex abutting the street with flames leaping from the front entrance. A crowd was gathering in the street. Some made vain attempts to fight the blaze, using cardboard scraps to toss dirt and sand onto the fire. Most were merely spectators. The MPs leapt into action, responding like the well-oiled machine they were. Ferris directed the patrol's two gunners, Specialist Zachary Smith and Private First Class Adam Pope, to seal off the area, positioning the Humvees to block the road. Smith was already ahead of the lieutenant. Once he determined their grid, he grabbed the radio handset to call in their discovery to Excalibur TOC, requesting help from the Iraqi Police Service and the fire department.

By that time, Staff Sergeants Roman Waldron and Robert Smith and Sergeant Eric Bertoni were emptying their fire extinguishers onto the blaze, a fire that now seemed to consume the entire front of the structure, its flames licking dangerously close to the adjoining buildings, which were separated only by a narrow alley. Ferris wasted no time in clearing the adjacent build-ings, kicking down doors when no one answered, flushing one family into the street. When Specialist Smith saw others in the crowd slipping in and out of the buildings to grab their belongings, he and Pope motioned them away from the structures.

After emptying their extinguishers, Waldron and Bertoni headed back to the Humvees while barking instructions to the crowd, their interpreter translating as best he could. They spotted several Iraqis pointing frantically toward the roof. "Baby, baby," one cried to Staff Sergeant Robert Smith, crossing his arms as if cradling an infant. At the same instant, Waldron looked up and caught a glimpse of two Iraqis waving wildly from the roof-top. He immediately headed down the alley with Sergeant Smith at his heels, both looking for some way to get to the roof. They found a stairway that was already beginning to fill with smoke, and without hesitation, they dove into the smoke and worked their way up the three flights as quickly as pos-sible, with Smith holding onto Waldron's gear to stay in contact. As they arrived at each landing in succession, they pounded on the door and called out to ensure no one was inside. Finally, they reached the roof.

Back in the street, Ferris and Bertoni, satisfied the adjacent buildings were cleared, also headed for the roof, plowing through the same smoky stairway discovered by Waldron. By the time they reached the terraced roof, Smith and Waldron had already corralled the young men they had spotted from the street and were preparing to head back down. There was only one way out, and that was back down the same stairway, now filled with a dense, dark smoke. Waldron motioned the Iraqis toward the stairs. "Oxygen, oxygen," one Iraqi screamed in panic. Waldron grabbed the Iraqi, pulled him tight to his body, and lurched down the stairwell. Bertoni latched onto the belt of the Iraqi Waldron was pulling along, with the other Iraqi following. Smith and Ferris brought up the rear. The human column raced down the stairwell, each man holding on tight to the man to his front. It was impossible to see and nearly impossible to breathe. Finally, they stumbled one by one into the alley, their faces blackened, coughing and gasping for air, calling out for water.

Ferris immediately took a head count after emerging from the conflagra-tion, even while Specialist Smith called in an "all clear" to Excalibur. By that time, Pope and Zach Smith had flagged down a passing water truck. Several Iraqis commandeered it and began hosing down the blaze. Moments later, Ferris and Bertoni forced their way into an adjacent building to make sure it was also empty. Waldron and Smith did the same for another house, bursting into a room to check for occupants, then retreating just long enough to catch their breath before moving to the next room. Meanwhile, Iraqis were dousing the front of the building. By the time the MPs completed their fourth trip, they were exhausted but satisfied that the building was empty.

The Iraqis had the blaze under control when a contingent of Iraqi police (IPs) arrived on the scene. (The fire department never did arrive.) Sergeant Waldron was ready for the IPs, having already conducted his own investigation into the cause of the fire. It was started, he concluded, by a faulty oil heater in the street-level apartment. Lieutenant Ferris and his interpreter did their best to comfort the building's owner, an older woman who was near shock from her misfortune. Feeling helpless, Ferris dug out a full case of MREs and several packets of powdered drink mix from the back of his Humvee and handed it over to the woman.

In total, the MPs helped save ten people that day, five adults and five children. Just as important, they were able to prevent the fire from spreading to nearby buildings. For their actions, Ferris, Bertoni, Waldron, and Robert Smith were submitted for Soldiers Medals. Specialist Zach Smith and Private First Class Pope, who alertly flagged down the passing water truck and kept headquarters informed, all the while struggling to contain the crowd, were put in for Army Commendation Medals. Their awards were disapproved by higher headquarters.[1]

The Adjutant General's Visit

Brigadier General Randall Thomas, Illinois' adjutant general and therefore the commander of the state's National Guard, finally gained approval to travel to Iraq with several other state adjutants general. Central Command was nervous every time a group of VIPs headed to Iraq, knowing full well the propaganda nightmare they would face if something happened to them while in theater. The group landed safely at Baghdad International Airport (BIAP) on December 11 for a carefully orchestrated three-day tour.

Word soon came down to the 233rd to send a contingent of soldiers to Camp Victory, located near BIAP, to meet with General Thomas. Sergeant First Class Jim Hobbs was chosen to take the 233rd contingent over to meet with the general, but given the unit's operations tempo, he struggled to find enough soldiers to accompany him. Thinking the general was on a fact-finding tour, he eventually picked maintenance and supply representatives as well as others he knew wouldn't be shy about voicing their concerns to the general. When they arrived at Camp Victory, they were surprised to discover General Thomas had made the trip without his normal entourage. The MPs and soldiers from other Illinois units met with the general in one of Saddam's former presidential palaces. They enjoyed their conversation, finding the general to be personable and engaging. Still, they were disappointed that no staff officers accompanied him, which gave them little chance to pass on their issues.

For his part, General Thomas thoroughly enjoyed his trip, relishing his chance to talk with his soldiers. The troops were positive and upbeat, and they looked great. When he asked about their issues and concerns, he got an earful. He left with an extensive list—promotions problems, equipment issues, pay snafus, and more. But more than anything, the troops wanted the folks back home to know that they were representing America well, and that they thought the real heroes were their families. They also wanted people back home to understand that things were going better than the news often suggested.

Once their visit was over, the MPs grabbed lunch at Camp Victory, then hustled back to Viper Base. Things were going crazy out in Baghdad. Saddam Hussein had just been captured in a spider hole near his hometown in Tikrit. As they drove past the gate to Camp Victory, they heard the distinctive sound of celebratory gunfire.[2]

A Rooftop Proposal

Captain Royer signed out of the company area on November 30, marking the beginning of his long-anticipated leave. But as much as he missed his wife and infant son, he hated leaving the company behind. His soldiers' safety and welfare were his responsibility. But there were also matters to attend to back in the States, and he was confident that Lieutenant Ferris could handle the command in his absence. Signing out on leave that same day were Specialist Nicole Hammack (Sarah Schmidt's confidant), Specialist Blake Mays, a gunner with the Crusaders, and Jake English, who was growing apprehensive about meeting his family now that they knew about his Baghdad romance.[3]

By this time, his relationship with Sarah had grown into a full-fledged romance. Months before, he took a big step and told Sarah he loved her. Her response that first time, and for every time thereafter, always included a question for Jake. "Forever?" she asked coyly, driving home her commitment to him. Jake had even asked Sarah to move in with him when they returned to the States. For Sarah, that was a very good sign, but the old doubts still lingered.

As Jake relished the comfort of his airline seat, he reflected on what he wanted to do when he got back home. He mentally added "buy a ring" to his list of things to do; he'd concluded that Sarah was the one for him—forever. And during his two weeks at home, the topic of Sarah and his intention to ask her to marry him came up repeatedly, especially with his family. He even revealed his plans to a group of grade-school kids during a visit to his cousin's fifth-grade classroom in Loami, a small town 6 miles west of Springfield. Leah Friedman, a reporter from the *Journal-Register*, was also there to write an article about Jake's visit. Because Jake knew that Sarah and everyone else in the 233rd read the paper online, he cornered Friedman after the presentation. "My brother was a reporter for two years," he told Friedman firmly. "I know how you guys work, and I need to know that that's not going in there!" She agreed, and his plans remained secret.

Ironically, it was Jake who could not keep a secret. He called Sarah the same day he bought her ring. "I got you a surprise," he revealed. "I hate surprises. Give me a hint," came the reply. "Well, it's round, and its permanent," he answered. Sarah knew what she wanted his surprise to be, but she had harbored too many doubts about Jake's intentions over the months. After the call, she went back to her quarters and found Moma and Harris, Jake's best friends in Baghdad, lounging on their cots. "What do you think it is, guys?" she asked. "Isn't it obvious?" they answered in unison. "Well, maybe it's a house key," she responded as the two rolled their eyes.

Jake returned to Baghdad on December 20, intent on popping the question on Christmas Day. That night, he sat in the TV room with his roommates, regaling them with colorful stories about his leave. But as the night drew on and with a hard day ahead of them, one by one they headed for bed. Even Sarah fell asleep after Jake left to take a shower. Jake, deciding that tonight was the night, headed to the roof. He spread out a blanket and lined it with flashlights to create atmosphere. Then he went downstairs and woke Sarah. "Come to the roof with me," he whispered softly. She roused herself and pulled on a sweatshirt, a gift from Jake that proved just the thing to ward off the night chill, then followed him to the roof. She was amazed by the scene that Jake had so carefully prepared for her—and by the things Jake now was saying to her, the kind of sentiments he never said. Then he dropped to one knee. "Will you marry me?" "Yes," she said emphatically. "Don't you want to see the ring?" "I don't care, I don't care," she replied immediately, overwhelmed by the moment. The two stared at the stars and talked late into the night, interrupted only occasionally by a Black Hawk helicopter streaking through the night sky.[4]

Christmas in Baghdad

"MERRY CHRISTMAS!!!" began Top Elmore in his holiday e-mail to the States. "Although we still had patrols going out, escort duties and base defense duties, many soldiers were able to participate" in the unit's holiday festivities, he told the unit's families and friends back home.

Back in March, when the 233rd was training at Fort McCoy, most of the MPs were confident they would be home long before Christmas. That illusion was destroyed by the Sanchez letter. But the MPs had accepted their fate long before the holidays rolled around, and they made the best of their Christmas in Iraq. Lieutenant Ferris led a handful of hearty souls on a Christmas "fun run." More people participated in a Christmas pageant, with Shannon Clark-son as the narrator and Cynthia Hilliard playing Mary, accompanied by a choir in the background. Bain, of course, was in charge of the scenery. There was also a flag-football tournament and a movie marathon for those not on duty, plus a bonfire on Christmas Eve. The dining facility served a traditional Christmas feast, and the compound was awash with cookies, hot chocolate, s'mores, and sodas. Colonel Glaser made an appearance on Christmas day dressed as Santa, but the highlight for many in the compound was when David Letterman showed up for autographs and pictures. Joshua Waters, on a lark, called in a spot report to the battalion, declaring that there was something or someone flying through the air, giving a grid coordinate to lend authenticity to his Santa Claus sighting. The night shift hooted it up when the battalion was slow to catch on. Even with all of this activity, however, spending Christmas in Baghdad so far from home was hard. Most of the MPs found their own private moments to open the presents and cards sent from home, and to place that all-important telephone call to the States.[5]

Chaplain Reck started his day by traveling to the Mother Teresa Orphan-age, where he linked up with three buses sent to pick up the 519th's guests for the day: the children from the orphanage plus all the neighborhood kids and their parents, 105 people in all. The party was the idea of several MPs from the 32nd MP Company, and they had spent weeks arranging for a lav-ish celebration at a convention center in the heart of the Green Zone. Santa Claus and several elves greeted the kids as they flowed into the building's conference room, a room dominated by a Christmas tree surrounded by presents and an abundance of stuffed animals. The room was decked out with festive decorations, and Christmas carols filled the air. The children gleefully made their way through a series of stations set up by the MPs, each featuring a different game or activity. All in all, the Christmas party was a wonderful success, and the MPs' efforts were rewarded on Reck's next visit to the orphanage. The nuns greeted him enthusiastically, thanking him for the day, telling him that many of the parents "couldn't believe how normal we were and how grateful they were for allowing them to be a part of the celebration." Their modest gesture of Christmas cheer had helped build a bridge across cultures.[6]

Lieutenant Rice

Staff Sergeant Fritzsche awoke on December 26 to a stabbing pain in his back. He'd suffered for several weeks already, but when the pain got progressively worse, he finally sought Specialist Jamie McCurry, one of the company's medics, for help. She gave him some Flexeril to ease the pain, but it had little effect. By the end of December, his back was so bad that he could barely walk without intense pain. As much as he had hoped to avoid it, he resigned himself to visit the troop medical clinic the next morning if the pain still persisted. But the TOC's mission list for December 27 showed him leading a morning patrol. He talked over his predicament with Lieutenant Rice. If the pain persisted, they decided, the lieutenant would go in his stead. It was really no big deal. Rice was planning to accompany one of the day's patrols anyway.

Lieutenant Stephen Rice was no different from the rest of his fellow lieutenants in the 233rd; he thrived on action. Trim and athletic, he was invariably intense and focused when on missions—a Gillette in the making, according to some of the 233rd's NCOs. Rice hailed from Alton, Illinois, a river town a few miles north of St. Louis. He earned his commission from Illinois State University in August 2002, branched with the military police, and was subsequently assigned to the 233rd.

As the 27th dawned, Fritzsche's back still throbbed. That clinched it. Lieutenant Rice would lead the day's patrol, which was scheduled to head east toward the New Baghdad police station, and from there through the neighborhoods on the east bank of the Tigris River. The Hogs' patrol that day consisted of three Humvees and nine personnel. With so many soldiers on leave, putting together enough people for the daily patrols was a struggle. Sergeant Hodges served as Rice's driver that day, while Sergeant Haworth filled in as their gunner. Sergeants Robert Spence and Dan Hinds commanded the other two Humvees. As the convoy cleared the front gate at 0720 hours, Lieutenant Rice contacted Excalibur TOC. Sergeant Hodges raised a silent prayer as she exited the gate, asking for a safe and calm day. The prayer was part of her daily ritual, one she especially observed when departing on morning patrols. It was, after all, IED time in Baghdad, the insurgents' favorite time to trigger attacks—the first couple of hours after morning prayers. As much as the MPs liked to vary their routine, and especially their routes, there were only a couple of bridges leading into the Green Zone.

The convoy was still working its way through the Green Zone when the TOC contacted Rice. A patrol of MPs had just been hit by an IED attack near a highway overpass. The TOC seemed confused about which MP unit was involved—the 143rd MP Detachment maybe, or perhaps the 32nd, but they included a grid along with instructions to rush to the area to help establish security and offer medical assistance to an injured MP. Within moments, the convoy crossed the 3rd Infantry Division bridge and sped through Baghdad's black market district on their way to the downed MPs.

It was 0733 hours when Rice brought the convoy to a halt on an entrance ramp to Highway 8. One hundred meters to their front was the injured American soldier, lying next to a disabled Humvee. What struck Rice most, however, was the eerie quiet. Normally, these kinds of incidents drew a crowd, especially during what passed for Baghdad's rush hour. To their rear was a gas station, with scores of cars lined up for gas. To their right, next to the interstate, was a large, open space filled with mounds of rubble and trash, the city's idea of garbage disposal. Within seconds of stopping, the entire team went into action. Rice contacted the TOC, reported their arrival, and requested a medevac. The Humvees formed a triangle, and the convoy's gunners immediately swung their weapons toward their respective sectors of fire. Simultaneously, Hinds, Hodges, and Specialist Ruyle were advancing in wedge formation toward the downed MP. With his report sent forward, Rice also dismounted and moved toward the disabled Humvee, with Sergeant Spence trailing him at a distance.

Rice was halfway there when an explosion ripped through the air. It was all too obvious what had happened. An insurgent had patiently waited for this moment before setting off the second IED. The MPs threw themselves to the ground, then scanned the area looking for the enemy. Hinds was hit in the left thigh, the force of the impact throwing him to the ground. "I'm hit by something!" he yelled to Ruyle, but seeing no blood, he lifted himself up, then heard gunfire as he moved out again. Sergeant Hodges felt a tiny fragment of shrapnel crease the back of her neck, but she was otherwise OK. She picked herself up and continued forward, making it to the injured MP just as she heard Stephanie Stretch, the lead vehicle's gunner, calling out behind her. "The LT's hit! The LT's hit!"[7]

Rice never had a chance to dive for cover. He heard a deafening explosion even as he was slammed to the ground. The blast had gone off to his right. Schrapnel ricocheted off a cement wall before striking his left side, ripping his M-16 from his grasp. His left leg immediately began to throb with pain. Rice instinctively brought his hand to his face and then pulled it away, recoiling from the sight of his own blood. He spotted his shattered rifle a few feet away and instinctively reached out for it until the pain caused him to draw back. Then he thought of his squad. Were any others hit? Were they all right? He prayed for their safety as he struggled to look around, realizing that they were in the middle of a kill zone. His ears rung from the force of

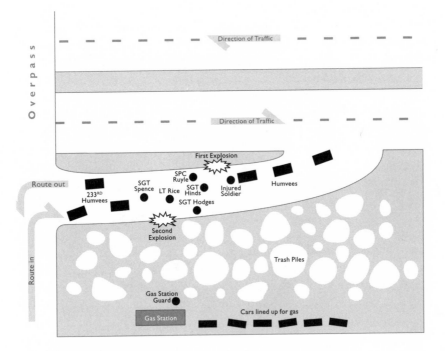

The LT Rice Incident

the blast as he struggled to make out voices. He thought he heard gunfire. "It . . . sounded like I was in some kind of a tunnel."

Sergeant Spence was the first to reach the lieutenant. He too was anxious to get the squad out of the kill zone, but his first concern was to see if the LT could be moved. Blood covered Rice's face from the lacerations, but it was immediately obvious that his lower left leg had gotten the worst of it. Even so, Spence decided he could be moved. He grabbed the back of Rice's web gear and dragged him toward the relative safety of their Humvee perimeter, where Specialist Herren was already calling for a medevac. Halfway there, Hodges reached the two and also grabbed hold. With Rice inside their make-shift perimeter, Hodges cut away the trouser leg and split open his boot, revealing the extent of Rice's injuries. What she discovered was bad, but not life-threatening. A piece of shrapnel had sliced into his boot, nearly severing his big toe. Another chunk of shrapnel tore clear through his ankle, shattering bone, muscle, and sinew as it passed through. Indeed, his entire left side was peppered with shrapnel, including one chunk embedded in his knee and another that had ripped into his quadriceps muscle. The right side of his face was also lacerated, but these were only superficial wounds. Finally, his flak vest had stopped another chunk of shrapnel, probably saving his life. Hodges cleaned around the wounds as best she could before applying bandages to his injuries, and then hooked up an IV. She knew there wasn't much she could do for him here. They had to get him to a hospital as soon as possible.

The medevac Lieutenant Rice had requested when he first arrived at the scene was still not airborne, and the prospects for one arriving soon did not look good, so Sergeant Spence made a key decision. He realized that the surrounding terrain offered few places for a helicopter to land, and with the 28th Combat Support Hospital (CSH) just a ten-minute drive away, he decided to drive the lieutenant in. That meant retracing their route, something they normally avoided, but time was of the essence, and getting to the Green Zone over another bridge probably meant a thirty-minute delay—a crucial thirty minutes. Even half-conscious, Rice knew that it was the right decision. Spence and Hodges lifted Rice into the back of the Humvee. Hodges jumped behind the wheel as Sergeant Haworth assumed his post in the vehicle's cupola. Rice remained conscious through it all, fighting to stay as alert as possible, despite the searing pain. As the Humvee lurched into gear, Haworth yelled down to the lieutenant, "Sir, just hold onto my leg—just hold onto my leg." Rice did as he was told as the convoy raced back toward the Green Zone.[8]

From Baghdad to Germany

The 28th CSH, the first destination for all Americans wounded in Baghdad, operated out of what was formerly Saddam's private hospital.[9] When the convoy arrived at the gate, an earnest young private, believing that casualties only arrived by air, barred their entrance. It took some firm persuasion from Spence before the gate guard waved them through. Once inside, they took Rice to the emergency room, where the hospital staff immediately went to work, removing his clothes and setting up another IV plus something for the pain that increasingly wracked his body. Rice retained consciousness, holding tightly onto the hand of Staff Sergeant Embry, a Special Forces medic assigned to the 32nd MP Company. "Everything looks good," Embry told Rice, keeping him updated on his condition, telling him that the blood supply looked good. Embry knew Rice well enough to give it to him straight, so he told Rice about his shattered ankle. "Man," Rice said, "just don't let them take my foot! Don't let them take my foot!"

He was still conscious when Sergeant Gillette stopped by with several Hogs in tow. The group included Sergeant Fritzsche, who was visibly disturbed to see Rice—the person who had gone on the patrol in his place—stretched out in front of him. "You're a mess," Fritzsche mumbled before telling the lieutenant that the troops wanted to see him. Rice protested, not wanting them to see him in his present state, but Fritzsche persevered, knowing the rest of the platoon would feel better when they saw that their lieutenant would make it. Fritzsche tipped a bottle of sterile water into a ball of gauze and began cleaning the blood and sweat from the lieutenant's face. Rice had had his differences with Fritzsche in the past, the inevitable tensions of combat, but in that moment he was overwhelmed by a powerful sense of camaraderie. Soon, several others from the 3rd Platoon began filtering by, one by one, to say good-bye. Specialist Stretch felt tears welling up in her eyes when her turn came. From her vantage point as the lead vehicle's gunner, it had been her fate to witness Rice hit by the blast. First Sergeant Elmore also stopped by. Could Top call his mother in Bunker Hill, Illinois? Rice asked. Top did, but only after he pestered the medical personnel attending to Rice for more information on the lieutenant's condition.

At 1:00 A.M. Illinois time, the first sergeant reached Ruth Rice. She had gone to bed early that night, fighting the early onset of the flu, and was barely able to talk. She wasn't startled by the sound of the phone ringing. Stephen often called at this time, and she welcomed all of his calls, regardless of the time. She especially loved the times when she could watch him over an Internet connection, munching on a cookie as he talked to her about life in Baghdad. She took comfort in his description of Sergeant Gillette, Stephen's platoon sergeant, whom he described as one of the best soldiers he knew. She prayed for him nightly but had faith and pride in his abilities. "He is a natural-born leader," she explained to friends. "Stephen always knew what he wanted and stayed focused." But the voice she heard tonight was unfamiliar. "Is this Ruth Rice?" she heard the voice ask. "Yes, it is," she replied. "This is First Sergeant Robert Elmore. Your son is alive." Top did the best he could to let her know that Stephen was going to be OK even as he described her son's condition. Stephen had been hurt in an IED attack, he explained, and his left big toe was severed. That same leg suffered other serious injuries. Stephen would soon be medevaced to Germany for treatment. Without much else to tell, the conversation ended abruptly.

Ruth immediately placed a call to Rich, Stephen's father, in Alton, Illinois. The two had divorced shortly before Stephen deployed to Iraq. That explained why she was new to the tiny southern Illinois community of Bunker Hill, although by virtue of her job as a police dispatcher and with a son serving in Iraq, she had quickly become something of a celebrity in town. Ruth's next call was to her daughter Suzi, who lived near her dad. Suzi soon headed over to her dad's house to help him deal with the news. Next came a call to her neighbor and best friend, Betty Phelps, followed by several more calls to friends and relatives. Before she was done, her voice was nearly gone.

Back in Baghdad, when the medical team completed their prep work on Lieutenant Rice, an attendant wheeled Steve off for a CT scan, then to the operating room for the first of what would be many surgeries. The medical team's initial order of business was to reattach his big toe. But the presiding surgeon also determined that there was little else they could do for Rice's mangled ankle in Baghdad. They needed to get him to Germany, and quickly.

It was about 6:00 P.M. when Rice awoke after surgery. As he opened his eyes, he saw Colonel Glaser leaning over him, looking forlorn. Glaser told Rice how proud he was, then pressed his unit coin into Rice's hand and asked if Rice wanted to call home. Even though he was groggy from the effects of anesthesia and morphine, Rice did want to call home to reassure his parents that he was all right. He made three calls in all, the first to his mother, then his father. Colonel Glaser placed the last call for him, this one to Captain Royer, who was still on leave in Springfield. He had been injured, Rice told Royer, and would soon be flown to Germany where they could begin to work on rebuilding his ankle. It was, by necessity, a short conversation. It was also, for Royer, the worst moment of the entire year. One of his soldiers had been seriously injured, and he wasn't even in country. He felt totally helpless.[10]

That evening, the 28th CSH loaded Rice up for the ride to BIAP to catch the first possible flight to Germany. Rice was soon joined by several other casualties in the holding area, including several Poles stationed at Karbala injured that day in a car bomb explosion. He also joined the injured MP he had gone to rescue that morning. The medical staff kept a close watch over Rice, and when a nurse became alarmed about a low blood oxygen count, they administered 2 liters of blood. He stayed conscious, but barely, as he lay on the stretcher. "This lieutenant needs to go, and these Polish guys need to go," he heard someone say. He was still conscious when they wheeled him into a waiting C-130 for the flight to Ramstein Air Base in Germany.

It was early Sunday morning back in Bunker Hill when Betty arrived at Ruth's front door with a steaming bowl of chicken soup. There wasn't much Betty could do to comfort her, but for Ruth, it was enough that she was there. By that time, Ruth was losing her battle with the flu. There was no way Ruth would be attending a party that evening at a nearby restaurant where Ruth's brother-in-law Mark played piano. Instead, Betty would use the occasion to tell their friends about Stephen's injury.[11]

The Midtown Restaurant in Alton, Illinois, was crowded that evening, filled with customers singing along as Mark played their requests. By chance, Stephen's old boss from his high school days was there with his family, as were others who knew Stephen. During a break in the music, Betty stood up to make her announcement. The crowd fell silent when they heard Stephen's name. He was seriously injured, Betty stated, but should be all right. With that, she passed the hat, a spontaneous gesture to help Ruth pay for the travel and related expenses that Betty knew were coming. Family, friends, and strangers all contributed generously that night, the beginning of an incredible outpouring of support Ruth received from all quarters.[12]

The next morning, Ruth and Betty began a determined effort to wrench whatever information they could on Stephen's condition out of the Army. By that time, Ruth's laryngitis and the strain of the last two days had taken their toll, and she gladly let Betty place most of the calls. They started first with Fort Leonard Wood, the MP schoolhouse and the site of most of Stephen's training. It took three calls before they found someone who claimed to have a record of a Second Lieutenant Rice. He'd been deployed to Afghanistan, the voice said, and subsequently died in a mortar attack. Ruth knew better, but she still found the news more than a bit disconcerting. Later that day, she received a call from the Department of Casualties in Washington, D.C., the official Pentagon agency responsible for notifying next of kin. Stephen was now in Landstuhl, a sergeant told her before passing on a toll-free number to call for information on his condition. Ruth could call that number, the sergeant explained, and the call would then be transferred to Landstuhl.

Lieutenant Rice's final destination in Germany was the sprawling Landstuhl Regional Medical Center, the largest American hospital outside of the United States. The facility had a first-class staff and excellent facilities, but the doctors already knew that this too was only a waystation for the lieutenant. Their job was to install an external fixator onto his leg, a contraption that looked more like an erector set than a medical device. The fixator was designed to stabilize the bones in his shattered ankle until orthopedic surgeons at Walter Reed could begin the reconstructive surgery. It was used as an alternative to a cast while his ankle wounds healed. But first they had to get him stabilized, and in that, Rice was not cooperating.

It was December 30 before the doctors finally operated on the leg, this time merely to clean his wounds and examine them more fully. The wound area had become inflamed with an infection peculiar to Iraq. The infection traveled quickly through his bloodstream and settled into his lungs. He developed double pneumonia and acute respiratory distress syndrome. His blood oxygen levels plummeted, and his temperature climbed to dangerous heights. From the surgery room, Stephen headed to the hospital's intensive care unit (ICU), where he spent the next several days. He awoke in the ICU hungry, thirsty, and mad at the staff for refusing to feed him. Mostly, he worried about losing his lower leg despite the staff's assurances to the contrary.

Keeping vigil at his bedside was Lieutenant Joy Hess, a classmate from his officer basic course who was stationed nearby. It meant the world to Steve to see her there, fretting over him. It meant even more to Ruth back in Illinois because Joy sent Ruth a series of e-mails that provided updates on Stephen's progress after the operation. Before Joy's e-mails, Ruth's efforts to find out about Stephen's condition had largely been an exercise in frustration. Ruth had little trouble contacting the staff at Landstuhl. The problem was that the Health Insurance Portability and Accountability Act of 1996, known in the medical community as HIPAA, prevented the staff from updating Ruth on his condition. Because Stephen was over eighteen, they were prohibited from telling her anything. The law said that they could inform a wife about her husband's condition, but not parents. Only Stephen could do that. But on the rare occasions when Ruth did talk to Stephen, he couldn't tell her much. He received regular doses of morphine to combat the intense pain, so Joy's regular e-mails were a godsend. Ruth faithfully forwarded the message to everyone in her e-mail address book. "We covet your prayers for his healing," she told her family and friends.

Rice spent the next several days in the hospital's ICU, hooked up to oxygen, receiving a strong antibiotic and morphine through an IV drip. Not until January 5, with his pneumonia under control and his temperature back to normal, did the doctors finally install the external fixator.[13]

The Recovery

Ruth Rice was more than a bit apprehensive when she arrived at Walter Reed Medical Center to see Stephen for the first time since his injury. Stephen had spent two full weeks at Landstuhl, including several days in the hospital's ICU. When his condition finally stabilized in early January, the Army transferred him to Walter Reed, the military's premier medical facility. Stephen's father, sister, and brother-in-law had already made the trip to D.C., but Ruth's budget had been tight since her divorce. She couldn't afford the trip until Operation Hero Miles stepped in to pay her fare.

Stephen progressed well once at Walter Reed. When he arrived, the doctors thoroughly cleaned his wound, then adjusted his fixator to ensure the foot was in the proper position before making repairs on his left knee. They soon had him up and moving, with the help of a walker. Ruth found Stephen in good spirits. He appreciated the visits from his family, as well as a surprise visit from NASCAR driver Jeff Gordon and 3 Doors Down, a rock group. But no visit buoyed Stephen's spirits more than the one from his old ROTC classmate, Jim Hannagan, who had driven halfway across the country to see his buddy.

The real work for his recovery was yet to come, Steve told his mother. He figured to be released from the hospital by the end of January for a one-month convalescence leave. After that, he would return to Walter Reed and the doctors would remove the fixator and replace it with a surgical boot before sending him back home again for six weeks. That wait was necessary to allow the screw sites around the ankle to heal completely. Then, and only then, could they operate on the ankle, and no one could say how much mobility Stephen would have until after that. He faced a long recovery, into May at least—well after the 233rd was due home.[14]

Addressing the State Legislature

As one of Illinois' most serious casualties to date, Lieutenant Rice became something of a celebrity when he arrived home for convalescence leave in early February. State Senator William Haine, a Democrat from Rice's hometown of Alton, caught wind of Rice's story and invited him to the state's senate chamber on February 10, where he planned to read a special proclamation honoring Rice's service and sacrifice. On the drive up to Springfield, Rice wondered whether Haine expected him to make a speech. The senator had hinted at the possibility, so Rice scribbled out a short speech just to be safe. When he arrived in the senate chamber, General Thomas personally escorted the lieutenant up to the dais, where Stephen was joined by Sergeant Jay Fritzsche, who was home on leave. Thomas then took his seat in the gallery, next to Ruth and her friend Betty.

Senator Haine's proclamation was full of the flowery language and platitudes one expected from a politician. Lieutenant Rice's comments were more memorable, delivered as he balanced on a pair of crutches. "I stand before you today kind of out of place," he began, speaking in understated tones, "away from the soldiers I made a promise to lead, so it's got me a little bit down." As he spoke, General Thomas gave Ruth a reassuring pat on her hand. She surrendered to her emotions, feeling her throat tighten, unashamed of the tears welling up in her eyes. "Your Illinois soldiers," Stephen continued,

[are] doing an amazing job under extraordinary conditions. Their mission is extremely stressful and their days are long, but remember that positive things are happening. It's too easy to watch the news and see the horrific images of yet another soldier being injured or killed by a roadside bomb or mortar fire or ambushes. We get accustomed to the shock value of our news media and we tend to overlook the accomplishments that our soldiers are making every single day. We forget about the numerous police stations, hospitals and schools that have been reinstituted since the beginning of the war. We don't get to see the forged bonds between soldiers, communities and neighbors that's taking place every day. So please remember the good things that your soldiers are doing, your Illinois soldiers, and take comfort in knowing that through mutual support of one another they're going to make it home safe—and before you know it.

It was an inspirational address. "We could not have scripted anything better," said General Thomas with obvious pride. "He spoke from the heart, representing Illinois' soldiers." Senator Adeline Geo-Karis of rural Zion agreed: "Lieutenant Rice, to me, represents the best of America."[15]

It was high and heartfelt praise from representatives of the nation Rice had sacrificed to protect. But ahead lay many operations and months of painful recovery, all for an uncertain future. Rice already knew the best he could hope for: his foot permanently fixed at a 90-degree angle. What he couldn't foresee were the weeks and months where he would feel forgotten and abandoned by the Army he had served so well in Iraq, languishing at Fort McCoy with nothing to do but mull over how dramatically his life had changed in those few seconds back in Baghdad. But all of this was in the future and on that day in February, when he addressed the state senate, he felt proud, but also guilty for abandoning his platoon. He marveled at how quickly these senators had transformed him from just a regular soldier into a hero. He was not comfortable with the transformation.[16]

14

Turf Battles

The MPs were not the only Americans patrolling the streets of Baghdad in early 2004. In fact, they were a distinct minority, for the soldiers of the 1st Armored Division and the 2nd Light Cavalry Regiment patrolled the neighborhoods as well. For that reason, Captain Royer, rejuvenated by his leave, made daily trips to Mule Skinner to coordinate with the maneuver units so they could avoid bumping heads on the streets—that was the theory, at least. Even so, there had been times where the MPs' most memorable encounter for the day wasn't with Iraqis, but with other Americans.

Copley reporter Marcus Stern got a firsthand lesson in inter-Army rivalries while accompanying a patrol led by Sergeant First Class Gillette. The Hogs were on a routine daylight patrol and heading back to Tombstone after making a stop at a local bank where Iraqis were anxiously exchanging their Saddam-era dinars for the new currency. 1st Armored Division tankers stood guard at the bank, and it was the Hogs' job to check in once an hour to make sure the money exchange was going well. As they pulled away from the bank, Specialist Stephanie Stretch, from her vantage point in the gunner's cupola, heard the telltale sounds of gunfire in the distance. "Let's go find them," said Gillette immediately. No one was surprised. Gillette always rode to the sound of the guns.

It didn't take long to find the source of the gunfire. The patrol pulled to a stop when they discovered a crowd of Iraqis milling about in the street. Across the street were a couple of Humvees belonging to the 2nd Battalion, 37th Armored Regiment, the maneuver unit responsible for this section of

Baghdad. Both groups began to investigate the incident, working on opposite sides of the street. After a few minutes, the armor lieutenant caught up with Sergeant Gillette in the middle of the street. "There's nothing here," he told Gillette matter-of-factly. "Everybody's gone. It's done." With that, the tankers piled back into their vehicles and drove off in a crescendo of noise and plume of dust and diesel exhaust, leaving the MPs on the street, still interviewing citizens. As they left, one tanker swung about in his turret and extended his arm in defiance, giving Sergeant Gillette the finger as they drove off. Gillette caught a glimpse of the insulting gesture but was already focused on what Sergeant Batterson was telling him. He'd discovered a large pool of blood, Batterson explained, plus a telephone line lying on the ground. A trail of blood led toward a nearby building.

By the time the Hogs were done with their investigation, they knew the identity of the injured man, who was already on his way to a local hospital. They also found two AK-47s still hot to the touch, and thanks to the cooperation of several Iraqi witnesses, they were able to take the shooter into custody. It was nothing more than routine police work—the job the MPs were trained to do.

Marcus Stern, who observed the incident from his vantage point in Gillette's Humvee, was struck by the irony of it all. Two groups converged on the scene—Regular Army tankers and the National Guard MPs in their lightly armored Humvees. When the tankers found "nobody to fight with, they left," Stern recalled. "And in leaving they expressed their contempt for the MPs, the National Guard unit." The MPs were too busy to reciprocate. They had a crime to solve.[1]

Friction

The incident that day was more than just the manifestation of ancient prejudices between the regulars and guardsmen. It also stemmed from the vague and overlapping missions the two groups received, for both worked the same turf in Baghdad, and the lines of responsibility were not always clearly defined. It was also a clash of cultures, not between guardsmen and regulars so much as a clash between the war fighters—the tankers, infantrymen, and cavalrymen of the Army—and those who were not.

Officially, the guidance each group received was straightforward. The maneuver units (the military's official jargon for the war fighters) were the official land managers in the city. The 3rd Infantry Division had divided Baghdad into sectors, assigning each of its fighting brigades a slice of the city to manage. These in turn were subdivided between the infantry and armored battalions and companies. The MPs were given primary responsibility over the police stations and for training the new police force. But in performing their duties, they patrolled the same streets assigned to the maneuver units. That fact necessitated careful coordination between the maneuver folks and the MPs—coordination that was the job of commanders and staff officers. There was some butting of heads between the MPs and 3rd Infantry Division soldiers during the early and chaotic days in Baghdad. It could hardly have been otherwise, given the nature and complexity of their missions. But as far as the MPs were concerned, relations headed south when the 1st Armored Division replaced the 3rd Infantry Division as the city's main occupying force.

Attached to the 1st Infantry Division was the 2nd Armored Cavalry Regiment (Light), recently deployed to Iraq from Fort Polk, Louisiana. (The 2nd was "light" by virtue of losing their tanks and armored personnel carriers when the unit moved from Germany to the States in the 1990s.) The cav had trained hard for their mission in Iraq, concentrating on fighting in an urban environment and training in one of the best urban training centers in the Army, the Military Operations in Urban Terrain (MOUT) site at Fort Polk, Louisiana. Fort Polk's MOUT featured a small city complete with buildings, sewers, and rubble—even well-trained aggressors serving as the enemy. The cav troops practiced both hard entries (busting down doors) and soft entries (knocking on doors before entering). They repeatedly drilled on how to search a building, stacking the team as the troops moved from one room to the next with rifles at the ready. They also received training in Iraqi and Islamic culture, and they went into Iraq with a 700-page book on Iraq that fit conveniently into their cargo pockets. They were honed to a fine edge when the Army called. Within ninety-six hours, the entire regiment, equipment and all, was on the ground in Kuwait, flown there by a fleet of C-5s, C-141s, and C-130 aircraft.[2]

America's Cavalrymen

The friction between the cavalrymen and the MPs was probably inevitable, working as they were in such close proximity. Part of the explanation lay in the cavalryman's role in life. An American cavalryman had one of the toughest and most dangerous jobs in the U.S. Army. In an offensive, he served at the tip of the Army's spear, ranging far ahead of the main forces—the eyes and ears of the commanding general. It was his job to find and fix the enemy, and as much as possible, to deceive the enemy into thinking that he represented the main American force. He wasn't supposed to slug it out, only to draw first blood and wait for the main body to arrive. But no branch loves its brawls more than the Cavalry. As one cavalryman described it, your typical cavalryman is "a guy with a big set of balls, goes out in front of everybody. I hunt the enemy down and I kill him. That's what I do."[3]

It wasn't that the average cav troop was bloodthirsty, just that the modern battlefield was brutally uncompromising. It was either kill or be killed where the cav fought their battles, and they had no intention of dying for their country. Military cynics measure their life expectancy in minutes and hours, not days, weeks, or months. This reality permeates the cavalrymen's mentality. Their intense training focused on crushing the enemy through speed and audacity. Cavalrymen are, by training and temperament, cocky, arrogant, supremely confident of their abilities, disdainful of weakness, and unconcerned about the subtleties of diplomacy. That mentality was a big part of why the war's combat phase went so well.

The very attributes that made the Cavalry soldiers so successful during the combat phase were precisely the traits that could undermine their effectiveness when patrolling the streets of Baghdad, where restraint, subtlety, and diplomacy were the order of the day. The job of pacifying Baghdad, of establishing a police presence even while presenting a friendly face to the Iraqi people, was one much better suited to the MPs and to the Army's civil affairs units. "We teach [MP] recruits that in dealing with civilians, they use the minimum amount of force. With us, force is like a rheostat," explained Colonel Joseph Rapone II, an official at the MP school at Fort Leonard Wood, Missouri. But in 2003, those units were scarce. By necessity, the war fighters took the lead. In the sector in which the 233rd operated, that unit was a squadron from the 2nd Light Cavalry Regiment. Attached to them was one tank company from the 2nd Battalion, 37th Armored Regiment.

The differences in the maneuver unit's training and mission translated into different approachs when working with the local Iraqis. The cavalrymen and tankers were there to keep order, but also to root out any cells of resistance. They frequently went looking for a fight, and sometimes they found it. The insurgents especially liked to take shots at the Abrams tanks, usually with rocket-propelled grenades, figuring that a tank kill was the ultimate coup. It wasn't that the cavalrymen didn't do their share of humanitarian work—opening schools, building soccer fields, passing out candy. They did. And over time, they learned when to knock on a door rather than breaking it down. They learned that a smile and an unexpected act of kindness could go much further than harsh treatment. They even proved themselves to be able and compassionate humanitarians, but in general, they used a more heavy-handed approach when performing their duties, especially early on.[4] If combat was what you wanted, then these were some of the best soldiers in the world. But that was not why they were in Baghdad. They were ill-suited to their new role as occupiers.

Their approach often elicited a response from the Iraqis different than what the MPs saw. "My MPs would drive through a neighborhood and people would wave at them," recalled Royer, "and then some cav scouts would drive through the same neighborhood ten minutes behind us and get lit up." Staff Sergeant Robert Smith of 1st Platoon lived that reality firsthand. "We were told pretty bluntly by some of the people in the neighborhood. They'd see the crossed pistols [on the Humvees]," and "the insurgents wouldn't shoot at us because we treated the people there fairly." In his end-of-tour after action report, written for the benefit of his replacement, Royer wrote, "People in our zones have learned the difference between the maneuver elements and the MP. The people have come to recognize the MP brassard and are even able to tell the difference in the vehicles. We have treated the people with respect, and it has most assuredly saved lives."[5]

Bumping Heads

The problem, as far as the Hogs were concerned, was that their buddies in the cav and armor units were not MPs and were not much interested in becoming ones. They reached that conclusion after a series of incidents where Cavalry or Armored patrols had taken Iraqis into custody and then, anxious to get rid of their prisoners, unceremoniously dumped them off at Tombstone. "What did they do?" the Hogs would ask their American counterparts, and the patrol leader would gladly fill them in. "Where's your evidence? Where's the incident report?" they then asked. As often as not, the answers they heard were far from satisfactory. "We're too busy for that" and "that's not our job" were par for the course. What the MPs needed from their counterparts to make an arrest stick was a capture tag, a form generated by the Coalition Provisional Authority, plus a minimum of two sworn statements and whatever other evidence had been collected. Faced with no evidence and no reports, there was little the Hogs could do but release the prisoners back into the streets. Such incidents happened so frequently that the Hogs began documenting them. That documentation gave Royer and 519th staff officers the ammunition they needed to lodge their complaints to the chain of command. Not surprisingly, the Cavalry and Armored troops had their own complaints—allegations that the MPs consistently failed to coordinate their "presence" patrols, and as a consequence, their patrols often interfered with Cavalry operations. There was truth in both sides of the argument, but with perseverance from commanders and staff, the situation improved.[6]

Royer eventually forged an especially strong relationship with the commander of the 237th Armor, Lieutenant Colonel Pat White, a soldier he held in high regard. But under the surface was still a reservoir of ill feelings, especially between the 3rd Platoon "Hogs" and the Cavalry. And once Lieutenant Rice was injured and out of the picture, the 3rd Platoon's relations with their local Cavalry element went downhill.[7]

A Botched Raid

The 2nd Light Cavalry Regiment had been working on a raid for months, the culmination of an extensive intelligence effort to root out a suspected cell of al-Qaeda operatives and Wahabi radicals living in the al-Jadidah neighborhood of Baghdad. A total of nine raids were planned on Iraqi homes in the 2nd Light Cavalry Regiment's area, all set to begin precisely at 0100 hours on January 20. The detailed plan involved elements from several units in the 2nd Light Cavalry Regiment sector. The 233rd's slice of the mission was to raid two houses and assist in securing the surrounding area during the operation. Royer assigned Lieutenant Flack to lead a team from 4th Platoon against one house, and Lieutenant Ferris led a team hitting another house.

The MPs were no strangers to such operations. Raids weren't an everyday occurrence, but they'd participated in enough to feel confident in their role. But for Lieutenant Ferris, this raid felt different. He was convinced his house was the wrong house, and as he took his people through their precombat checks late that night, that thought haunted him. He had discovered the discrepancy earlier that day. The battalion intelligence officer had given him aerial photographs of the house his team was supposed to hit, plus a street address. He wanted to know what the house looked like from the street—whether there was a walled courtyard, and how far the house was set back from the gate. Three interpreters he trusted implicitly volunteered to get the information he sought. Equipped with Staff Sergeant Jimmie Mayes's home video camera, the interpreters drove a POV past the house while one of them cradled the camera in his arms so as not to draw attention. It wasn't the same house, the interpreters told Ferris excitedly when they returned. The house in the photograph was next door. The interpreters made two more trips to the neighborhood to confirm their findings, each time videotaping the houses from three different angles. They insisted that the residents of this house were innocent.

Armed with the information, Ferris went to Captain Royer, who in turn talked to the intelligence officer for the 2nd Battalion, 37th Armored. The answer Ferris got back late in the day was disconcerting. "We're going to hit both houses to make sure we get everybody," he was told. His team would hit the house belonging to the address, and an ad hoc group from the cav with no real experience in raids would hit the house in the photograph. Specifically, his team was looking for an al-Qaeda operative who was suspected of manufacturing and planting improvised explosive devices.[8]

Ferris selected his team carefully. He chose Staff Sergeant Waldron, an experienced police officer in the States, to lead the house entry team, assisted by Sergeant Eric Bertoni, Sergeant Jimmie Mayes, Specialist Chris Ater, and an interpreter. Heading up the security team and tasked to stay with the vehicles was Staff Sergeant Robert Smith, one of the platoon's best navigators, who would also guide the raid team to the objective. Ferris, of course, would accompany the entry team, along with Specialists Shawna Keith and Joshua Crutchley.

All nine raid teams that night linked up at the operation's rally point, a vacant lot behind the New Baghdad police station. They synchronized their watches before departing for their individual raid sites. Minutes later, Ferris stood in front of a black wrought-iron gate with his entry team clustered about him, watching the seconds tick down to 0100 hours. Although he suspected this was the wrong house, he was in no mood to take chances. That attitude could put him and the entire team at risk if he was wrong and insurgents were waiting for them inside. Through the gate, he could make out a large courtyard, with the modest two-story house situated about 20 feet back. Suddenly, from next door, he heard the distinct sound of wood and glass breaking, and strident voices. The team next door had triggered their raid early, kicking in the door and in the process rousing the entire neighborhood, including an excitable little dog, which yelped wildly inside the MPs' target house. Moments later, a young man in his thirties, obviously awakened by the commotion, stumbled into the courtyard and limped to the gate. "Chellum, chellum," he yelled, referring to the barking dog. Ferris reacted instinctively, pulling out his 9-millimeter pistol and leveling it at the man's forehead. With his left hand he grabbed the man's shirt and yanked him violently into the iron gate, adrenaline pumping. "F*** the chellum. Open the f***in' door," he screamed. The man, near panic, managed to pull up the iron rod that secured the door, swinging the door in. Instantly, Ferris had him on the ground while Sergeant Smith secured his hands with Flex-Cufs. While Ferris and Smith were busy outside, Sergeant Waldron led the rest of the raid team into the house.

Once inside, they rounded up and secured the occupants in the kitchen, a group that included an older woman in her fifties, plus four young women and a small girl. While Mayes's team cuffed the women and patted them down, Sergeant Waldron and his crew searched the house, moving methodically from room to room, weapons at the ready, using the stack formation they had employed so many times before. Once the first-floor rooms were searched for insurgents, they moved to the second floor, and then to the roof. When they were confident that the rest of the house was empty, they headed back downstairs and searched the entire house again, this time taking their time, methodically searching each room for contraband.

By then, Ferris, along with his interpreter, had taken one of the women to an adjacent room for interrogation. "Are there any weapons in the house?" he asked her. "Why are there so many women living in the house together?" "How is everyone related?" "What is her occupation?" "What is their religion?" Ferris fired off the questions in quick succession. After discovering nothing from the first woman, he waved the second woman into the room and subjected her to the same barrage of questions. Through it all, the second young woman retained her composure. Ferris guessed her to be in her thirties, and he noted that she was very attractive, despite her lack of makeup and unkempt condition. There was no denying it—she had a regal air about her. She spoke excellent English, and during the questioning, she revealed that she was the daughter of the older women and that the others were her sisters and brother. She was forthright when she answered, and she treated him more cordially than the circumstances warranted. Before the war, she explained, she had worked as a veterinarian. Her brother worked as a DJ and a keyboard player. They were Christians, she went on, Syrian Christians to be exact, although the family had lived in Iraq for many years. Even so, they didn't associate with their neighbors very much. As he questioned her, Ferris allowed his eyes to wander, examining the room more closely. The room, indeed the whole house, was spotless. As he continued his visual sweep of the room, a picture caught his eye. There, on the wall behind the woman's head, was a painting of the Virgin Mary. The doubts that had haunted him before the raid now struck him full force. They had hit the wrong house. He was sure of it now. There would be no more interrogations that night.

Ferris motioned the woman back to the kitchen, where the rest of the family was assembled. He and Sergeant Mayes relaxed slightly but were startled when a huge German shepherd suddenly appeared, striding casually through the kitchen. This was not the dog that had made such a commotion when they first pounded on the door. This dog could have done serious damage if he'd been provoked. Fortunately, he passed through the room with no sign of aggression and was soon gone. Once the dog left the room, Ferris and Mayes breathed a sigh of relief.

While Ferris talked to the family members, they occasionally heard the sounds of breaking glass emanating from the houses down the street. Sergeant Waldron continued his methodical room-by-room search. As a trained policeman, he knew the clumsy techniques used next door not only antagonized those being searched, but were also a lousy way to find contraband and compromised any evidence they might find. He, Bertoni, and Ater worked meticulously, first through the downstairs rooms, then heading upstairs to check the bedrooms. They found nothing of interest, not even any weapons, the item almost all Iraqis had somewhere in their homes. When Waldron completed his search, Ferris gathered up his men, and as they left, he did his best to apologize to the woman and her family.

Once outside, Sergeant Smith brought the lieutenant up to speed on the action next door. That patrol had found nothing of value in their house, Smith explained, but someone did implicate another family two houses down. The soldiers then hit that house, kicking in the door just as before, and departing minutes later with four Iraqi men in custody.

As the Reapers pulled away from the house and turned toward Viper Base, Ferris mulled over the entire mission. Just as he feared, they had raided the wrong house. His lame apology hardly made up for the disruption they had inflicted on this woman and her family. The Reapers prided themselves in treating the Iraqis they encountered with respect. They, like everyone in the 233rd, believed that approach explained why they could travel through some of Baghdad's toughest neighborhoods unmolested. Now they had burst into the home of a perfectly innocent family in the middle of the night. He even threatened a man's life! Ferris resolved to return the next day and make things right.

When he encountered Captain Royer later that night, he vented his frustrations. He was angry at the clumsy way the patrol next door had conducted their business. Most of all, he was angry at himself. Venting to the captain was his way to purge the shame and anger he felt for the grief they had inflicted on this family. Royer understood.[9]

A Return Visit

The next morning, Lieutenant Ferris led a three-vehicle convoy back to the same neighborhood. This time, they came not to search for contraband, but to make amends to the woman and her family. They had loaded up with food, powdered drink mix, medical supplies, personal hygiene items, "everything we could get our hands on." Lieutenant Ferris led their delegation to the door, a group that included Sergeants Waldron and Smith. Sergeant Mayes stayed with the gunners to set up security in the street.

The woman was startled when she saw the Americans at her door. Ferris offered another apology, mustering up as much sincerity as he could, then offered their gifts as restitution, including a lock to replace the one broken during the raid. She graciously invited them in and gestured for them to sit around her living room table, then busily went to work preparing coffee for her guests. All of this was done in the spirit of hospitality in the finest tradition of Arab culture. It wasn't long before the formality melted away. She appreciated the Americans' gesture, she said with a smile; the Saddam-era police would never have done such a thing. And this second visit she counted as an honor: the Americans had visited her not as conquerors, but as friends, an act that was bound to draw the attention and even envy of her neighbors. Their visit would restore her family's standing with the neighbors, she explained, and for that she was grateful. She was flattered when Sergeant Waldron offered to help her find a job, perhaps as an interpreter, given her excellent mastery of English. This was not possible, she patiently explained. She feared the job might subject her and her family to reprisals. Indeed, she suspected that one of her neighbors had turned them in as a vendetta. The MPs then offered to help secure a job with the new Ministry of Health as a veterinarian, and they gave her a point of contact with the agency. The woman seemed overwhelmed. She had been rudely awakened in the middle of the night and subjected to a frightening search. Now, hours later, here were the same Americans, offering restitution.

Out in the street, neighbors approached Sergeant Mayes. They were curious about the Reapers' return to their neighborhood. Why did they come back? one neighbor asked. Because we interrupted a perfectly innocent family's sleep for no reason, and we wanted to make it right, Sergeant Mayes explained. When Lieutenant Ferris emerged from the home, other Iraqis pressed in around him. Will he visit them as well? they asked expectantly. No, he told them, another unit had hit their home, not his. Where were the four taken away the night before? He didn't know, and he told them as much.

Moments later, Ferris directed the patrol to mount up, and they soon sped away. This time, however, Ferris felt much better. They had made amends, and in the process, they had forged a new friendship in Baghdad. They had even been invited back for dinner. He declined, of course, but the gesture heartened him.[10] As for the four Iraqis who were seized by the other patrol, they were eventually released after the interrogators determined they were innocent.

15
Winding Down

Baghdad was growing steadily more violent in early 2004. The unit's daily briefings reinforced that harsh reality, but it was Lieutenant Rice's injury that drove the point home for those in the 233rd. The MPs grew especially concerned when their interpreters, so critical to their success, increasingly became terrorist targets.[1]

With violence in Baghdad on the rise, the MPs happily greeted the day in early February when they swapped the bulk of their Humvees for armored versions. The armored Humvees came from the 59th MP Company, an active Army unit that for the past year had pulled the force security mission at Camp Victory. Because the 59th rarely left their compound, they could no longer justify using armored Humvees and were ordered to turn them over to the 233rd. Royer wondered why it took the Army so long to figure that one out, but he was thankful to receive them nonetheless. Armored Humvees were a rare commodity in Baghdad, and he knew his soldiers would be that much safer while driving through Baghdad.

Sergeant Mike Whited, the unit's assistant maintenance sergeant, took charge of the Humvee swap since Staff Sergeant Hildebrandt was home on leave. Whited had worked as a shop foreman for the Buske Trucking Line back in the States, giving him a wealth of experience in maintaining heavy equipment. He was the ideal backup to Hildebrandt.

The unit didn't replace its entire inventory of Humvees—only twenty-two out of their authorized fleet of forty-seven, enough to give four or five armored Humvees to each platoon, plus one to the commander. Each platoon leader determined which Humvees to turn in, selecting those not already configured for operations in Baghdad. In return, Whited suspected he would get some of the 59th's worst vehicles, typical of such operations in the Army. He also knew that both sides would scrutinize the other unit's equipment before accepting it, so he and his mechanics, supplemented by several MPs detailed from the platoons, worked far into the night preparing their turn-ins. Sergeant Joel Mauney, a GM-trained mechanic stateside, was especially welcomed to the task.

When the day came for the swap, the 59th drove their offerings to Viper Base. For the next several days, Whited and his mechanics pored over the 59th's Humvees while the 59th's mechanics did the same with theirs. It did not take long before Whited was bending Royer's ear about their lousy condition. In all, Whited's folks deadlined nearly every armored Humvee, indicating that they failed to meet the Army's maintenance standards without extensive repairs. Three needed new radiators, almost all had bad hub seals and worn brake shoes, and more than a few needed new tires. Several came with cracks in their 4-inch-thick bulletproof windshields—an expensive repair item. Of the vehicles Whited turned in, the 59th deadlined two. Captain Royer raised the issue with Colonel Glaser but was soon overruled. These Humvees were armored, came the reply, and safer than what they had, regardless of their condition. Whited signed for all twenty-two, and his mechanics rolled up their sleeves and went to work.

The 233rd's mechanics were no strangers to hard work, and this far into the unit's deployment, they had developed quite a reputation for resurrecting vehicles thought to be beyond repair. As it turned out, these new Humvees challenged their scrounging and trading skills more than their maintenance expertise. The 519th helped locate the radiators they needed, and Whited canvassed other units in the Green Zone for more parts. In several cases, units that were preparing to leave Baghdad were more than happy to give him the parts he sought. In a few cases, they traded for what they needed. In the end, the hard work was worth it. Within a week, all twenty-two armored Humvees were traveling the streets of Baghdad.

Once repaired, every 233rd patrol that left the gate rode in armored Humvees. Their new vehicles were designed and built from the ground up to handle the extra weight of the armor plating. They were equipped with a more powerful engine, a robust suspension system, bulletproof glass, side plates, and flooring of hardened steel. They were also air-conditioned due to the need to button up in the event of a chemical or biological attack. Since the MPs drove through the streets with the gunner sitting in the open cupola, the air conditioning was basically worthless.

It wouldn't be long before the armored Humvees proved their worth.[2]

Battle Handoffs

The Humvee swap corresponded with another important event for the 233rd. On February 11, Lieutenant Colonel Dave Glaser, the much-loved commander of the 519th MP Battalion, turned over MP operations in eastern Baghdad to the commander of the 759th MP Battalion, newly arrived in theater from Fort Carson, Colorado. The handover was significant in a couple of respects. First of all, from top to bottom, the 233rd hated to see Lieutenant Colonel Glaser and the 519th leave. Glaser was admired and respected by the entire command. He was the kind of leader everyone wanted to serve with—intelligent, compassionate, not afraid to make hard decisions. "I had worked with the greatest battalion commander in the world," said Royer with complete sincerity. "When I would do something wrong and would be reprimanded by Colonel Glaser, which was not often, . . . I felt more like I had disappointed my father than I had done something wrong." Glaser would be sorely missed.[3]

But not only Glaser was leaving. When he arrived, he arrived as an individual replacement. But the Army had been stung hard during the Vietnam war by its policy of rotating individuals through the war zone on one-year tours. That policy destroyed unit cohesion and morale. It turned every soldier who arrived in Vietnam into the F***in' New Guy, or FNG for short. It created an environment where many soldiers worried much more about surviving their year in Vietnam and too little about accomplishing the mission. It turned every Vietnam-era veteran into a "days" counter. After the war, the Army brass did some sober reflection and reached the conclusion that the individual rotation policy was exactly the wrong way to run a war. The better way, they concluded, was to regularly rotate entire units through the war zone, and in that way, they could maintain unit cohesion and the soldiers' fighting edge. An outgrowth of that decision was that more units were needed to rotate through the theater—in other words, the regulars needed National Guard and Reserve units to fill out their troop rotation plan.

When the 519th departed Iraq a few days after their battle handoff, the 233rd became the sole tenant on Viper Base. The MPs felt a bit lonely without their neighbors, but by March, they had other things on their mind. They too would soon be heading home, back to their loved ones, to cool breezes and green grass. Anticipation was building.

Saved by a Day

Sergeant Rich Carroll spent much of his year in Baghdad escorting Colonel Glaser and 519th staffers around town. That wasn't his team's exclusive mission, but the 2nd Platoon "Punishers" often drew Glaser's name. When the 759th took over from the 519th, it was only natural that the Punishers be the ones who escorted the new commander around town.

This was Carroll's second tour in Iraq. He'd served with the 233rd during Desert Storm. He got out of the National Guard in 1995 to concentrate on his work as a police officer in Lansing, Illinois. Then the terrorist attack on 9/11 happened, and he knew he had to get back in. Carroll enlisted into the 233rd on October 15, 2001, betting that they'd eventually be sent back to Iraq. "I felt like we left some unfinished business after the first gulf war," he explained matter-of-factly.[4]

March 7 found him leading the 1st Squad, assigned to escort the new commander around Baghdad. That date also marked the debut for the team's newly acquired armored Humvees. Like most patrols with the battalion commander, they started at the police academy, where the colonel routinely coordinated with the Iraqi Police Service (IPS) hierarchy, then headed to Provider for lunch.

After lunch, Sergeant Carroll met with the colonel to discuss their mission. The colonel told Carroll he wanted to see a cache of weapons and ordnance stored at a police station on the other side of Mule Skinner. Because Mule Skinner was frequently mortared, he wanted to check out the information he'd received from the Iraqi police (IPs) before lunch. If they found the weapons cache, the colonel continued, he planned to call in an explosive ordnance demolition team to take care of it. But he had no location for the police station. Instead, an IPS major would guide them to the station on the east side of Baghdad.

Nothing about the mission sat well with Carroll, and he told the colonel as much. It wasn't a good idea, Carroll argued, to follow an Iraqi policeman he neither knew nor trusted to an undisclosed location on the other side of town. Carroll had learned to be suspicious, and now he feared that the IP might lead them into a trap. There was nothing new, after all, about weapons caches at police stations. They all claimed that distinction. Carroll suggested that they check on the station tomorrow. The colonel was inclined to agree, but he decided to check it out anyway.[5]

As the convoy pulled out, Carroll was plagued by a premonition. "I'm just the biggest cliché for every military movie there is," he mused. "Who gets killed? I'm short and I have a kid on the way. . . . I'm just begging for it!" They were off nonetheless, with an IPS pickup in the lead, followed by the colonel's Humvee, then Sergeant Carroll's Humvee, and behind him Sergeant Sean Meyer and his team. Bringing up the rear was Specialist Richard Helkey's team. Helkey was getting some well-deserved on-the-job training as a team leader.

They headed east from Provider for the first leg of their journey, plowing their way through heavy traffic, keeping the interval close to prevent a car from slipping into their formation. They soon passed Mule Skinner and then drove over what they jokingly called the Banana Bridge, named after the vendors who always clogged it, before turning south on main supply route Pluto. Because the traffic was thinning out, Specialist Mike Thompson, Carroll's seasoned driver, automatically stretched out the interval. Specialist John Stonewall, from his vantage point behind the SAW, kept a close watch on the right side of the road, his sector of responsibility. For a time, the convoy fell in behind an engineer convoy, then was on its own again when the engineers turned off. Within moments, Carroll picked up the distinctive crack of a primer, immediately followed by a tremendous explosion some 20 meters to their front left. The blast bisected the distance between his and the lead Humvee, and it instantly turned a nearby car into a fireball.

"Go, go, go!" he screamed to Thompson, hoping his voice carried over the explosion. The Humvee carrying the 759th's commander swerved to the right as if pulling to a stop. Instinctively, Thompson closed in on the Humvee's rear, ready to push it out of the kill zone if necessary. At the last moment, the commander's vehicle lurched forward again and sped down the road. Carroll screamed into his Motorola, then barked instructions to Meyer and Helkey to watch for other IED explosions, rocket-propelled grenades, or machine gun bursts. He next twisted in his seat to check on Stonewall, ready for the worst because the gunner's left side had been exposed to the blast. Stonewall looked a bit dazed but otherwise seemed OK, and he responded quickly to Carroll's commands to keep a close watch on his sector of fire.

The convoy continued down the road for a few hundred meters before finally skidding to a stop. As he exited the Humvee, Carroll spotted the IPs who had led them here, and he couldn't help but notice their air of apathy: "They seemed completely unsurprised . . . about the attacks." But his attention was soon pulled elsewhere. He set out security and then raced forward to the lead vehicle to make sure the commander and his crew were all right. The colonel had a slight limp but insisted that he was OK. Stonewall complained that his ears were ringing severely, that Carroll's voice sounded robotic, but he otherwise appeared unscathed. Not until Carroll slipped back into his own seat to call the TOC did he notice the shattered windshield directly in front of his face, the pane of armored glass bulging ominously toward him. He immediately stepped out to check the damage. Amazingly, lying on the Humvee's hood was a golf-ball-sized chunk of shrapnel. Based on the telltale signs of machining, it obviously came from a mortar or artillery shell. Carroll made some mental calculations to determine its trajectory. The shrapnel had sliced through an air intake pipe on the right side of the hood before burrowing deep into the bulletproof glass. Shards of glass were fused into the shrapnel, and underneath the impact point lay a thin layer of finely pulverized glass. He pushed his finger into the divot in the windshield, amazed as he watched his second knuckle disappear into the hole. But the glass had held—it had absorbed the force of impact. Only later did Carroll understand that the windshield had saved his life. That chunk of shrapnel had his name on it.[6]

Shortly after the convoy stopped, the IPs went back to the site of the blast, then returned to rejoin the patrol. Carroll was not the only one suspicious of the IPs that day, but after a brief discussion about whether to take them to Mule Skinner to be interrogated, the IPs were released. "I have my suspicions to this day," stated Carroll months later.

Relief in Place with the 984th

On March 13, the 984th MP Company, one of the 759th's subordinate companies back in Colorado, arrived from Fort Carson to replace the 233rd. A patrol from the 233rd escorted the 984th from Baghdad International Airport to Mule Skinner, the base of operations they were to share with the 759th while stationed in Baghdad.

Before Colonel Glaser had turned over his own command, he ordered his company commanders to prepare information packets for their replacement units—what the Army called continuity books. Royer's version, much of it assembled by TOC personnel, ran to 14 pages of single-spaced text and covered everything from detailed training advice for surviving in Baghdad, to cultural insights, to advice on managing leaves and the importance of Family Readiness Groups, to the enemy's tactics and techniques. It was a thorough how-to guide for any new commander. But that was just the start for the relief-in-place (RIP) plan Royer designed for the two companies. He was determined to pass on as much life-saving knowledge as he could in the time they had left in country. Royer's battle handover plan was based on a model that almost everyone in Baghdad used. The 984th's company commander would shadow Captain Royer as he made his rounds. Likewise, the unit's first sergeant would accompany First Sergeant Elmore, with the same concept being used at the platoon level as well.

As far as Colonel Glaser was concerned, the 984th could not have found a better unit with which to RIP. "Jeff didn't lose a soldier because Jeff's guys were that good," explained Glaser months later. "Every day they went out they were vigilant. They knew where the danger areas were. They put overwatch out. They worked the local populace for the intelligence. They probably found more IEDs than . . . any company I had . . . and that was because of their interaction with the community and the police that they worked with who, honestly, loved them." It was high praise from someone so well respected. The 233rd had a lot to teach the 984th.

Once the 984th settled into their new residence, the RIP began in earnest. Royer still lacked a firm departure date for the unit, but he assumed that they'd be out of Baghdad no later than April 6, their 365th day in theater. That meant they had just two weeks with the 984th. The RIP went as planned for the first few days, with the Fort Carson troopers eager to learn the routine while absorbing the insights the 233rd MPs offered up. Toward the end of their first week, however, tensions began to surface between the two commands. The 984th's commander was getting anxious to cut the tether. She ended the RIP one week into the exercise and directed her soldiers to begin operations on their own, without the aid or advice of the Illinois guardsmen.

Whatever her reasoning, almost everyone in the 233rd believed the 984th had lost a golden opportunity. The MPs took comfort in knowing that the soldiers of the 984th, by and large, were as solid a bunch of MPs as they had encountered in Iraq. And for their part, the soldiers of the 984th reciprocated that respect. Some even continued to link up with the 233rd MPs for patrols, unbeknownst to their commander. One 984th noncommissioned officer (NCO) paid his 233rd counterpart a high compliment: "The 233rd has completely changed [my] opinion of the National Guard," he stated with complete sincerity.[7]

Training Pennsylvania's Redlegs

In the midst of the 233rd's RIP, the 759th's commander tasked the 233rd with a new mission: Captain Royer detailed three NCOs to work with a field artillery battery newly arrived in Baghdad. Battery B of the 1st Battalion, 109th Field Artillery Regiment, was a Pennsylvania Army National Guard unit from Nanticoke, Pennsylvania, located in the heart of the state's coal mining district near Wilkes-Barre. The unit was loaded with "skis"—young men who were the sons and grandsons of Polish coal miners, men who still clung to a hard-working, blue-collar mentality. A third of the soldiers were college students before the war. Now they were in Iraq, serving not as artillerymen but as "shake-and-bake" MPs, fresh from a crash course in military police duties at Fort Dix, New Jersey. They reluctantly gave up their designation as a battery, a term unique to artillery units, and became known as B Company, the MP equivalent. Their reclassification illustrated just how desperate the Army had become for MPs.[8]

As fate would have it, Bravo Company backfilled the 549th MP Company, a Regular Army unit from Fort Stewart, Georgia. The 549th was responsible for Sadr City, the volatile neighborhood in eastern Baghdad that was now home to 2 million impoverished Shia Muslims. To heighten Bravo Company's challenge, the unit got shortchanged on its RIP; they spent only six days with the 549th. Even worse, because Bravo Company inherited the 549th's equipment, most of their time together was spent inventorying equipment and moving that equipment from a compound in Sadr City to Bravo Company's home at Mule Skinner. Indeed, the move to Mule Skinner was the only time Bravo Company's NCOs got a chance to ride with the 549th through Sadr City. The colonel knew the former Redlegs (the soldiers' term of endearment for artillerymen) needed much more help than that.[9]

So it was that Captain Royer ordered Staff Sergeants Jim Nayonis, Jim Batterson, and Jeremie Mayes (Jimmie's brother) to report to the 759th's operations sergeant for detailed instructions. Batterson, Mayes, and Nayonis represented some of Royer's most seasoned NCOs. Each was an experienced law-enforcement officer back in the States. More importantly, they knew how to maneuver through the city, how to relate with the citizens of Baghdad, and had a solid rapport with the city's nascent police force. When they met with the operations sergeant, her instructions were simple enough: stay with the Redlegs until you feel "comfortable that they can patrol by themselves," accompany them on patrols, supervise their training, and teach them how to be MPs.[10]

Sergeant Nayonis harbored serious misgivings about their new mission, but he kept his feelings to himself. They were dispelled when he met with Captain Robert Ohl, Bravo Company's commander. Ohl, a class of '94 West Point graduate who had transferred to the Pennsylvania National Guard when the Army downsized in 1996, was a mature and level-headed officer. He was backed by a solid supporting cast, including a first sergeant with over thirty-four years of experience. As a West Pointer, Ohl had heard his share of National Guard horror stories while on active duty. He'd been weaned on tales of fat, out-of-shape, slipshod guardsmen—weekend warriors who were dangerously ignorant of their jobs. But after one visit with the 109th in 1996, he "realized this wasn't your typical Guard unit," and he signed up with the Pennsylvania National Guard. He never regretted his decision, and he now found himself in command of a company with one of the toughest gigs in Baghdad.

The Redlegs' mission was complicated by the fact that the battalion commander and the staff of the 759th obviously doubted their abilities. It wasn't just the presence of Batterson, Mayes, and Nayonis that led Ohl to that conclusion; Ohl welcomed their help. There was also the fact that the colonel refused to allow Bravo Company's twelve overweight soldiers to leave the compound. The young captain appealed that decision, arguing that although his overweight soldiers might not have the best appearance, they were otherwise solid soldiers who knew their jobs. Furthermore, confining them to base would wreak havoc with the cohesiveness and integrity of his teams. The colonel was unconvinced, and the decision stood. There was also a flap over issuing maps to Pennsylvanians who did not have security clearances. The commander stepped in to expedite that issue. Finally, there was the commander's refusal to allow Ohl's troops to wear MP brassards, insisting he would only issue them when they had proven themselves as MPs. It was a little thing, Ohl told himself, but it grated on him. They were doing the job of MPs, putting their lives at risk every day. And because the Iraqis understood what the brassards meant and treated the MPs accordingly, wearing the brassard could only help. From Nayonis's perspective, the Redlegs were "getting set up for failure."

Nayonis, Batterson, and Mayes spent nearly three weeks with Bravo Company and found the experience immensely satisfying. They started with the notion that "if it's not broke, why fix it," and after accompanying Bravo Company's first patrol, they noted plenty of things that the Redlegs were doing well. More importantly, they were extremely receptive and eager to absorb the lessons the MPs offered up. "You can learn from our mistakes," Nayonis told the unit's leadership after the first patrol, then ran through a list of areas where they needed to improve.

After their first formal after action review (AAR) with the unit's leadership, the MPs split the Redlegs into three groups, drivers, gunners, and team leaders, for a more detailed discussion. Nayonis took the drivers, stressing the importance of maintaining a proper interval between Humvees on patrols. He explained how they could dominate the road while patrolling and how to peel off traffic to the curbs while driving; he discussed the need to constantly scout for avenues of escape in the event they were boxed in, and he suggested ways to prevent Iraqi vehicles from slipping into their convoy. All of his comments were designed to keep the convoys moving—and to keep the Redlegs alive. Batterson and Mayes's comments to the gunners and team leaders were much the same, delivered to a receptive audience.

Each day, the trio accompanied three different patrols and ended the day with a "hot wash," an in-depth AAR. There was plenty of give and take at these sessions. The Redlegs fired off questions and offered their own observations and suggestions, and as they did so, they mastered the skills they needed to survive and succeed in Sadr City. Captain Ohl was especially concerned about establishing a solid rapport with the Iraqi police, and Batterson, Mayes, and Nayonis did not disappoint, filling the Redlegs in on the nuances of relating with the Iraqis. Through it all, Nayonis marveled at how quickly the Redlegs were learning, and how much he learned from them.[11]

By the second week, Nayonis, Mayes, and Batterson concluded that Ohl's troops were ready to patrol the streets on their own—that their own work was done. But each time they said as much to the operations sergeant, she came up with new areas of concern, followed by instructions to work on those. It only reinforced Nayonis's earlier observation that the 759th simply did not trust the Pennsylvania guardsmen. Were the 759th's doubts a result of deeply ingrained friction between regulars and guardsmen, he wondered, or because these were not school-trained MPs? Many of the 233rd's enlisted men thought it was the former—that ancient Regular Army prejudices against guardsmen were on display, even though their own relationship with the 519th had been so positive. Their experiences with the 759th and the 984th reinforced that conclusion. Staff Sergeant Nayonis chalked it up to the fact that these were shake-and-bake MPs, having heard as much from senior NCOs in the 759th. "They're not true MPs, you know," the 759th sergeant major was apt to remind him.

Captain Ohl, a West Pointer in command of guardsmen, believed both issues played a role. Yet after some reflection, he concluded the animosity was more a regular versus National Guard thing than an MP thing. Operating as they were in the pressure cooker of Baghdad, where failure had such dire consequences, there were plenty of opportunities for misunderstandings. As professionals, whether regulars and guardsmen, MPs or artillerymen, their mission was to work through the difficulties and get the job done. At the end of the day, Captain Ohl was determined that his men would overcome whatever obstacles were thrown their direction, whether those obstacles came from the Iraqis or from his own chain of command.

The three 233rd NCOs continued to work with Ohl's soldiers until it came time for the 233rd to head home. They returned to Viper Base just in time to help transfer the 233rd's equipment to the 759th MP Battalion at Mule Skinner. As they did, four MP teams from the 32nd MP Company (Wisconsin National Guard) arrived in Bravo Company's area to pick up where the 233rd NCOs had left off. The colonel was still not ready to let the Redlegs operate independently.[12]

16

Going Home

"Fourteen days and a wake-up 'til we fly home," began First Sergeant Elmore's March 22 e-mail to the Family Readiness Group (FRG). "We are scheduled to roll out of Baghdad on the fourth, which may fluctuate a day or two, and we fly out on the sixth, which also might fluctuate a day or two. . . . There will be several variables," he continued, but "one way or another, we are coming home." Ironically, the families had gathered at the Northenders VFW Club only the day before, 125 of them hanging onto every shred of information that Colonel Dennis Celletti, the state's chief of staff, and other National Guard officials offered up. Colonel Celletti gave them plenty of information, but no dates. Elmore's e-mail finally provided that, although they knew it might be subject to change. Even so, the official countdown was on, both in Baghdad and half a world away in Illinois.[1]

Staff Sergeant Randy Camden was growing busier as the 233rd closed in on their redeployment date. As the company's supply sergeant, it was his job to account for every piece of unit equipment in Baghdad, from the 233rd's wrecker to the smallest tool in the maintenance section's toolbox, all in preparation to hand the unit's equipment over to the 759th. Normally such inventories took a week or more. He was given only two days with the 759th supply sergeant, March 30 and 31, all while the unit was expected to maintain an ambitious schedule of patrols. Camden spent the weeks before the inventory assessing the gear the platoons never used, securing it in conexes as he accounted for it. Meanwhile, Sergeant Hildebrandt's mechanics spent long hours fixing as many maintenance discrepancies as possible. When the date for the actual turnover arrived, the whole operation went remarkably smoothly. It helped that the 759th's supply sergeant didn't insist on counting every tool and widget in the 233rd's many tool kits, trusting that the shortage annexes Sergeant Hildebrandt had prepared were accurate. That trust was born of one of the realities of war. The Army was always more forgiving about lost equipment during a war; they were usually willing to chalk up losses to the chaos of battle and the cost of waging war. Still, both sides were as meticulous as time would allow. Once the 759th supply sergeant accepted the equipment, several of the vehicles and radios were immediately signed back over to the 233rd so the platoons could continue conducting patrols.[2]

March 31 was also the day Royer sent a three-man advance party to Balad Airbase, a Ba'athist-era airfield located 68 kilometers north of Baghdad on a nondescript patch of desert. Co-located with the airbase was Camp Anaconda, a sprawling tent city where those awaiting flights were billeted. The advance party consisted of Lieutenant Flack, Staff Sergeant Lawrence Wilson, and Specialist Brad Clark. It was their job to wrangle the earliest flight out, to "G-2" the customs process, and to find billeting for the unit. Camp Anaconda offered decent amenities for the troops while they waited: a well-stocked PX, a theater, a phone bank, an Internet café, good chow, and even a swimming pool. What it did not have were air-conditioned barracks—only tents. Thankfully, it was April. Sergeant Wilson found the whole experience exhilarating. He took pride in being detailed to this most important of missions. And after months toiling in the TOC on the night shift, working in daylight was an unexpected delight.[3]

Last Patrols

On April 2, the platoons visited their police stations one last time. Saying goodbye to the Iraqi police and interpreters they had grown to trust and admire was a bittersweet experience for both sides. The MPs knew they would never see these men again, and that many might soon die. The interpreters were a favorite target of the insurgents, but the police officers—in fact, anyone who "collaborated" with the Americans—also risked their lives. Most of the Iraqis they worked with took on these jobs because of the money; they needed it to feed their families. But they also dreamed of making Iraq a better place to live. And now their partners in that shared dream were heading home, leaving behind the chaos and pervasive threat of death that was Iraq. More than a few of the Iraqi police shed tears during their farewells with the men and women of the 233rd. And more than a few of the MPs felt a tinge of guilt along with an intense sense of pride in a job well done. As they left, they were cautiously optimistic about the future of the country. They knew it would take years to build a truly free and independent country—not a carbon copy of the United States, certainly, but a nation where the Iraqi people could flourish. They held few illusions about the challenges that faced Iraq. Most MPs thought the nation would not achieve its full potential while the current generation was still in charge, but they held out hope for the next generation—the kids in the street who greeted them so warmly, the students in the schools who always rushed to meet them. The MPs hoped those kids would remember the MPs' acts of kindness, and that because of their work, the seeds of hate would fail to take root.[4]

The next morning, the MPs convoyed the remainder of their vehicles to Mule Skinner. Then it was the 984th's turn to transport the MPs back to Viper Base. The 233rd was now the lone tenant at their old compound, stranded with no transportation of their own. They were both excited and apprehensive. They'd been extended too many times to put much faith on any promises from higher headquarters. Only when they were wheels-up would they allow themselves to believe they were actually going home.

Late in the day, Captain Royer received the call they all awaited. Lieutenant Flack reported that he had locked in a flight for April 10, plus billeting for the company while they waited. And if the unit came up immediately, reported Flack, they might get lucky and catch a flight out as early as the 6th.[5]

The Wake-up—Heading Home

Captain Royer immediately arranged for transportation to Balad, requesting a departure time of 0500 hours the next morning, but the battalion commander insisted on seeing them off personally, which postponed their departure until 1000 hours. While they waited, they made last-minute arrangements. They shipped most of their baggage home separately and turned in their excess ammunition. Soldiers could keep only two 30-round magazines, plus 200 rounds for the squad automatic weapons. The colonel arrived on schedule and gave a short speech thanking them for their service in Iraq. Then they were off, riding to Balad in the back of a fleet of cargo trucks. They arrived at the airfield a couple of hours later, anxious to begin out-processing.

Al-Sadr Uprising

The 233rd left behind a city in turmoil. Just days before their move to Balad, four American contractors were brutally murdered in Fallujah; they were burned and dismembered before their corpses were hung from a bridge.

That news put everyone on edge. When the MPs finally arrived at Camp Anaconda, they were met with more disconcerting news. Shia militiamen, followers of the radical cleric Muqtada al-Sadr, had gone on a rampage in Sadr City and were seizing control of several Shia-dominated cities south of Baghdad. As the day dragged on, the news only worsened. There were unsubstantiated reports that al-Sadr's militiamen attacked police stations throughout the city, and that in some cases, the Iraqi police fled the stations rather than fight it out. Unconfirmed reports filtered in that police stations rebuilt after the invasion were once again looted by angry Iraqis. The MPs knew not to take the information at face value. They were confident that the police they trained had stood their ground. (Three police stations in Sadr City were temporarily taken over by Shi'ite militiamen, but none of those affiliated with the 233rd was affected.) The MPs could not fail to see the irony of it all. They had just risked a year of their lives to help the Iraqis build a modern police force, and now, if the reports were true, it had all unraveled on the very day they left the city. Still, their overriding emotion as they absorbed the day's news was not anger or disappointment, but fear that they might be sent back in. It was, they believed, someone else's fight now. They just wanted to get home.[6]

The brass had different concerns, of course, and officials at Balad and back at Scott Air Force Base in Illinois, where all military flights were ultimately cleared, scrubbed all scheduled flights from Iraq. The 233rd no sooner arrived at the airfield than their name was wiped off the flight board. Even more disconcerting was the discovery that several planes were actually turned around in midflight. "Here we go again," they said to each other. They prayed that they somehow might be spared a similar fate and sweated out the next few days.

Their fears were well justified. Four Illinois National Guard units with April departure dates were abruptly extended for ninety days, including the 233rd's sister MP companies, the 933rd from Chicago and the 333rd from Freeport. The 32nd MP Company from Wisconsin was also extended. Tragedy struck that unit on April 9, when Specialist Michelle Witmer died of injuries sustained after insurgents attacked her Humvee. Almost everyone in the 233rd knew her, and they knew that Michelle's sister also served with the 32nd, while her twin sister was assigned as a medic in another unit. Theirs was a small, tight-knit community, so they shared the 32nd's grief. The news was a reminder of just how lucky they had been to escape a similar fate.[7]

On the 10th, the MPs watched what was supposed to be their flight depart from Balad empty. Shortly after that, the word they'd waited for finally came down: they were once again cleared for departure. Because their equipment had already been distributed to other units, the 233rd was spared.

After a year of extensions and uncertainty, their relief and joy was palpable. All they had to do now was snag a flight out. That proved no easy task.[8]

Stranded at Anaconda

Things finally started to go the MPs' way on April 15, when the 233rd once again appeared on the flight board for a departure that day. The troops left tent city and rushed to the airfield, gladly dumping out their duffel bags for the customs inspection. They were almost through when the word came down that their flight had been diverted to take out a unit from the 82nd Airborne Division by virtue of its status as a rapid deployment force. They sullenly crammed their gear in their duffel bags and shuffled back to tent city. Their emotional roller-coaster ride was far from over.

Royer grew discouraged as he watched flight after flight diverted to other uses. It was one thing to see flights turned into medevac missions to Germany. But other planes left empty lest they pose a target to insurgent missiles, and many flights were diverted to the 82nd's use since the division had two full brigades to fly out. His mood didn't improve when he realized that the Air Force personnel worked a lot harder to get the 82nd Airborne out of the country than they did to find aircraft for one lowly National Guard company. "We fought every step of the way to get flights," he explained later. "It was a matter of networking, good old National Guard know-how and networking." While they waited, Anaconda endured daily mortar attacks, earning the derisive name "Mortaritaville" from the troops. Each mortar attack put Royer and Elmore on edge, especially because their troops were usually scattered all over the base.[9]

Their worst scare occurred when a mortar round hit tent city, splitting the distance between First Sergeant Elmore and Robert Junior. Top was especially unsettled when he realized the round hit in the precise spot where he'd stood only seconds before. The reaction from everyone nearby was immediate and instinctive. Most ran from the scene, exiting the danger zone. But when Elmore looked up, he saw one figure streaking toward the site of the attack, toward the injured soldiers who now lay sprawling on the ground. It was Dana Hodges, who once again reverted from her role as an MP to her secondary duty as medic. Elmore saw her again a few minutes later, her arms covered with blood, her hand shaking slightly as she raised it to take a deep drag on her cigarette.[10]

Two days later, the unit cleared out of the tents that had been their home for nearly two weeks and once again headed to the customs area. They divided into two chalks; the first consisted of 110 personnel, and the second comprised the remainder of the company, including half of 3rd Platoon and all of the 4th. Captain Royer penciled himself onto the second manifest. Again the first chalk dumped its gear for the customs officials to inspect, hopeful that their luck would finally hold. It did, and the first chalk passed into the sterile area to await boarding procedures. That was the cue for the second chalk to dump their gear for the customs inspection.

While the second chalk waited, Captain Royer stepped out of the customs area to coordinate with Air Force personnel, leaving Lieutenant Ferris and Sergeant Gillette in charge of the customs inspection. It was then that a young Army specialist approached Ferris. "Sir, are you in charge of this group?" she asked. Ferris didn't like the sound of that. Both flights were scrubbed, she told him in tones loud enough for those nearby to hear. Ferris felt his gut turn over with the news. He hustled out to find the captain, leaving the news to spread like wildfire back in the customs tent. That news sent the company's morale into a tailspin. Ferris likened it to "someone just kick[ing] the last breath out of your lungs." "Don't do anything stupid or crazy," Royer and Ferris told the troops. The rest of their instructions were more explicit. Take some time to collect your thoughts, explained Top, before letting your families back home know what's going on, then get some sleep. It was good counsel, for they were powerless to change their fate. The best they could do was just deal with it. "I went to bed that night very down," Ferris recalled.

Thankfully, "Mr. Murphy," the fictitious guy who predicted that whatever can go wrong, will go wrong—the guy who everyone in the Army knew so well—took the next day off. The unit awoke to the sounds of First Sergeant Elmore's voice booming throughout their makeshift sleeping quarters. The first chalk had a flight, he bellowed, but no one knew how long that would hold—in other words, they needed to hustle over to customs before the higher-ups changed their mind. The troops were at the customs inspection point within minutes, and as soon as their gear was cleared, they eagerly pitched in to help some Air Force loadmasters maneuver their baggage onto several waiting pallets.

Sam Woods, one of those on the first chalk, stood on the tarmac as the first chalk watched the C-17 Globemaster make its landing approach. He watched as it loitered high in the air, then finally swooped down for a landing. Suddenly, it banked hard to the left, spewing a volley of white flares from its belly as it maneuvered. The lumbering aircraft climbed again, then circled once more before dropping down abruptly, landing, and rolling to a stop near the cluster of MPs. Woods cornered one of the flight crew as they waited to board. "What's with all the flares?" The answer Woods got was hardly encouraging. "That's an emergency system," the crewman explained, "a system that's incorporated into the plane" whenever it "gets painted."

The first chalk was soon airborne, but even then, they worried that the plane would return to Anaconda. Nearly everyone raised a silent prayer that it would stay the course to Germany. They did, and the realization finally dawned that they were truly heading home. Not so for the second chalk. No sooner had the first chalk lifted off the tarmac than the word came down that the second flight was canceled. "Pack your bags and head back to tent city," they were told unceremoniously. For how long? they asked. It may be another week before the Air Force could get them out, came the reply.[11]

Royer was happy for the first chalk, but figured that as far as his group was concerned, "Murphy was working overtime." "Well, sir," stated Sergeant Mauney matter-of-factly, "I guess we've used up all our luck." He couldn't argue with Mauney's observation. To have endured what they did for a year in Baghdad and suffer only one casualty and no deaths was just short of a miracle. Royer was convinced their luck was partly due to those crossed pistols stenciled on the sides of their Humvees—that the people of Baghdad knew who they were and respected them. How else to explain incidents where 233rd patrols drove through a neighborhood, only to have another unit pass through the same streets minutes later and come under fire?

At the time, however, that was small consolation. Once back at the tent city, Royer turned the MPs loose. Most headed to the phone bank to report their grim news to the folks back home.[12]

First Contingent

The first chalk departed Balad at 1450 hours on April 18 and headed for Rhein-Main Airbase in Germany. Back at Balad, Captain Royer got the word that someone had taken pity on the MPs and found a flight for the second chalk—a flight scheduled to leave within hours. There was one hitch, however. It was headed to Kuwait first, then Germany. That was good enough for Royer, who had just resigned himself to another week at Anaconda. Together with Sergeant Gillette, the senior NCO in the second chalk, they rounded up the troops, tossed their personal gear onto the back of a 5-ton truck, and headed back to the customs station for the third time. Twelve hours after the first group departed, the second contingent was airborne and headed for Kuwait.

By that time, the first chalk was coursing its way home. The web seating wasn't exactly comfortable, but they were far better than those on the older C-130 aircraft, and for that the MPs were grateful. Many slept during their ride to Germany, some even stretching out on the floor. Their thoughts invariably turned to the reception that awaited them in Wisconsin, and to their plans once they got home. The plane landed at Rhein-Main Airbase, near Frankfurt, late in the afternoon of the 18th. They were on the ground just long enough to stretch their legs and get a nicotine fix before reboarding. The next leg took them to the Bangor International Airport in Maine, a civilian airfield that received a steady stream of military flights carrying veterans from Iraq. The MPs arrived in Bangor shortly after midnight. Even at that hour, they were greeted by local members of the VFW as they deplaned. The men and women of the VFW welcomed them home with hugs, handshakes, coffee, and donuts. They even passed out cell phones so the troops could call home. The MPs were on the ground just long enough to contact someone at Volk Field, the airbase that supported Fort McCoy. Then the first chalk was airborne again, with an anticipated arrival time in Wisconsin of 4:00 A.M. local time.[13]

The Reunion

Waiting for the first chalk at Volk Field were scores of families and friends, who eased their anticipation by sharing stories of their own painful odysseys over the past several days. Among them was Lisa Higginson, Tammy Hughes (Sergeant Lawrence Wilson's fiancée), and Deanna Victor. They'd spent the previous evening in a local restaurant, swapping stories and talking about their plans for the next few days, more animated than usual. As chance would have it, they were joined by Sergeant Larry Hundsdorf's fiancée, Melanie England. The women started the evening as strangers, but quickly forged a bond of friendship based on shared circumstances.

When Lisa Higginson recounted her roundabout trip to Wisconsin, the story was familiar to all. She had departed Springfield for Fort McCoy a couple of days before, only to get a call from Ed telling her to head back home; he was stuck in Iraq for a couple of more days. Understandably disappointed, she turned around. She stewed for most of her drive back to Rantoul, where she'd left her daughter, Amber, with her grandparents. "I'm just going back to Springfield in the morning," she told her dad in frustration. "I'm not going to Fort McCoy to see him. He gets home when he gets home!"

The next morning Lisa received two calls, one from Ed in Germany with the news he was coming home and the other from Tammy Hughes, trying to convince her to head once more to McCoy. She soon found herself packing, mumbling to herself, "I'm not going to go—I'm not going to go." By the time her father found her, she'd experienced a change of heart. "Damn it, I'm going."[14]

Now the four of them stood together at the edge of the tarmac, along with scores of others, on a decidedly cold April morning. They waited for a Globemaster to appear at "Oh-dark-thirty," as veterans said. It finally did, circling briefly before swooping down for a landing. As it taxied to a stop about a quarter mile from the waiting families, the crowd broke into a cheer. It took a long time for the soldiers to deplane, and even when they did, it was impossible in the darkness to identify anyone. All they could see were the dark outlines of soldiers filing past a military van as they turned in their weapons. Then the MPs formed into a loose file of twos, and Lieutenant Ferris barked out orders that sent them marching toward their families and friends.

The MPs peered hard into the darkness, hoping to catch a glimpse of their families, able only to see a dark line of figures silhouetted in front of a glaring bank of lights. Ed Higginson heard the crowd long before he could make anyone out; he strained hard to find Lisa. He marveled at how many were waiting to greet them so early in the morning—a crowd that included dozens of children. Just short of the crowd, Lieutenant Ferris gave them the order they had all waited to hear for over a year: "Go to your families." With that, the two groups merged, lost in the moment. Even soldiers who had no one waiting for them found plenty of hands to shake and embraces to share.[15]

Second Contingent

Even as the first chalk approached Wisconsin, another C-17, loaded with the remainder of the 233rd, was taxiing to a stop in Kuwait City. As they disembarked, Royer got the word that their aircraft was broken, that they'd be stranded in Kuwait for a couple of days while the Air Force flew in the parts needed to fix their bird. The MPs settled into tent city in an ugly mood, and Royer immediately hit the phones, scrambling to find anything that could get them home earlier. He got a lead on a C-17 that was leaving Kuwait empty, heading to Frankfurt and then across the ocean, terminating in the state of Washington. That was the opening he was looking for. He explained his predicament to a blue-suiter (Air Force personnel), who knew someone with a friend at Scott Air Force Base, the military's version of a mission clearinghouse. Because the plane was flying directly over Wisconsin, it made no sense to fly it empty when it could take his soldiers home. "Don't stop—we'll jump," he said, only half in jest.

Royer's persistence paid off, and the Air Force agreed to reroute the flight to Volk Field. Once again, Royer and Gillette rounded up their soldiers.

They transferred their baggage from one plane to another as the flight's ground crew marveled at their teamwork. In all, the second chalk was stuck in Kuwait for a little over a day and arrived at Rhein Main at 10:00 A.M. on the 20th after a six-hour flight.

That's when Royer received the next piece of bad news: crew rest. Air Force regulations prohibited the flight crew from continuing to the States until they got some sleep, and no one had thought to plan for another crew. Royer was tired, smelled pretty ripe after forty-eight hours without a shower, and was more than a little agitated when he heard that their gear had to be offloaded. Nor was he amused when a major informed him that his troops would be bused to tent city while they waited: "I pretty bluntly told this major that . . . he wasn't taking my gear off that airplane." And because there was a light dusting of snow in the air, a trip to tent city wasn't cutting it either. Instead, the MPs loitered in the terminal area and called their families with their latest update. Some found their way to a barracks and helped themselves to its laundry facilities. Others walked to the base exchange. Mostly, they caught up on their sleep in the terminal area.[16]

The second chalk spent a half-day at Rhein Main before it finally reboarded for the flight to Bangor. They flew across the Atlantic in the dead of night, curled up in their sleeping bags, some taking hits on bottles of NyQuil that passed from soldier to soldier. As the flight approached the coastline, a crew member passed out customs declaration forms. They dutifully filled them out and resigned themselves to yet another customs inspection once they landed. Moments after the plane glided to a stop, a customs official boarded the plane and asked everyone to pass their forms forward, thanking them for their trouble. Thankfully, that was the extent of their customs inspection.

Royer felt exhilarated. Finally, after a tumultuous year in Baghdad, the entire unit was back in the States. As they deplaned for a quick stretch, they were greeted by the Bangor VFW, old-timers who had seen their own war, now greeting each MP with a hearty handshake and a cup of coffee. It was the middle of the night, yet they were there to meet every flight arriving in country. It was a small gesture that meant the world to Royer and the rest of the MPs. They were home!

Still, their journey had one more leg before they too could greet their loved ones, and their flight was going nowhere until someone at Volk Field answered the telephone. "Why not spend a day here!" thought Sergeant Mauney sarcastically. "We've been delayed a day every time we stopped." But the MPs took the initiative one more time, grabbing cell phones in a determined attempt to rouse someone—anyone—at Volk Field. Meanwhile, Sergeant Weber called Pamela to tell her of yet another delay. She was thrilled nonetheless. "He's in country—I can drive there," she murmured to herself.

It was Gillette who finally raised Volk Field, and the group was once again airborne after a little more than an hour on the ground. They landed three hours later and deplaned into an early morning mist, then met with the same fanfare experienced by the first chalk. Waiting for them at Volk Field were most of their comrades from the first chalk, along with family members and the unit's entire chain of command, from their battalion commander all the way up to General Randy Thomas, the state's adjutant general.

General Thomas was content to wait in the background, relishing the moment. He marveled at how disciplined and professional the MPs conducted themselves, even as their loved ones stood only a couple of hundred yards away. As they deplaned, they turned in their 9-millimeters and M-16s, then formed up and fixed their attention on Sergeant Gillette and Captain Royer. With that, crisp orders were issued and the group marched through a gate toward their waiting families. Finally, Captain Royer gave the order to dismiss the troops. Only then did he head to his own family.[17]

Home at Last

On Wednesday, April 21, the entire company began its formal demobilization process at Fort McCoy. The process consisted of a series of briefings, lectures, and a physical for everyone in the unit. The Army viewed the demobilization process as a critical step in taking care of its veterans, but most of the MPs saw it as nothing more than a hassle. The MPs took issue with one step of the demobilization process, however. When told they would receive only a cursory physical examination, the company's leadership took strenuous exception, insisting that each MP receive a thorough physical. Even with that, however, blood samples were not drawn. For the rest of the demobilization process, the MPs cooperated but endured the process with little enthusiasm, eager only to head home.

On early Sunday morning, the company boarded a fleet of five commercial buses for the final leg of their journey: the drive back to Springfield. Unbeknownst to them, Major Michael Bierman, the MP's battalion executive officer, in coordination with the FRG, had arranged for a memorable reception in Springfield. Bierman contacted Lieutenant Colonel George Rakers, a veteran of the 233rd during Desert Storm who now worked full-time for the secretary of state police. Could Rakers help arrange a police escort into town? asked Bierman. Rakers was more than happy to oblige. He placed calls to the state police, secretary of state police, the Springfield police department, and the Sangamon County sheriff's office, arranging for squad cars to pick them up at Lincoln some 30 miles north of town. From there, the idea took on a life of its own. As far as the Springfield police department was concerned, these were fellow police officers, and several other departments from the surrounding area felt the same way. (Fourteen police departments were represented in the 233rd.) They all eagerly signed on.[18]

For the MPs, the drive south through the rich farmlands of Wisconsin and Illinois presented a stark contrast from the harsh landscape of Iraq. Royer marveled at the sight of clouds dotting the sky, fat with the promise of spring rains. Dana Hodges relished the smell of fresh air, so welcome after the pervasive stench of Baghdad. They were all struck by the lack of traffic and by the clean and uncluttered streets and highways. More than a few found themselves unconsciously scanning the roadsides, still looking for danger, then reminding themselves that they were no longer in Iraq. Adjusting to that reality, Lieutenant Ferris realized, would take time—you couldn't just throw a switch and immediately turn off old habits. Sergeant Camden told himself he'd have to start obeying the traffic signals again lest one of his police buddies remind him with a ticket. More than anything, they all soaked in the verdant greens of the countryside and relished the sight of freshly tilled fields of rich, dark soil stretching to the horizon. "It was like somebody was massaging my eyeballs," Paul Hildebrandt remembered fondly.[19]

As the bus convoy crossed the Wisconsin border into Illinois, a state police patrol car pulled in front of the convoy. When they approached Bloomington, about 70 miles out from Springfield, a squad car driven by Officer Kurt Kaufmann, a former member of the unit, joined the procession. By the time they reached the intended pickup point near Lincoln, their escort had grown to several squad cars. And as they drew closer to Springfield, they spotted clusters of people on the overpasses, cheering and waving flags as they passed underneath. It seemed that with each passing mile, another police car pulled into the convoy. By the time they reached the city limits, five buses and nearly forty police cars pulled off Interstate 55 for the 5-mile trek across the north side of Springfield, headed toward Camp Lincoln.

As they coursed their way through Springfield, it looked as though "every police car, every fire truck, everything you can imagine was out [there] with their lights going." But that wasn't all. From the moment the convoy entered the city limits, there were people lining the streets, often several deep. Many waved homemade signs proclaiming "Welcome" and "Thank you" as the buses passed. They spotted older residents holding their hands over their hearts, while others saluted. Young children waved, and almost everyone cheered. It was an amazing show of support, especially surprising considering the coverage the MPs saw on CNN and Fox while in Baghdad. "What makes the news," reflected Specialist Bradley Marcy later that day when interviewed by a local reporter, "is people back home protesting, everyone questioning why we're there. Then when you get home . . . you see everyone happy and saying we did a good job. . . . That's awesome!" Indeed, for everyone on those buses that day, the ride through Springfield was one of their most emotional and memorable experiences of a very eventful year. More than a few were speechless, embarrassed to find a lump in their throat, overwhelmed with emotion as they sat quietly and soaked up the scene outside their windows. It was one more experience they shared. It was part of what bound them together.[20]

Finally, the moment had arrived. The buses pulled into Camp Lincoln. Lieutenant Rice was there to greet Captain Royer as he stepped off the bus, saluting as he reported back to duty even while balancing on a set of crutches. Top wasted no time in getting the rest of the company off the buses. They filed smartly into the armory and formed into platoons.

Waiting in the armory were over 400 people, mostly families and close friends. Clustered in the background were General Thomas, Command Sergeant Major Bingse Young, the state's senior NCO, and a small group of National Guard officials. The crowd buzzed with excitement as they watched the company move smartly onto the drill floor and form up, culminating with Lieutenant Rice once again assuming his place in front of 3rd Platoon. Facing the company, Royer never spotted the podium in the corner of the drill floor, but it wouldn't have mattered if he had. He was in no mood for long speeches, nor was anyone else.

"You did it," he proclaimed as he addressed his troops for the last time. "Hoo-ah," came the rousing response. "Job well done," he continued. "Mission accomplished." And then he gave them the order everyone wanted to hear: "Company dismissed!" With that, the gymnasium erupted in cheers, and the families rushed forward to greet their warriors in glorious pandemonium.[21]

17
Conclusion

Saturday, August 14, 2004, was a gorgeous day for Springfield—an unseasonably cool day in a town known for its stifling August weather. The sun shone brightly and a cool breeze blew, barely rustling the ranks of corn and soybeans in the rich farmland that surrounded the state capital. Many in Illinois liked to think they lived in a modern-day Garden of Eden, blessed as they were with some of the world's richest soil and abundant rainfall. And central Illinois in 2004 was uncommonly green. For the men and women of the 233rd, the contrast with Baghdad could not be more pronounced. August 14 marked the first time the MPs gathered for a unit drill following their return from Iraq nearly four months before.

In honor of the occasion, the adjutant general and his staff held an official welcome ceremony for the troops. Since 2004 was an election year, the ceremony was as much a campaign event as it was a salute to the MPs. Governor Rod Blagojevich was there, along with U.S. Senate candidate Barack Obama, who had recently gained national notoriety at the Democratic National Convention. Several other dignitaries also crowded the podium. To the left of the podium was a handsome desk bearing the governor's seal, placed there for a bill-signing ceremony scheduled to follow the opening remarks. In the audience were approximately 150 family members, patiently waiting for what they thought would be an award ceremony for the troops. In the background was a smattering of local reporters. The crowd fell silent when Captain Royer marched his soldiers onto the cavernous drill floor. They filed in smartly, then fell in beside rows of tightly packed chairs arrayed on the drill floor, taking their cue from their commander to "take seats!"

Four politicians addressed the assemblage in quick succession, starting with a legislator from Aurora and ending with the governor. All four thanked the soldiers for their service and dedication, then congratulated each other on passing the Citizen Soldier Initiative, a piece of legislation designed to protect the employment, housing, and credit rights of Illinois' guardsmen and reservists. After the speeches, Governor Blagojevich moved to the desk to sign the legislation, accompanied by a cluster of media and a score of family members armed with cameras. After the signing ceremony, Governor Blagojevich and Senate candidate Obama walked over to the soldiers, now standing at attention. The two politicians shook hands and chatted with each soldier in the first rank, then moved across the isle to talk to the soldiers' parents, spouses, and friends. "You are going meet the rest of the soldiers, aren't you, governor," chided one spectator. "Of course," he immediately replied. For the next hour, Blagojevich and Obama did just that.

While the politicians worked their way through the crowd, a family member proudly flashed a crudely made sign bearing the slogan "Vote Republican." Outside in the parking lot was an SUV sporting a computer-generated sign in the rear window that read "Iraqi Veterans Against Bush." And through it all, in the back row of the company, separated by two empty rows of chairs, sat First Sergeant Elmore, silently surveying the entire scene. "The ceremony's for the troops," he insisted laconically.

Later that evening, the governor surprised the troops when he crashed their unit party at the Northenders VFW club in Springfield. Beer flowed freely that night as the governor worked his way through the room like the seasoned politician he was. When Top Elmore ribbed him about drinking Busch Beer, he was quick to reply, "I'm nonpartisan." "Yeah, right!" others responded when hearing of the exchange.[1]

Adjusting to Home

By the time their August drill occurred, the MPs were well on their way to readjusting to the real world. Sergeant First Class Kevin Weber started his adjustment when he first spotted evergreen trees in the distance after landing in Germany. In Iraq, "everything was in various shades of tan or brown," he explained. The lush greens of Germany were a wonderful contrast, something they all soaked in. When Captain Royer finally arrived home, one of his most welcome sites, outside his family, were the clouds that hung in the Illinois sky. "I didn't see clouds for seven months over there."[2]

Adjusting to home wasn't all welcome home parties, home-cooked meals, and uninterrupted nights. For many, adapting to the rhythms of life back home included unexpected challenges. Jeff Royer didn't care at all for the Fourth of July celebrations, and his standing joke with wife Sonia was that he was going to keep a lawn mower running outside his window at night to lull him to sleep, a fitting substitute for the ubiquitous generators in Baghdad. Keith Hildebrandt loved spending time with his fiancée and thought he was adjusting nicely until he went driving one day. As he cruised down the road, he caught sight of a McDonald's bag lying innocuously alongside of the road. He instinctively jerked the steering wheel hard to the left, giving the bag a wide berth. A second later, he realized he was back home. "Whoa!" he thought to himself. "You're not in Baghdad any more." Some changes were more obvious, and not as distressing. As Sergeant First Class Ryan Machin explained it, the year in Baghdad "made me appreciate . . . the things we have here in the United States, the things that everybody takes for granted, the simple things—electricity at all hours of the day, even something as simple as colors . . . It made me much more appreciative of my family."[3] His comments were echoed by many in the unit.

Changes

The truth was, most of the MPs were just beginning to come to terms with the way their year in Baghdad had changed them. For the old hands, MPs like Sam Woods and Jim Hobbs, both retiring after long careers in the National Guard, the experience didn't change them much. But Hobbs and Woods spent most of their time in the tactical operations center (TOC) and rarely ventured out into the streets of Baghdad. The younger MPs, especially those who spent plenty of time on the streets, found themselves changed in more profound ways.

Most of the MPs spent their year in Baghdad living on the edge, their senses perpetually on the alert while fighting to keep a lid on their emotions. They lived for the moment, knowing danger might be waiting for them around the next corner. Once they returned to the States, more than a few MPs discovered it was difficult to ratchet down their lives. Specialist Adam Moma, who was only eighteen when he deployed to Iraq, found it tougher to relate to his peers when he returned to Western Illinois University. "I don't feel like I fit in with my own age very much any more," he stated regretfully. Moma wasn't the only one who recognized that his time in Baghdad had changed his outlook. Keith Hildebrandt felt very much the same way—and not just because he planned to marry his high school sweetheart, Trisha, upon his return. "I changed," Keith said emphatically. "I became more confident, more independent."[4]

Sergeant Camden noticed he developed more patience while overseas, the kind of patience a supply sergeant needs when there's nothing you can do except wait for the Army to come through with much-needed supplies. For Captain Royer, who carried the burden of command, whose decisions meant life or death for his soldiers, the experience affected him differently. "They say I don't laugh as much anymore, . . . that I'm more cynical," he commented in a moment of reflection. "I have a lot less tolerance . . . with people doing stupid things."[5]

Sergeant Dana Hodges and Specialist Richard Williams, who experienced the UN bombing close up, struggle to put that day behind them. Williams admits that he doesn't get as excited about the little things since Iraq, that his life in the States simply does not compare with the intensity of his life in Baghdad. Hodges believes her year in Iraq has changed her for the better. Still, old friends sometimes remark how her "eyes look like they're a thousand years old."[6]

The MPs experienced more obvious changes as well. Like their fathers, uncles, and grandfathers from previous wars, many were eager to get on with their lives in more meaningful ways. They were ready to settle down, get married, and start raising a family. Keith Hildebrandt was one of those, and Jimmie Mayes, who got engaged just one month after returning home, was another. For Mayes, absence did indeed make the heart grow fonder.

Several marriages resulted because of the deployment. Jake and Sarah English were the first to marry upon returning home. They tied the knot on May 28 in a simple ceremony at the English family home in Jacksonville. Their story even caught the attention of a programmer for CBS's *Early Show* who was looking for a "positive story from Iraq." He thought the Englishes filled the bill nicely. The couple lost their chance for national notoriety, however, when Ronald Reagan died on Saturday, June 4, preempting their appearance the next Monday. Jake was greatly relieved. Much more important to him were the two planks added to the family's signpost at Lake Jacksonville bearing his and Sarah's names.

Sergeant Robert Spence and Specialist Blanca Valdez, who had been engaged when they deployed to Iraq, married shortly after returning to the States, and Specialists Danielle Middleton of 1st Platoon and Craig Davis from the 4th also married upon returning stateside. Rebecca Power, a medic attached to the 1st Platoon, met Specialist Ommy "Izzy" Irizarry, a popular and well-respected mechanic from the 519th who hailed from Puerto Rico, at Viper Base. The two continued their relationship upon returning home, and their baby, Oceana Grace, was baptized at Springfield's Atonement Lutheran Church in June 2005. The two were married a month later under a gazebo in Annacoco, Louisiana, near Fort Polk. The ceremony was both romantic and bittersweet. Izzy, still with the 519th, headed back to Iraq three months later while Rebecca and Oceana returned to Illinois to wait for his return. (Izzy was based at Camp Mule Skinner—now renamed—and made frequent jaunts into Baghdad to recover downed or destroyed vehicles.) Finally, Sergeant Gillette, the Hogs' platoon sergeant, married medic Jamie McCurry in May 2005.

Perhaps inevitably, the unit's year-long deployment strained several marriages to the breaking point, often aggravating tensions that existed even before the troops shipped out. Laura Thomason's marriage was among that group. She credits her squad mates in the operations section with helping her cope with a deteriorating marriage while in Iraq. She was divorced shortly after returning home and quickly reclaimed her maiden name, Gant. Medic Richard Williams was another. His time overseas only aggravated problems that existed before he left, and the marriage ended a year after he returned. Jay Fritzsche, who married just nine days before his deployment date, found it difficult to pick up his marriage where the two newlyweds had left off. Both had changed during his absence, and after his return, they "slowly grew apart." Jay was divorced in 2005, his marriage a casualty of the deployment.[7]

Many in the 233rd looked forward to resuming their schooling—schooling that was abruptly interrupted when the unit deployed in 2003. Among these was Abraham Bain, who was elated when he turned in his gear after completing his six-year hitch with the National Guard, tired of seeing class after class at Southern Illinois University in Carbondale pass him by. He returned to school in the fall of 2004, ready to focus all his energies on an industrial design degree, looking forward to begin his sophomore year in college—for the third time.

Lieutenant Joel Ferris was another of those eager to move on with his life, "maybe have a family, finish my masters." Joel knew he had changed. He felt more mature and grounded. The fact that he also came back with a Bronze Star helped patch up an often troubled relationship with his father. There had always been a distance between the two when Joel was growing up—tensions that resulted in part because of his father's own experiences in Vietnam. But now they had something in common. They were both combat veterans, and because of that, they shared a bond forged in two wars a generation apart. "I now can relate to my father," reflected Ferris proudly. "He has a Bronze Star—I do too."

Joel soon made his way back to his old job at the Social Security Administration in St. Louis. It wasn't long before the agency's executives took note of his management potential and started to groom him for more challenging positions. Joel also started dating Leigh Boyer, an old high school acquaintance. The relationship had been kindled a year ago, just one week before

Joel headed to Iraq, after a chance encounter at a Mount Olive bar. Once in Iraq, Joel put the encounter behind him, but six months into his tour, a letter unexpectedly arrived from Leigh. He wrote her back, and as the weeks and months slipped by, their correspondence continued—first letters, then e-mails that grew more and more frequent, then phone calls. By the time he arrived back home, he was ready to get more serious about this relationship as well. On August 7, 2005, Jayden Patrick Ferris was born, and Leigh began working toward her nursing degree. Joel was thrilled with how his life was shaping up.[8]

The 233rd After Iraq

At the unit's September drill, Captain Royer distributed a fistful of awards to unit members. Still working its way through the Army's bureaucracy were four Soldiers Medals—the highest award possible for humanitarian actions—recommended for the unit's four firefighters, Lieutenant Ferris, Staff Sergeants Waldron and Robert Smith, and Sergeant Eric Bertoni. By September, the unit resumed its hectic schedule, made even more so because of their success in Baghdad. Several MPs headed to Poland for a couple of weeks to help Polish Army units prepare for their own hitch in Iraq. They were also pressed into service to train Illinois units headed overseas. And when hurricanes Katrina and Rita slammed into the Gulf Coast, no one was surprised when several MPs volunteered to head south and help.[9]

The 233rd experienced a dramatic personnel turnover during its first year back from Iraq. There was nothing unusual about that. Change is a constant in the Army, and it was no different for the 233rd. By April 2005, over a third of the company's Iraqi veterans were no longer with the unit. Captain Royer was one of the first to rotate out, having exceeded the average command tour by a sizable margin. He handed over the reins of command in December 2004 to Captain Kate Atterbury, herself a former platoon leader with the unit before moving to a staff position with the state headquarters. Sergeants Jim Hobbs and Sam Woods, the two full-timers who'd seemingly been with the unit forever, both retired.

Thirty of the 233rd's members left the Army entirely, having reached the end of their tours. Most of these had been extended through the duration of the deployment by virtue of the stop-loss program. Among this group were Ed Higginson, Paul Hildebrandt, Abraham Bain, and Jay Fritzsche. They harbored no regrets about going to Iraq but were eager to get on with their lives. For Ed and Lisa Higginson, that included a church wedding on their one-year anniversary, and on May 17, 2005, came a new baby boy, who, according to Ed, was "quite possibly the cutest baby on the planet."[10]

Another twenty-three MPs transferred to other units. Most of these joined other Illinois National Guard units, including Keith Hildebrandt, who landed an assignment with a Springfield-based maintenance company, and Randy Camden, who transferred to the state's military academy, along with Kevin Weber. Joel Mauney backfilled Camden as the unit's new supply sergeant. Marc Victor found a position with the 183rd Fighter Wing, an Air National Guard unit located at Springfield's airport. Three MPs found full-time jobs with the state's recruiting and retention command, and four, including Quintrell Crayton and newlyweds Danielle Middleton and Craig Davis, made their way to Alaska and full-time positions with the Alaska National Guard.

Sergeant Lawrence Wilson, the TOC night shift's ace operations sergeant, was promoted to Sergeant First Class and became the 233rd's full-time Readiness NCO after their return, then in mid-2005 was transferred to the 33rd MP Battalion in Bloomington, the 233rd's battalion headquarters. Wilson saw plenty of familiar faces when he arrived at the 33rd, including Captain Royer and Lieutenants Ferris and Flack.

First Sergeant Elmore continued on as the 233rd's First Sergeant even as many others in the 233rd came and went, providing continuity as Captain Atterbury took command. But by late 2005, Top Elmore decided it was time to make some changes in his own life as well. He enrolled in the Illinois Department of Corrections training program to become a parole officer—a job where he could take full advantage of his years of military experience. And after twenty years in the Army National Guard, he decided to retire and pass the first sergeant baton to the next generation. Accordingly, December 2005 marked his last drill, a nostalgic and emotional occasion for many in attendance. John Gillette, newly promoted to master sergeant, became the 233rd's new first sergeant, adding a diamond to his new E-8 stripes.

Jeff Royer was also weighing his options as 2005 drew to a close. He served as the 33rd MP Battalion's S-2 (intelligence officer) at the time, but he soon decided to transfer to the 85th Training Division in the Army Reserve, where he'd have a better chance for promotion to major, and even more appealing, help train units deploying to Iraq.

But even with all the changing faces, the essence of the 233rd remained, carried forward by those who stayed with the unit. Among that group were Jake and Sarah English. Josh Holder, the reluctant hero who thwarted the attack on al-Mesbah, also stayed on board. By Josh's own admission, life has not been kind to him since his return, but by late 2005, he was working hard to change that, working toward a promotion to sergeant while he also attended Southern Illinois University (in spring 2006), majoring in forensic science. Joshua Waters, who had kept things interesting in the TOC night shift, was another who stayed with the unit, still assigned to the operations section. Ryan Machin, newly promoted to master sergeant, was one of many who moved up in the unit's hierarchy, slotted against one of the vacated operations sergeant positions. Roman Waldron, Jim Nayonis, Jim Batterson, and Jeremie Mayes took over vacated platoon sergeant positions. Jimmie Mayes also got an additional stripe when he moved to the TOC. Sergeant Robert Spence was among several who took over as squad leaders and earned a staff sergeant rocker in the process.

Finally, Richard Carroll, who fought to get back into the unit after 9/11, earned a promotion to staff sergeant and took over as squad leader for 1st Squad of 4th Platoon after deciding to stay in. His wife, Marcia, gave birth to daughter Olivia in June, one of several children the MPs conceived during their midtour leaves. Of all the souvenirs Rich brought back from Iraq, none is more cherished than the chunk of shrapnel that almost claimed his life. Carroll was unable to find a jeweler who could convert the shrapnel into crosses. (The shrapnel is made from the kind of tempered steel suitable for munitions.) In the meantime, he keeps it safe in a dresser drawer.

Some of those who served with the 233rd in Baghdad will soon be heading back overseas. Headquarters Company of the 33rd MP Battalion, the new home for Flack, Ferris, and several others, was due to rotate to Iraq in September 2006. Leading that group was Lieutenant Colonel George Rakers, who went to the gulf in 1990 with the 233rd and in 2004 helped organize the 233rd's reception back from Iraq. Those who had already served in Iraq were told they could opt out of the 2006 rotation. For Flack, awaiting promotion to captain, his thinking changed when he discovered that his wife was pregnant, with their son due in February 2006. So too for Lieutenant Ferris, with a newborn son at home and his career with the Social Security Administration taking off. There was even talk of taking over as the next commander of the 233rd. For both officers, it was time to give their families higher priority.[11]

Those the MPs Left Behind

The MPs kept close tabs on American and Iraqi friends they left behind in Iraq. Captain Ohl and the Redlegs of Bravo Company found themselves in the midst of the al-Sadr uprising when the 233rd departed for Balad Airbase. Within a week, the Redlegs finally received their much-coveted MP brassards, then were abruptly transferred to a new mission located 70 miles north of Baghdad. Ohl appreciated the change in mission because the new assignment was less dangerous, but more than a few of his Redlegs "missed the glamour and excitement of rolling through the streets of Baghdad and Sadr City."[12]

As for the MPs of the 984th, the Fort Carson unit that replaced the 233rd, they also completed a successful tour in Baghdad, matching the 233rd's accomplishment by bringing everyone home safely in February 2005. The 519th MP Battalion headquarters, which beat the 233rd home by a couple of months, experienced even more dramatic personnel changes upon arriving home, as is typical for active-duty units. Chaplain Brian Reck transferred to Fort Bliss, Texas, where he was assigned to an air defense artillery training unit. Considering his repeated deployments to Korea, Afghanistan, and Iraq, his family had coped well during his long absences. By late 2005, it was his turn to take care of them, especially after his wife Kari was diagnosed with vulvar cancer. Even with that, Brian also found time to write about his own experiences in both Afghanistan and Iraq. His book, *A Chaplain Experience,* was published in 2005.[13]

Lieutenant Colonel David Glaser stayed in command of the 519th for another sixteen months after the unit returned to Fort Polk. He also set up a training program to train National Guard units—soldiers like the Pennsylvania artillerymen—in basic military police skills. In June 2005, he turned over command and was reassigned to an important position as the chief of the MP branch for the human resources command. His goal is to command an MP brigade. His old command, the 519th, returned to Baghdad in October 2005, with maintenance sergeant Ommy Irizarry in tow.

Izzy was not the only person with 233rd connections serving in Iraq at that time. Ironically, both Terry Lucas, the unit's very first commander, and Tom Bowman, who turned over command of the unit just weeks before the gulf war, also spent 2005 in Iraq. Lucas, long since retired from the Guard, arrived in October 2005, assigned as an operations officer for the Department of Justice assisting the regime's crime liaison office, where he helped ferret out criminals from the former regime. Colonel Tom Bowman arrived in Iraq on June 11, 2005, in command of a group of seventeen Illinois guardsmen who serve as liaisons with the multinational division, dominated by the Poles and other central Europeans.[14]

Difficult Adjustments

When the 233rd returned safely to Springfield in the spring of 2004, Captain Royer was certain of a couple of things. He was certain that some of his soldiers would struggle to come to terms with their experiences in Baghdad—that the 233rd would have its share of post-traumatic stress disorder

(PTSD) cases. His soldiers simply had seen and experienced too much for that not to be the case. Royer also knew that some of those who most needed help would be reluctant to seek it. For that reason, the unit's monthly drills became opportunities for the chain of command to assess how the troops were doing. When someone exhibited warning signs of PTSD, the leadership gently pushed them toward treatment.

Family members, for their part, had been coached at their Family Readiness Group meetings not to press their loved ones about their experiences. Some things, they were told, their soldiers might be willing to talk about—some things they might never discuss. The senseless death and destruction, the arbitrary and capricious nature of tragedy they witnessed, the intense rush of adrenaline when in danger, the exhilaration when they triumphed, the agonizing pain when they fell short—these realities were as old as war itself. They were also things that only someone who experienced them firsthand could ever truly understand. Accordingly, family members were warned not to press their loved ones too much. The soldiers would choose their own time and place to talk about them.

For Staff Sergeant Joel Mauney, there were "some things you want to talk about, and some things you don't want to talk about at all." Mauney was struck by the advice a seasoned Vietnam veteran gave him when he returned to work. "Just make friends with it," his buddy told him with no elaboration. Mauney returned to that phrase repeatedly over the next few days, struggling with it until he found his own meaning to his friend's words of advice. "Don't hide from it," Mauney concluded. "Don't keep it inside. Try and talk about it as much as you can." Still, there were things he knew he would never tell Sarah—things he hoped never to recall again.[15]

Kristina Ward, one of the first to struggle with combat stress early in her tour in Baghdad, adjusted well to her life once returning stateside. By late 2005, Kristina was engaged and excited about being a new mom. She gave birth to Brayden in August 2005. She also reenlisted for another six-year tour with the Illinois National Guard.

Specialist Stephanie Stretch's experiences in Baghdad were typical of many. She spent her entire tour in Baghdad as a SAW gunner in 3rd Platoon. After returning to the States, she was excited about getting back to her college education at Southern Illinois University, but she soon discovered that a good night's sleep was frustratingly elusive. Her nights were plagued by flashbacks from Baghdad, including the day Lieutenant Rice was cut down by an improvised explosive device. Even during the day, innocuous things like trash along the road often triggered disturbing thoughts. Stephanie and roommate Nicole Hammack finally sought counseling at a nearby veteran's hospital in October 2004. Stephanie filled out the mandatory forms, but because of the Veterans Administration's (VA) mounting backlog, she was unable to get an appointment with a counselor until February 2005. Two months later, Senator Dick Durbin encountered Stephanie and three other Iraqi veterans with PTSD at a forum sponsored by John A. Logan College. Senator Durbin and a staffer took note of Stephanie's maturity and her obvious composure when speaking during that meeting. On August 1, 2005, she testified before a Senate subcommittee investigating the nation's VA hospitals, which by that time were overwhelmed by PTSD patients from Iraq and Afghanistan. That evening, she also appeared on ABC news, giving an articulate voice to the problems of Iraqi veterans dealing with PTSD.[16]

Specialist Lucas Jockisch was another MP who struggled with PTSD upon returning to the States. At first, he looked forward to resuming his schooling, following his squad leader, Sergeant Jason Haworth, to Western Illinois University. But Lucas was unable to get a good night's sleep and soon began drinking heavily. There were lots of incidents that Jockisch tried to blot out, but one in particular was hard to shake. It was the day Sergeant Haworth led a patrol through a neighborhood of Baghdad, with Jockisch at his usual post, hunkered down behind the lead vehicle's SAW. When Haworth heard shots up ahead, the patrol sped to the scene. As the vehicles approached, Jockisch spotted an Iraqi man standing on the running board of a semi tractor, brandishing an AK-47. As the lead Humvee closed the gap, the gunman raised his rifle and pointed it directly at Jockisch. The two locked eyes, and Jockisch instinctively pulled the trigger on his SAW, watching a stream of 5.56-millimeter bullets tear into the man's torso. The Iraqi died instantly.

In the subsequent investigation, the MPs learned the gunman had stopped his semi at an Iraqi police (IP) checkpoint, then suddenly ripped the AK-47 out of the startled IP's grip. The IP took off running full speed down the street. That's when the MPs showed up. Only Jockisch's quick thinking prevented the gunman from cutting down the fleeing IP. But that fact, and the vociferous praise the IPs showered on Jockisch afterward, did little to comfort him months later. He had killed a man at close range, even as he looked into his eyes. It was the kind of thing that stayed with you.

Sergeant Jim Batterson first noticed changes in Jockisch during a weekend drill—changes that suggested he suffered from PTSD. Batterson pulled Jockisch aside and encouraged the young soldier to get some help. Finally, in the spring of 2005, Jockisch decided to take his sergeant's advice and checked in with the VA. Gradually, with the help of the VA doctors, Lucas began to put his life back together. By late 2005, he was even looking for opportunities to return to Iraq, possibly accompanying the 33rd MP Battalion if they'd have him, and if not, wait until the 233rd returned. For Jockisch, life in Iraq seemed to have more meaning, more relevance, than his mundane life in the States.[17]

Lieutenant Steve Rice had his own challenges to overcome—challenges that were more physical than mental. After the operation in May 2004 that permanently fixed his left foot at a 90-degree angle and fused his big toe to his foot, Rice was posted to Fort McCoy while he waited for the Army to make a final decision on his medical status. The Army's system for dealing with those recovering from serious injuries had been designed with active-duty soldiers in mind. Because Fort McCoy was where he deployed, and because he was still on active duty, McCoy was where the Army insisted he wait while they evaluated his case. But for Rice, it made no sense to post him there, hundreds of miles from his family, with nothing to do.

Rice spent six long weeks at McCoy—weeks filled with boredom, frustration, and indecision. He worked on his recovery in the same way he approached his job as an MP—aggressively. After pestering anyone who would listen, he discovered it could take many more months before the Army's cumbersome medical evaluation system would adjudicate his case. In the meantime, the Army physicians and bureaucrats who now controlled his life gave him very little to do but to sit and wait. Rice wasn't good at either. Instead, he petitioned anyone and everyone he could about his plight, contacting his chain of command at Fort McCoy and back in the Illinois National Guard. When his efforts failed to get results, he attempted to contact the adjutant general's office while simultaneously writing the office of Lieutenant Governor Pat Quinn. Staffer Eric Schueller did what he could to resolve the issue. Rice finally got some satisfaction when the Army put him into the Community-Based Health Care Organization, a pilot program specifically designed for cases like his. They transferred him to his hometown of Godfrey, Illinois, and found work for him at the 1151st Transportation Company in nearby Granite City. Meanwhile, Rice continued with his physical therapy at a local hospital. The new arrangements were a huge improvement over the months he had languished at Fort McCoy, and for that he was grateful.[18]

By the time Steve moved back to Illinois, he grew increasingly discouraged by the notion of living the rest of his life with his left foot fixed permanently at a 90-degree position. He also suffered from near-constant pain associated with his injuries. By the end of 2004, he made an important decision. He'd seen more than his share of amputees at Walter Reed and was generally impressed at how well they were able to adjust to their new prosthetic devices. Gradually, he warmed to the idea of living with a prosthetic leg instead of a foot that never moved. On January 12, 2005, the surgeons at Walter Reed amputated his left leg below the knee and fitted Steve with a prosthetic device. Within days, he began the long process of physical therapy, learning to master getting around on his new leg with a renewed determination and with his spirits buoyed. By the summer of 2005, he had progressed enough to participate in a fund-raiser for disabled veterans, riding his bike across Kansas, Missouri, and part of Illinois to raise money for the Wounded Warrior Project and Soldier Ride. On November 28, 2005, he was medically retired from the Army, eager to begin his new life in Maryland as a Department of Defense employee. Between those two events, he sandwiched in a week of skiing in Colorado.[19]

And what of Dana Hodges, who saw so much blood spilled during her tour in Iraq, pulling double duty as a team leader (her official assignment) and medic? On the surface, Dana impressed people with her uncommon frankness and confidence. Most who met her came away convinced that Dana was the kind of MP you wanted to have with you when things got tough. She was, but the self-assurance masked the pain she carried. Before going to Iraq, Dana had contemplated a future in medicine. Afterward, she admitted to friends that her time in Baghdad had changed her. She now was unsure of what lay in her future—law enforcement perhaps, or maybe medicine. She was even thinking about going on active duty, but added this as an afterthought. "I'd like to . . . stay [away] from the blood and guts for a little bit."

In the months after her return to the States, Dana struggled to find her way, especially when the opportunity to go on active duty didn't pan out. It took a change of scenery before she got her life back on track. By late 2005, her days of uncertainty were behind her. She landed on her feet in Las Vegas, finding work in the region's booming real estate business.[20]

Future of Iraq

The men and women of the 233rd were typical of most of their generation. They generally claimed to be largely disinterested in politics. They followed the news no more and no less than most Americans. But serving in Iraq put them at the center of the world's attention. It made them participants in the greatest political debate of our time.

It helped that the vast majority of them believed in their mission. They saw firsthand the devastation that Saddam had wrought on Iraq, the crushing poverty and repression his Ba'athist thugs imposed on the Iraqi people, and deemed their task justified. "If you were over there and saw the way the people were living, you'd agree that we needed to be there," stated Specialist Jockisch without a moment's hesitation. His sentiments were echoed by almost all of the MPs. "I hated being there," admitted Staff Sergeant Mark Walden, "but do I think it was a waste of time. No! I think we needed to be there, and I think it needed to be done." Ryan Machin, a veteran of the first gulf war, was even more emphatic. "It was the right thing to do and I'll stand by that until the day I die."[21]

They were not a bit bothered by the fact they found no weapons of mass destruction. Weren't the 3rd Platoon "Hogs," after all, exposed to some kind of radioactive contaminant at Diyala Bridge? That and the occasional radio traffic they overheard of reported discoveries of mustard gas and other agents led them to conclude that Saddam did have a few WMDs, just not on the massive scale that so many had predicted before the war. More importantly, they saw themselves as necessary agents of change, bringing democracy and freedom to a troubled corner of the world.

Most MPs predicted a better future for Iraq, but several voiced doubts about whether the Iraqi people were up to the task, especially because the country was riddled with corruption and torn by religious and ethnic divisions. When they had reason to reminisce about their time in Iraq, flipping through photographs of themselves with smiling IPs, they were inevitably reminded of the incredible challenges the Iraqis now faced. Too many of the Iraqi police and interpreters in those photos were dead now, victims of terrorists who targeted anyone who worked with the Americans. Even the House of Love Orphanage became a target for the terrorists, just as Sister Beth had feared. Nothing made less sense to the MPs than to target those destitute, handicapped children.

But the MPs also had reason for hope. Iraq possesses a relatively well-educated population desperate for change. The MPs agreed that Iraq's transformation would be slow and painful and that Americans would need to be involved for many years to come. Most believed it would take a generation or more for the Iraqis to create a truly open and democratic society. The real hope, they insisted, rested with the children of Iraq, the very kids who mobbed them wherever they went, who never failed to meet them with a smile and an innate curiosity. "It won't happen overnight," reflected Lieutenant Ferris, "it won't happen in the next five years. . . . It will take the children growing up." Sergeant Hodges agreed. "It's going to have to be the children to build the society up, but I think they're going to be able to do it."[22]

Still, it would be wrong to suggest that believing in the mission was what sustained them during their year in Baghdad. Even more important was the intense camaraderie they shared with each other. Stephen Rice expressed it best: "We were told to go, and once you're in a combat zone, all the politics and BS goes out the window real fast and there's only one thing left. That's your family. . . . That's my platoon! . . . My world revolved around those 33 soldiers. . . . It's not about oil, it's not about Saddam Hussein, it's not about weapons of mass destruction, it's about my guys and getting them home alive."

Rice's comment speaks volumes about the intense bond the members of the 233rd shared with each other and for their unit. As far as they were concerned, there was no better unit in Iraq than their unit, and no finer soldiers than their comrades. "I'd go back in a heartbeat as long as it was with the same unit," stated Laura Gant, sharing a sentiment expressed by many in the unit. Joel Mauney took it a step further. "I would put our unit up against any other MP company in the Army." Their esprit de corps was unmistakable. Marcus Stern, the Copley reporter who spent a week with the unit, felt it, and so did Colonel Glaser. "The 233rd," Glaser stated with complete sincerity, was "as good or better than any company I'd been around."[23]

Deanna Victor felt the same deep affection for her fellow members of the "Band of Sisters," Monica Hildebrandt, Tammy Hughes, and Sarah Mauney, who shared their year together waiting and worrying about their loved ones overseas. "The bond that we have I will never have with anyone else," she explained to a newspaper reporter. "You can't understand how this feels unless you experience it yourself. We hang on each other. When one is weak, the other is strong." Monica Hildebrant felt exactly the same. "That friendship I formed with those three women . . . is something special that we will have with each other forever."[24]

Conclusion

It is hard to imagine a more important mission in Iraq after the fall of Saddam's regime than the one the 233rd and her sister MP companies drew. They were charged with creating stability out of anarchy, and with building an honest and responsive police force from one of the most corrupt and brutal police forces in the world. There were many other vital missions to be accomplished during those crucial early months of occupation: rebuilding the nation's crumbling infrastructure and oil industry, kick-starting the economy, beginning hundreds of ambitious humanitarian projects, and, perhaps most important, forging the first democratic government in the Arab world. It soon became apparent that all of these depended on the military's ability to impose security on a nation that formerly knew only brutal repression. At the heart of that effort was the 233rd and a handful of other MP companies.

It is also hard to imagine a group of soldiers more ideally suited to their task than the men and women of the 233rd. They possessed the perfect combination of police experience, intuition, maturity, and plain old-fashioned common sense needed to pull it off. They approached their job aggressively, even while demonstrating an admirable empathy for the Iraqi people and the Iraqi police with whom they worked. More than anything, they proved remarkably resilient. "I think a soldier is the most adaptive person in the world," explained Lieutenant Rice with obvious conviction. "When given a really crappy hand, they can make the best of it." The soldiers of the 233rd proved that many times over. They were by no means perfect, but even when they failed, they generally did so with a commendable humility and grace.[25]

What is perhaps most remarkable about them, however, is just how ordinary they are—how the soldiers of the 233rd are typical of all of America's young men and women fighting in the nation's war on terror. The same stories could be told, with obvious variations, about the 32nd MP Company, or the 204th, or 812th, or about scores of other units serving in Iraq, active, reserve, or National Guard, infantry, engineers, or transportation. America's soldiers are both idealistic and pragmatic, unrelenting in the pursuit of their mission yet generally restrained in their execution of that mission. They represent the very best of America, and as in all wars, they occasionally exhibit some of our worst traits as well. Most of them serve in anonymity and will remain forever lost to history. Their accomplishments will never be written about. Their sacrifices will be taken for granted—or even worse, forgotten by future generations. Their stories, no doubt, are every bit as compelling as those presented here.

But this is not a story about all Americans serving in Baghdad. It's the story of the men and women of the 233rd MP Company during one incredible year in the unit's distinguished history. They lived, for that year, with an intensity that most of us will never experience. In the process, they exceeded everyone's expectations but their own, and got everyone back home alive. Their memories of those experiences and the bonds that they formed will illuminate the rest of their lives in ways that those who were not there, who were not part of it, will never be able to fully understand or appreciate. They are different people because of that year, and for the most part, they are better for it.

The soldiers of the 233rd who served in Iraq are an amazing group. But what is perhaps most noteworthy about them is not how extraordinary they are. Ultimately, they are no different than the rest of us. They are ordinary people who rose to the challenge that their nation thrust on them and accomplished remarkable feats.

The men and women of the 233rd possess all of the admirable strengths and most of the regrettable flaws and failings to which humanity is subject. They are no more worthy of God's grace than you or me. But because of their struggles and sacrifices during their year in Baghdad, they deserve our deepest respect and admiration. They faced the greatest challenge of their lives and triumphed—not for themselves or even for their families, but for the American and Iraqi people they served.

233rd Military Police Company Roster

There were 157 soldiers who deployed to Kuwait in April 2003 with the 233rd MP Company, with 156 making the trip north to Baghdad, and six more who joined the unit in September, for a total of 162 men and women who served with the unit in Iraq. The following MPs authorized their name to be released.

SPC Christina Ashley	4th PLT	SPC Quntrell Crayton	3rd PLT
SPC Christopher Ater	1st PLT	SPC Joshua Crutchley	1st PLT
SPC Abraham Bain	HQs	SGT Christopher Cunningham	HQ
SPC Justin Bandy	2nd PLT	SPC Craig Davis	4th PLT
SGT Matthew Bandy	1st PLT	SGT Jameson Denagel	1st PLT
SPC Grant Barnes	HQ	SPC Christopher Dennison	1st PLT
SSG James Batterson	3rd PLT	SPC Brandon Douglas	2nd PLT
SGT Jennifer Batterson	2nd PLT	MSG Roger Ducharme	HQ
SGT Jacob Baucom	2nd PLT	1SG Robert Elmore	HQ
SPC Adam Bauer	HQ	SPC Robert P. Elmore	2nd PLT
SPC Jeffrey Bennett	HQ	SPC Jacob English	HQ
SGT Phillip Berriman	4th PLT	1LT Joel Ferris	1st PLT
SGT Eric Bertoni	1st PLT	1LT Mark Flack	4th PLT
SPC Jacob Blome	3rd PLT	SSG Jeremiah Fritzsche	3rd PLT
SGT Robert Bowser	HQ	SPC Robert Gasen	1st PLT
SPC Jason Brown	1st PLT	SGT Ryan Getz	1st PLT
SSG Randall Camden	HQ	SFC John Gillette	3rd PLT
SSG Brian Campbell	HQ	SPC Timothy Gilmore	2nd PLT
SPC Steven Carmody	1st PLT	SGT Kurtis Glosser	4th PLT
SPC Angela Carner	2nd PLT	SGT Brandon Golden	2nd PLT
SGT Richard Carroll	2nd PLT	SPC Nathan Grissom	1st PLT
SSG Deborah Carter	HQ	SPC James Hamilton	4th PLT
SGT Shauna Cashion	1st PLT	SPC Nicole Hammack	HQ
SPC Brad Clark	4th PLT	SPC Anthony Hanks	2nd PLT
SPC Erica Clark	2nd PLT	SGT Matthew Harris	HQ
SPC Geoffrey Clarkson	3rd PLT	SGT Jason Haworth	3rd PLT
SGT Shannon Clarkson	HQ	SGT John Hayes	4th PLT
SPC Joshua Crawford	4th PLT	SPC Richard Helkey	2nd PLT

SPC Mitchell Herren	3rd PLT	SSG Jeremie Mayes	2nd PLT
SGT James Herrick	2nd PLT	SPC Blake Mays	4th PLT
SPC Harry Hibbs	3rd PLT	SPC Linda McCarter	HQ
SGT Edward Higginson	HQ	SGT Mamie McCurry	HQ
SSG Keith Hildebrandt	HQ	SPC Mark McManaway	1st PLT
SGT Paul Hildebrandt	1st PLT	SGT Sean Meyer	2nd PLT
SPC Cynthia Hilliard	4th PLT	SPC Danielle Middleton	1st PLT
SGT Matthew Himpelmann	HQ	SPC Randall Miller	2nd PLT
SGT Dan Hinds	3rd PLT	SPC Adam Moma	HQ
SFC James Hobbs	HQ	SPC Andrew Moore	4th PLT
SGT Dana Hodges	3rd PLT	SPC Raymond Moore	HQ
SPC Joshua Holder	1st PLT	SSG Lisa Morrison	4th PLT
SGT Phillip Holt	4th PLT	SSG James Nayonis	4th PLT
SGT Joshua Hubbard	4th PLT	SFC Michael Parkin	1st PLT
SGT Larry Hundsdorfer	3rd PLT	SPC Dillard Patterson	3rd PLT
SGT Marvin Iffert	2nd PLT	PFC Adam Pope	1st PLT
SPC Christopher Jockisch	2nd PLT	SPC Rebecca Power	1st PLT
SPC Lucas Jockisch	3rd PLT	SPC Michael Racki	1st PLT
SGT Mark Johnson	4th PLT	SPC Michael Ravenscraft	1st PLT
SPC Eric Jones	2nd PLT	SPC Ryan Ray	3rd PLT
SGT Matthew Kampfl	HQ	SPC Roger Reed	4th PLT
SPC Shawna Keith	1st PLT	SSG Kenneth Reiterman	2nd PLT
SPC Steven Keith	3rd PLT	2LT Stephen Rice	3rd PLT
SPC David Kinley	1st PLT	CPT Jeff Royer	Cmdr
SPC Dennis Kirchgesner	HQ	SPC Dustin Ruyle	3rd PLT
SGT James Kollins	4th PLT	SSG Kenny Santiago	3rd PLT
SPC Joseph Layman	3rd PLT	SPC Sarah Schmidt	HQ
SPC Michael Leverich	HQ	SPC Megan Schukar	3rd PLT
SPC William Lipcamon	2nd PLT	SGT Nicholas Shasteen	3rd PLT
SPC Paul Lorenz	2nd PLT	SPC Phillip Shipley	4th PLT
SPC Benjamin Lynch	3rd PLT	SPC Ayrielle Singley	HQ
SFC Ryan Machin	2nd PLT	SSG Cindy Singley	HQ
SGT Clinton Mansholt	HQ	SSG Robert Smith	1st PLT
SPC Bradley Marcy	2nd PLT	SPC Zachary Smith	1st PLT
SGT George Martin	1st PLT	SGT Robert Spence	3rd PLT
SGT Joel Mauney	3rd PLT	SPC Jennifer Stamer	4th PLT
SPC Louis Maxedon	HQ	SPC Naythan Stewart	4th PLT
SSG James Mayes	1st PLT	SPC Jon Stonewall	2nd PLT

SPC Zachary Street	1st PLT	SSG Rusty Walker	2nd PLT
PFC Stephanie Stretch	3rd PLT	SPC Kristina Ward	4th PLT
SGT Nicholas Strode	1st PLT	SPC Joshua Waters	HQ
SPC Janet Sutter	2nd PLT	SGT Craig Watkins	3rd PLT
SPC Laura Thomason	HQ	SFC Kevin Weber	4th PLT
SPC Michael Thompson	2nd PLT	SPC Deirdre Weide	HQ
SGT Timothy Tolbert	4th PLT	SGT Michael Whited	HQ
SPC Damien Tucker	3rd PLT	SPC Richard Williams	3rd PLT
SGT Christopher Turner	1st PLT	SSG Lawrence Wilson	HQ
1LT Jacob Vahle	2nd PLT	MSG H. Samuel Woods	HQ
SPC Blanca Valdez	2nd PLT	SPC Paul Woolsey	4th PLT
SGT Marc Victor	HQ	SPC William Woolsey	4th PLT
SPC Raine Vonnida	4th PLT	SGT Sean Wright	4th PLT
SSG Mark Walden	4th PLT	SPC Trevor Wright	3rd PLT
SSG Roman Waldron	1st PLT		

Notes

Availablitiy of Interviews: The interview tapes and digital recordings, transcripts for most of the interviews, and interviewees release forms are available to the public at the Illinois Military Museum located at Camp Lincoln in Springfield, Illinois.

Preface

1. Interview with SPC Joshua Holder and SPC Joshua Crutchley, March 12, 2005.

2. Rich Miller, "Rich Miller's 'vacation'—report from Iraq," City2 E-News, http://www.city2e-news.com/miller9.html. Rich Miller, "Wrong moves, right moves," *Illinois Times*, September 18–34, 2003.

3. Miller, "Wrong moves," 7.

Chapter 1. The Early Years

1. Mark R. DePue, *Lineage and Honors of the Illinois Militia and National Guard* (Springfield: Illinois National Guard and Militia Historical Society, 2004), 161–62.

2. Interview with LTC (Retired) Terry Lucas, September 9, 2004.

3. Lucas.

4. Lucas. Interview with COL Tom Bowman, August 26, 2004. Years after the Cuban refugee mission at Fort McCoy, the MPs still proudly displayed a collection of handmade knives and other weapons seized from the Cubans in the 233rd orderly room.

5. Bowman.

6. Bowman.

7. Interview with LTC Kevin Keen, August 2, 2004. Conversation with SSG Lawrence Wilson, May 20, 2005 (not recorded).

8. Interview with MAJ Wendell Lowry, January 19, 2005.

Chapter 2. Mobilization and Train-up

1. Interview with Sister Beth Murphy, January 17, 2005. Springfield *State Journal-Register,* October 24, 2003, 1.

2. Interview with SGT Paul Hildebrandt and Monica Hildebrandt, August 28, 2004.

3. Interview I with CPT Jeff Royer, July 22, 2004. "Timeline Iraq," http://timelines.ws/countries/IRAQ_B.html. Department of the Army, First U.S. Army Permanent Order 035-55, February 4, 2003.

4. Paul and Monica Hildebrandt.

5. Royer I. Interview I with 1SG Robert Elmore, July 15, 2004. STARC-IL Warning Order 03-001, January 28, 2003. Conversation with SSG Lawrence Wilson, May 20, 2005. Several soldiers actually volunteered to be transferred to the 333rd and 933rd MP Companies when these units were alerted several days before the 233rd's alert.

6. Conversation with CW4 Jack Pascoe, January 19, 2005.

7. "233rd leaving for active duty," Springfield *State Journal-Register,* February 10, 2003, 1, 6. Royer I. Elmore I. Paul and Monica Hildebrandt.

8. Royer I.

9. Elmore I. Springfield *State Journal-Register,* October 23, 2003, 1, 6. "View from the Top," Springfield *State Journal-Register,* October 25, 2003, 1, 4.

10. Assorted 233rd MP Company personnel records. Elmore I.

11. Royer I. *233rd Military Police Company Modified Table of Organization and Equipment,* Department of the Army, October 4, 2001.

12. Royer I. Elmore I. Interview with 1LT Joel Ferris, August 17, 2004. Interview with SFC Jim Hobbs, January 7, 2005.

13. Royer I. Ferris.

14. Royer I. Elmore I. Interview with SFC Ryan Machin, August 11, 2004. Interview with SSG James Nayonis, September 12, 2004. Conversation with SSG Lawrence Wilson, February 24, 2005.

15. Elmore I.

16. Interview with 1SG (Retired) Jerry Calbow, September 22, 2004. Paul and Monica Hildebrandt. Interview with 1LT Jennifer Fallert, February 13, 2005.

17. Royer I. Elmore I. Interview with SPC Joshua Holder, August 15, 2004. Interview with SGT Ed Higginson and Lisa Higginson, September 15, 2004. Paul and Monica Hildebrandt.

18. "Troops' efforts praised at rally," Springfield *State Journal-Register,* March 30, 2003, 1, 12. Interview with Monica Hildebrandt, Tammy Hughes, Sarah Mauney, and Deanna Victor, November 7, 2005.

Chapter 3. Into Iraq

1. CPT Lesley Kipling and COL Ted Spain, "From Kuwait to Baghdad," *Military Police Magazine,* April 19, 2004. (COL Spain, the article's coauthor, was also the brigade commander for the 18th MP Brigade.) Paul and Monica Hildebrandt. Royer I. Elmore I. Interview with 1LT Steven Rice, August 17, 2004. Interview with CPT (Chaplain) Brian Reck, February 11, 2005.

2. Royer I. Interview IV with CPT Jeff Royer, August 12, 2004. Interview with LTC David Glaser, August 4, 2004.

3. Royer I. Elmore I. Paul and Monica Hildebrandt.

4. Interview with 1LT Joel Ferris, August 17, 2004. "Joint effort stands up Iraqi air base," http://www.Af.mil/news/story.asp?storyID, January 12, 2005.

5. Federal Research Division, U.S. Government, *Iraq: A Country Study* (Washington, D.C.: U.S. Government Printing Office, 1990), 86–96.

6. Interview II with CPT Jeff Royer, July 27, 2004. Ferris. Interview with SFC Jim Hobbs and SSG Robert Smith, January 7, 2005.

7. Royer IV. Elmore I. Interview with SSG Keith Hildebrandt, September 13, 2004.

8. Hildebrandt.

9. Hildebrandt.

10. Interview with MSG Herbert "Sam" Woods, September 24, 2004. Elmore I. Interview II with 1SG Robert Elmore, August 2, 2004. Interview with SSG Lawrence Wilson, August 26, 2004. Interview III with CPT Jeff Royer, August 3, 2004.

11. Interview with 1SG (Retired) Jerry Calbow, September 22, 2004.

Chapter 4. Early Operations

1. Presentation by 1SG Robert Elmore to the Springfield Breakfast Optimists Club, November 19, 2004.

2. Interview V with CPT Jeff Royer, August 30, 2004. Ferris. Wilson. CPT Jeff Royer, "TTP's (Tactics, Techniques and Procedures) for Operations in Baghdad AO (Area of Operation)," January 22, 2004, 2. (This document was a Memorandum for Record that CPT Royer wrote for the commander of the unit replacing the 233rd.)

3. The 3rd Infantry Division included one MP company, but its operations after the fall of Baghdad were centered on airport security. Several MPs recall them waving as the 233rd left BIAP, heading for the heart of Baghdad.

4. Wilson. Royer V. Interview with SSG Jeremiah Fritzsche, February 17, 2004.

5. Interview II with 1SG Robert Elmore, August 2, 2004. Attachment 1, "Vignettes Clarifying Rules of Engagement Pertaining to Fleeing Ambush Attackers and Pursuit," to Brigade FRAGO 122, June 26, 2003,

6. Royer II. Elmore I. Interview with SGTs Daniel Hinds, Dana Hodges, and Robert Spence, August 14, 2004. Personal notes provided by SSG Jeremiah Fritzsche, February 17, 2005.

7. Royer II. Interview I with 1LT Mark Flack, August 14, 2004.

8. Elmore II. Hinds, Hodges, and Spence. Shortly after LTC Glaser arrived in Iraq, the Army discontinued the practice of rotating individual personnel into Iraq, rotating entire units instead.

9. Interview IV with CPT Jeff Royer, August 12, 2004. Telephone interview with SGT Shauna Cashion, November 2004. Interview with SPCs Adam Moma and Laura Thomason (Gant), September 11, 2003. Interview with SPC Jacob English and SPC Sarah English, August 14, 2003.

10. Royer II. Flack I.

11. Interview with SFC John Gillette, September 12, 2003. "Sworn Statement," by SFC John Gillette dated April 28, 2003.

12. Gillette.

13. E-mail from SFC John Gillette, July 28, 2005. "Sworn Statement" by Gillette.

14. Fareed Zakaria, "What We Should Do Now," *Newsweek,* September 1, 2003, 23–24. CPT Lesley Kipling and COL Ted Spain, "From Kuwait to Baghdad," *Military Police Magazine,* April 19, 2004. Harry Levins, "Shortage of MPs, Army leans on reserve forces," *St. Louis Post-Dispatch,* December 4, 2003. After the end of the cold war, senior leaders argued over how the Army should restructure itself. The Army dramatically downsized, but as it did so, the brass became reluctant to shed the Army's fighting units. Pentagon planners increasingly pushed to eliminate the National Guard combat divisions. These units were deemed to be irrelevant

to any future fight because it took too long to prepare them for war, they argued. The National Guard's leadership, however, insisted the divisions should be retained, arguing that the Guard divisions were much cheaper. Regular Army senior leaders insisted that these "excess" infantry and armor units should be converted to combat support units, thus creating more of the transportation, logistical, civil affairs, and MP units the Army now needed. The state adjutant generals, and by extension their governors, pleaded with Congress to protect them. At the end of the day, the states retained the bulk of their fighting formations. The debate over increasing the number of MP units in the Guard and Reserve ended when an insightful staff officer argued that the Guard could use the infantry battalions it retained to serve as MP units in a crunch. (The above comments are based on my own experience as the Force Integration Readiness Officer for the Illinois National Guard from 1997 to 2001.)

15. Tommy Franks, *American Soldier* (New York: Regan Books, 2004), 416.

16. James T. Quinlivan, "The Painful Arithmetic of Stability Operations," *Rand Review,* summer 2003. "Frontline: Rumsfeld's War: Paths to Power," Public Broadcasting System, http://www.pbs.org/wgbh/pages/frontline/shows/pentagon/paths/bush2.html. Franks, *American Soldier,* 419, 524. Eric Schmitt and David E. Sanger, "Looting disrupts detailed U.S. plan to restore Iraq," *New York Times,* May 19, 2003, 1, 10. Nancy Gibbs, "Unfinished Business," *Time,* April 28, 2003, 43–44. Brian Bennett, "Sorting the Bad from the Not so Bad," *Time,* May 19, 2003, 42–44. Interview with LTC Chris Hall, September 15, 2004, and July 27, 2005. (LTC Hall served as a National Guard liaison officer to the CENTCOM staff during 2002 and 2003.) James Fallows, "Blind into Baghdad," *Atlantic Monthly,* January–February 2004, 7. Ahmad Chalabi, the Iraqi expatriate who sat out much of the Saddam regime in London and returned to Iraq after the war as head of the Iraqi National Congress, predicted that the Iraqis would be quick to rise up and take control of their country. He was a popular figure in Congress and the Pentagon, and his belief in a quick resurrection by the Iraqis became part of the Bush administration's postwar assumptions. Many believe that key administrative figures were essentially guilty of believing what they wanted to believe. http://www.iraqinews.com/people_chalabi.shtml.

17. Franks, *American Soldier,* 524–26. Fallows, 19–20. The State Department began working on postwar plans fully one year before the war. Seventeen working groups, many involving Iraqi expatriates, labored to address the mind-boggling array of economic, social, security, and political issues that a freed Iraq would face. The end product was a 2,500-page report of mixed quality. The CIA, USAID, and nongovernmental organizations with extensive experience in nation building and humanitarian relief also produced voluminous studies. No document proved more useful and prescriptive than one generated by a team of Army War College faculty members headed by Dr. Conrad Crane and Dr. Andrew Terrill. After months of intensive work, the group published its recommendations in a 78-page document entitled "Reconstructing Iraq: Insights, Challenges, and Missions for Military Forces in a Post-Conflict Scenario." The document addressed in detail the "Challenges of a Military Occupation of Iraq." It concluded with a "Mission Matrix," a prioritized list of 135 tasks that the occupation forces would need to address, divided into twenty-one categories. The matrix even included which agency or organization should be responsible for each of the 135 tasks during four distinct phases of the occupation. Task 7A, "Establish & Maintain Police Systems and Operations," was cited as a "critical

task" for the occupying forces, a job for which the "Coalition Military Forces" were primarily responsible. The final document was published in early 2003, posted on the War College's Web site, and widely distributed throughout the Department of Defense. It was a veritable blueprint for planning the occupation of postwar Iraq, available to everyone in the military. James Fallows, "Blind into Baghdad," *Atlantic Monthly*, January–February 2004, 4–20. Conrad C. Crane and W. Andrew Terrill, "Reconstructing Iraq: Insights, Challenges, and Missions for Military Forces in a Post-Conflict Scenario," Army War College, February 2003.

Pentagon and CENTCOM planners largely ignored the War College documents and other postwar planning studies. Also ignored were the studies' consistent findings that substantially more troops were needed for the postwar occupation than were needed to win the war itself. "How could the Administration have thought that it was safe to proceed in blithe indifference to the warnings of nearly everyone with operational experience in modern military occupations," asked Fallows in his *Atlantic Monthly* article on prewar planning. Fallows, knowing the controversial nature of his article, went to great lengths to vet his story. Deputy Secretary of Defense Paul Wolfowitz, when pressed by the House Budget Committee about troop levels before the war, revealed the administration's logic. "I am reasonably certain that [the Iraqis] will greet us as liberators, and that will help us to keep requirements down. It's hard to conceive that it would take more forces to provide stability in post-Saddam Iraq than it would take to conduct the war itself." Fallows concluded that senior administration officials believed that any mention of the challenges posed by a postwar occupation was actually an argument against liberating Iraq—or at the very least, as an argument for delaying the attack until an adequate postwar plan could be developed. Senior officials characterized such talk as defeatist. Fallows, "Blind into Baghdad," 3, 25–28.

18. Fallows, "Blind into Baghdad," 3, 25–28. Fallows asserts that "neither the Army nor the other services moved very far past Phase III (decisive operations) thinking." CENTCOM essentially started its postwar planning from scratch. Further compounding the problem was the tendency to focus too much time and energy on the war itself.

19. Schmitt and Sanger, "Looting disrupts detailed U.S. plan," 1, 8. Fareed Zakaria, "What We Should do Now," *Newsweek*, September 1, 2003, 22–25.

20. Schmitt and Sanger, "Looting disrupts detailed U.S. plan," 1, 10. Fallows, 20.

21. Conversation with SSG Roman Waldron, March 2, 2005. Jay Garner led a planning group that began its work in the fall of 2002, but his plan, like others developed, was rejected.

22. Royer II. Elmore I. http://timelines.ws/countries/IRAQ_B.HTML.

23. Operations Order 519-002 (Viper Strike), April 29, 2003. This document, updated daily in a series of Fragmentary Orders (or FRAGOs), remained in effect for several months.

24. Fritzsche. 233rd MP Company Operations files, Report (handwritten report with no heading), May 5, 2003.

25. 233rd FRAGO 4 (Daily Rollup) to OPORD 519-02 (Viper Strike), May 6, 2003. Royer II. "American Morning—interview with Ahmed Kadhim Ibrahim," January 1, 2004, CNN.com, http://transcripts.cnn.com/TRANSCRIPTS/0401/01/ltm.13.html. CPT Royer last encountered General Ahmed Kadhim months after

Royer returned to the States, while he was watching the NBC evening news. There, suddenly, was General Kadhim at the United Nations, being interviewed, obviously still in a position of influence in the new Iraqi government.

26. 233rd FRAGO 3, May 4, 2003. 519th FRAGO 13 to OPORD 519-02, May 3, 2003.

27. Ferris. Interview with SFC Ryan Machin, August 11, 2004.

28. Flack, I. E-mail from 1LT Mark Flack, June 4, 2005.

29. Flack, I. Flack e-mail.

30. Ferris. Interview with SSG Roman Waldron, August 15, 2004.

31. 1LT Mark Flack, "Iraqi Police Station Assessment Form," al-Mesbah and al-Kerada police stations, May 6, 2003. 1LT Mark Flack, "Iraqi Police Station Assessment Form," Al-Mesbah police station, May 8, 2003.

32. Interview with SSG Dan Hinds, November 4, 2005. Conversation with SFC John Gillette, November 6, 2005.

33. 233rd FRAGO 5 (Daily Rollup) to OPORD 519-02 (Viper Strike), May 6, 2003.

34. 233rd FRAGO 8, May 9, 2003.

35. 233rd FRAGO 1, May 1, 2003. Interview with SSG Roman Waldron on March 2, 2005 (no transcript available). Flack I.

36. Interview with SSG Mark Walden, April 27, 2005.

37. Wilson. Glaser.

38. Interview with MSG Herbert "Sam" Woods, September 24, 2005.

39. Calbow. Elmore II. E-mail from 1SG Robert Elmore to the FRG, "Greetings to all 233rd families and friends," circa June 2003.

40. FRAGO 26 (Change) to OPORD 519-02 (Viper Strike), June 9, 2003. Royer, TTP, 10. Many of the Americans on the ground maintain that the insurgency started in May, after the flawed decision to disband the Iraqi army. Four days later, the first bombs went off in Falluja.

41. Glaser. Royer IV. Machin, 8. E-mail from LTC David Glaser, October 26, 2005. The 1st Armored Division was first alerted during the buildup to war. They were ordered to stand down when the Pentagon determined that they would not be needed for the initial occupation.

42. Royer IV. Elmore II. E-mail from LTC Glaser, October 26, 2005. Shortly after LTC Glaser arrived in Baghdad, the Army changed its troop rotation policy for units in Iraq. From that time forward, those assigned with a unit when it arrived in country would stay with the unit until the entire unit rotated out. It was a lesson the brass had learned the hard way in Vietnam. Allowing individual rotations to occur in the midst of the war did nothing but destroy the unit's cohesion and morale.

Chapter 5. Forging a New Baghdad Police Force

1. Federal Research Division, U.S. Government, *Iraq: A Country Study* (Washington, D.C.: U.S. Government Printing Office, 1990), 251–53. 233rd MP Company Files, Spot Reports, "Background," circa July 2, 2003. At the top of Saddam's internal security pyramid stood the Ministry of the Interior, a department that included the Police General Directorate, the Traffic Police General Directorate, the Civil Defense Directorate (a branch that controlled citizenship and immigration issues),

and the Mukhabarat, or Department of General Intelligence, the most notorious of Saddam's policing agencies—his eyes and ears for keeping track of the Iraqi public. In Iraq, one never knew who might be a Mukhabarat informant.

2. "Background." Sean Flynn, "Baghdad: How Do You Police the Un-Policeable," *Gentleman's Quarterly,* June 2004, 183. Glaser. Royer, TTP for Operations, 9. Royer II.

3. Flynn, "Baghdad," 183. Elmore I. Royer II. Interview with SFC Robert De-Hart, October 22, 2004.

4. "U.S. overhauls administration to govern Iraq," *New York Times,* May 12, 2003, 1. "New policy in Iraq to authorize G.I.s to shoot looters," *New York Times,* May 14, 2003, 1. "Iraq's slide into lawlessness squanders good will for U.S.," *New York Times,* May 18, 2003, 1.

5. FRAGO 29 (Change) to OPORD 519-02 (Viper Strike), June 10, 2003.

6. FRAGO 25 (Daily Rollup) to OPORD 519-02 (Viper Strike), May 1, 2003. FRAGO 29 (Change) to OPORD 519-02 (Viper Strike), June 10, 2003. Interview with SSG Roman Waldron, March 2, 2005. Glaser. E-mail from LTC David Glaser, October 26, 2005. Royer IV.

7. SFC James Hobbs, memorandum, "Status of Iraqi Police Stations," June 18, 2003.

8. FRAGO 29 (Change) to OPORD 519-02 (Viper Strike), June 10, 2003. Telephone conversation with LTC Kevin Moffett, November 16, 2005. (LTC [then MAJ] Moffett served as the 519th Battalion's S-3 for the unit's entire duration in Iraq.)

9. Military enlistment contracts are for six to eight years, with soldiers serving those years in a variety of ways. It is typical that soldiers serve the first two to three years on active duty before finishing the remainder of their time in service in one of the Reserve components. Many satisfy the remainder of their contract in either the National Guard or Reserve, but others transfer into the Inactive Ready Reserve. In this status, they are assigned to no unit and attend no military training, but are still subject to being called up in the event they are needed.

10. Ferris. E-mail from 1LT Joel Ferris, June 9, 2005.

11. Ferris. Interview II with 1LT Joel Ferris, May 28, 2005.

12. Rice. Flack I.

13. Ferris e-mail, June 9, 2005.

14. Ferris II.

15. Ferris. Rice. Interview II with SSG Roman Waldron, August 15, 2004. Interview with Mike Jijika, January 19, 2005. (Jijika, an Iraqi expatriate who took up residence in Michigan after the first gulf war, served as an interpreter for the 519th MP Battalion.)

16. Machin.

17. Nayonis. Interview with SFC Kevin Weber, April 28, 2005.

18. Ferris e-mail, June 9, 2005.

19. CPT Jeff Royer, memorandum, "Actions Needed for Police Stations to Progress to Monitoring Stage," July 14, 2003. Flynn, "Baghdad," 182–84. SGT Mark S. Rickert, "First Baghdad police graduate civil retraining," Army News Service, July 18, 2003. http://www4.army.mil/ocpa/print.php?story_id_key=5061.

20. Interview with SSG James Nayonis, September 12, 2004. Interview with SFC Ryan Machin, August 11, 2004.

21. Weber. Flynn, "Baghdad," 181.

22. Royer, "Actions Needed for Police Stations." Flynn, "Baghdad," 182–84. Rickert, "First Baghdad police graduate civil retraining."

23. Ferris II. Ferris e-mail, June 9, 2005.

24. FRAGO, 10 May, 2003. Ferris. Flynn, "Baghdad," 181. Machin. Royer II.

25. David Washburn, "Contractor Titan's hiring faulted," http://www .signonsandiego.com/news/world/iraq/20040521, May 21, 2004. Azad was hired by the Titan Corporation, the American corporation responsible for supplying interpreters to the CPA. CPT Royer assigned Azad to the Reapers when they decided to replace Farouq, who was generally effective, but also unreliable.

26. Conversation with SFC Lawrence Wilson, August 27, 2005.

27. Weber. Flack I. FRAGO 78, August 1, 2003. FRAGO 81, August 4, 2003. Waldron. Royer II. The 233rd had a police dog team attached to the unit. The first person the dog bit when under the MPs' control was an Iraqi policeman rioting over his lack of pay.

28. Holder. 233rd MP Company files, Spot Report, statement by SGT Ryan Getz on the incident, July 3, 2003.

29. Ferris e-mail, June 9, 2005.

30. Royer III. Glaser. E-mail from LTC David Glaser, December 6, 2005.

31. Interview with SGT Joel Mauney, August 23, 2004.

32. 233rd MP Company files, Situation Report, September 2, 2003.

33. Glaser.

Chapter 6. Anything but Routine

1. 1SG Robert Elmore e-mail, July 15, 2003.

2. Gillette. Interview with SSG Lawrence Wilson, August 26, 2003. Interview with SGT Joel Mauney, August 23, 2004. Hodges. Interview with SGT Chris Cunningham, August 23, 2005.

3. Royer II, 12. FRAGO 56 to OPORD 519-02, July 13, 2003. "Standard Operating Procedures for Searching Local National Females," June 21, 2003. Attachment 1 to FRAGO 136, August 22, 2003.

4. Interview with SGT Christopher Cunningham, August 23, 2005. Company files, "Sworn Statement," by 1SG Robert Elmore dated July 15, 2003. Telephone conversation with 1SG Robert Elmore, September 9, 2005. After the raid, the MPs discovered that the al-Sa'adoun police station had not come under mortar attack; the source of the explosion was actually a hand grenade.

5. The CPA strictly forbade Iraqi citizens from carrying handguns. Cunningham. Telephone conversation with 1SG Robert Elmore, September 9, 2005. Conversation with SGT Jacob English, October 9, 2005.

6. Cunningham.

7. Interview with SSG Randall Camden, September 16, 2004.

8. Paul and Monica Hildebrandt.

9. Interview with SFC Kevin and Pamela Weber, March 15, 2005. E-mail from SFC Kevin Weber, September 5, 2005.

10. Higginson.

11. Royer III. Elmore II. Interview with SSG Mark Walden, April 28, 2005. Kevin and Pamela Weber.

12. Victor.

13. E-mail from SFC Kevin Weber to Pamela Weber, May 25, 2003. E-mail from SFC Kevin Weber to Pamela Weber, July 16, 2003. Elmore II. Royer IV.

14. "Army study of Iraq war details a 'morass' of supply shortages," *New York Times*, February 3, 2004.

15. SSG Hildebrandt.

16. Elmore II. FRAGO 102, August 22, 2003. The U.S. Army had armored Humvees nearby in Bosnia but decided not to send these to Iraq.

17. The standard operating procedure for such incidents was to order any suspects to dismount with their hands over their heads, with the command given in both Arabic and English.

18. Interview with SSG Jay Fritzsche, February 17, 2004. Conversation with SSG Daniel Hinds, November 5th, 2005.

19. Fritzsche.

20. 1LT Stephen Rice, Incident Report, July 7, 2003. Interview with SGT Dana Hodges and SPC Richard Williams, September 20, 2004. Conversation with SSG Hinds, November 5, 2005.

21. SSG Cindy Singley was struck by a round from celebratory fire as it fell to the ground while she was walking across the compound.

22. Robert F. Worth, "7 G.I.s wounded in 3 violent incidents in Iraq," *New York Times*, July 9, 2003, 10.

23. 233rd Spot Report, August 7, 2003. 233rd Situation Report, August 7, 2003. Royer II.

24. Ed and Lisa Higginson.

Chapter 7. Bombing at the UN

1. Evan Thomas, "Groping in the Dark," *Newsweek*, September 1, 2003, 27–31. Fareed Zakaria, "What Should We Do Now," *Newsweek*, September 1, 2003, 23. Joshua Hammer, "Countdown to Mayhem," *Newsweek*, September 1, 2003, 35–37.

2. 233rd MP Company Spot Report files, July 12, 2003. Spot Report files, August 2, 2003.

3. Michael Elliott, "America Stretched Thin," *Time*, September 1, 2003, 30. Hammer, 36–37.

4. Interview with SSG Jay Fritzsche, February 17, 2005.

5. Interview with SGT Dana Hodges and SPC Richard Williams, September 20, 2004. Incident Report, "Bombing of the UN HQ," August 19, 2003.

6. Hodges and Williams.

7. Interview with SPC Stephanie Stretch, August 24, 2005. Conversation with SSG Hinds, November 5, 2005.

8. Hodges and Williams. Incident Report, "Bombing of the UN HQ."

9. Headquarters, Combined Joint Task Force 7 memorandum, "OIF Rotation and Mobilization Policy," September 8, 2003.

10. 1SG Elmore II33. Interview with SGT Joel Mauney, August 23, 2004. CPT Royer IV. Interview with SFC Kevin and Pamela Weber, March 15, 2005. Interview with SSG Lawrence Wilson, August 26, 2004.

11. Elmore II. Kevin and Pamela Weber.

12. Extract from Situation Report, September 19, 2003. Interview with 1SG Robert Elmore and SFC John Gillette, March 12, 2005.

13. 233rd MP Company Spot Report files, July 15, 2003. 1SG Elmore and SFC Gillette.

14. Elmore and Gillette.

Chapter 8. Midtour Leaves

1. Higginson. E-mail from SGT Higginson, August 21, 2005.

2. FRAGO 136 (Environmental Leave) to OPORD 519-02 (Viper Strike), September 23, 2003. Spot Report File, Environmental Leave Policy, about September 24, 2003. Spot Report File, Environmental Leave—Senate Bill, September 30, 2003.

3. Royer IV. Ferris. Flack.

4. Royer IV. Royer, TTP for Operations, 13. Telephone interview with SPC Adam Bauer, August 3, 2005.

5. Higginson. Spot Report File, e-mail from SGT Higginson to 1SG Elmore, September 28, 2003.

6. Higginson.

7. Paul and Monica Hildebrandt. Greg Cima, "Families still wait: concern mixes with confidence in Springfield's 233rd," Springfield *State Journal-Register,* July 12, 2003, 1, 4.

8. Abbey Brown, "Soldier holds his daughter for first time," Springfield *Journal-Register,* October 12, 2003, 1.

9. Paul and Monica Hildebrandt.

10. Interview with SSG James Nayonis, September 12, 2004. Paul and Monica Hildebrandt.

11. Fritzsche.

12. Wilson.

13. Wilson. Hinds, Hodges, and Spence. Royer III.

14. Wilson. Mauney.

Chapter 9. Hearts and Minds

1. Royer III.

2. "Rewriting History—And More," *U.S. News and World Report,* May 12, 2003, 20. "Hopes deferred as school begins in Baghdad," Iraq Foundation, October 3, 2003, http://www.iraqfoundation.org/news/2003/joct/3_school.html.

3. Interview with SSG Roman Waldron, June 22, 2005. Mayes.

4. Interview with SSG Mark Walden (4th Platoon), April 27, 2005. The Hogs of 3rd Platoon did not get involved with any schools in their neighborhood. Theirs was more of a commercial neighborhood, and it was also more hostile toward the American presence.

5. Waldron.

6. Waldron.

7. Waldron. Mayes.

8. Telephone interview with 1SG Robert Elmore, April 18, 2005.

9. Mayes. Waldron.

10. Waldron. Ferris. Mayes.

11. Interview with CPT (Chaplain) Brian Reck, February 11, 2005.

12. Reck. The Americans knew the orphanage as Mother Teresa's Orphanage, the name posted on a sign outside the orphanage gate. On its Web site, however, the orphanage is known by the name Dar al-Mahabha (House of Love) Orphanage.

13. "Iraqi in America," September 28, 2004, http://fayrouz.blogspot.com/2004/09/mother-teresa-and-iraq.html. Ragged Edge Online, April 2, 2003, http://www.raggededgemagazine.com/extra/baghdad1.html. "Saint Anthony's charities *Messenger*," June 13, 2004, http://www.caritasantoniana.org/ing/progetto1.asp. Sister Beth Murphy.

14. Reck. Interview with SPC Adam Moma and Laura Thomason, September 11, 2004. Telephone interview with 1SG Robert Elmore, April 18, 2005.

15. Moma and Thomason.

Chapter 10. An Embedded Reporter

1. Ginny Skalski, "233rd living in an Iraqi palace," Springfield *State Journal-Register,* May 18, 2003, 1, 4.

2. Elmore II. Robert Elmore, "Life in Iraq in the words of a 233rd sergeant," Springfield *State Journal-Register,* August 10, 2003, 1, 9. Interview with Mike Kienzler, September 14, 2004. Greg Cima, "Families still wait," Springfield *State Journal-Register,* July 12, 2003, 1. By October 12, Monica Hildebrandt's picture had appeared four times on the front page of the *Journal-Register.*

3. Kienzler.

4. Interview with Marcus Stern, August 16, 2004. "1998 Eugene Katz Award for Excellence in the Coverage of Immigration," Center for Immigration Studies, September 1998, http://www.cis.org/katz1998.html.

5. Stern.

6. Stern.

7. Kienzler. Stern. Marcus Stern, "Daily operations: challenges, rewards part of patrolling Baghdad," Springfield, *State Journal-Register,* October 19, 2003, 1, 17.

8. Stern, "Daily operations," 7.

9. Springfield *State Journal-Register,* October 19–26, 2003.

10. Kienzler. Stern.

11. Stern, "Daily operations," 4–6, 9–10. Interview with SSG Mark Walden, April 27, 2005.

12. FRAGO (Daily Rollup) to OPORD 519-02 (Viper Strike), July 12, 2003. FRAGO 140 (Daily Rollup) to OPORD 519-02 (Viper Strike), September 26, 2003. "Media Relations," document filed in 233rd unit files under folder marked Spot Reports, circa September 16, 2003. FRAGO 167 (Daily Rollup) to OPORD 519-02 (Viper Strike), October 24, 2003.

13. Glaser. Royer, TTP, 6. LT Gen Ricardo S. Sanchez, Coalition Forces Memorandum, "Dignity and Respect while Conducting Operations," December 13, 2003. Royer III. Royer IV. Gillette.

14. Dexter Filkins and Alex Berenson, "Suicide bombers in Baghdad kill at least 34," *New York Times,* October 28, 2003, 1, 8. The official reports on the time of

the attempted attack on the New Baghdad station vary widely. The 233rd files contain three reports on the incident, with three different times (0900, 0930, and 0940 hours). The *New York Times* gives the time of the attack as 10:15 A.M.

15. Weber. 233rd unit files, Incident Reports, E10-086, October 27, 2003.

16. Weber. Spot Report, October 27, 2003. Filkins and Berenson, "Suicide bombers," 8.

17. Filkins and Berenson, "Suicide bombers," 1, 8. Glaser. E-mail from LTC David Glaser, December 5, 2005.

Chapter 11. A Typical Day

1. Interview with MSG Herbert "Sam" Woods, September 24, 2004. Waters. Higginson.

2. Interview with SSG Lawrence Wilson, August 26, 2004. Interview with SSG James Batterson, May 19, 2005.

3. Woods. Waters. Higginson.

4. Waters.

5. 233rd unit files, "Combat Power Chart," November 22, 2003. 233rd unit files, "Mission Tracking," November 22, 2003.

6. Higginson. Waters. Woods.

7. Waters.

8. Flack.

9. 233rd unit files, "Combat Power Chart."

10. Interview with SPC Jacob English, April 29, 2005.

11. Berriman. Royer II.

12. Berriman. Flack.

13. Telephone interview with SPC Stephanie Stretch, August 24, 2005.

14. Berriman. Rice. 233rd unit files, Incident Report E11-046, November 22, 2003.

15. Rice interview file. 1SG Robert Elmore interview file.

16. Flack II. Incident Report E11-048, 22 November 2004.

17. Riot control training consisted of forming the MPs into a wedge, with the troops equipped with billy clubs, body shields, and face shields. They then practiced what they affectionately called the "stomp and drag," which was nothing more than a solid wedge of soldiers moving forward one step at a time, pushing the crowd back as they went. The theory was that a crowd would eventually be intimidated by the soldiers' discipline and disperse, but the MPs had serious doubts about these tactics. "This would never work for the Iraqis," contended Royer. Said MAJ Zane Jones, the 519th's operations officer, "When the other guy has a gun, that's not riot control; that's combat." The company leadership brainstormed new tactics more suited for the realities of Baghdad. Instead of the human formation, they planned to stretch a roll of concertina wire between two Humvees and use this contraption to push the crowd down a street. Additionally, they considered backing this up with a phalanx of MPs armed with shotguns loaded with nonlethal beanbags.

18. 233rd unit files, "Combat Power Chart," November 22, 2003. 233rd unit files, "Mission Tracking," 22 November 2003.

19. Ibid.

20. Interview with SPC Lucas Jockisch, November 6, 2005. Hinds, Hodges, and Spence.

21. Interview with MAJ Zane Jones, November 3–4, 2004. Fritzsche.

22. 233rd unit files, "Combat Power Chart," November 22, 2003. 233rd unit files, "Mission Tracking," 22 November 2003. 233rd unit files, planning documents, etc.

Chapter 12. *Down Time*

1. SSG Lisa Morrison, "How to Feel Like Your MP in Baghdad," 233rd Unit files.

2. Interview with SPC Abraham Bain, April 29, 2005. Conversation with SSG Lawrence Wilson, April 27, 2005.

3. Interview with SPCs Adam Moma and Laura Thomason, September 11, 2004.

4. Interview with Jacob English, April 29, 2005. Interview with Sarah English, May 14, 2005.

5. Jacob English.

6. Ibid.

7. Marcus Stern, "Keeping connected," Springfield *State Journal-Register,* October 22, 2003, 1, 4. Abbey Brown, "Morale, missions and Iraqi toilets," Springfield *State Journal-Register,* October 12, 2003, 1, 4.

8. Chaplain Reck. Chaplain Reck e-mail, September 21, 2005.

Chapter 13. *"The LT's Hit!"*

1. 233rd MP Company unit files, sworn statements, November 28, 2003, by 1LT Joel Ferris, SSG Robert Smith, SSG Roman Waldron, SGT Eric Bertoni, SPC Zachary Smith, and PFC Adam Pope. Interview with SSG Robert Smith, January 7, 2005. Waldron.

2. Interview with BGen Randall Thomas, August 18, 2004. Interview with SFC Jim Hobbs, August 25, 2005.

3. 233rd MP Company unit files, Leave Records.

4. Interview with SPCs Jacob and Sarah English, August 14, 2004. Leah Friedman, "No place like home," Springfield *State Journal-Register,* December 11, 2003, 1, 8. Chris Terry, "Love and rockets," Springfield *State Journal-Register,* May 2004, 1, 8.

5. E-mail from 1SG Robert Elmore, December 25, 2003. Woods.

6. E-mail from Reck, September 21, 2005.

7. After SGT Hinds regained his feet, he spotted a machine gunner from the other element firing toward a rooftop. Hinds hollered out and finally convinced him to stop; he feared that the indiscriminate fire might hit a civilian. Hinds ended up with a large bruise, but whatever hit him did not break the skin. Conversation with SSG Hinds, November 5, 2005.

8. Hinds, Hodges, and Spence. Rice. Shawn Clubb, "Alton guardsman recovering from wounds suffered in Iraq," *Telegraph,* January 14, 2004, http://www.zwire.com/site/news.cfm?newsid. E-mail from Ruth Rice, December 28, 2003. E-mail from Stephen Rice, August 24, 2005.

9. Dan Baum, "Annals of War—Two Soldiers: How the Dead Come Home," *New Yorker,* August 9, 2004.

10. Rice. Royer IV. E-mail from Stephen Rice, August 24, 2005. Stretch.

11. Rice. Calbow. E-mail from Ruth Farmer, August 20, 2005. Email from Stephen Rice, August 24, 2005.

12. Telephone interview with Ruth Farmer, May 10, 2005. E-mail from Ruth Farmer, August 20, 2005. E-mail from Stephen Rice, August 24, 2005.

13. Rice, 20–25. E-mail from Ruth Farmer, December 30, 2003. E-mail from Ruth Farmer, August 20, 2005. E-mail from Stephen Farmer, August 24, 2005.

14. Rice, 25–28. Clubb, "Alton guardsman recovering from wounds." Steve Horrell, "Wounded soldier to be honored by Haine," *Edwardsville Intelligencer,* February 10, 2004. Operation Freedom Miles Web site, http://www.heromiles.org. Operation Freedom Miles is a nonprofit organization founded in September 2003 by several U.S. airlines and Congressman Ruppersberger, which allows private citizens to donate their frequent-flyer miles to soldiers returning home on leave. After December 2003, the program was expanded to fly family members to military hospitals where their loved ones recuperated.

15. 2LT Jason Celletti, "State senate honors guardsman wounded in Iraq explosion," Illinois Army National Guard, February 26, 2004, http://www.il.ngb.army .mil/publicaffairs/Work%20Files/html/stories/stry022604.html. Stephen Rice speech, February 10, 2004, Illinois state senate archives. E-mail from Ruth (Rice) Farmer, August 20, 2005. E-mail from Stephen Rice, August 24, 2005.

16. E-mail from Stephen Rice, August 24, 2005.

Chapter 14. Turf Battles

1. Stern. Gillette II.

2. DeHart.

3. DeHart.

4. DeHart. Glaser. SSG Robert Smith. Harry Levins, "Short of MPs, Army leans on reserve forces," *St. Louis Post-Dispatch,* December 4, 2003.

5. Royer, TTP for Operations, 6. Royer III.

6. Telephone interview with 1LT Stephen Rice, May 11, 2005. SFC John Gillette, memorandum to Commander 233rd, "2LCR Maneuver Elements," August 22, 2003. Interview with SSG James Batterson, May 19, 2005.

7. Royer II. Glaser.

8. Ferris. Smith. Notes from SSG Roman Waldron, August 2005.

9. Ferris. Smith. Interview with SSG James Mayes, May 13, 2005. Notes from SSG Roman Waldron, August 2005.

10. Ferris. Smith.

Chapter 15. Winding Down

1. FRAGO 248 to OPORD 519-02 (Viper Strike), December 30, 2003. FRAGO 249 to OPORD 519-02 (Viper Strike), December 31, 2003. FRAGO 265 to OPORD 519-02 (Viper Strike), January 15, 2004. FRAGO 328 to OPORD 519-02 (Viper

Strike), March 17, 2004. Interview with Mike Jijika, January 19, 2005. Jijika was an Iraqi émigré and American citizen who arrived in the United States in 1996 after spending three years in Germany awaiting a visa, having escaped from Iraq in 1993. He accompanied the American forces into Baghdad, and he served with the 519th MP Company as an interpreter.

2. Interview with Keith Hildebrandt, June 28, 2005. Interview with SGT Michael Whited, July 1, 2005. Glaser. The Humvees were delivered in two installments. Eight were initially delivered, and the remainder were delivered several days later.

3. Glaser. Royer IV.

4. Interview with SGT Richard Carroll, September 2, 2005.

5. Carroll.

6. Carroll. SGT Richard Carroll, sworn statement, March 8, 2004.

7. Glaser. Royer IV. Ferris I. Nayonis I. 759th Military Police Battalion Web site, http://www.carson.army.mil/759thMP/history.htm.

8. Army planners now plan to double the size of the MP corps within the next couple of years, increasing the force from 38,000 to 70,000 MPs. SPC Kevin Stabinsky, "Becoming MPs," *Soldier Magazine*, July 2005, 36–39. LTC David Glaser was quoted in this article, having given up his command of the 519th MP Battalion, then taking command of the 509th MP Battalion. Receiving a second battalion command in the contemporary Army is almost unprecedented.

9. Interview with CPT Robert Ohl, July 5, 2005. The unit was renamed Company B because the term "battery" was the field artillery's equivalent of a infantry or MP company.

10. Ohl. CPT Ohl worked as a facilities maintenance supervisor for Corning Incorporated, the world-famous glassware manufacturer. Ohl was the corporation's first employee to deploy to Iraq, and the company was incredibly supportive, even ensuring that the snow was removed and the lawn mowed at Ohl's home in Corning, New York. No doubt they were motivated in part by the fact that Ohl's son was born just two days before his deployment overseas. Nayonis. Jim Nayonis served on the Monticello, Illinois, police department, and Jeremy Mayes was one of many from the Springfield police department. Jim Batterson was a corrections officer at a prison in Jacksonville.

11. Nayonis.

12. Ohl. Nayonis. Interview with SGT Ryan Getz, July 1, 2005.

Chapter 16. Going Home

1. E-mail from 1SG Robert Elmore, March 22, 2004. John Reynolds, "They'll be home soon," Springfield *State Journal-Register*, March 22, 2004, 1, 4.

2. Interview with SFC Randall Camden II, July 13, 2005. Interview with SSF Keith Hildebrandt, June 28, 2005.

3. Wilson. Royer V.

4. Machin. Royer III. Royer V. Ferris. Flack I. Waldron I.

5. Royer V.

6. Royer V. "No Easy Options," *Time*, April 19, 2004, 35–48. "Uprising spreads: Rumsfeld sees it as 'test of wills,'" *New York Times*, April 8, 2004, 1, 8. E-mail comments from 1LT Joel Ferris, August 2005. Mahdi Army, http://en.wikipedia.org/wiki/Mahdi_Army.

7. "Periscope," *Newsweek,* May 10, 2004. Carrie Antifinger, "Wisconsin Army National Guard Spc. Michelle M. Witmer," http://www.militarycity.com/valor/257274.html.

8. E-mail from LT Flack, July 24, 2005. E-mail comments from 1LT Joel Ferris.

9. Royer V. Mauney. John Reynolds, "233rd coming home—four other Illinois units to stay in Iraq," Springfield *State Journal-Register,* April 16, 2004, 1, 5.

10. Conversation with 1SG Robert Elmore.

11. E-mail comments from 1LT Joel Ferris, August 2005. 1LT Ferris e-mail, September 20, 2005.

12. Mauney. Royer III, 17.

13. E-mail from LT Ferris, September 21, 2005.

14. Higginson.

15. Higginson. Wood.

16. Royer V. Mauney.

17. Mauney. Interview with BGen Randall Thomas, August 18, 2004. Royer V. Kevin and Pamela Weber.

18. Calbow.

19. Royer V. Camden. Ferris I. Kevin and Pamela Weber. Hinds, Hodges, and Spence. Machin. Paul and Monica Hildebrandt.

20. Interview with LTC George Rakers, August 20, 2005, 1–7 minutes. (Rakers currently serves as the commander of the 33rd MP Battalion, the 233rd's stateside higher headquarters unit.) Nayonis. Wood. Kevin and Pamela Weber. Royer V. Abbey Brown, "Mission accomplished," Springfield *State Journal-Register,* April 26, 2004, 1, 4, 5.

21. Royer V. Thomas.

Conclusion

1. Waldron. Nayonis.

2. Weber. Royer V.

3. Royer V. K. Hildebrandt. Machin.

4. Moma. K. Hildebrandt.

5. Camden. Royer V.

6. Williams and Hodges. Hinds, Hodges, and Spence.

7. Conversation with SGT Richard Williams, November 5, 2005. E-mail from Jay Fritzsche, November 25, 2005.

8. Ferris. E-mail from Joel Ferris, August 7, 2005. Telephone conversation with CPT Joel Ferris, November 30, 2005.

9. The 233rd received the Army's Valorous Unit Award for its service in Iraq.

10. E-mail from Edward Higginson, October 31, 2005.

11. CPT Joel Ferris took command of the 233rd MP Company in March 2006.

12. E-mail from Robert Ohl, November 3, 2005.

13. Dick Foster, "Fort Carson welcomes home 984th MP Company," *Rocky Mountain News,* February 9, 2005, http://www.rockymountainnews.com. E-mail from Brian Reck, October 31, 2005.

14. E-mail from COL Tom Bowman, October 31, 2005.

15. Mauney.

16. Interview with SPC Stephanie Stretch, August 24, 2005. Nicole Sack, "Beginning the healing: Durbin speaks to local vets about post-traumatic stress," *Southern Illinoisan,* April 2, 2005.

17. Interview with SPC Lucas Jockisch, November 6, 2005.

18. E-mail from 1LT Stephen Rice, August 24, 2005.

19. E-mail from 1LT Stephen Rice, November 13, 2005.

20. Hinds, Hodges, and Spence. Telephone conversation with Dana Hodges, December 28, 2005.

21. Jockisch. Walden. Machin.

22. "Mother Teresa and Iraq," September 28, 2004, http://fayrouz.blogspot.com/2004/09/mother-teresa-and-iraq.html. Ferris. Hinds, Hodges, and Spence.

23. Rice, 33. Moma and Gant. Mauney. Glaser. Stern.

24. Abbey Brown, "Local families caught off guard by length of deployment," Springfield *State Journal-Register,* September 13, 2003, 1, 4. Paul and Monica Hildebrandt.

25. Rice.

Index